A History of Alcohol and Drugs in Modern South Asia

At the beginning of the twenty-first century, alcoholism, transnational drug trafficking and drug addiction constitute major problems in various South Asian countries. The production, circulation and consumption of intoxicating substances creates (and responds to) social upheavals in the region and had widespread economic, political and cultural repercussions on an international level. This book looks at the cultural, social and economic history of intoxicants in South Asia, and analyzes the role that alcohol and drugs have played in the region.

The book explores the linkages between changing meanings of intoxicating substances, the making of and contestations over colonial and national regimes of regulation, economics, and practices and experiences of consumption. It shows the development of current meanings of intoxicants in South Asia – in terms of politics, cultural norms and identity formation – and the way in which the history of drugs and alcohol is enmeshed in the history of modern empires and nation states – even in a country in which a staunch teetotaller and active anti-drug crusader like Mohandas Gandhi is presented as the 'father of the nation'.

Primarily a historical analysis, the book also includes perspectives from Modern Indology and Cultural Anthropology, and situates developments in South Asia in wider imperial and global contexts. It will be of interest to scholars working on the social and cultural history of alcohol and drugs, South Asian Studies and Global History.

Harald Fischer-Tiné is Professor of Modern Global History at the Swiss Federal Institute of Technology (ETH-Zürich), Switzerland.

Jana Tschurenev is a Research Fellow at the Centre for Modern Indian Studies at the University of Göttingen, Germany.

Routledge studies in the modern history of Asia

1 **The Police in Occupation Japan**
Control, corruption and resistance to reform
Christopher Aldous

2 **Chinese Workers**
A new history
Jackie Sheehan

3 **The Aftermath of Partition in South Asia**
Tai Yong Tan and Gyanesh Kudaisya

4 **The Australia–Japan Political Alignment**
1952 to the present
Alan Rix

5 **Japan and Singapore in the World Economy**
Japan's economic advance into Singapore, 1870–1965
Shimizu Hiroshi and Hirakawa Hitoshi

6 **The Triads as Business**
Yiu Kong Chu

7 **Contemporary Taiwanese Cultural Nationalism**
A-chin Hsiau

8 **Religion and Nationalism in India**
The case of the Punjab
Harnik Deol

9 **Japanese Industrialisation**
Historical and cultural perspectives
Ian Inkster

10 **War and Nationalism in China, 1925–1945**
Hans J. van de Ven

11 **Hong Kong in Transition**
One country, two systems
Edited by Robert Ash, Peter Ferdinand, Brian Hook and Robin Porter

12 **Japan's Postwar Economic Recovery and Anglo-Japanese Relations, 1948–1962**
Noriko Yokoi

13 **Japanese Army Stragglers and Memories of the War in Japan, 1950–1975**
Beatrice Trefalt

14 **Ending the Vietnam War**
The Vietnamese communists' perspective
Ang Cheng Guan

15 **The Development of the Japanese Nursing Profession**
Adopting and adapting Western influences
Aya Takahashi

16 **Women's Suffrage in Asia**
Gender nationalism and democracy
Louise Edwards and Mina Roces

17 **The Anglo-Japanese Alliance, 1902–1922**
Phillips Payson O'Brien

18 **The United States and Cambodia, 1870–1969**
From curiosity to confrontation
Kenton Clymer

19 **Capitalist Restructuring and the Pacific Rim**
Ravi Arvind Palat

20 **The United States and Cambodia, 1969–2000**
A troubled relationship
Kenton Clymer

21 **British Business in Post-Colonial Malaysia, 1957–70**
'Neo-colonialism' or 'disengagement'?
Nicholas J. White

22 **The Rise and Decline of Thai Absolutism**
Kullada Kesboonchoo Mead

23 **Russian Views of Japan, 1792–1913**
An anthology of travel writing
David N. Wells

24 **The Internment of Western Civilians under the Japanese, 1941–1945**
A patchwork of internment
Bernice Archer

25 **The British Empire and Tibet 1900–1922**
Wendy Palace

26 **Nationalism in Southeast Asia**
If the people are with us
Nicholas Tarling

27 **Women, Work and the Japanese Economic Miracle**
The case of the cotton textile industry, 1945–1975
Helen Macnaughtan

28 **A Colonial Economy in Crisis**
Burma's rice cultivators and the world depression of the 1930s
Ian Brown

29 **A Vietnamese Royal Exile in Japan**
Prince Cuong De (1882–1951)
Tran My-Van

30 **Corruption and Good Governance in Asia**
Nicholas Tarling

31 **US–China Cold War Collaboration, 1971–1989**
S. Mahmud Ali

32 **Rural Economic Development in Japan**
From the nineteenth century to the Pacific War
Penelope Francks

33 **Colonial Armies in Southeast Asia**
Edited by Karl Hack and Tobias Rettig

34 **Intra Asian Trade and the World Market**
A. J. H. Latham and Heita Kawakatsu

35 **Japanese–German Relations, 1895–1945**
War, diplomacy and public opinion
Edited by Christian W. Spang and Rolf-Harald Wippich

36 Britain's Imperial Cornerstone in China
The Chinese maritime customs service, 1854–1949
Donna Brunero

37 Colonial Cambodia's 'Bad Frenchmen'
The rise of French rule and the life of Thomas Caraman, 1840–1887
Gregor Muller

38 Japanese–American Civilian Prisoner Exchanges and Detention Camps, 1941–45
Bruce Elleman

39 Regionalism in Southeast Asia
Nicholas Tarling

40 Changing Visions of East Asia, 1943–93
Transformations and continuities
R. B. Smith, edited by Chad J. Mitcham

41 Christian Heretics in Late Imperial China
Christian inculturation and state control, 1720–1850
Lars P. Laamann

42 Beijing – A Concise History
Stephen G. Haw

43 The Impact of the Russo-Japanese War
Edited by Rotem Kowner

44 Business–Government Relations in Prewar Japan
Peter von Staden

45 India's Princely States
People, princes and colonialism
Edited by Waltraud Ernst and Biswamoy Pati

46 Rethinking Gandhi and Nonviolent Relationality
Global perspectives
Edited by Debjani Ganguly and John Docker

47 The Quest for Gentility in China
Negotiations beyond gender and class
Edited by Daria Berg and Chloë Starr

48 Forgotten Captives in Japanese Occupied Asia
Edited by Kevin Blackburn and Karl Hack

49 Japanese Diplomacy in the 1950s
From isolation to integration
Edited by Iokibe Makoto, Caroline Rose, Tomaru Junko and John Weste

50 The Limits of British Colonial Control in South Asia
Spaces of disorder in the Indian Ocean region
Edited by Ashwini Tambe and Harald Fischer-Tiné

51 On The Borders of State Power
Frontiers in the greater Mekong sub-region
Edited by Martin Gainsborough

52 Pre-Communist Indochina
R. B. Smith, edited by Beryl Williams

53 **Communist Indochina**
R. B. Smith, edited by Beryl Williams

54 **Port Cities in Asia and Europe**
Edited by Arndt Graf and Chua Beng Huat

55 **Moscow and the Emergence of Communist Power in China, 1925–30**
The Nanchang Rising and the birth of the Red Army
Bruce A. Elleman

56 **Colonialism, Violence and Muslims in Southeast Asia**
The Maria Hertogh controversy and its aftermath
Syed Muhd Khairudin Aljunied

57 **Japanese and Hong Kong Film Industries**
Understanding the origins of East Asian film networks
Kinnia Shuk-ting

58 **Provincial Life and the Military in Imperial Japan**
The phantom samurai
Stewart Lone

59 **Southeast Asia and the Vietnam War**
Ang Cheng Guan

60 **Southeast Asia and the Great Powers**
Nicholas Tarling

61 **The Cold War and National Assertion in Southeast Asia**
Britain, the United States and Burma, 1948–1962
Matthew Foley

62 **The International History of East Asia, 1900–1968**
Trade, ideology and the quest for order
Edited by Antony Best

63 **Journalism and Politics in Indonesia**
A critical biography of Mochtar Lubis (1922–2004) as editor and author
David T. Hill

64 **Atrocity and American Military Justice in Southeast Asia**
Trial by army
Louise Barnett

65 **The Japanese Occupation of Borneo, 1941–1945**
Ooi Keat Gin

66 **National Pasts in Europe and East Asia**
P. W. Preston

67 **Modern China's Ethnic Frontiers**
A journey to the West
Hsiao-ting Lin

68 **New Perspectives on the History and Historiography of Southeast Asia**
Continuing explorations
Michael Aung-Thwin and Kenneth R. Hall

69 **Food Culture in Colonial Asia**
A taste of empire
Cecilia Leong-Salobir

70 **China's Political Economy in Modern Times**
Changes and economic consequences, 1800–2000
Kent Deng

71 **Science, Public Health and the State in Modern Asia**
Edited by Liping Bu, Darwin Stapleton and Ka-che Yip

72 **Russo-Japanese Relations, 1905–1917**
From enemies to allies
Peter Berton

73 **Reforming Public Health in Occupied Japan, 1945–52**
Alien prescriptions?
Christopher Aldous and Akihito Suzuki

74 **Trans-Colonial Modernities in South Asia**
Edited by Michael S. Dodson and Brian A. Hatcher

75 **The Evolution of the Japanese Developmental State**
Institutions locked in by ideas
Hironori Sasada

76 **Status and Security in Southeast Asian States**
Nicholas Tarling

77 **Lee Kuan Yew's Strategic Thought**
Ang Cheng Guan

78 **Government, Imperialism and Nationalism in China**
The Maritime Customs Service and its Chinese staff
Chihyun Chang

79 **China and Japan in the Russian Imagination, 1685–1922**
To the Ends of the Orient
Susanna Soojung Lim

80 **Chinese Complaint Systems**
Natural resistance
Qiang Fang

81 **Martial Arts and the Body Politic in Meiji Japan**
Denis Gainty

82 **Gambling, the State and Society in Thailand, c.1800–1945**
James A. Warren

83 **Post-War Borneo, 1945–1950**
Nationalism, Empire and State-Building
Ooi Keat Gin

84 **China and the First Vietnam War, 1947–54**
Laura M. Calkins

85 **The Jesuit Missions to China and Peru, 1570–1610**
Ana Carolina Hosne

86 **Macao – Cultural Interaction and Literary Representation**
Edited by Katrine K. Wong and George Wei

87 **Macao – The Formation of a Global City**
Edited by George Wei

88 **Women in Modern Burma**
Tharaphi Than

89 **Museums in China**
Materialized power and objectified identities
Tracey L-D Lu

90 **Transcultural Encounters between Germany and India**
Kindred Spirits in the 19th and 20th Centuries
Edited by Joanne Miyang Cho, Eric Kurlander and Douglas T. McGetchin

91 **The Philosophy of Japanese Wartime Resistance**
A reading, with commentary, of the complete texts of the Kyoto School discussions of "The Standpoint of World History and Japan"
David Williams

92 **A History of Alcohol and Drugs in Modern South Asia**
Intoxicating affairs
Edited by Harald Fischer-Tiné and Jana Tschurenev

93 **Military Force and Elite Power in the Formation of Modern China**
Edward A. McCord

94 **Japan's Household Registration System and Citizenship**
Koseki, identification and documentation
Edited by David Chapman and Karl Jakob Krogness

A History of Alcohol and Drugs in Modern South Asia

Intoxicating affairs

Edited by Harald Fischer-Tiné and Jana Tschurenev

Routledge
Taylor & Francis Group
LONDON AND NEW YORK

First published 2014
by Routledge

2 Park Square, Milton Park, Abingdon, Oxfordshire OX14 4RN
711 Third Avenue, New York, NY 10017

Routledge is an imprint of the Taylor & Francis Group, an informa business

First issued in paperback 2017

British Library Cataloguing in Publication Data
A catalogue record for this book is available from the British Library

Library of Congress Cataloging-in-Publication Data
A history of alcohol and drugs in modern South Asia : intoxicating affairs / edited by Harald Fischer-Tiné and Jana Tschurenev.
pages cm. — (Routledge studies in the modern history of Asia ; 92)
Includes bibliographical references and index.
1. Substance abuse—South Asia—History. 2. Drug traffic—South Asia—History.
3. Alcoholism—South Asia—History. 4. South Asians—Drug use—History.
5. South Asia—Social life and customs. I. Fischer-Tin?, Harald. II. Tschurenev, Jana.
HV5840.S64H57 2014
362.290954—dc23

2013025461

ISBN: 978-0-415-84263-1 (hbk)
ISBN: 978-0-8153-7341-4 (pbk)

Typeset in TimesNewRomanMTStd
Project Managed and Typeset by: diacriTech

Contents

List of Contributors

Jana Tschurenev is a Research Fellow at the Center for Modern Indian Studies, University of Göttingen. After gaining her PhD from Humboldt University Berlin, she worked as Assistant Professor at the ETH-Zurich, doing research on the history of education, moral reform campaigns, and global movements.

Harald Fischer-Tiné is Professor of Modern Global History at the Swiss Federal Institute of Technology (ETH-Zürich). He has published extensively on South Asian colonial history and the history of the British Empire. Currently, he is doing research on the history of the YMCA in India.

James McHugh is Assistant Professor in the School of Religion at the University of Southern California, Los Angeles. His first book *Sandalwood and Carrion: Smell in Indian religion and culture* was published by Oxford University Press in 2012, and he is currently working on a monograph on alcohol in South Asia.

Amar Farooqui is Professor of History at Delhi University, India, and has been Fellow of Nehru Memorial Museum and Library, New Delhi. He has published extensively on the opium trade in South Asia.

Tobias Delfs is a Research Assistant in the Department of Northern European History at Kiel University, Germany, and works on his doctorate for the University Research Priority Program 'Asia and Europe' at the University of Zurich, Switzerland.

Maria Moritz is a Research Associate at the Department of Education Studies of Humboldt University, Berlin, researching in the history of schooling in nineteenth century India. She has specialized in Indian colonial and global history and is currently working at the publication of her PhD thesis on Indian intellectuals and the Theosophical Society.

Kawal Deep Kour is a Research Scholar at the Department of Humanities and Social Sciences, Indian Institute of Technology, Guwahati. Her research interests include the socio-economic and political history of narcotics and public policy on drugs. She is presently writing her doctoral dissertation on the history of the opium poppy in Assam.

Maria Framke is a historian of modern South Asia. She received her doctorate from Jacobs University Bremen with a thesis on Indian engagements with Fascism and national socialism in the inter-war period. Since 2013 she is based at ETH Zurich with her post-doctorate project on South Asian humanitarianism in armed conflicts.

R. Eric Colvard received his PhD from the University of Iowa in 2013. He is an Assistant Professor of History at Wayne State College, in Nebraska.

Carolyn Heitmeyer is a Research Fellow at the University of Sussex. Her doctoral work focused on Muslim identity, nationalism and violence in Gujarat. Her current research interests include biomedical governance and biotechnology.

Edward Simpson is Senior Lecturer in Social Anthropology at the School of Oriental and African Studies, University of London. He has written on religion and politics in Gujarat.

Claude Markovits is Senior Research Fellow Emeritus at the Centre of Indian and South Asian Studies, Paris. His publications include *The Global World of Indian Merchants* (Cambridge University Press, 2000), *The Un-Gandhian Gandhi: The life and afterlife of the Mahatma* (Permanent Black, 2004), and *Merchants, Traders, Entrepreneurs* (Palgrave Macmillan, 2008).

Acknowledgements

The idea for this volume sprang from a panel on the history of alcohol and drugs in South Asia, which the editors co-convened in 2010 at the 21st European Conference on Modern South Asian Studies in Bonn; while Hope Marie Childers, Jim Mills, and Erica Wald did not contribute to this volume, we gained important inspiration and insights from their presentation during the panel session. Claude Markovits not only offered fruitful remarks and critique on the presentations in the panel, we are happy and grateful that he also took the time to read the contributions to this volume and write an afterword. We would like to cordially thank Nikolay Kamenov and Francesco Spöring for discussing the introductory essay with us and, especially Vasudha Bharadwaj for her critical comments and revisions on the whole manuscript. We are also very grateful to Paromita Dasgupta and Janine Wilhelm for their copy-editing work. Especially Janine's patient and meticulous work on the manuscript has been of tremendous help for us. Finally, our thanks go to Routledge's anonymous reviewers for their supportive commentaries, to Dorothea Schaefter and Jillian Morrison for the unstinting support from the publisher's side, as well as to the *Journal of Imperial and Commonwealth History* for granting us permission to include Harald Fischer-Tiné's article on 'The Drinking Habits of our Countrymen'.

Introduction

Indian anomalies? – Drink and drugs in the land of Gandhi

Jana Tschurenev and Harald Fischer-Tiné

A few days before Christmas 2011 an incident that occurred in the Indian province of West Bengal made it to the breaking news of the national news-chains. From there it circulated to the bulletins of international television chains like BBC and *Al Jazeera* and reached a global audience within a few hours.[1] The events reported from a rural district in the densely populated Indian region bordering Bangladesh were most dreadful: more than 160 people had died following the consumption of adulterated *cholai*, a local variety of *desī dārū* or bootlegged Indian 'country liquor'. Some of the foreign commentators expressed their astonishment about the obvious popularity of strong drink among India's rural population. Their bewilderment must have grown when they learned that this mass poisoning was by no means a singular event: 107 people were listed as victims of bad moonshine in the southern state of Karnataka three years previously and more than 130 deaths from the same cause were recorded in July 2009 in Gujarat, the last of the Indian states to still be officially 'dry' today.[2]

What makes the event in West Bengal so intriguing is, then, not only the scale of the tragedy but also that it reminded a world-wide audience of a fact that is hardly part of the public image of India projected to the outside world, although well-known in the region itself. Contrary to popular perceptions, alcohol consumption is (and has been for centuries) a regular if problematic feature of the country's social life. The relative absence of alcohol and drinking in popular western imaginings of India is not least the result of the legacy of the powerful attempt at editing out the role of drink, initiated by a diverse range of historical actors from the late nineteenth century onwards. At the height of India's independence movement during the 1920s and 1930s, M.K. Gandhi and other spokesmen of the Indian National Congress (INC) were at pains to present India as a country of teetotallers, the positive antithesis of a debauched 'western civilization'.[3] Implicitly or explicitly, the increased consumption of alcohol among Indians and the problems resulting thereof were often cast by nationalists advocates of abstinence as mere consequences of pernicious European influence and the ensuing 'westernization' of the Indian educated classes in particular.[4] This interpretation was also compatible with the discourse of the international temperance movement. As early as 1887, a worker of the US-American Woman's Christian Temperance Union commented upon the prospects of expanding the organization's work in India that 'it is the Anglo-Indian rather than the native Hindu who needs reformation'.[5] Needless to say, such reductionist representations of India's 'alcohol problem' were ideally suited to lend credibility to the Indian nationalists' own temperance agitation. It is curious to note also that a similar rhetoric is revived in recent debates about India's 'new' middle class that has rapidly grown in the last two decades as a result of the politics of economic liberalization adopted in the late 1980s. In the vein of the earlier nationalist propaganda, it is often deplored nowadays that alcohol abuse is no longer predominantly a problem of the poor, as was assumed even in the medical literature until fairly recently,[6] and that the drinking habits of the country's well-heeled middling sorts damage 'India's reputation as a country with a culture of abstinence especially in matters regarding alcohol'.[7]

Having said that, it is important to mention that in portraying drink as alien to Indian society, the INC activists of the interwar period and today's admonishers of westernization had powerful allies. They could draw on a religious rhetoric that was popularized even earlier by a rather unlikely coalition of adherents to reformed Hinduism in India, Christian missionaries, as well as devotees of various esoteric groups and sects in the West. For very different reasons, representatives of all these groups had an interest in presenting alcohol consumption in general and excessive drinking in particular as part of the 'shallow materialism' that allegedly prevailed in the rapidly modernizing and secularizing countries of the West and had no moorings in 'spiritual' India.

Astonishingly enough, we find rather the reverse picture when it comes to the issue of more 'exotic' stimulants, namely psychoactive substances like cannabis and opium. For centuries, the subcontinent had come to be regarded and represented in the West as a site of intense drug consumption.[8] Even according to the conventional wisdom of the early twentieth century, Indians (much like the Chinese) could indulge in their 'distinctive vice'[9] largely unhindered by moral restraints or legal interventions of the (despotic oriental) state. This view was particularly influential among colonial administrators. Thus, a British surgeon writing in 1868 presented the drug habits of the 'native' population of East Bengal in crudely generalizing and essentializing terms, stating that 'Mahomedans are addicted to opium eating and in Dacca all adults of above forty years of age become slaves to this drug.' Probably even more shocking for an western audience he added that 'Mahomedan mothers almost invariably give infants, from the fortieth day after birth, until they are three years old a small quantity of opium daily.'[10] Yet, while such ascriptions or, for that matter, Indian self-representations to the effect that 'opium may be regarded as the parallel to wine and beer in Europe and America'[11] were rarely brought into question among European commentators, there existed a tremendous variety in the ways in which this stereotype was received in the West. During the eighteenth and early nineteenth centuries many European servants of the English East India Company quickly adopted the opium filled *hookah* (water pipe) as one of the more agreeable features of oriental culture, even though this practice of smoking opium instead of eating it was regarded as 'degenerate' at home.[12] Reflecting the impact of an increasingly medicalized global crusade against mood altering substances, some tourist guide books, *vademecums* and medical treatises of late nineteenth and early twentieth century, by contrast, painted a rather gloomy picture of the emaciated 'drug addicts' in the opium dens of Indian port towns. In a book on the 'by-ways of Bombay', for instance, British police commissioner S.M. Edwardes took his readers into one of the 'clubs in the city where a man may purchase nightly oblivion for the modest sum of two or three annas'[13] and provided them with the following noteworthy account:

> The room is not a large one, for the habitual smoker prefers a small apartment, in which the fumes of the drug hang about easily; and its reeking walls are unadorned save with a chromo plan of the chief buildings at Mecca, a crude portrait of a Hindu goddess, and oleographs of British royalty. It were all the same if these were absent; for the opium-smoker comes not hither to see pictures, save those which the drugged brain fashions, and cares not for distinctions of race, creed or sovereignty. The proprietor of the club may be a Musalman; his patrons may be Hindus, Christians or Chinese; and the dreams which riot across the semi-consciousness of the latter are not concerned as a rule with heroes of either the spiritual or temporal kind.[14]

When Edwardes's book was first published in 1912, his depiction of oriental 'drug habits' – and the resulting blurring of racial and cultural boundaries– was certainly designed to shock an European visitor to India. Half a century later, however, his colourful narrative would possibly have added to the attraction of the country for a new generation of western travellers who visited the subcontinent precisely because of the lax attitude *vis-à-vis* the consumption of intoxicants that supposedly prevailed there. The American Beat poet Allen Ginsberg, for instance, famously confessed that it was not least the expectation to encounter the (drug-induced) 'living transmission of spiritual and visionary energy'[15] that made him spend a year in India in 1962/63, thus paving the way for countless young Westerners who would criss-cross the subcontinent during the next two decades in search of drugs and spirituality – a phenomenon whose 'pre-history' is further explored by Maria Moritz in this volume.

Building on these impressionistic observations on some popular representations and perceptions of the use of intoxicants in India, then, one could frame an argument regarding the somewhat paradoxical situation that the subcontinent has been simultaneously constructed as a site of abstinence (when it comes to alcohol) and a site of intense and unrestricted consumption (when it comes to opium or cannabis). However, such a dichotomy of 'Western' and 'Eastern' substances, of 'legal' and 'illegal' intoxicants is misleading. In a pioneering article, American historian Marc Jason Gilbert has recently observed that 'liquor and opium use, licit and illicit, have always had a place in the Indian economy'.[16] The same holds true, one might add, when it comes to Indian culture. Nonetheless, differential treatment of alcohol and 'exotic stimulants' seems to structure historical research on intoxicants in the Indian subcontinent. This, at least, is a conclusion one would be tempted to draw when contrasting the relatively rich body of literature on the history of drugs like opium with the scarce writings on alcohol consumption in South Asia. The present volume, therefore, is an attempt to bring together fresh research on all varieties of mood altering substances in modern India and analyze them in a common framework through a set of what we feel are meaningful analytical categories and critical questions. It is our primary objective to provide a corrective for oversimplifications and generalizations that still have an astonishing currency when it comes to issues of alcohol and drug consumption in South Asia by historicizing and contextualizing the role that intoxicants have played in the region over the past 200 odd years. In doing so the book is not only designed to fill a gap in South Asia related historiography, it also wants to build on and contribute to the exciting and constantly growing field of literature on the global history of alcohol and drugs more generally.[17] We feel that the opening of a narrow 'area studies' perspective on intoxicants in South Asia through comparisons with other world regions but also through the analysis of actual interactions and entanglements with other parts of the globe within and beyond the British Empire provides a much more accurate and complete picture of the problematic.

The politics of drink and temperance: Historical research on alcohol in South Asia

While it has been often repeated that the brahmanical textual tradition and Islamic law prohibited alcoholic beverages,[18] sources such as the epics *Ramayana* and *Mahabhahrata* indicate that drinking was common in *kshatriya* milieus. During the Mauryan period (fourth century BCE), a governmental system of regulating the production and sales of alcohol seemed to have been in place.[19] Wine-drinking was common practice at the Mughal court, as in other contemporary Muslim courts.[20] The autobiographies of Mughal emperors Babur and Jahangir reveal that both were 'great lovers of alcohol', even if from time to time suffering 'pangs of guilt about their drinking habit.'[21] Moreover, as Meera Khare shows, in an environment inspired by Sufi mysticism, the image of the wine cup in Mughal paintings could assume a variety of spiritual-religious meanings.[22]

While wine was thus appreciated within court culture, social drinking was (and still is) an essential part of rural life, as for instance David Hardiman's seminal study on peasant drinking patterns in South Gujarat shows.[23] 'What wine is to a Frenchman ..., and beer to the German or Englishman', the liquor contractor A.M. Dalal testified in 1923 in front of the Bombay excise committee, 'toddy is to a poor husbandman, a Bhil, a seafaring Kharwa, a Koli and a hardworking labourer.'[24] Toddy, i.e., the fermented juice from certain kinds of palm trees, was used as an 'aid to digestion', and a 'substitute for both food and water' in times of economic hardship.[25] Village-manufactured toddy and *dārū*, the 'country liquor' made from the Mahua flower (*Bassia latifolia*),[26] were offered to guests as token of hospitality, sealed the decisions reached at *panchayat* meetings, and were consumed at feasts and celebrations.[27] While drink was most important as a mark of friendship and an expression of solidarity, tribal religion also included drink offerings in acts of worship. Alcohol served as 'food of the gods', and was used by spirit mediums to enhance their state of trance. Hardiman quotes a 'local proverb' saying 'God gave the brahman ghi and the Bhil liquor.'[28] Drinking in South Gujarat was not confined to the Adivasi peasants; even the Parsis, who often acted as liquor contractors in the framework of the colonial excise policy, 'were well known for their love of toddy and country liquor'.[29] Thus when arguing 'that drink was alien to Indian culture', Hardiman concludes, the middle class social reformers who started to advocate temperance and prohibition from the mid-nineteenth century onwards 'confused their own élite values with Indian culture as a whole'.[30]

In the wake of the nationalist movement, the promotion – quite successful, as we have seen – of the image of India as an abstinent culture had allowed for the nationalist elite's assertion of moral superiority against the intemperate colonizers.[31] Moreover, the prohibition of alcoholic drinks, a forceful demand of nationalists and temperance activists since the 1900s, was a means to severely diminish the colonial state's resources. The taxation of psychoactive substances was not only a 'fiscal cornerstone of the modern state' in general, but also 'the chief financial prop of European colonial regimes'.[32] Boycotting liquor, imported spirits, and toddy was a prominent strategy within the *swadeshi* campaign of 1905, which sought to further economic self-sufficiency and national identity.[33] As John Rogers and others have persuasively argued, a close connection between the temperance movement and nationalist mobilization also existed in Ceylon. International organizations such as the Theosophical Society promoted temperance within the Buddhist revival movement. Abstaining from drink, in this context, became a marker of a Buddhist-Singhalese cultural-national identity, also against the Tamil population. Thus, in this instance, the 'alcohol question' came to fuel communal conflict.[34]

In India, the standard of abstaining from alcoholic beverages was closely linked to various efforts to appropriate or impose upper caste norms, which became part of modern middle class culture. Lucy Carroll has shown that early temperance associations were formed in the wake of an influential writer-caste's – the *kayasthas* – struggle for self-improvement.[35] While she rejects a classical Sanskritization thesis as a viable interpretative framework for such efforts, continuities between caste politics and social reform campaigns in the modern public sphere can clearly be detected.[36] When nationalists mobilized the Indian public against the production, sale, and consumption of alcohol as part of their anti-colonial agitation, this implied the enforcement of brahmanical values among other social classes.[37] Social boycott, caste sanctions, and other coercive measures were at times applied to punish transgressors against the nationalist course.[38] What Ian Tyrrell has observed looking at the 'imperial feminism' of the World Woman's Christian Temperance Union, is hence also valid for the nationalist movement in India: 'history is replete with ironies in which the dominated become agents of domination'.[39]

Conflicts arising from nationalistic efforts to impose Sanskritic norms of abstention on groups which do not conform to them are still to be observed, as Peggy Froerer's study on Hindu nationalism in rural India demonstrates.[40] Alpa Shah's study on the Maoist anti-drinking campaign in Jharkhand in 2000, however, argues against 'binaries of "sanskritisation" versus *adivasi* assertion' by pointing to a generational division in the conflicts over Adivasi drinking.[41] The Maoist campaign revealed their leaders' ambiguous stance toward Adivasi lifestyles. Similar to the image of tribal 'wildness' in colonial discourse, Maoist leaders viewed Adivasi culture as characterized by both, masculine valour and a 'natural' propensity for insurgency on the one hand, and 'barbarous' tendencies in need of taming on the other hand. In the main, it was well-entrenched stereotypical images of tribal drinking, such as the figure of the wife-beating male drunkard that fuelled the latter aspect. Thus, the Maoist campaign targeted the common home-made drinks of the Adivasis, *hadia*, a beer made from rice, and *mahuā kā pānī*, but not the 'foreign varieties' of alcohol preferred by the higher caste rural elite. The Adivasi response to the new norms was marked by a generational differentiation. While the Maoists alienated the older generation, who sought to uphold social drinking, a new generation of educated Adivasi youth would rather emulate the rural elite, change their drinking pattern, and support the Maoist efforts.[42]

It would be misleading, therefore, to interpret temperance agitation solely in terms of upper caste/middle class politics of distinction, and/or cultural hegemony. Otherwise, it would be difficult to explain that campaigns against drinking have been a part of many of the Adivasi rebellions which were at the centre of early subaltern studies research.[43] In 1895, 1905, and 1922–3, popular temperance movements occurred in South Gujarat, partially in resistance to the colonial taxation policy; the last one, the Devi movement, was the most influential anti-liquor movement in the history of the region.[44] In 1878, the colonial administration started to implement new excise regulations in the Bombay presidency. The idea behind the Abkari Act of 1878 was to extract maximum revenue from a minimum consumption of intoxicating liquors. Under its provisions, the production of mahua liquor (*desī dārū*) was to be confined to central distilleries, where the excise duty was to be levied before the liquor left the distillery. Moreover, toddy-tapping was to be licensed and the palm trees taxed under excise. Both liquor and toddy were only to be sold in licensed shops.[45] In this way, drink was made a standardized commodity from which regular rates of excise could be expected. The process of commodification 'drove the people out of the fields to the shop',[46] resulting in a de facto prohibition and the criminalization of what was before common practice. Not surprisingly, this was met with 'organized, collective resistance'[47] from the side of the peasantry – people took refuge to illicit tapping, distillation and smuggling. Moreover, protests against the Abkari legislation were issued from the English and vernacular press, as well as from nationalist organizations.[48] These protests deserve some emphasis since they point to the fact that, besides there being in general a strong link between nationalist mobilization and temperance, even colonial measures limiting the accessibility of alcoholic drink could face nationalist opposition. For the Adivasi peasants, the commodification of liquor often led to increased debt and, consequently, loss of land. To jump on the temperance bandwagon, therefore, could prevent further pauperization. Taking a vow to abstain in the future from toddy and *dārū* showed commitment to the cause of communal advance and allowed people to express their protest against colonial taxation, as well as against money-lenders who often were at the same time liquor sellers.[49]

A more recent, and quite successful, case of a popular movement against alcohol occurred in Andhra Pradesh in the 1990s. Women, many of them with a low caste background, organized themselves to fight the effects of arrack on their families and communities.[50] The 'alcohol question' had proved quite important in the history of women's political mobilization and activism in India. Many women participated in the Congress's measures of boycotting liquor during the Indian independence movement.[51] It is important to note that this was perfectly in line with a broader global trend that can be traced back to the late nineteenth and early twentieth century. For example, in the USA and British settler colonies, fighting 'the devil of the domestic sphere'[52] (in Andhra the women would 'slay' a 'spirituous demon')[53] proved quite an important entry point for women into the public sphere.[54] As Karin Rosemblatt's case study on Chile in the 1930s and 1940s shows, women's organizations actively promoted the norm of the male bread-winner family, which implied a new code of responsible and temperate masculinity as well.[55]

The National Literacy Mission also prepared the ground for the rural women's political articulation in Andhra Pradesh. Domestic violence and the wasting of families' resources in the liquor store were concerns which sparked the anti-arrack agitation in 1990. As the movement progressed, the activists raised demands of total prohibition, and formed political alliances which helped to achieve this goal in 1995.[56]

Among other things, one must note that, as in other parts of the world, the 'alcohol question in South Asia was crucially linked to employers' and social reformers' concerns over the morality, discipline, and efficiency of the working class, and the establishment of modern labour regimes.[57] In 1880, the English daily *The Englishman* published a letter that vividly complained about 'grog shops' which were to be found 'at the gates of every tea garden of

Assam', which tended 'to attract the coolies away from their work, to increase sickness in our lines and difficulty in the management of labour'.[58] Work spaces such as plantations, factories, and mines, around which labourers (and, at times, their families) build their social lives, became privileged sites for limiting alcoholic drink, or the establishment of 'dry zones'.[59] Such efforts were often contested by labourers, who insisted on their leisure habits, but were also made difficult by the long practice of paying labourers partially in rum and liquor.[60]

Taken together, the literature on drink and temperance points towards the complexity of the co-existing norms and practices of drinking in colonial and postcolonial South Asia, in which colonial domination and its contestation intersected with struggles along the lines of caste, class and gender. The picture would, however, remain incomplete without considering the drinking behaviour of Europeans in South Asia, British and otherwise, and pointing to the conflicts that surrounded it. Recent research by proponents of a 'new military history', for example, has shown that drunkenness (and the resulting 'vices') of British troops alarmed colonial policy makers.[61] While the behaviour of an unruly and disorderly colonial underclass of (partially) European descent particularly seemed to threaten claims to British civilized superiority,[62] they were not the only ones to blame when it came to heavy drinking – points which the contributions of Fischer-Tiné and Delfs in this volume will explore, and which might further help to historicize the formation of the contrasting images of drinking Europeans and abstaining Indians.

Historical research on opium and cannabis in South Asia

In contrast to the still rather fragmented studies on alcoholic drink, the literature on hallucinogenic substances in South Asia is as diverse as it is copious. The approaches vary from economic history to cultural history, religious studies to Indology. The only comprehensive monograph attempting to deal with all major aspects of the topic was penned by the Bangladeshi scholar Emdad-El Haq. It was published in 2000 under the title *Drugs in South Asia*.[63] In his subtitle, the author promises to cover the period 'from the opium trade to the present day', and it is precisely this overambitious aspiration that leads to the shortcomings of Haq's work. Despite the author's command of a wide array of sources, it ultimately proves to be impossible to write with an equal degree of authority about the opium policy of the English East India Company in the 1790s and the growth of a 'narco-democracy' in Pakistan in the 1990s. Not surprisingly, therefore, the historical part of the book remains somewhat superficial. Haq, who is a political scientist and devotes the bulk of his volume to post-independence developments, has consequently been accused of 'presentism' by some historians.[64] In an attempt to avoid these pitfalls, we do not even try to review the vast body of literature on drugs in South Asia over the last couple of centuries. In what follows, we rather confine ourselves to a brief discussion of some of the major trends of research focussing on opium and cannabis during the colonial period, which provides the temporal framework for most contributions in this volume.

Given its economic significance from the late eighteenth to the early twentieth century, it is hardly surprising that opium has received by far the most attention by historians to date. By the early twentieth century, several authors – some of whom were still working within the framework of British imperialism while others were related to the anti-opium movement – already reconstructed the genealogy of the poppy plant in South Asia.[65] According to their findings, opium came to the subcontinent with the Arab arrival in Sindh in the early eighth century. Initially it was predominantly used for medical purposes, being an important element of the pharmacopeia used in the Islamic healing system of *Unani-tibb*.[66] By the fifteenth and sixteenth centuries, however, the widespread 'recreational and semi-medicinal use'[67] of the drug amongst Hindu and Muslim elites is well documented. Particularly the affinity of the Mughal nobility towards opiate use (and abuse) has attracted some scholarly attention,[68] although an in-depth study of the phenomenon still remains a desideratum.

As far as the colonial period is concerned, research about opium in South Asia has been largely dominated by economic historians. From the 1920s onwards, the British monopoly of the opium trade in Bengal has been discussed controversially among them. Whereas early imperialist historiography was apparently at pains to stress that the British were only continuing the opium policy of the Mughal emperors,[69] David Owen's pioneering work on the imperial drug trade maintained that even though the British might not have introduced the drug to India, it was nonetheless their 'talent for organization that made of it a world problem'.[70] Needless to say, that this 'world problem' affected some parts of the globe more severely than others. Owen clearly alludes here to a second focus of the literature: the opium exports from British India to South East Asia and, above all, China.

Whereas a number of studies published in the 1950s and 1960s offered greater insights into the organization of the colonial opium economy in this wider political and economic framework, it was a more far-reaching argument brought forth by David Washbrook in the 1990s that would provoke a renewed interest in the economic and political significance of opium in colonial India and beyond. According to Washbrook, 'Company India was engaged in building perhaps the world's first "narco-military" empire, an empire in which power and profit remained as closely linked as ever they had been in the Mercantilist Age of the eighteenth century'.[71] The coupling of poppy policy and empire building was also the starting point for Carl Trocki's influential study, which argued that not only was opium the 'keystone' of colonial empires in Asia in the long nineteenth century, it was also 'vital to the capitalist transformation of the local economies'.[72] Most recently a similar argument has been forcefully reiterated in the 800 odd pages of Dutch historian Hans Derks' colossal monograph on the *History of the Opium Problem*.[73]

Whereas Trocki and Derks look at the wider framework of European opium trading in Asia, and devote only a few chapters to India, some studies have focused exclusively on the South Asian context during the past two decades. The work of our author Amar Farooqui is particularly noteworthy in this regard. Farooqui shifted the focus away from the well documented and intensely studied 'official' trade in Bengal opium as monopolized by the EIC,[74] and explored instead the agency of Indian actors who controlled the 'Malwa trade' in central and western India. From his detailed case studies he derived a broader theory, arguing that opium has been a key factor not only in the emergence of Bombay as a commercial centre and metropolis but also in the making of an indigenous capitalist class.[75] Amar Farooqui further develops this point in his contribution to the present volume, defending it against criticism that has recently been levelled against his far-reaching conclusions drawn from the analysis of indigenous opium dealings in western India by French historian Claude Markovits.[76] The debate partly continues in the pages of this book, since Claude Markovits uses his afterword to engage with Farooqui's reply to his criticism.

Besides the complexities of the political economy of the production and trade in the Indian subcontinent, the question of the 'moral economy' of opium has also turned out to be a fruitful area of research. One important focus of interest has been the Royal Commission on Opium which toured India in 1893/94 and the impact of its multi-volume report published in 1895.[77] In earlier literature, the Commission, whose members eventually arrived at the conclusion that neither opium production nor the consumption of the drug were harmful for the subcontinental population's economic and physical well-being, has been accused of whitewashing Britain's ruthless drug business in the subcontinent.[78] In a widely-circulated article, John F. Richards, by contrast, presented the Commission's recommendations as a culturally sensitive intervention of the colonial state, protecting the Indian populace from the 'cultural imperialism' of the protestant anti-opium movement.[79] This positive assessment provoked immediate criticism. Pratik Chakrabarti, for instance, critiqued Richards's lack of distance from his sources.[80] Criticism of a similar kind is also implicit in a comprehensive study on the Commission by Paul C. Winther, who argues that the British constructed a 'scientific' argument to cloak their economic interests in the opium trade.[81] As Winther shows in great detail, opium production and consumption in India was defended not least by Anglo-Indian surgeons on the grounds of the drugs putative potency in preventing malaria.[82]

While the activities of British merchants and officials as well as the interventions of western missionary or other civil society organizations thus continue to be an important topic for historians of South Asia, Indian actors in the opium trade or the fight against it have received comparatively little attention. This is surprising, not least because – analogous to what we have seen with respect to alcohol – the struggle against the colonial government's liberal opium policy was also discovered by Indian nationalists to be an issue on which their own agenda of social reform and moral purity could be combined with an attack on an immoral colonial regime. It is well known, for instance, that Mohandas Gandhi strongly opposed the use of opium for non-medical purposes and used the anti-drug rhetoric also on a metaphorical level, comparing the relationship of the Indian people to their British colonizers to that of a drug addict to his dealer.[83] Furthermore, his illustrious British follower '*dīnbandhu*' C.F. Andrews forcefully campaigned against the state monopoly and advocated Britain's responsibility in combatting the 'opium evil' in India.[84] Despite the involvement of such renowned leaders of the freedom movement, the existing literature on this topic, however, is rather sparse and the chapters by Kawal Kour and Maria Framke in this volume can help to close the existing gap.

In contradistinction to opium, Indian hemp has for a long time been completely neglected by South Asianists. This research lacuna is astonishing considering the fact that the cultivation of the *cannabis sativa* plant and the consumption of its leaves, blossoms and resin in the local forms of *ganjā*, *bhāng* and *chāras* have a long tradition in the region.[85] It is only in recent years and largely due to the single-handed effort of Glaswegian historian James H. Mills that we have by now a fairly nuanced understanding of the uses of Indian hemp and the politics of regulating its production, trade and consumption during the last two centuries. Mills first explored the relationship between cannabis and the psychiatric diagnosis of madness in a chapter of his monograph on lunatic asylums in colonial India.[86] In his subsequent in-depth study *Cannabis Britannica*[87] as well as in a number of articles he has further explored various facets of the drug's history in British India and beyond. The scope of his interests is remarkable: besides early British medical experiments with 'gunjah'[88] and international 'high politics' on cannabis,[89] James Mills has also critically examined the impact of specific groups and political agendas on the Indian Hemp Drug Commission (IHDC) 1893/94, a body set up almost simultaneously with the Opium Commission. According to Mills, the story of the IHDC likewise reflected the growing influence of the evangelical temperance lobby in British and imperial politics.[90] His findings once more underline the necessity to analyze the fight against alcohol and drugs in a common analytical frame rather than in isolation. This insight has apparently also guided the research undertaken by Michael Agrosino, who explores subaltern drug practices, demonstrating that intoxicating substances are highly interchangeable not only in the eyes of elite 'anti-vice' activists but also for consumers from the lower social orders.[91] In a fascinating case study on South Asian indentured labourers in Trinidad, the US-based anthropologist has shown how the habit of consuming *ganjā*, initially prevalent among the 'coolies', was gradually replaced with a fancy for rum. However, Agrosino's case study not only reminds us once more that the widespread idea that intoxicating substances possess a sort of a 'natural cultural habitat' is utterly misleading. The fact that this change in the coolies' recreational practices was pushed by their employers in the sugar plantations simultaneously points to the close inter-linkages between the regulation of access to intoxicants and the disciplining of labour that have been outlined above. In addition, Agrosino's study of a migrant community illustrates how fruitful it can be to widen the geographical frame of analysis. In the next section we will therefore sketch out more systematically the global contexts in which the South Asian contestations over intoxicants were enmeshed.

Drink and drugs in a global context

As the international literature on the history of alcohol and drugs suggests, cultural norms and governmental regulations regarding different psychoactive substances are often closely related. Such relations include the establishment of analogies between substances and their presumed social or medical effects, as the case of the medicalization of the alcohol problem in the US shows. Alcohol was the first substance the properties of which were deemed 'addictive', a paradigm which was then used to frame the understanding of opiates and cannabis.[92] Moreover, to moral and social reformers in the US and Latin America as well as in Britain and other European countries, intoxicants were at the core of urban 'vice constellations',[93] which also included prostitution and gambling.[94] An integrative research approach can thus show how different intoxicants are placed in a common interpretative framework. The framework emerging in the late nineteenth century was shaped by a biological view of the human and eugenicist concerns over the inheritability of damages caused by drink and narcotics as 'racial poisons'.[95] Moreover, such an approach can reveal how certain intoxicants came to be privileged over others, such as in the ban on substances of non-European origin in modern Western Europe and the US on the one hand, and their coming to terms with alcoholic drinks on the other.

Thus, while this volume brings together research on drinking norms and practices of different groups in South Asian history through studies on the use of *ganja* and the economics and regulation of opium, it locates them in the framework of wider geographical entanglements. The global economic process that Courtwright described as 'the confluence of the world's psychoactive resources'[96] made a wide range of increasingly potent intoxicants available to a broadening range of consumers. Moreover, as we have already indicated, they proved to be crucial for the building of overseas-empires.[97] How closely the history of alcohol and drugs is tied to the political and moral economies of modern colonial empires has most recently been shown in the seminal volume edited by James Mills and Patricia Barton.[98] Against the background of the global dimension of the production, trafficking, and consumption of various psychoactive substances as capitalist commodities, the efforts to contain and limit them also took shape internationally.

Further, we have emphasized the close connection between temperance agitation and nationalist mobilization in India as well as Ceylon in this volume. While the 'fight against alcohol' and other 'vices' certainly figured prominently in many projects of national 'regeneration' and integration in South Asia and elsewhere,[99] a strong international civil society movement offered legitimacy, material resources, and moral support to temperance workers in all lands.[100] 'Large-scale temperance behemoths such as the International Order of Good Templars (IOGT), the Blue Cross and the World Woman's Christian Temperance Union (WWCTU)',[101] together with a broad variety of local and regional, professional, children's, and students' organizations provided important channels of communication. International congresses and conventions provided the platform to discuss scientific theories which supported the demand for abstinence, to formulate policy recommendations and build pressure on national and colonial governments and the League of Nations.[102] Though driven by diverse motives, many anti-alcohol activists displayed a kind of 'unitary humanity model' or 'one-worldism'[103] that framed alcohol as an enemy to the progress of the human race as a whole. In the early decades of the twentieth century, many of them broadened their agenda to also campaign against opium or cigarette smoking.

The first modern organized temperance movements, which occurred in the context of the evangelical revival in the US and Britain, stressed the promotion of virtues of individual self-control.[104] However, while signing a pledge of total abstinence remained the basic form for joining any voluntary association dedicated to temperance, activists increasingly shifted their focus to the demand for state intervention.[105] Thus, the global wave of national prohibition legislations (c. 1914–30) was partially due to an influential transnational advocacy network.[106] The advocates of prohibition in India were well aware of these global currents and were very interested in the success especially of the most prominent case, namely American prohibition (1920–33).[107] At the same time, the temperance activities of Gandhi and other Indian nationalists were enthusiastically reported upon in international publications such as the *Union Signal*, issued by the American WCTU.[108] Through a close alliance with British and American missionaries and international organizations such as the WCTU (which had had an active 'national' chapter in India since 1893), Indian nationalist temperance advocates were part of a powerful international activist network.[109]

The anti-alcohol 'crusade' can be interpreted as one of the first global issues, a problem that was assumed to be manageable only by means of worldwide cooperation or, to use a popular current term, global governance. The 'infamous liquor traffic' which appeared to threaten especially the 'native races' of Africa was driven by imperial competition and transcended any national boundaries.[110] As a consequence, only an international regulatory regime would be able to control and restrict it. As early as in the 1880s, international negotiations went on between several imperial powers to regulate the influx of 'trade spirits' to West Africa and Cameroon.[111]

Around the same time, the international regulation of opium also gained momentum. While the lax attitude towards opiate use characteristic of early nineteenth century Britain and France was slowly replaced by a more critical and anti-permissive stance from the 1860s onwards,[112] the arrival of the United States on the world stage ensured that the global anti-opium lobby eventually took off around 1900. Historians have provided several persuasive explanations for the fact that the USA became the driving force of a world-wide anti-drug regime in the twentieth century. First, the emergence of a growing minority of Chinese labourers on the Pacific coast and along the railway confronted federal and state governments with a novel drug problem that soon spilled over to other communities too.[113] Secondly, the proselytizing efforts of US missionaries in China were severely hampered by the image of Westerners as 'drug-dealers',[114] and as a result, a strong evangelical lobby tried to influence US foreign policy. Lastly, and perhaps most importantly, the problem acquired new dimensions soon after the Americans attained the colonial territory of the Philippines after the Spanish-American War of 1898, and with it tens of thousands of opium consumers in the local population. The US colonial authorities soon realized that they could not suppress consumption through the implementation of a colonial law. The Philippines were only one nodal point in a worldwide web of drug trafficking and efficient countermeasures therefore had to be taken on an international level.[115] As has been shown in great detail by historians of various backgrounds, British India – the world's largest producer of raw opium at the time – became a major target of the ensuing US anti-drug crusades. In the first international opium conferences of Shanghai (1909), The Hague (1912) and Geneva (1924–5), regarded today as milestones in the evolution of an international drug-regulation regime, zealous American prohibitionists frequently clashed with representatives of the Raj, at least some of whom remained eager to protect one of their most vital sources of tax revenue.[116]

Against this general background, it is one of the objectives of the present volume to analyze the history of intoxicants and intoxication in modern South Asia within the framework of imperial and international connections. This approach not only takes into account cultural encounters and the drawing of racial and class boundaries within the colonial social formation,[117] but also global reform movements, travellers' experiences, international diplomacy and institution-building with respect to both opium and alcohol.

Chapter previews

In the first chapter, James McHugh explores the historiography and selected sources on 'Alcohol in Pre-Modern South Asia.' He first provides an overview on the cultural norms surrounding a number of alcoholic beverages in the Sanskrit tradition, exploring concepts such as *surā*, *soma* and the generic term *madya.* He considers texts which comprise both normative-ethical as well as medical materials. He points to the function of alcohol as a social marker in early India, and how the ethics of consumption and the restrictions attached to social hierarchies were based on gender and caste. Referring to the *Caraka-Saṃhitā Agniveśa*, an early Ayurvedic text, the author shows how intoxicating drinks were assumed to exert varying effects on different bodily constitutions while the ideal drink was expected to bring about 'happiness, sexual potency, and corpulence'.

After shortly discussing alcohol in the Mughal court culture, McHugh also analyzes some of the myths relating to alcohol production and consumption in early India. The secondary literature on the subject includes romantic claims that Vedic people were more than aware of the evils of alcohol, as well as conjectures that early 'brahmin settlers' indulged heavily in *soma* beer. McHugh introduces the controversy surrounding the question of when the technique of fermentation first occurred in South Asia. Such controversies come as a reminder of the need for a detailed, context-sensitive study of the available sources instead of overarching generalizations on alcohol in or essentialist constructions of 'pre-modern India'.

That the production and sale of opium was a cornerstone of the British imperial economy is well known. Amar Farooqui's paper 'Opium, the East India Company and the "Native" States' examines the colonial policy towards the production and trade of opium that was *not* under British control. As early as 1800 the East India Company had a system in place under which the opium production of eastern Uttar Pradesh (under the brand name 'Banaras opium') and Bihar ('Patna opium') were shipped to Calcutta, where they were auctioned and subsequently shipped to the Chinese market. The opium production of what is today's Madhya Pradesh, broadly designated 'Malwa opium', however, posed a fundamental challenge to this trade system. The region consisted of a number of princely states which found it more lucrative to ship their opium production through an alternative trade network to China, via Pali in Rajasthan, Karachi and Daman, rather than to sell it to the East India Company. Farooqui's paper analyzes in detail how the agents of the Company sought to gain control over this trade with the help of bilateral treaties. Capt. J. Caulfield, for example, signed a contract with Madho Singh of the Kota state, proposing to buy 4,000 *man* of opium every year. A similar contract was signed by Gerald Wellesley and the state of Indore. Having a profound knowledge of the trafficking process 'on the ground', company agents tried to impede opium smuggling through contracts that promised a stable market. The contracts were met with skepticism in the company's headquarters at first, but with time similar orders were actually enforced. Farooqui thus points at the agency of the princely states in the networks of opium trafficking within the British Empire and beyond.

Tobias Delfs' chapter on 'Drunkenness and mission in eighteenth century Danish East India' breaks new ground by looking at a European colonial power that is often forgotten in conventional accounts of the period. The small Danish enclaves in the subcontinent are nonetheless important in that they provided a crucial hub for ambitious missionary activities that would have a pivotal impact on the way India's encounter with European modernity took place in the eighteenth century. Delfs explores the social history of the representatives of Danish-English-Halle Mission in the Danish territory of

Serampore in Bengal and reveals that there existed a widespread drinking problem in missionary circles. He first attempts to reconstruct the general attitude towards alcohol that prevailed in the German and Scandinavian Pietist milieu from which the missionaries were recruited, and then shifts to the actual drinking practices in the colonial periphery of Europeans in general and missionaries in particular. In a marvellous example of micro-history, the author eventually zooms in on the biography of the Danish missionary Lambert Christian Früchtenicht (1772–1806), who served in India for more than five years and was eventually expelled from the mission because of his excessive drinking and undisciplined behaviour. Delfs' piece opens up a window onto the everyday life of 'white subalterns' in India and thus feeds into a new current of imperial history concerned with the social history of Europeans from the lower orders in the colonies, and the ideological consequences that their transgressive behaviour had on various projects designed by the colonial elites.

Harald Fischer-Tiné's contribution 'Liquid Boundaries: race, class and alcohol in British India' dovetails nicely with the previous chapter in that it also looks at the effects that European alcohol consumption had on both, colonial ideologies as well as actual governance. However, the focus shifts from Danish missionaries in the eighteenth century to the middle and lower ranks of the non-official community in British India during the heyday of empire in mid-nineteenth century. The chapter starts with a brief section providing information on the evolution of a European drinking problem in the Company era and the emergence of moral and medical discourses on alcohol (and abstinence) among the colonial elites. The subsequent parts focus on particular communities that were often associated with the 'liquor question'. The first group under scrutiny are European sailors and pilots. Similar to 'white' soldiers, the representatives of maritime professions were not only mainstays of the colonial projects of expansion, control and exploitation, they were also regarded as 'naturally' prone to the temptations of drink. The next section looks at the 'wrong sorts' of non-official European community transcending the maritime periphery of the subcontinent: European planters and vagrants. Particularly the latter group of peripatetic 'white subalterns' came to be seen as fundamentally dangerous to colonial self-legitimizing ideologies through their mere existence. As was the case with the planters, part of their negative image derived from their drinking culture and the implications of their 'drunk and disorderly behaviour', particularly their propensity for uncontrolled aggression and violence against the 'natives' when intoxicated. As is demonstrated in detail in the case studies, this perceived link between alcohol consumption and 'white violence' was regarded as one the main reasons for the colonial government to regulate the alcohol consumption of certain segments of the European population in British India. The anti-alcohol campaigns that were launched by the colonial state and civil society organizations thus constituted an important aspect of the wider imperial project.

Maria Moritz's chapter shifts the focus from alcohol to the consumption of cannabis, or *ganja*. Her paper 'Looking for Spirituality in India' closely examines two years (1894–6) in the life of German theosophist, trader and transnational citizen Wilhelm Hübbe-Schleiden to illuminate the connections between increasing global travel, information exchange and commodification of drugs. Making use of Hübbe-Schleiden's personal papers and published materials, Moritz reconstructs how Hübbe-Schleiden's spiritual quest lead him from a European interest in 'Indian religion', through experimenting with yoga, *ganja* and asceticism with his 'guru' Pasupati Deva in Uttarpara near Calcutta, to disillusionment with 'Indian spirituality'. Around this core focus, Moritz draws together secondary literature from German and English-speaking historians to show how Hübbe-Schleiden's experiences in India were formed in the context of new historical entanglements of tourism, exchange of spiritual ideas and drug-taking. Drawing our attention to the late-twentieth century phenomenon of 'finding oneself in India' with the help of intoxicants and spiritual techniques, Moritz persuasively argues that the phenomenon of 'drug tourism', though it seemed to have emerged in the late Cold War global economy, was in fact part of a historical tradition with deep roots in the colonial period.

The paper of Kawal Deep Kour, 'The Opium Question in Colonial Assam', is a close examination of the Assam Opium Enquiry Committee Report from 1933 and the shifting attitudes towards opium in Assam in the late nineteenth century that led to its formation. The so-called 'Maximum Revenue from the Minimum Consumption' policy of the colonial government in Assam, as Kour shows, was based on the liberal-colonial principle of 'non-interference' with local custom, a broad belief in the therapeutic qualities of opium and even a 'lesser of two evils logic' that, influenced by the massive temperance campaigns, found opium less dangerous than alcohol, at least for Indians. Between the years 1900 and 1921, however, Assam witnessed a dramatic change in its attitude toward opium. Partially due to international developments, a number of anti-opium societies emerged in Assam. M.K. Gandhi's tour through the interior in 1920 and the subsequent launch of a temperance movement in Assam also contributed to the change of attitude against opium. Towards the end of the 1920s, efforts spearheaded by the League of Nations to check the global proliferation of opium further strengthened enforcement efforts in Assam. The pinnacle of efforts was marked by the 1933 Committee, which conducted an official enquiry by travelling through Assam and interviewing opium eaters, among others. The Committee's findings repudiated the discourse of medical and therapeutic use of opium and argued for a closer restriction of the population's access to opium.

The links between the League of Nations opium policy and colonial and national debates in India are further explored by Maria Framke. Her paper 'Internationalizing the Indian War on Opium: colonial policy, the nationalist movement and the League of Nations' introduces the global anti-opium movement, which was formed towards the end of the nineteenth century to challenge the market-driven expansion of this drug. In the wake of this movement, three international conferences took place at The Hague before the First World War, culminating in the first international drug control treaty in 1912. After the end of the First World War the issue of drug control was taken up by the League of Nations which emerged as a global drug regulating institution. The Genevan body's initiatives to curtail the manufacture, internal consumption and trade of opium produced ambivalent reactions in British India. The colonial government in Delhi was reluctant to implement a ban on the drug trade. The Indian nationalists, however, showed a keen interest in this aspect of the work of the League, which otherwise was often critically seen as an appendix to British politics. Framke analyzes colonial and national responses to the League's anti-opium stance against the backdrop of the colonial government's economic interests and diplomatic efforts, as well as the growing rejection of the League's authority by the nationalist movement in India.

Robert Eric Colvard's paper '"Drunkards beware!": Prohibition and nationalist politics in the 1930s' examines the virulent struggles over alcohol from the beginning of the Civil Disobedience Movement in 1930 to the end of Congress-led provincial governments in 1939. Colvard explores the close connection between anti-alcohol agitation and nationalist mobilization, linking picketing and other anti-alcohol action to the Congress' struggle for both national independence and cultural hegemony. He does not, however, stop with nationalist rhetoric and politics but seeks also to put those in perspective by contrasting them to interests and activities of other actors such as 'liquor men', and analyzes the conflicts arising from the orientation and means of nationalist mobilization. Colvard argues that tensions increased dramatically in the 1930s between nationalists devoted to the prohibition of drink on the one hand, and the sellers and buyers of liquor on the other. The growing hostility between the nationalists and a colonial government fighting tooth and nail against them manifested itself in debates regarding access to drink. These tensions led to a crisis point forcing drinkers to decide whether to stop drinking and support the nation, or continue their habit and implicitly support the colonizers. When the Indian National Congress joined the government in the provincial assemblies in 1938, it used the power of the state to begin the long fight of eradicating the alcohol menace from India. In the process, drinkers found themselves subject to moral criticism from nationalist leaders and the full might of Congress-led provincial governments. An independent India appeared poised to destroy the existing drink-producing industry and to force drinkers to conform to the social mores of the upper castes.

Carolyn Heitmeyer and Edward Simpson pick up on the Indian National Congress' involvement in anti-alcohol campaigns and take the narrative into the postcolonial phase. Concentrating on Gujarat, Gandhi's home state and a long time stronghold of the Congress party, they lay bare the ambivalences characteristic of official anti-alcohol policies in India. Gujarat, the only Indian state with a continuous prohibition policy throughout its history and currently the only 'dry state' in the country, offers a splendid example of the complex religious, social, economic and political agendas that converge in the anti-alcohol discourse. Starting with the hypothesis that ever since prohibition was enforced, it has been more of a political statement than a social and cultural reality, Heitmeyer and Simpson first analyze the religious discourses on which the anti-alcohol agenda in the region rests, drawing mostly on anthropological literature. They then move on to more mundane realities by providing a sketch of the flourishing bootlegging industry and its multifaceted entanglements with politicians and the police. The rhetoric of abstinence thus emerges as a symbolic discourse that has remained powerful in Gujarati society because it links to the ideals of self-control and purity that have deep roots both in local religious cultures and the hegemonic version of the history of India's freedom struggle. Thus, according to Heitmeyer and Simpson, giving up prohibition would be read in Gujarat as distancing oneself from the moral aspirations it stands for and hence discredit the person or party who advocates it, even though everyone knows that it has no relation to the actual levels of alcohol consumption.

In his short afterword, Claude Markovits, finally, provides carefully calibrated comments on the book in its entirety as well as on the various contributions and indicates possible avenues for future research. Most importantly, he contrasts the picture emerging from the case studies presented in the present volume with the theories David Courtwright has developed for the global history of intoxicants. He finds Indian specificities to be more striking than commonalities with transnational phenomena and global trends.

Taken together, we hope that the chapters of this anthology shed new light on the development of current meanings of intoxicants in South Asia in terms of politics, cultural norms and identity formation. We also hope to underline the way in which the history of drugs and alcohol is enmeshed in the history of modern empires and nation states even in a country in which a staunch teetotaller and active anti-drug crusader like Mohandas Gandhi is presented as the 'father of the nation'. In slight tension with Claude Markovits' conclusions, the editors feel that the findings presented here hardly leave a doubt that, at least in this respect, arguments positing an 'Indian exceptionalism' must be critically interrogated.

Notes

1 Cf. BBC, 'Toxic alcohol kills 143 in West Bengal'. Online. Available HTTP: <http://www.bbc.co.uk/news/world-asia-india-16174531> (accessed 6 December 2012) and *Al Jazeera*, 'Tainted alcohol kills scores in India'. Online. Available HTTP: <http://www.aljazeera.com/news/asia/2011/12/20111215633291 8171.html> (accessed 6 December 2012).

2 Cf. Channel NewsAsia, 'Hooch tragedy kills 122'. Online. Available HTTP: <http://www.channelnewsasia.com/stories/afp_asiapacific/view/441568/1/.html> (accessed 10 June 2013).

3 D.M. Fahey and P. Manian, 'Poverty and purification. The politics of Gandhi's campaign for prohibition', *The Historian*, 67, 3, 2005, 489–506.

4 M.K. Gandhi, *Key to Health*, Ahmedabad: Navajivan Publishing House, 1948, pp. 32–3.

5 Letter from Mrs Joseph Cook, dated 24 February 1887, 23 Beacon Street, Boston to Francis Willard. Manuscript collection of the Francis Willard Archives, Evanston, Illinois.

6 Cf., for instance, G. Gaunekar, V. Patel and A. Rane, 'The impact and patterns of hazardous drinking amongst male industrial workers in Goa, India', *Social Psychiatry and Psychiatric Epidemiology*, 40, 4, 2005, 267–75 and P.C. Gupta, S. Saxena, M. Pednekar et al., 'Alcohol consumption among middle-aged and elderly men: a community study from Western India', *Alcohol and Alcoholism*, 38, 4, 2003, 327–31.

7 R. Prasad, 'Alcohol use on the rise in India', *The Lancet*, 373, 9657, 2009, 17.

8 While analytically alcohol and other intoxicating substances might well be grouped together, we chose to apply a conventional distinction in historiography between alcohol and drugs (as used, for instance, by the Alcohol and Drugs History Society), the latter term referring to substances such as opiates, cannabis, and coca-based products.

9 D.E. Owen, *British Opium Policy in China and India*, New Haven: Yale University Press, 1933, p. 2.

10 J.F. Wise, 'Notes by Dr. J.F. Wise, Civil Surgeon of Dacca on the Sanitary State of the Station', in Government of Bengal, *First Annual Report for 1868*, Calcutta: Government Press, 1869, pp. 97–129, p. 101.

11 This was a statement made by one of the delegates of British India in the League of Nations. 'The world and India. Speeches by the Jam Saheb', *The Times of India*, 17 November 1922, p. 11. Cf. also Maria Framke's chapter in the present volume.

12 E.M. Collingham, *Imperial Bodies: the physical experience of the Raj (1800–1947)*, Oxford: Polity, 2001, pp. 30–1 and B. Milligan, *Pleasures and Pains: opium and the Orient in 19th-century British culture*, Charlottesville, London: University Press of Virginia, 1995, p. 115.

13 S.M. Edwardes, *By-Ways of Bombay*, Bombay: D.B. Taraporevala Sons & Co., 1912, p. 21.

14 Ibid.

15 S. Ganguly, 'Allen Ginsberg in India: an interview', *ARIEL: A Review of English Literature*, 24, 4, 1993, 23–4.

16 M.J. Gilbert, 'Empire and excise: drugs and drink revenue and the fate of states in South Asia', in J.H. Mills and P. Barton (eds) *Drugs and Empires. Essays in modern imperialism and intoxication*, Houndmills, New York: Palgrave Macmillan, 2007, pp. 116–41, p. 137.

17 Particularly noteworthy in this respect are the multifarious activities of the Alcohol and Drugs History Society, which include the publication of a journal devoted exclusively to the social and cultural history of substance consumption. Cf. http://alcoholanddrugshistorysociety.wordpress.com/shad-journal/

18 For a historiographical discussion cf. James McHugh's chapter in this volume.

19 H.K. Sharma, B.M. Tripathi and P.J. Pelto, 'The evolution of alcohol use in India', *AIDS and Behavior*, 14, 1, 2010, 8–17.

20 M. Khare, 'The wine-cup in Mughal court culture – from hedonism to kingship', *The Medieval History Journal*, 8, 1, 2005, 143–88.

21 P. Chatterjee, 'The lives of alcohol in pre-colonial India', *The Medieval History Journal*, 8, 1, 2005, 189–225, 190.

22 Khare, 'The wine-cup in Mughal court culture'.

23 D. Hardiman, 'From custom to crime. The politics of drinking in colonial South Gujarat', in R. Guha (ed.) *Subaltern studies IV. Writings on South Asian history and society*, Delhi: Oxford University Press, 1985, pp. 165–228; cf. also P. Froerer, *Religious Division and Social Conflict. The emergence of Hindu nationalism in rural India*, New Delhi: Social Science Press [et al.], 2007, pp. 221–55; A. Shah, 'Alcoholics anonymous: the Maoist movement in Jharkhand, India, *Modern Asian Studies*, 45, 5, 2011, 1095–1117, especially 1107–10.

24 D. Hardiman, 'From custom to crime', in Guha, *Subaltern Studies*, p. 176; for a similar quote from the Abbe Carre, travelling in India in the 1670s, cf. Chatterjee, 'The lives of alcohol', p. 211.

25 D. Hardiman, 'From custom to crime', in Guha, *Subaltern Studies IV*, pp. 176–7.

26 I. Munshi, 'On drinking and "drunkenness". History of liquor colonial India', in M. Dossal and R. Maloni (eds) *State Intervention and Popular Response. Western India in the nineteenth century*, Mumbai: Popular Prakashan,1999, pp. 127–46, p. 128; Froerer, *Religious Division and Social Conflict*, p. 221.

27 D. Hardiman, 'From custom to crime', in Guha, *Subaltern Studies IV*, pp. 174–5.
28 Ibid., pp. 173–4; for Adivasi drinking culture cf. Shah, 'Alcoholics anonymous', pp. 1107–8.
29 D. Hardiman, 'From custom to crime', in Guha, *Subaltern Studies IV*, pp. 170–1.
30 Ibid., p. 167.
31 Fahey and Manian, 'Poverty and purification'.
32 D.T. Courtwright, *Forces of Habit. Drugs and the making of the modern world*, Cambridge, Mass.: Harvard University Press, 2001, p. 5. Cf. also M.J. Gilbert, 'Empire and excise', in Mills and Barton, *Drugs and Empires*.
33 R. Guha, *Dominance without Hegemony. History and power in colonial India*, Cambridge, Mass. etc.: Harvard University Press, 1997, pp. 100–51.
34 J.D. Rogers, 'Cultural nationalism and social reform. The 1904 temperance movement in Sri Lanka', *Indian Economic and Social History Review*, 26, 3, 1989, 319–41; cf. M. Frost, "Wider opportunities": religious revival, nationalist awakening and the global dimension in Colombo, *Modern Asian Studies*, 36, 4, 2002, 937–67; A.P. Kannangara, 'The riots of 1915 in Sri Lanka: a study in the roots of communal violence', *Past and Present*, 102, 1984, 130–65.
35 L. Carroll, 'Origins of the Kayastha temperance movement', *Indian Economic and Social History Review*, 11, 1974, 432–47.
36 L. Carroll, 'The temperance movement in India. Politics and social reform, *Modern Asian Studies*, 10, 3, 1976, 417–47.
37 Therefore, temperance agitation and boycott also met with resistance from the people economically affected by them (cf. Robert Eric Colvard's chapter in this volume).
38 Guha, *Dominance without Hegemony*, pp. 100–51.
39 I. Tyrrell, *Woman's World, Woman's Empire. The Woman's Christian Temperance Union in international perspective, 1880–1930*, Chapel Hill: University of North Carolina Press, 1991, p. 6.
40 Froerer, *Religious Division and Social Conflict*, pp. 221–55.
41 Shah, 'Alcoholics anonymous', p. 1098.
42 Ibid., pp. 1104–12.
43 Ibid., p. 1097.
44 D. Hardiman, 'From custom to crime', in Guha, *Subaltern Studies IV*, pp. 213–14; idem, 'Adivasi assertion in South Gujarat: the Devi movement of 1922–23', in R. Guha (ed.) *Subaltern Studies III*, New Delhi: Oxford University Press, 1984, pp. 196–230.
45 I. Munshi, 'On drinking and "drunkenness"', in Dossal and Maloni, *State Intervention and Popular Response*, pp. 129–30.
46 Frederick Lely, assistant collector of Surat district, on the effects of the regulations of 1878, in Hardiman, 'From custom to crime', p. 194.
47 I. Munshi, 'On drinking and "drunkenness"', in Dossal and Maloni, *State Intervention and Popular Response*, p. 131.
48 Ibid., p. 135.
49 D. Hardiman, 'From custom to crime' in Guha, *Subaltern Studies IV*, p. 212. For a critical comment on the Subaltern Studies perspective on peasant consciousness in connection to the Adivasi anti-drinking movements cf. Shah, 'Alcoholics anonymous', pp. 1099–1103.
50 B. Sarveswara Rao and G. Parthasarathy, *Anti-arrack Movement of Women in Andhra Pradesh and Prohibition Policy*, New Delhi: Har-Anand Publications, 1997.
51 R. Kumar, *The History of Doing. an illustrated account of movements for women's rights and feminism in India, 1800–1990*, New Delhi: Kali for Women, 1993.
52 S.C. Martin, *Devil of the Domestic Sphere. Temperance, gender, and middle-class ideology, 1800–1860*, DeKalb: Northern Illinois University Press, 2008.
53 K. Balagopal, 'Slaying of a spirituous demon', *Economic and Political Weekly*, 27, 46, 1992, 2457–61.
54 P. Bunkle, 'The origins of the women's movement in New Zealand: the Women's Christian Temperance Union 1885–1895', in P. Bunkle and B. Hughes (eds) *Women in New Zealand Society*, Auckland: George Allen & Unwin, 1980, pp. 52–76.
55 K.A. Rosemblatt, 'Domesticating men. State building and class compromise in popular-front Chile, in E. Dore and M. Molyneux (eds) *Hidden Histories of Gender and the State in Latin America*, Durham: Duke University Press, 2000, pp. 262–90.

56 R. Pande, 'From anti-arrack to total prohibition: the women's movement in Andhra Pradesh, India, *Gender, Technology and Development*, 4, 1, 2000, 131–44.

57 J. Tanner, 'Die "Alkoholfrage" in der Schweiz im 19. und 20. Jahrhundert', *Drogalkohol*, 3, 1986, 147–68; K. Transchel, *Under the Influence. Working-class drinking, temperance, and cultural revolution in Russia, 1895–1932*, Pittsburgh: University of Pittsburgh Press, 2006.

58 Cited in N. Varma, 'For the drink of the nation: drink, labour and plantation capitalism in the colonial tea gardens of Assam in the late nineteenth and early twentieth century', in M. v. d. Linden and P. Mohapatra (eds) *Labour Matters. Towards global histories. Studies in honour of Sabyasachi Bhattacharya*, New Delhi: Tulika Books, 2009, p. 295.

59 T. Klubock, *Contested Communities. Class, gender, and politics in Chile's El Teniente copper mine, 1904–1951*, Durham: Duke University Press, 1998.

60 E. Akyeampong, 'What's in a drink? Class struggle, popular culture and the politics of *akpeteshie* (local gin) in Ghana, 1930–67, *The Journal of African History*, 37, 2, 1996, 215–36.

61 E. Wald, 'Health, discipline and appropriate behaviour: the body of the soldier and the space of the cantonment, *Modern Asian Studies*, 46, 4, 2012, 815–56 and D.M. Peers, 'Imperial vice: sex, drink and the health of British troops in North Indian cantonments, 1800–1858', in D. Killingray (ed.) *Guardians of Empire. The armed forces of the colonial powers c. 1700–1964*, Manchester: Manchester University Press, 1999, pp. 25–52.

62 Cf. H. Fischer-Tiné, *Low and Licentious Europeans: race, class and white subalternity in colonial India*, New Delhi: Orient Longman, 2009 and idem, 'Britain's other civilising mission: class-prejudice, European "loaferism" and the workhouse system in colonial India', *Indian Economic and Social History Review* 42, 3, 2005, 295–338.

63 M. Emdad-ul Haq, *Drugs in South Asia: from the opium trade to the present day*, Houndmills, New York: Palgrave, 2000.

64 J.F. Richards, '"Cannot we induce the people of England to eat opium?" The moral economy of opium in colonial India', in Mills and Barton, *Drugs and Empires*, pp. 73–80, p. 74.

65 Cf., for instance, H.B. Dunnicliff, 'The Indian opium trade: a historical review', *Asian Review*, 34, 1938, 349–59 and J. Rowntree, *The Imperial Drug Trade: a re-statement of the opium question in the light of recent evidence and new developments in the East*, 2nd edn, London: Methuen & Co, 1906.

66 S. Tibi, *The Medicinal Use of Opium in Ninth Century Baghdad*, Leiden: Brill, 2006.

67 Emdad-ul Haq, *Drugs in South Asia*, p.14.

68 For a detailed but rather descriptive account see S.P. Sangar, 'Intoxicants in Mughal India', *Indian Journal of History of Science* 16, 2, 1981, 202–14. Cf. also S. Dale, *The Garden of the Eight Paradises: Babur and the culture of empire in Central Asia, Afghanistan and India*, Leiden: Brill, 2004 and S. Honchell, 'Pursuing pleasure, attaining oblivion: the roles and uses of intoxicants at the Mughal Court', unpublished MA-thesis, University of Louisville, KY, 2010.

69 R. Dane, 'The Indian opium trade: a historical review', *Asian Review*, 23, 1938, 61.

70 D.E. Owen, *British Opium Policy in India and China*, New Haven: Yale University Press, 1934, p. 18.

71 D. Washbrook, 'India 1818–1860: the two faces of colonialism', in A. Porter (ed.) *The Nineteenth Century (= Oxford History of the British Empire, IV)*, Oxford: Oxford University Press, 1999, pp. 395–421, p. 404.

72 C.A. Trocki, *Opium, Empire and Global Political Economy. A study of the Asian opium trade 1750–1950*, London, New York: Routledge, 1999.

73 H. Derks, *History of the Opium Problem: the assault on the East, c. 1600–1950*, Leiden: Brill, 2012.

74 Cf., for instance, R.E. Kranton and A.V. Swamy, 'Contracts, hold-up, and exports: textiles and opium in colonial India', *American Economic Review*, 98, 5, 2008, 967–89; J.F. Richards, '"Cannot we induce the people of England to eat opium?"', in Mills and Barton, *Drugs and Empires*; J.F. Richards, 'The opium industry in British India', *Indian Economic and Social History Review*, 39, 2–3, 2002, 149–80; idem, 'Indian empire and peasant production of opium in the nineteenth century', *Modern Asian Studies*, 15, 1, 1981, 59–82; E.N. Baker, 'The opium industry', *The Economic Journal*, 6, 21, 1896, 114–22.

75 A. Farooqui, 'Opium and the trading world of western India in the early nineteenth century', in Mills and Barton, *Drugs and Empires*, pp. 83–100; idem, *Opium City: the making of early Victorian Bombay*, Gurgaon: Three Essays Collective, 2006; idem, *Smuggling as Subversion: colonialism, Indian merchants and the politics of opium, 1790–1843*, rev. and updated ed., Lanham: Lexington Books, 2005; idem, 'Opium enterprise and colonial intervention in Malwa and western India, 1800–1824', *Indian Economic and Social History Review*, 32, 4, 1995, 447–73.

76 C. Markovits, 'The political economy of opium smuggling in early 19th century India: leakage or resistance?', *Modern Asian Studies*, 43, 1, 2009, 89–111.

77 J.F. Richards, 'Opium and the British Empire: the Royal Commission of 1895', *Modern Asian Studies*, 36, 2, 2002, 375–420; K.L. Lodwick, *Crusaders against Opium: protestant missionaries in China, 1874–1917*, Lexington: University of Kentucky Press, 1995, pp. 85–109.

78 Cf., for instance, V. Berridge, *Opium and the People: opiate use and drug control policy in nineteenth and early twentieth century England*, rev. ed., New York, London, 1999, pp. 173–94 and J.B. Brown, 'Politics of the poppy: the Society for the Suppression of the Opium Trade 1874–1916', *Journal of Contemporary History*, 8, 3, 1973, pp. 97–111.

79 Richards, 'Opium and the British Empire', pp. 418–19.

80 P. Chakrabarti, 'The empire of trade and the morality of science', June 2004, review of P.C. Winther, *Anglo-European Science and the Rhetoric of Empire: malaria, opium, and British rule in India, 1756–1895*, New York, Oxford: Lexington Books, 2003. Online. Available HTTP: http://www.h-net.org/reviews/showrev.php?id=9508 (accessed 10 June 2013).

81 P.C. Winther, *Anglo-European Science and the Rhetoric of Empire: malaria, opium and British rule in India, 1756–1895*, Lanham: Lexington Books, 2003. On the popular varieties of the medicinal use of opium cf. also A. Farooqui, 'Opium as a household remedy in nineteenth-century western India?', in B. Pati and M. Harrison (eds) *The Social History of Health and Medicine in Colonial India*, London: Routledge, 2009, pp. 229–37.

82 Winther, *Anglo-European Science*, pp. 234–42.

83 M.K. Gandhi, 'Hind Swaraj', in *Collected Works of Mahatma Gandhi*, vol. X, Ahmedabad: Government of India, The Publications Division, 1983, p. 22 (the pamphlet was first published in 1909).

84 C.F. Andrews, *The Opium Evil in British India: Britain's responsibility*, London: Student's Christian Movement, 1926.

85 D. Wujastyk, 'Cannabis in traditional Indian herbal medicine', in A. Salema (ed.) *Ayurveda at the Crossroad of Care and Cure*, Lisbon: Universidade Nova, 2002, pp. 45–73.

86 J.H. Mills, *Madness, Cannabis and Colonialism. The 'native only' lunatic asylums of British India 1857–1900*, London, Basingstoke, 2000, pp. 43–65.

87 J.H. Mills, *Cannabis Britannica. Empire, trade and prohibition*. Oxford: Oxford University Press, 2003. Cf. also idem, 'Globalizing ganja: the British Empire and international cannabis traffic, *c.*1834–*c.*1939', in G. Goodman, P.E. Lovejoy and A. Sherrat (eds) *Consuming Habits: global and historical perspectives on how cultures define drugs*, 2nd edn, London, New York: Routledge, 2007, pp. 178–93. Most recently, Mills concluded his cannabis trilogy with a volume that focusses on the drugs career in Britain during the twentieth century. J.H. Mills, *Cannabis Nation. Empire, control and consumption in Britain, 1928–2008*, Oxford: Oxford University Press, 2013.

88 Mills, *Cannabis Britannica*, pp. 17–46 and 140–9.

89 J.H. Mills, 'Colonial Africa and the international politics of cannabis: Egypt, South Africa and the origins of global control', in Mills and Barton, *Drugs and Empires*, pp. 165–84.

90 J.H. Mills, 'Cannabis in the commons: colonial networks, missionary politics and the origins of the Indian Hemp Drugs Commission 1893–4', *Journal of Colonialism and Colonial History*, 6, 1, 2005, 1–26. The IHDC is also analyzed in R. Shamir and D. Hacker, 'Colonialism's civilizing mission: the case of the Indian Hemp Drug Commission', *Law and Social Inquiry*, 26, 2, 2005, 435–61.

91 M. Angrosino, 'Rum and ganja. Indenture, drug foods, labor motivation, and the evolution of the modern sugar industry in Trinidad', in W. Jankowiak and D. Bradburd (eds) *Drugs, Labor, and Colonial Expansion*, Tucson: University of Arizona Press, 2003, pp. 101–16.

92 H.G. Levine, 'The discovery of addiction. Changing conceptions of habitual drunkenness in America', *Journal of Studies on Alcohol and Drugs*, 39, 1, 1978, 143–74; M. Valverde, *Diseases of the Will. Alcohol and the dilemmas of freedom*, Cambridge: Cambridge University Press, 1998.

93 D.T. Courtwright, 'Mr. ATOD's wild ride: what do alcohol, tobacco, and other drugs have in common?', *Social History of Alcohol and Drugs*, 20, 2005, 105–40, 110.

94 D.J. Guy, *Sex and Danger in Buenos Aires. Prostitution, family and nation in Argentina*, Lincoln, Neb.: University of Nebraska Press, 1995; B. Donovan, *White Slave Crusades. Race, gender, and anti-vice activism, 1887–1917*, Urbana, Ill.: University of Illinois Press, 2006; J. Grosse, F. Spöring, and J. Tschurenev (eds), *Biopolitik und Sittlichkeitsreform. Kampagnen gegen Alkohol, Drogen und sexuelle Devianz in globalhistorischer Perspektive*, Frankfurt, New York: Campus (forthcoming 2014).

95 M. Valverde, 'Racial poison. Drink, male vice, and degeneration in first-wave feminism, in I.C. Fletcher, L.E.N. Mayhall and P. Levine (eds), *Women's Suffrage in the British Empire. Citizenship, nation and race*, London: Routledge, 2000, pp. 33–50.

96 Courtwright, *Forces of Habit*, pp. 9–66.

97 Courtwright, 'Mr. ATOD's wild ride', p. 121.

98 Mills and Barton, *Drugs and Empires*.

99 N. Kamenov, 'Globale Ursprünge und lokale Zielsetzungen: Die Antialkoholbewegung in Bulgarien, 1890–1940, in S. Marung and K. Naumann (eds) *Vergessene Vielfalt. Territorialisierung und Internationalisierung in Ostmitteleuropa von 1850 bis zum Beginn des 20. Jahrhunderts*, Vandenhoeck und Ruprecht (forthcoming); D.J. Guy, *Sex and Danger in Buenos Aires*; W.G. Mills, 'The roots of African nationalism in the Cape Colony. Temperance, 1866–1898', *International Journal of African Historical Studies*, 13, 2, 1980, 197–213.

100 D.M. Fahey, 'Temperance internationalism. Guy Hayler and the World Prohibition Federation, *The Social History of Alcohol and Drugs*, 20, 2006, 245–75.

101 J.S. Blocker, D.M. Fahey and I.R. Tyrrell (eds), *Alcohol and Temperance in Modern History. An international encyclopedia*, Santa Barbara, Calif.: ABC-CLIO, 2003, p. 318. On the IOGT cf. D.M. Fahey, *Temperance and Racism. John Bull, Johnny Reb, and the Good Templars*, Lexington: University Press of Kentucky, 1996; A. Forel, *Der Guttemplerorden. Ein sozialer Reformator, seine Geschichte, sein Zweck, seine Grundsätze, seine Organisation und seine Tätigkeit. Im Auftrage der Schweizerischen Grossloge des I.O.G.T. verfasst ...*, Schaffhausen: Schweizer Grossloge, s.a.; on the WCTU cf. Tyrrell, *Woman's World, Woman's Empire*; M. Ogawa, 'The "White Ribbon League of Nations" meets Japan. The trans-pacific activism of the Woman's Christian Temperance Union, 1906–1930', *Diplomatic History*, 31, 1, 2007, 21–50.

102 F. Spöring, '"Du musst Apostel der Wahrheit werden": Auguste Forel und die Karriere des sozialhyienischen "Evangeliums der Geistigkeit" im wissenschaftlichen Anti-Alkohol-Diskurs, 1886–1931, in Grosse, Spöring and Tschurenev, *Biopolitik und Sittlichkeitsreform*.

103 Y.S. Kim, 'Constructing a global identity. The role of Esperanto', in J. Boli and G.M. Thomas (eds) *Constructing World Culture. International nongovernmental organizations since 1875*, Stanford, Calif: Stanford University Press, 1999, pp. 127–48.

104 B.H. Harrison, *Drink and the Victorians. The temperance question in England, 1815–1872*, 2nd edn, Hartnolls: Keele University Press, 1994.

105 I. Eisenbach-Stangl, 'From temperance movements to state action: an historical view of the alcohol question in industrialised countries', in R. Müller and H. Klingemann (eds) *From Science to Action? 100 years later – alcohol policies revisited*, Dordrecht: Springer, 2004, pp. 15–28.

106 M.L. Schrad, *The Political Power of Bad Ideas. Networks, institutions, and the global prohibition wave*, Oxford: Oxford University Press, 2010.

107 N. Singh, *Dry America. An object lesson to India*, Madras: Ganesh, 1921.

108 Emma Price, 'India's new day', *Union Signal*, May 20, 1920, 7; Anon., 'Christian missionaries, Mohammedans and Hindus unite for prohibition in India', *Union Signal*, May 20, 1920, 15; Taraknath Das, 'Progress of prohibition in India', *Union Signal*, September 29, 1921, 6; Anon., 'Begam of Bhopal declares prohibition in her state', *Union Signal*, April 26, 1923, 3.

109 Francis Willard, 'President's address. Before the second biennial convention of the world's W.C.T.U. and the twentieth annual convention of the national W.C.T.U.', in *Minutes of the Second Biennial Convention and Executive Meetings of the World's Woman's Christian Temperance Union, Chicago, 1893*, Chicago: Woman's Temperance Publishing Association, pp. 56–7.

110 A. Olorunfemi, 'The liquor traffic dilemma in British West Africa. The southern Nigerian example, 1895–1918, *International Journal of African Historical Studies* 17, 2, 1984, 220–42; D. van den Bersselaar, *The King of Drinks. Schnapps gin from modernity to tradition*, Leiden: Brill, 2007.

111 L. Pan, *Alcohol in Colonial Africa*, Helsinki: Finnish Foundation for Alcohol Studies, 1975.

112 H. Padwa, *The Culture and Politics of Opiate Control in Britain and France, 1821–1926*, Baltimore: The Johns Hopkins University Press, 2012, pp. 50–85; V. Berridge, *Opium and the People: opiate use and drug control policy in nineteenth and early twentieth century England*, rev. ed., London: Free Association, 1999.

113 Emdad-ul Haq, *Drugs in South Asia*, pp. 36–41; D.L. Ahmad, *The Opium Debate and Chinese Exclusion Laws*, Reno, Las Vegas: University of Nevada Press, 2007, pp. 1–50; N. Shah, *Contagious Divides: epidemics and race in San Francisco's China Town*, Berkeley, CA: University of California Press, 2001, pp. 77–104; and M. Aurin,'Chasing the Dragon: the cultural metamorphosis of opium in the United States, 1825–1935, *Medical Anthropology Quarterly*, 14, 3, 2000, 414–41.

114 F. Dikötter, L. Laamann and Z. Xun, *Narcotic Culture. A history of drugs in China*, London: Hurst and Company, 2004, pp. 100–1.

115 A.L. Foster, 'Opium, the United States and the civilizing mission in colonial South East Asia', *Social History of Alcohol and Drugs*, 24, 1, 2010, 6–19; K. Meyer and T. Parssinen, *Webs of Smoke: smugglers, warlords, spies, and the history of the international drug trade*, Lanham, ML: Rowman & Littlefield, 2002, pp. 20–2; and A. Baumler, *The Chinese and Opium under the Republic: worse than floods and wild beasts*, Albany: State University of New York Press, 2007, pp. 66–9.

116 On the diplomatic history of the international regulatory regime with respect to opium and cannabis cf. Mills and Barton, *Drugs and Empires*, chapters 10–13; Meyer and Parssinen, *Webs of Smoke*, pp. 15–35; W.B. McAllister, *Drug Diplomacy in the Twentieth Century: an international history*, New York, London: Routledge, 2000, pp. 41–102 and A.H. Taylor, *American Diplomacy and the Narcotics Traffic 1900–1939: a study in international humanitarian reforms*, Durham NC: Duke University Press, 1969.

117 M. Sinha, *Colonial Masculinity. The 'manly Englishman' and the 'effeminate Bengali' in the late nineteenth century*, Manchester: Manchester University Press, 1995.

Part I

Trajectories: Reconstructing the history of intoxicants in the pre-colonial and early colonial periods

1 Alcohol in pre-modern South Asia

James McHugh

Introduction

There is a very long history of the production and consumption of alcoholic drinks in pre-modern South Asia. In the texts called the Vedas, our earliest surviving textual sources for South Asia, there are references to what is evidently a fermented and intoxicating drink called *surā*. For later periods, references to intoxicating, alcohol-containing drinks are numerous in many genres. A number of sugars and grains were available in South Asia, and thus from around the turn of the Common Era many varied intoxicating drinks are named, and in many cases described, as being made from wheat, rice, barley, palm sap, sugar cane products, honey, flowers, and fruits, including dates and grapes. Texts on religious law and on statecraft legislate the consumption and sale of these drinks, and medical texts describe the virtues and dangers of intoxicating drinks in some detail. Literary texts in Sanskrit sometimes portray scenes of drunkenness, a state that often has erotic and humorous associations.

Intoxicating drinks were apparently frowned upon in some contexts, yet in others they are presented as acceptable and even useful. The ethical-legal and medical discourses show that the world of intoxicating drinks was socially complex: not all people were socially permitted or physically suited to drink intoxicants, and those who could do so could not always drink the same types of beverage owing to caste restrictions and the varied constitutions of people's bodies. Thus, as we shall see below, in some texts intoxicating drink is presented as a bad thing, and in others it is praised. While not universally condemned, alcohol was never universally celebrated. Sanskrit texts that discuss alcohol not only display variety in terms of genre and social/sectarian context, but such texts were also produced, expanded, and interpreted over many centuries. We therefore find there to be significant diachronic change in the manner drinks are represented.

In the second millennium CE Muslim rulers and Islamic cultures became increasingly prominent in South Asia. As in the earlier medieval period, the status of alcohol was ambiguous in these contexts because of the prohibition of alcoholic drinks in Islam. As before, disapproval amongst certain clerics by no means led to universal abstinence, and from our sources it seems that many elite and powerful Muslims in South Asia quite openly engaged in drinking alcohol: indeed, the wine cup was endowed with powerful symbolism in Indo-Persian culture. It appears that it was also during this period that the various beers, wines and toddies of early medieval South Asia came to be distilled, producing a stronger product – a type of arrack – than had previously been available.

In this short survey of alcohol in pre-modern South Asia I shall first orient the reader to certain debates and questions that have dominated secondary scholarship. In particular I will examine the question of the history of distillation. I shall then provide an overview of the history of intoxicating drinks in South Asia prior to the presence of Islam in the region, pausing to examine a few genres of texts in a little more detail. Finally, I shall briefly discuss the status of alcohol in Islamic cultures in pre-modern South Asia. The history of alcohol in this region is vast and complex, and much remains to be discovered, translated, and theorized. This chapter is only the very start of a longer project in which I intend to write a far more comprehensive account of this topic.

'Spirituous liquor', distillation, and moral judgments

In South Asia, during the period under consideration – approximately the first millennium CE until the mid-second millennium CE – there is no concept of a substance equivalent to our 'alcohol' as present in various drinks. Rather, certain drinks are understood to have a potency to intoxicate, a state most commonly designated in Sanskrit by means of various forms derived from the verbal root √*mad*, which can mean amongst other things 'to be drunk' or 'to be intoxicated', as well as 'to be exhilarated' or 'to be glad'. The most general term for drinks that create this intoxicated state in people, the term used in legal texts for example, and a term that does not imply any particular ingredient used (such as grains or grape juice), is *madya*, 'intoxicating [drink]'. The power of certain drinks to intoxicate is explained as the spontaneous result of combining certain materials. As I shall discuss below, a sort of fermentation starter called *kiṇva* (also sometimes called *surābījam*) is sometimes mentioned in the context of making intoxicating drinks, but there was no concept of yeast. Indeed, in many early Indic recipes for grain-based drinks there appear to be no malted grains, so in these cases the starter might have been the sort of dried cakes containing saccharifying moulds, fermentation yeasts, and supplementary herbs one still sees used in the production of rice wines throughout much of Asia.[1]

Until around the thirteenth century CE, South Asian sources do not mention distillation of alcoholic drinks. However, scholarly writing on alcohol in pre-modern South Asia is not infrequently characterized by what are arguably anachronistic and loose translations that imply drinks were distilled products, something that is further complicated by the lively debate as to whether distillation was practised at a very early date in South Asia.

In his still commonly used Sanskrit-English dictionary, composed in the late nineteenth century, Monier Williams translates *madya* as 'any intoxicating drink, vinous or spirituous liquor, wine' and he translates a term meaning 'a jar for *madya*' as 'a vessel for intoxicating liquors, brandy jar'.[2] Another important late nineteenth-century dictionary, that of Apte, also translates *madya* as 'spirituous liquor, wine, any intoxicating drink'. Indeed, Apte even foregrounds the term 'spirituous'. Thus some readers and translators of Sanskrit texts that mention these drinks might well be tempted to think they were reading about a distilled drink at all times and in all places.

The reasons why these scholars translated these Sanskrit words with English terms that suggest distilled drinks are a worthy subject for study. I would tentatively suggest that for traditional scholars educated in Sanskrit in India in the nineteenth century, *madya* and other words for intoxicants might well have referred to distilled drinks, as such drinks were available in India and had been so for many centuries. For example, in what remains perhaps one of the more thorough surveys of Sanskrit texts for references to intoxicating drinks, Rajendralal Mitra in 1873 routinely used the term 'spirituous drinks' to refer to very early sources.[3] This continues today, and Om Prakash, an authority on food and drink in India, wrote in 1961 that 'Another beverage of the Vedic period was *Surā* (intoxicating liquor) which was prepared from fermented barley or wild paddy after distillation.'[4] South Asian scholars of Sanskrit could well have understood *madya* to cover various distilled arracks for quite a long time, as below we shall see that distilled alcoholic drinks had been recorded as being produced since approximately the thirteenth century CE. So, in Sanskrit texts *as composed or as read* in the nineteenth century *madya* might well refer to some sort of arrack, and given the well-established nature of these products and the lack of a detailed history of intoxicants in South Asia, it would seem reasonable for these scholars to understand very early references to *madya* as referring to such a product.

This tendency to translate terms for intoxicating drinks with English terms that suggest distillation would appear, at least in the nineteenth century, to be a separate issue from the vigorous, and very historically aware, discussion concerning the origins of distillation in South Asia. It appears that we can trace this latter controversy to the publication in 1951 by Sir John Marshall of an illustrated account of archaeological excavations at the ancient city of Taxila, in what is now Pakistan.[5] Here, he reported finds of some pottery vessels dating from around a century before or after the turn of the Common Era, which he lists as 'water-condensers'. About these vessels he says the following: 'The precise use made of these vessels is not certain, but it seems probable that the condensing was done as shown in the sketch.' The sketch in question is in the accompanying volume of illustrations. Here three vessels are illustrated both separately and also in a diagram that shows two of them assembled into a still that also utilizes other types of vessels. Notably, Marshall does not mention alcohol, and instead mentions steam distillation, a process that could, of course, have many other applications. It is important to note here that from Marshall's description it is clear that the three vessels were not all found together in the same area: rather they appear to have been found in different locations of the site and also in different strata.

In 1979 the late F.R. Allchin, an important archaeologist of South Asia, published a paper entitled 'India: The Ancient Home of Distillation' in which he considerably expanded Marshall's theory of such vessels being water condensers.[6] Allchin notes that over a hundred vessels similar to the still 'receiver' were found at another Indo-Greek archaeological site, Shaikhan Dheri, and these vessels could be dated from c. 150 BCE until the end of the occupation of the site in the fourth or fifth century CE.[7] He also notes that, since the work of Marshall, other scholars have suggested that his proposed distilling apparatus could well have been used for making alcoholic drinks. For example, Mahdihassan, in discussing such vessels, takes for granted that early textual references to *madya* and *surā* refer to distilled drinks, and it is possible here that he relies on such nineteenth century translations of these terms as I discussed above.[8] If Marshall's vessels and reconstruction were all we had to work with, the case for distillation would still be very conjectural, but Allchin believed he could make a stronger case. He thus introduces two other pieces of evidence that he believes make it quite likely that distillation of alcohol was discovered in India.

First, Allchin appears to hold a theory to the effect that the presence of a certain technology amongst a primitive people in a certain area suggests its great antiquity in that area. He notes the abundance of ethnographic evidence for distillation technology amongst 'primitive people' in India today. Presumably he holds that it is unlikely that such people might ever learn a new technology, and therefore this technology for distilling alcohol must be quite ancient. He notes that there are, however, no references to this sort of distillation in early and medieval Indic textual sources, as I shall discuss below. This leads Allchin to note the following: 'There is thus an unresolved difference between the textual evidence and the inferences which may be drawn from ethnographic observation.'[9] His argument is as follows: primitive people nowadays in India distil alcohol. Therefore distillation is an ancient practice in South Asia. But there are no early textual references to this process. Therefore, in order to find this 'missing distillation', we need to look to other non-textual forms of evidence, such as the evidence of archaeology, and also we should look harder at the texts, as perhaps distilled alcohol was in fact hiding there all along.

I have already mentioned the archaeological materials that Allchin brings to his case, namely the 'receivers' that have been found in early Indo-Greek sites. His newly discovered textual evidence also relates to these same archaeological materials. Observing that, in the reconstructed stills, the condenser somewhat resembles an elephant's head and trunk, he observes that one word associated with drinking intoxicants in Sanskrit is *śuṇḍa*, a term that also means 'elephant's trunk'. Thus he concludes that the use of this term ('elephant's trunk') in contexts related to intoxicating drinks did in fact refer to the products of distillation made with a still that looked like the one both Marshall and Allchin wish to reconstruct: an *elephant's head-shaped* still. And he thus concludes that 'Indian literature does, after all, contain numerous references to distillation, although one could scarcely have recognized them until the archaeological evidence was available.'[10] The reluctance of authors of Sanskrit texts to furnish explicit descriptions of distilled alcohol can, he claims, be attributed to three facts. First, Sanskrit texts are generally reluctant to discuss alcohol, even fermentation. Secondly, such sources do not discuss craft practices. And thirdly, there was a general secrecy surrounding alcohol owing to its 'ritual and sacramental aspect'.[11]

As we shall learn from the brief survey below, Allchin's claim about the lack of representations of intoxicating drinks in Sanskrit texts is incorrect, and we still possess many technical and non-secretive discussions of these drinks and how to make them. Moreover, I am not at all convinced by the argument Allchin makes to the effect that the word for 'trunk' suggests the shape of a still, and was therefore also used to refer to the consumption of distilled alcohol, at least for early periods. The two words could be quite distinct, or the reason for the polysemy here could be quite different - we simply do not have enough detailed philology on the terminology for intoxicating drinks in early South Asia to pass judgment on this at the present time. And the extremely hypothetical nature of the material reconstruction of this type of 'still' should be quite clear from the brief account I gave above. That is to say, the debate all dates back to Marshall's assembly of a 'still' from quite diverse pots, most of which are not particularly remarkable in form, and which, even if correctly reconstructed, might well not have been used for condensing alcohol.

Needham, in *Science and Civilization in China*, reviews these and other materials taking a balanced view of the matter, though ultimately he seems cautiously convinced by Allchin's 'elephant's trunk' theory and Marshall's reconstruction.[12] Thus, although by no means all scholars are convinced by this material, the thesis that 'distillation is strangely absent in early texts' persists and Marianne Oort, in a paper from 2002, refers to the above theories of early distillation in South Asia in order to support a 'distillation reading' of a hymn from a very early Sanskrit text called the *Atharvaveda*.[13]

In reading secondary scholarship on the history of alcohol in pre-modern South Asia it is useful to be aware of the above debates and uncertainties surrounding the precise nature of what these drinks were and how they were made, as most scholars have consciously, or unconsciously, subscribed to a quite distinct position on these questions. Furthermore, it is also important to note that some scholars working in South Asia took a rather dim view of the consumption of alcohol, and in their writing they sometimes present this history in a somewhat polarized manner. For example, V.G. Rahurkar, writing in 1974, notes that a certain Sanskrit term 'shows that the Vedic people were conscious of the evil effects and the detestable character of wine …' though I might add that the presence of such a bias should not put the scholar off reading such works, as they often collect and present many valuable sources.[14] Rajendralal Mitra, on the other hand, adopted a thoroughly and consciously (even mischievously) 'rational' approach and was quite comfortable to assert that 'The Earliest Brahmin settlers were a spirit-drinking race, and indulged largely both in Soma beer and strong spirits',[15] but this should not surprise us from a scholar who only the previous year had written a famous article on 'Beef in Ancient India',[16] where he asserted that in earlier periods beef was an acceptable food in Hindu circles. Thus in secondary scholarship we frequently see a tension between a desire to locate the discovery of alcoholic distillation in South Asia and a discomfort with any tendency to celebrate alcohol cultures in the same region.

The history of alcohol in South Asia rouses strong passions, and indeed this should not surprise us, as these drinks have always been somewhat controversial in certain circles even within South Asia, as I shall now explain.

Surā and the ethics of drinking in early South Asia

The earliest textual evidence for an intoxicating drink in South Asia is to be found in the large collection of Sanskrit texts called the Vedas which date from before the Common Era. These texts mention two types of intoxicating drinks. The most important and esteemed of the two is a drink called *soma* that is prepared from a plant that is also called *soma*. Soma is also presented as a god in the Vedic texts and the *soma* drink is itself an important and much praised offering to the gods in some of the sacrifices described in these texts. The topic of *soma* – what sort of plant it may have been, its significance in the sacrifice and in Vedic texts, not to mention the interesting secondary scholarship on these matters – is quite enormous and I cannot even begin to discuss it here.[17] Instead I wish to focus on the other drink, a fermented alcoholic preparation called *surā*, which appears to have been made from grains (rice, barley, millet).[18]

As Malamoud notes in an excellent article on '*soma* and its counterpart', that is to say *surā*, this latter, fermented drink, far from being a sacrificial drink of the gods, is 'from the most ancient texts … denounced as that which impels man into sin and deprives him of self-control'.[19] There are two ritual occasions, however, when *surā* is drunk, which is perhaps surprising given that '... in a society legislated by the normative texts of Vedic and brahmanic India, the consumption of alcohol is quite generally and very vigorously condemned'.[20] In one of these rituals *surā* appears to function somewhat like a ritual antidote to excessive *soma* consumption, thus reinforcing its role as a ritual 'counterpart' of *soma*. In the second ritual, a royal consecration, *surā* is present precisely because it is normally excluded from sacred rites, because the king 'wishes to appropriate every rite to himself and to have all opposed pairs transform for him and though him …'.[21] In some Vedic rituals *surā* is therefore essential, but this only reinforces the idea that this drink is prohibited to brahmins, and literally quite opposed to the revered *soma*. By no means all parts of society, though, were engaged in performing or patronizing Vedic sacrifices, and certainly by a later date alcoholic drinks with other names were known. Therefore we might ask whether *surā* was prohibited for everyone. And, for those people who were forbidden to drink *surā*, were other alcoholic drinks likewise prohibited?

To answer these questions we need to turn from ritual texts to those that deal with Hindu religious law, *dharmaśāstra*. In his formidable study of *dharmaśāstra*, Pandurang Vaman (P.V.) Kane provided a thorough account of the complexities of traditional Hindu law with regard to alcohol.[22] As Kane notes, some authorities say that all intoxicating drinks (*madya*) are forbidden to all brahmins in all stages of life, and these authorities assert that drinking *surā* or *madya* is one of the 'great sins', along with killing a brahmin, theft, and sexual intercourse with the wife of the *guru*. Some authorities claim that the word *surā* is broad in scope and refers to several types of intoxicants (as the word '*madya*' does), whereas others claim that *surā* has a restricted meaning, being only that intoxicating drink made from flour. This *surā* made from flour, a sort of beer as it were, is, according to some authorities, forbidden to all of the higher three *varṇa*s (sometimes translated as 'castes'): brahmins, kṣatriyas and vaiśyas. Restrictions on brahmins are even more stringent – not only are they forbidden to drink *surā*, but *all* other intoxicating drinks (excluding, of course, *soma*) are also forbidden to them. For kṣatriyas and vaiśyas all other intoxicating drinks, made from flowers, molasses and other materials, are permitted. And the rest of society can apparently drink whatever it desires, including *surā*, though Kane does note one opinion that 'good śūdras [the lowest *varṇa*] should abstain from surā also …'.[23] I might briefly mention here that these prohibitions on drinking alcohol were exploited in practices that we would call tantric, in forms of ritualized drinking that deliberately inverted the norms of abstinence. Thus these restrictions on drinking helped shape the nature of ritual transgression in South Asian religions.[24] Of course, as should be evident by now, such tantric rites involving alcohol would only have seemed transgressive to a limited and elite part of society.

This ideal account of righteous society, according to which there is a stratified, inverse-hierarchical access to a variety of types of intoxicating drinks, no doubt does reflect a complex alcohol culture. Notably, the 'lower' parts of society had access to a far richer array of drinks. This complexity is also seen in other discourses that take a more ethically neutral stance with regard to intoxicating drinks, namely texts on statecraft, medicine, and on erotics and courtly pleasure that I shall now consider.

Taxes, spies, medicine, and erotic pleasure

An early Sanskrit text on statecraft, the *Arthaśāstra*, contains a section on the activities of a state official called the Superintendent of *Surā*.[25] This text is notoriously difficult to date but is seems to have been produced in the third century BCE with additions until the first century CE, though even within these vague limits we can still say that this is one of the earliest detailed accounts of drink and drinking culture in South Asia after the Vedas. Although *surā* appears to be a specific term for a fermented drink made of flour, the term is used here as a synecdoche to refer to intoxicants in general, for several types of drinks are described here and not just *surā*. As well as descriptions of drinks and the drinking establishment, the *Arthaśāstra*, in keeping with its wider economic and political concerns, also describes the control and taxation of intoxicating drink, in addition to relating how one should exploit the nature of drinking establishments for the purpose of intelligence gathering. This text makes it clear that at this period there was a trade in these drinks, and that it was legal and supervised by the government.

Six generic types of intoxicating drinks are described and the basic quantities of their ingredients are also listed. Ingredients include flour and also sugar-cane products, such as jaggery, along with various herbs and barks. The drink made from grape juice is here called *madhu*, an early term for an intoxicating drink that is also associated with honey – evidently in this context that association has been broken. Also notable here is the description of a drink called *maireya* that appears to have been quite a popular preparation in the centuries around the turn of the Common Era. The text also describes the preparation of the ferment starter (*kiṇva*). This substance was understood to be responsible for creation of the power to intoxicate in some drinks. In an account of a school of philosophy called materialism, a text called the *Sarvadarśanasaṃgraha* refers to *kiṇva* in order to show how the materialists argued that consciousness arises from the elements alone, in the form of a body, without the addition of an extra mental or soul-like entity: 'In that case the elements earth and the rest are the four *tattva*s; from them alone, transformed into the form of a body, consciousness is produced, like the power to intoxicate [is produced] from *kiṇva* etc. [when its components are assembled.]'[26] Thus, fermentation, understood as the creation of a power to intoxicate in a drink, was thought to derive solely from the combination of certain very specific materials left for a few days. I should also add that there is no mention of distillation in the *Arthaśāstra*, a text that certainly does not shy away describing the technicalities of making intoxicating drinks.

The description of the place for selling and serving drink in this text is very interesting: '[the superintendent of *surā* should have made] drink-houses (*pānāgārāṇi*) with several rooms, separate beds and seats, [and] drinking places with perfumes, garlands and water pleasant according to the season'.[27] Nevertheless, drinking was not terribly salubrious, but still it was legal and even useful to the state. There were controls, however, and the accumulation of intoxicating drinks is prohibited 'because of the danger of negligence by those assigned to works, because of the danger of respectable people (*ārya*) transgressing the limits of decorum, and because of the danger of the energy of fiery people'.[28] In terms of the organization of the text, the control of intoxicating drinks is listed after agriculture and precedes the sections on animal slaughter and courtesans, activities that would be considered either low class or of dubious respectability from the point of view of the brahminical ideals of behaviour promoted in texts on *dharmaśāstra*. This controlled trade in intoxicating drinks was nevertheless very useful for the purpose of gathering intelligence. Drinking places not only attracted a wide variety of characters, local and foreign, but also secret agents, and the attractive female servants of the trader could easily search the bodies and possessions of intoxicated people. As depicted in the *Arthaśāstra*, drinking houses were very cosmopolitan places, where all manner of strangers mingled, drank, became intoxicated and sometimes fell asleep. However, not all drinking took this form, for householders (*kuṭumbinaḥ*) are permitted to make certain drinks on occasion: white 'beer' (*śvetasurā*) for necessary business, and the herbal drinks called *ariṣṭa*s for medicine.[29]

Whereas in the *Arthaśāstra* the state-controlled business of selling intoxicating drink is a source of intelligence and revenue, medical texts in Sanskrit describe the pharmacological properties, health benefits, and dangers of the many types of drinks that were available. We possess a large number of these texts (not to mention commentaries) that date from several centuries BCE until the twentieth century. Like the *Arthaśāstra*, and quite unlike the brahmanical discourses on intoxicating drinks, these texts do not for the most part present a moralizing perspective on alcohol, a pragmatism we also see in this genre with regard to the consumption of meat and garlic. In this short chapter it is not possible to present these medical materials in their full complexity and diachronic development. Instead I shall describe the contexts of one early, important, and easily available foundational text of *Āyurveda*, *Caraka's Compendium*, the *Carakasaṃhitā*.[30] This text is complex: scholars believe the earliest version might date from the third or second centuries BCE and that it was last revised in the fourth or fifth centuries CE.[31] For our purposes here, however, we can simply classify this text, like the *Arthaśāstra*, as another rather early source on intoxicating drinks.

Caraka's Compendium discusses alcohol in detail in two places. First, in a description of varieties of food and drink there is a list of intoxicating drinks (generically called *madya*, 'intoxicant') together with brief statements of their qualities and medical indications. These drinks are beneficial for a great variety of complaints, from piles to fever. This passage does not provide any details of what the drinks are made of, but it does note some general qualities of intoxicants: 'Wine is exhilarating, nourishing, removes fear, grief and fatigue, provides boldness, energy, imagination, satisfaction, corpulence and strength. It is like nectar if used by persons predominant in sattva according to rules and with reasoning.'[32]

The second part of this text to discuss intoxicants concerns the treatment of excessive intoxication (*madātyayacikitsitam*). As we see in other medical texts, this section provides a wealth of information on drinks, on drinking practices, as well as a theory of how intoxicants function. Here *surā* is first celebrated and we are told that it 'should be used properly'.[33] The text describes an ideal drinking scene where the person who is perfumed and adorned should sit on a comfortable bed or seat, and drink from vessels of gold, silver or precious stones whilst being attended by beautiful, adorned women. One should also always drink wine together with various fruits, vegetables, and roasted meats.[34]

The text then describes how people of different bodily constitutions are affected in different ways by intoxicating drinks, and how people should therefore partake of drink in combination with certain foods and bodily preparations.[35] Intoxicating drink is said to possess both good qualities and faults. When consumed correctly it is like the nectar of immortality (*amṛta*), but when drunk together with an improper regime it acts like poison (*viṣavat*).[36] The text explains that intoxicating drink works by entering into the heart (*hṛdayam āviśya*). Then, having disturbed the ten qualities of a sort of bodily 'energy' called *ojas* by means of its own ten (opposed) qualities, the intoxicating drink changes (or 'agitates', 'perturbs') the mind (*svaguṇair ojaso guṇān daśabhir daśa saṃkṣobhya ceto nayati vikriyām*).[37] Several increasing stages of intoxication are described and explained, and then the qualities and dangers of drink are related in greater detail.[38] In general, the good qualities of drink appear to consist of the production of happiness, sexual potency, and corpulence. Different types of drinking parties (*āpāna*) are described, as well as ideal (and less than ideal) drinking companions.[39] Following this relatively positive account of intoxicating drink the text turns to the treatment of excessive intoxication, the nature and treatment of which occupies the remainder of the section.

This medical text, *Caraka's Compendium*, presents intoxicating drink as possessing good qualities and bad. In many ways the first half of the section paints a quite glowing picture of the joys and benefits of drinking alcohol, though the extensive discussion of the problems of excessive intoxication reveals that drinking is not without dangers. Nevertheless, in this text, alcohol drunk by the right person, in the right manner, with the right preparations, appears to be a wholly good thing, which is quite unlike the Vedic ritual context and the brahmanical legal context, where at best *surā* is a necessary counterpart to *soma*, and where other drinks are tolerated but by no means celebrated. According to *Caraka's Compendium*, in order to drink correctly and safely one nevertheless needs to understand all the variables that can be involved in producing the desirable effects.

Above I noted the capacity of intoxicating drink to create happiness and to increase virility (*pauruṣam*),[40] and this leads me to the next context where alcohol is important: sensual pleasure and erotics. One Sanskrit text on drinking and erotics begins as follows: 'The nectar-like juice produced of grapes is called '*kādambara*'; it arouses the penis. And it is extremely useful for the arts [found] in the texts on erotics, it is suitable for arousing Māra [that is to say, Kāma, the god of love], and eminently confers ability.'[41] Drinking parties with courtesans formed part of the pleasurable lifestyle of the man-about-town portrayed in that well-known Sanskrit erotic text, the *Kāmasūtra*.[42] This aspect of drinking intoxicants, an activity associated with erotic pleasure and the sociability of leisure, is also encountered in literary and poetic texts. For example, in an early poetic work by Aśvaghoṣa describing the life of the Buddha, the *Buddhacarita*, there is a scene in which the Buddha goes to a pleasure garden.[43] His father hopes that he will be distracted in that place by the erotic dalliances of the women there, so as to forget his new found awareness of old age, disease, and death. In the pleasure garden the women are intoxicated, flirtatious, and confused. Of course, in this case the erotic chaos contrasts with the heroic resolve of the Buddha not to become distracted, but in another later source we see a very similar scene presented in a more straightforwardly erotic light. The text in question is the *Delight of the Mind*, or *Mānasollāsa*, composed at the court of, and attributed to, the twelfth century Kalyāṇi Cāḷukya king, Someśvara III.[44] The greater part of this encyclopaedia of royal life is devoted to various sensual pleasures, sports, and games that the king should experience, watch, and play. One of the games is called the 'game of drinking intoxicating drinks' (*madirāpānakrīḍā*).[45] In the section describing this game, a number of drinks are described in some detail (none are distilled), as are various appetizers that one should eat with the drink. Then the party begins. Regarding the ideal location and purpose of the party we are told:

> In a grassy place in the forest, or on a sandbank by the river,
>
> in a garden filled with fruits and flowers, or in a well painted house,
>
> the king should have the womenfolk practice the game originating from drinking liquor,
>
> for their happiness of mind, and so he himself can watch them.[46]

Drinks are served in precious vessels of gold and silver, and of glass that is the colour of various gemstones, and the women get drunk. As with the women who surround the Buddha in the pleasure park, the drunk women at this party become what one might describe as charmingly confused, jealous and angry, and lustful towards the king, who has been left alone to be the sole spectator of this delightful, erotic chaos. Nowhere is there a suggestion that this play is immoral or unhealthy. Rather, in this context playing the game of drinking intoxicating drinks displays the king's competence in ruling and in enjoying his kingdom, not to mention his erotic desirability.

By the second millennium CE, however, the pleasures of royal drinking were no longer limited to the courts of kings who understood and practised drinking according to the conventions of Indic textual cultures. Muslim rulers also drank intoxicants, though of course the religious, ethical, and literary associations of drinking in these contexts were quite different. I shall now present a very brief account of this pre-modern Indo-Muslim drinking.

Drink in Indo-Muslim culture

Alcohol in South Asian Islamic culture has not been the subject of a single monograph, and in accounts of the period there is a tendency for scholars to focus on the drink and drug habits of important individuals, such as emperors and courtiers.[47] In part this is because the lives of such figures were more widely reported in what are nowadays better-known texts, but also the hedonistic exploits of these people can often make for a very lively, sometimes disparaging, historical narrative, something the early writers of chronicles no doubt intended. For example, in addition to opium, which I shall not discuss here, wine was popular with some Mughal emperors, though there was a tension here in an Islamic context: Shah Jahan is reported to have only drunk on certain occasions and Aurangzeb was apparently totally abstinent.[48] Other emperors, however, enjoyed a variety of wines and even accepted gifts of wine from a British ambassador.[49] Indeed, although alcohol was not considered by Europeans to be a serious commodity for major trade, as Chatterjee notes it played a very important role in processes of friendship and negotiation in the seventeenth century, not to mention in the exercise of royal power.[50] As we shall see below it is clear that strong arrack was available at this period, and so the fact that wine would still constitute a prestigious gift to an emperor suggests that such factors as rarity and flavour might have played a part in the evaluation of drinks during this period. As with the drinking game of King Someśvara, in these elite Mughal contexts the material culture of drinking played an important role, and the wine cup in particular was rich in symbolic associations.[51]

Accounts of the deeds of emperors are not terribly informative about the nature of drink in society at large. Thankfully, Irfan Habib provides an excellent discussion of distillation in later medieval and early modern South Asia, and other accounts of foreign travellers also enrich our understanding of the variety of drinks and drinking practices.[52] Habib believes that any early distillation in South Asia, the sort postulated by Marshall and Allchin, 'probably had no sequel'.[53] Distillation of alcohol does, however, appear to have taken off in South Asia during the period of the Delhi Sultanate. Habib quotes an account of distillation that Zia Barani composed in 1357, in writing about the time of Sultan Kaiqubad (1286-9): 'the wine makers of Kol and Meerut brought [to Delhi] distilled (*chakānīda*) sweet-scented unfermented (*be-khammari*) arrak (*'arq*), two or three years old, filling wine flagons with it'.[54] Habib presents another fascinating passage from the same text describing the later reign of 'Alā'uddīn Khaljī, when the sale of wine had been prohibited and people 'set up boilers (*bhaṭṭīs*) in their houses and made wine out of sugar (*qand*), and distilled it (*chakānidand*), drank it and sold it at high prices'.[55]

As Habib notes, these accounts constitute a very early attestation of distillation of alcohol on a commercial scale in an Islamic context. As well as sources composed by South Asian historians, Habib examines the descriptions of several foreign visitors, Chinese and European, to the region. From these accounts, and those discussed by Chatterjee, it appears that in the fifteenth to seventeenth centuries arrack was produced from sources such as rice, sugar, and toddy, which had long been used to manufacture a great variety of fermented but non-distilled drinks, possibly of a lesser prestige, more 'village drinks', than the sometimes imported grape wine.[56]

To return to the question I noted at the start of this chapter when discussing the manner in which some major Sanskrit dictionaries chose to translate a key term for 'intoxicating drink', it seems quite likely that distilled arrack has been manufactured in South Asia for approximately seven hundred (or more) years, and it appears that the fermented drinks that were thus distilled correspond quite closely with those produced in South Asia in earlier periods, being made from grains, sugar, and palm toddy. Quite possibly communities using Sanskrit (and also other languages) after this period might have adapted their previous terminology such that words that used to refer to products more like beers and wines came to refer to these far stronger drinks. Possibly, by the nineteenth century this adapted terminology had become so ingrained that somewhat anachronistic readings of earlier texts seemed quite natural. I should add that I state this theory quite tentatively, and that I intend to explore in far greater detail the impact of distillation technologies on Sanskrit learning in future works.

Conclusion

Although the discourse of the Vedic sacrifice and the laws of *dharmaśāstra*, not to mention the prohibitions of Islam, attempt to impose an apparently simple and rigid theory of intoxicating drinks onto society, the enduring impression one gets in reading the materials I have presented is that an enormous diversity, both of drinks and drinkers, resists and complicates these discourses at every turn. It is important to present these official, elite, and religiously orthodox discourses, but we should also try to read between the lines, and investigate other sources in order to understand what other parts of society drank, how they drank, and what they thought about drinking. For example, in the sources I have discussed the voice of the manufacturer and seller of intoxicating drink remains silent.

As is also clear, the debate on distillation that began with Sir John Marshall's famous reconstruction of a still haunts much of the secondary literature on this topic. Allchin's rather audacious 'elephant's trunk' theory of the forgotten references to distillation in Sanskrit texts highlights the fact that we need a nuanced, comprehensive, and diachronic philology of the language of intoxicating drinks in Sanskrit. Similar studies in other languages, such as Pali, and in vernaculars would also be invaluable in writing the history of alcohol in South Asia. Unfortunately for these early periods, the production of written texts is associated with an elite class, and whether they favoured drinking or abstinence, they evidently had quite distinctive approaches to alcohol – golden drinking cups and complete abstinence were quite probably not the norm. The work of Chatterjee and Habib shows that studying the reports of foreign visitors can be informative here, and Rudi Matthee, in his study of drugs and alcohol in Iranian history, likewise finds such foreign sources to be quite productive.[57] Materials relating to trade, such as those found in the Cairo Geniza might also be revealing. Of course in a post-orientalist world of scholarship we are only too well aware that these accounts need to be read with great care, but there is no doubt they can provide an alternative perspective on alcohol in South Asia, one that has different biases with regard to drink than the perspectives of authors of Sanskrit and Persian texts. We do possess a great number of such sources, in addition to those composed in South Asia, and thus with careful reading and very thoughtful translation of all these materials it should be possible to write a quite balanced and detailed history of alcohol in pre-modern South Asia.

Notes

1 K.H. Steinkraus (ed.), *Handbook of Indigenous Fermented Foods*, 2nd edn, New York: Marcel Dekker Inc., 1996, pp. 439–81.

2 It is worth noting that the so-called St Petersburg Lexicon of Böhtlingk and Roth, a major source for Monier Williams' dictionary, only gives 'an intoxicating drink' ('ein berauschendes Getränk') in this sense of *madya*.

3 R. Mitra, 'Spirituous drinks in ancient India', *Journal of the Asiatic Society of Bengal* 42, 1, 1873, 1–23, 58.

4 O. Prakash, *Food and Drinks in Ancient India (from earliest times to c. 1200 A.D.)*, Delhi: Munshi Ram Manohar Lal, 1961, pp. 24–5. This book is a very good source for the study of drinks in early South Asia, along with the same author's *Economy and Food in Ancient India*, parts 1 and 2 (Delhi: Bharatiya Vidya Prakashan, 1987). Another useful survey is P. Aalto, 'Madyam apeyam', in C. Vogel (ed.) *Jñānamuktāvalī: commemoration volume in honour of Johannes Nobel*, New Delhi: International Academy of Indian Culture, 1959, pp. 17–37.

5 J. Marshall, *Taxila: an illustrated account of archaeological excavations*, Cambridge: Cambridge University Press, 1951, vol. 2, pp. 420–1, vol. 3, plate 125.

6 F.R. Allchin, 'India: the ancient home of distillation', *Man*, New Series 14, 1, 1979, 55–63.

7 I might note that neither of the receivers in the primitive contemporary stills illustrated by Allchin and also Mahdihassan (see below) resemble the vessels found by Marshall, being instead simple vessels of no special design.

8 S. Mahdihassan, 'The earliest distillation units of pottery in Indo-Pakistan', *Pakistan Archaeology* 8, 1972, 159–68.

9 Allchin, 'India: the ancient home of distillation', p. 58.

10 Ibid., p. 62.

11 Ibid.

12 J. Needham, *Science and Civilisation in China*, vol. 5 *Chemistry and Chemical Technology*, part IV *Spagyrical Discovery and Invention: apparatus, theories and gifts*, Cambridge: Cambridge University Press, 1980, pp. 85–6, 131–2.

13 M.S. Oort, 'Surā in the Paippalāda Saṃhitā of the Atharvaveda', *Journal of the American Oriental Society* 122, 2, 2002, 355–60.

14 V.G. Rahurkar, 'The use and control of liquor in ancient India', *Vishveshvaranand Indological Journal, Acharya Dr. Vishva Bandhu Commemoration Volume*, Hoshiarpur: Vishveshvaranand Vishva Bandhu Institute of Sanskrit and Indological Studies, 1974, 286–300.

15 R. Mitra, 'Spirituous drinks in ancient India', p. 2.

16 R. Mitra, 'Beef in ancient India', *Journal of the Asiatic Society of Bengal* 41, 1872, 174–96.

17 Malamoud's excellent article on *soma* and *surā* provides some of the main bibliography for this vast topic, which unlike alcohol, has been thoroughly studied. C. Malamoud, 'Le soma et sa contrepartie: remarques sur les stupéfiants et les spiritueux dans les rites de l'Inde ancienne', in D. Fourier and S. D'Onofrio (ed.) *Le Ferment Divin*, Paris: Éditions de la Maison des sciences de l'homme, 1991, pp. 19–33.

18 Malamoud describes the preparation of *surā* (ibid., pp. 23–5). On *surā* see also M.B. Kolhatkar, *Surā: The Liquor and the Vedic Sacrifice*, New Delhi: D.K. Printworld, 1999.

19 Ibid., p. 22.

20 Ibid., p. 21.

21 Ibid., p. 31.

22 I base my account here on P.V. Kane, *History of Dharmaśāstra (Ancient and Mediaeval Religious and Civil Law)*, vol. II, part II, Poona: Bhandarkar Oriental Research Institute, 1941, p. 799. On the regulation of alcohol see also V.G. Rahurkar, 'The use and control of liquor in ancient India', pp. 286–300. For the case of Theravāda Buddhism monasticism see P. Kieffer-Pülz, 'Die Klassifizierung des Alkoholverbots in der buddhistischen Rechtsliteratur der Theravādin', in P. Schalk (ed.) *Im Dickicht der Gebote. Studien zur Dialektik von Norm und Praxis in der Buddhismusgeschichte Asiens*, Uppsala: Universitet, 2005, pp. 153–223.

23 Kane, *History of Dharmaśāstra*, p. 796.

24 For a translation of a short humorous play about the exploits of a drunken tantric adept that also sheds some light on medieval perceptions of drinking and drunkenness, see D.N. Lorenzen, 'A parody of the Kāpālikas in the *Mattavilāsa*', in D.G. White (ed.) *Tantra in Practice*, Princeton, N.J.: Princeton University Press, 2000, pp. 81–96.

25 *Arthaśāstra* 2.25. Kauṭalya, *The Kautilīya Arthaśāstra*, ed. R.P. Kangle, Bombay: University of Bombay, 1963. For the Sanskrit see part I, pp. 78–80. For the English translation of this whole section together with notes, see part II, pp. 153–6.

26 Mādhava, *Sarvadarśanasamgraha, Ānandāśramasamskrtagranthāvali* 51, Pune: Ānandāśrama Press, 1977, p. 1.
tatra pṛthivyādīni bhūtāni catvāri tattvāni tebhya eva dehākārapariṇatebhyaḥ kiṇvādibhyo madaśaktivac caitanam upajāyate …

27 My translation, Kauṭalya, *The Kautilīya Arthaśātra*, part I, p. 79.

28 My translation, ibid., p. 78.

29 Kauṭalya, *The Kautilīya Arthaśātra*, part II, p. 156.

30 *Caraka-Saṃhitā, Agniveśa's treatise refined and annotated by Caraka and redacted by Dṛḍhabala,* ed. and trans. P. Sharma, Jaikrishnadas Ayurveda Series, Varanasi, New Delhi: Chaukhambha Orientalia, 1981–1983, vol. I, pp. 209–10, vol. II, pp. 390–408.

31 D. Wujastyk, *The Roots of Ayurveda*, rev. ed., London: Penguin Books, 2003, p. 4.

32 *Caraka-Saṃhitā*, vol. I, p. 210.

33 *Caraka-Saṃhitā*, vol. II, p. 391.

34 Ibid., pp. 391–2.

35 Ibid., p. 392.

36 Ibid.

37 Ibid.

38 Ibid., pp. 393–6.

39 Ibid., pp. 397–8.

40 Ibid., p. 395.

41 Stanzas 1 and 2 of the *Kādambarasvīkaraṇakārikāmañjarī* which is given in *Kāmakuñjalatā*, ed. P. Ḍhuṇḍirājśāstrī, Varanasi: Chowlhamba Sanskrit Series Office, 1967.
mṛdvīkāyāḥ samudbhūto yo raso 'mṛtasannibhaḥ
kādambara iti khyāta udañjeḥ bodhakārakaḥ
kāmatantrakalāyāṃ tu atyantaṃ hitakārakaḥ
mārasyodbodhane dakṣa atisāmarthyadāyakaḥ

42 Vatsyayana Mallanaga, *Kamasutra*, trans. W. Doniger and S. Kakar, Oxford: Oxford University Press, 2002, p. 19.

43 Ashva Ghosha, *Life of the Buddha*, trans. P. Olivelle, New York: New York University Press: J.J.C. Foundation, 2007, Canto 4.

44 Someśvara, *Mānasollāsa of King Someśvara*, ed. G.K. Shrigondekar, Gaekwad's Oriental Series, vols. 28, 84, 138, Baroda: Oriental Institute, 1925–1961.

45 Ibid., vol. 3, p. 215.

46 Ibid.

47 For an excellent and broad-ranging account of alcohol in South Asia in the seventeenth century, including in European contexts, see P. Chatterjee, 'The lives of alcohol in pre-colonial India', *The Medieval History Journal* 8, 2005, 189–225.

48 A. Schimmel, *The Empire of the Great Mughals: history, art and culture*, London: Reaktion Books, 2004, p. 196.
49 Ibid., p. 198.
50 See Chatterjee, 'The lives of alcohol'.
51 M. Khare, 'The wine-cup in Mughal court culture - from hedonism to kingship', *The Medieval History Journal* 8, 1, 2005, 143–88.
52 I. Habib, 'Medieval technology: exchanges between India and the Islamic world', *Aligarh Journal of Oriental Studies* 1, 2, 1985, 197–222. See also Chatterjee, 'The lives of alcohol'.
53 Habib, 'Medieval technology', p. 205.
54 Ibid., pp. 207–8.
55 Ibid., p. 208.
56 Ibid., p. 209; Chatterjee, 'The lives of alcohol'.
57 R.P. Matthee, *The Pursuit of Pleasure: drugs and stimulants in Iranian history, 1500–1900*, Princeton, N.J.: Princeton University Press, 2005.

2 Opium, the East India Company and the 'native' states

Amar Farooqui

It is generally recognized that opium was vital for sustaining the British Empire throughout the nineteenth century. During the latter half of the eighteenth century, and most of the nineteenth, Indian opium was indispensable for promoting British imperial interests in Asia. Throughout this period Britain was the 'world's largest organized supplier of narcotics'.[1] India was the main supplier of opium to East and Southeast Asia, particularly China. Opium served three purposes: it was a major source of revenue for the colonial state in India; it paid for Chinese goods, principally tea, imported into Britain; and the commercial and financial operations connected with it provided avenues for remitting colonial plunder to the metropolis. The average annual opium revenue of the British Indian government for the 50 years from 1789–90 to 1838–9 was 6 per cent of total revenues; the average for the next half-century from 1839–40 to 1888–9 works out to 15 per cent.[2] This should be regarded only as a fraction of the wealth that opium generated for British imperialism.

Curiously, for all its importance to the colonial economy, there has not been much research on production and marketing of the commodity in India. The standard historical account of British opium policy, D.E. Owen's *British Opium Policy in China and India*, was published way back in the 1930s.[3] Subsequently, B.B. Chaudhuri's pioneering study of opium production in colonial eastern India probed the role of opium in the agrarian economy.[4] After Chaudhuri's work of the mid-sixties, there was virtual silence on the subject till J.F. Richards's 1981 article on peasant production of opium in nineteenth century India, focussing on the same area that Chaudhuri had studied, namely the Ganga region.[5] Over the next two decades Richards published several articles on various aspects of the history of the opium enterprise in the British Indian empire. The last piece he wrote on this theme before his sad demise in 2007 was a provocative polemical essay, 'The Moral Economy of Opium in Colonial India', in which Richards inverted critiques of the relationship between opium and imperialism by insisting that participation in the opium enterprise should not be seen as an ethical question; the drug had medical benefits and was useful for the Indian economy – whatever the consequences for China. In being generally critical of the opium trade we reproduce the discourse of evangelists and the late-nineteenth-century anti-opium lobby.[6]

Accepting their perspective is a form of cultural imperialism.[7] In the case of historical research on the opium produce of western India, the only significant contribution that one can think of, apart from Amalendu Guha's well-known articles of the 1970s on Parsi entrepreneurs (which we shall return to later), in which he explored the link between the opium trade and the rise of the Indian capitalist class, is Asiya Siddiqi's seminal essay of 1982, 'The Business World of Jamsetjee Jejeebhoy', based on the correspondence of the leading early nineteenth century west coast exporter of the commodity.[8]

It is often forgotten that 'Indian opium' was a generic name for two distinct 'brands' of the commodity, 'Bengal opium' and 'Malwa opium', with their own separate histories during the colonial period. One of the earliest measures taken by the East India Company following the conquest of Bengal was the establishment of a monopoly over the opium produce of Bihar, initially by the Company's servants in their private capacity and eventually as an official monopoly of the colonial state by the end of the eighteenth century. The monopoly was extended to Benaras-Ghazipur and other opium producing areas of the Ganga region when these came under the Company's control in the closing decades of the century. In 1797 the Company introduced a policy under which all the opium produced in its territories in eastern India was directly appropriated from the peasants. Opium cultivation was strictly regulated through the grant of licences to producers. Opium was procured in the raw, semi-liquid, state from poppy cultivators and processed by the Company in its own establishments. The bulk of this opium was intended for export, mainly to China. As is well known the Company's export opium was auctioned at Calcutta to private dealers who then took the risk of smuggling the drug into China.[9] The Company's opium was referred to as 'Bengal opium'. Bengal opium was of two varieties, 'Benaras opium' and 'Patna opium', the opium produce of eastern Uttar Pradesh and Bihar respectively. Strictly speaking these labels indicated the establishments, or opium agencies, that supplied the opium for the Company's auctions. Under the 1797 system (formalized through a regulation of 1799) two agencies had been established to oversee the procurement and processing of opium, one at Benaras (Varanasi) and the other at Patna.

It is indeed surprising that the Company should have been unaware at this stage of the possible competition that Bengal opium might have to contend with from another source of supply within India. The Malwa plateau (lying in the western portion of present-day Madhya Pradesh and some of the adjoining areas of Rajasthan), produced large quantities of opium (eventually designated as 'Malwa opium'). Malwa had been a major poppy growing tract since at least the sixteenth century. In the late pre-colonial period, European merchants, travellers, botanists and medical practitioners were quite familiar with the opium of western India. In the latter half of the eighteenth century the Portuguese had made use of their presence on the west coast of India to develop a network for the overseas export trade in Malwa opium. The success of the Portuguese initiative was facilitated by their possession of Macao in China. Macao was initially the principal base for smuggling the drug into mainland China. The Malwa opium export trade was already well-established by c. 1800, just around the time that the Company had put in place elaborate arrangements to secure its opium monopoly in eastern India.

It was in 1803 that the governor-general, Lord Wellesley, first learnt of the serious threat to its Bengal monopoly by exports from the west coast.[10] The Company's officials in Bombay were immediately instructed to ensure that the trade was extinguished. This was a goal that the Company was unable to attain. Rather, the trade in Malwa opium continued to expand rapidly. The Company was then forced to give up its objective of having a market exclusively for Bengal opium. Instead, it attempted to establish a monopoly over Malwa opium as well, by trying to procure the entire produce of the region and auctioning it along the pattern of Bengal opium. Malwa opium auctions commenced in 1821 and were held at Bombay (later, for a few years, simultaneously at Bombay and Calcutta). The auctions were discontinued after 1830 since the Company was unable to emerge as the sole supplier of the Malwa drug due to rampant smuggling of the commodity to China. From 1831 onwards private traders, both Indian and European, were allowed to export opium through Bombay on the payment of a moderate duty to the British Indian government.[11] Indian traders had demonstrated great ingenuity and resourcefulness in perfecting an alternative route for transporting opium from Malwa to the west coast. The route completely avoided British-administered territories. The main route ran from northern Malwa to Pali in Rajasthan; from Pali it proceeded via Jaisalmer to Karachi; and thence, by sea, to the Portuguese enclave of Daman, from where it was shipped to China. This route remained active till the end of the 1830s when the occupation of Karachi and the subsequent annexation of Sind finally put an end to it.

Malwa opium was produced entirely in princely or 'native' states which were under indirect colonial rule. It needs to be underlined that Malwa was a volatile region throughout the first half of the nineteenth century. The British had to wage two major wars – the second and the third Anglo-Maratha Wars – before they could subjugate the Malwa states. When the East India Company emerged as the paramount power in Malwa in 1818 following the third Anglo-Maratha war, it preferred placing the entire area under indirect rule. For the rest of the colonial period the numerous princely states of Malwa were governed by indigenous rulers who acknowledged overall British supremacy while retaining a measure of internal autonomy. Some of the prominent states of Malwa were the Maratha-ruled principalities of Gwalior (Sindia), Indore (Holkar), Dhar and Dewas; the Rajput-ruled principalities of Ratlam, Sitamau, and Rajgarh; and the Pathan-ruled principality of Bhopal. Gwalior was territorially the largest state in Malwa, and politically the most important in the region. Besides, there was the state of Kota in neighbouring Rajasthan.

The main problem which the Company encountered in procuring opium for its parallel auctions at Bombay was that it had to buy the Malwa drug at very high prices, leaving it with a very small margin of profit. Unlike the producing areas of the Ganga region, which lay in directly administered territory, the

Company had no control over opium production in Malwa. It was unable to purchase the drug straight from peasant producers who cultivated poppy and extracted the opium latex from the plant. Most of the opium produced in the region passed into the hands of wholesalers who operated as an informal syndicate. The transactions of this syndicate were coordinated from the city of Ujjain – the commercial and financial capital of Malwa.[12] The Company was forced to purchase opium for its auctions from the Malwa wholesalers who pocketed a significant portion of the earnings from the drug trade. Within just two years of its direct involvement with the Malwa opium business the Company decided to give up procurement in the open market. From 1823 onwards, it resorted to coercion in order to secure supplies of the drug at relatively lower prices. This it did by mounting pressure on the princely rulers of Malwa to use their respective state apparatuses to appropriate the greater part of the opium produce of the region for the benefit of the East India Company.

The Malwa opium syndicate was thus to be divested of its control over the commodity through political intervention. Negotiations were opened with the princely states of Malwa and Rajasthan for signing treaties whereby the producing states would hand over to the Company the bulk of the opium which these states produced, at a specified fixed price. The project, however, failed. Large quantities of the commodity remained within an indigenously controlled network. The Sindia state, the single largest producer of opium in the region, did not accept the restrictive measures that the Company had proposed, although negotiations with the Gwalior durbar dragged on till the end of the decade. The Company's strategy of imposing the 'opium treaties' could scarcely have been effective without the inclusion of the Sindia state. Most of the states which had actually agreed to sign the treaties had done so reluctantly and powerful opium lobbies in these states often had the backing of the rulers themselves in their endeavours to bypass the restrictive measures. A closer look at the process of negotiating the treaties reveals the extent to which opium was a contentious political issue. In formulating their responses on this question the princely states of Malwa articulated the interests of the various groups involved in the opium enterprise: petty-traders, wholesale merchants, bankers, speculators, commission agents, insurance firms, couriers and revenue farmers. At the same time these responses highlight the critical importance of opium as a source of earning for the respective states (often for rulers in their individual capacity as well), in an era of colonial domination that imposed severe constraints on their economies.

*****

In July 1823 the Calcutta authorities sounded the Company's senior officials posted in Malwa and Rajasthan on proposed treaties with the states to which these officials were accredited. The Company laid particular stress on 'giving native chiefs a direct interest' in controlling the transit of opium as well as restricting its cultivation.[13] Progress in negotiating the treaties was rather slow. This was not for want of enthusiasm on the part of the Company's officials, but due to the extremely hostile reaction of the states. It took considerable negotiating skill, and over two years, to pressurize the indigenous rulers and chiefs to put their signatures on the restrictive treaties. Most of the treaties were finally signed in 1826 by which time Calcutta was already beginning to have misgivings in the matter. The states with which it had been proposed to enter into opium agreements fell into three broad categories: (i) opium-producing states in southern, eastern and north-western Malwa; (ii) Rajasthan states through which the smuggling routes passed; and (iii) Kota, which was both a major point of transit and a leading producer of opium.

Negotiations had commenced in 1823–4 with several chiefs in Rajasthan being approached for entering into formal engagements to block transit routes. A weak Udaipur (Mewar) which had had its authority, resources and territory encroached upon by successive Sindia, Holkar and Kota onslaughts during the latter half of the eighteenth century was the first to succumb.[14] Udaipur was primarily a transit state.[15] Some opium was produced in the state, but it was confined to the Chittaurgarh strip on the Malwa-Udaipur border.[16] Its strategic location on the route from north-west Malwa to Pali gave it 'in a peculiar degree the power of checking the one great transit route by which opium found its way to the west coast'.[17] Entering into an agreement with Udaipur was crucial though not difficult to accomplish. Similar treaties were contemplated with Jodhpur, Jaipur and Bundi in Rajasthan. The successful conclusion of negotiations with Udaipur gave rise to a mood of optimism in Calcutta, the more so due to the traditional prestige enjoyed by Mewar among the Rajput-ruled states. By October 1824 it was more or less certain that Jaipur, Jodhpur and Bundi would definitely sign the treaties. Furthermore that the petty states of Dungarpur, Banswara and Jhabua on the Malwa-Gujarat border might also be roped in.[18] Jaipur eventually did not accept any opium treaty. Interest in Dungarpur and Banswara waned as the two states were rather insignificant from the point of view of the clandestine trade. Although Bundi signed a treaty in April 1825, this could hardly be regarded as a triumph since negligible quantities of the drug were produced in the state, and it did not possess commercial enterprise of much consequence.[19] By 1826 most of the *producing* states, barring Gwalior and the eastern Malwa states, had signed the treaties. The delay in the case of eastern Malwa was caused by the tardiness of the political agent entrusted with this task, who did not 'stir in the business' till very late. In any case the eastern Malwa states (Bhopal, Rajgarh, Narsinghgarh, and Khilchipur) produced only small quantities of opium.[20] Sindia's exception was, of course, an important one.

Of the agreements concluded by 1826 those with Indore and Kota were the most notable. The agreement with Kota, negotiated by the political agent Capt. J. Caulfield, provided the template for treaties with the leading producing states. Poppy was cultivated on a large scale in Kota. Zalim Singh (d. 1824), *de facto* ruler of the state, had been instrumental in promoting opium enterprise in his territories. His successor, Madho Singh, too was 'intimately connected with many of the most substantial business houses, and otherwise deeply involved in private mercantile speculation'.[21] The Kota treaty, signed in July 1825, stated that the Company would take up all 'good quality' opium that the state had to offer, at the rate of Rs 39.5 per *panseri* (1 *panseri* = 10 lbs avoirdupois).[22] In view of the fact that Kota had a large transit trade in opium, the British Indian government agreed to pay into the Kota treasury an amount equivalent to the annual revenue derived by the state from transit duties. The treaty was initially valid for a period of six months, with a provision for subsequent renewal.[23] It was when the time approached for renewal that the arrangement ran into trouble. As early as October 1825 Caulfield had reported that the sahukars of Kota were vehemently opposed to the renewal of the treaty.[24] When the treaty was initially signed in July, Caulfield had not anticipated that renewal would be a problem. He now regretted that he had not made the agreement valid for a period of at least one year. There was 'the possibility of the mercantile community of this Principality constraining the Raje Rana [Madho Singh] to remonstrate against the adoption of ... measures which they are persuaded will infallibly prove their ruin'.[25] Caulfield hinted at the growing isolation of Madho Singh who, 'it is insinuated', had sacrificed the 'interest of the saocars [sahukars] of the country ... to the wishes of the British Government'.[26] Madho Singh's alienation from the Kota sahukars was reflected in the fact that Bahadur Mal, the 'Rothschild of Malwa' and the leading opium dealer in Kota, 'refused to abide by his agreement through the Raj Rana' of selling opium to the Company on account of the Kota state at the agreed price of Rs 39.5 per *panseri*.[27]

Protests notwithstanding, Caulfield was eventually able to persuade Madho Singh to renew the treaty. A new agreement was signed in December 1825.[28] But this agreement was not without its problems. The Company now undertook to buy a specified amount of opium, 4,000 *man*, from the Kota state every year (a *man* or 'maund' of opium in Malwa was approximately 40 lbs av.).[29] The price at which the opium was to be bought was reduced from Rs 39.5 to Rs 30 per *panseri*. It was however stated in the treaty that an increase in the price at which the Company procured opium in other parts of Malwa would entitle the state to the same. Besides, the state was promised a bonus of five rupees per *panseri* on the quantity it supplied, if it actively prohibited the export of opium from its territories. Madho Singh had not capitulated without extracting some concessions. More importantly, the quantity of opium which the Company agreed to take from Kota was considerably higher than the total estimated produce of the state. Around 1820 it was estimated that Kota produced less than 1,600 *man* of opium.[30] Even allowing for an increase in production in the intervening period the figure of 4,000 *man* seems excessive. Bahadur Mal had been canvassing for the acceptance of this figure since early 1825. In a letter of February, the Malwa opium agent, Samuel Swinton, had quoted Bahadur Mal as stating that 4,000 *man* was the total produce of Kota. He commented that it was in Bahadur Mal's interest 'to rate it high, from his connection with the Raj Rana and the state'.[31]

In 1826 Madho Singh contracted with the principal sahukars of Kota for supplying to the state the stipulated quantity of 4,000 *man* of opium which the Company had agreed to buy under provisions of the treaty. Bahadur Mal alone got a contract to supply almost one-third of the total quantity. Madho Singh, who it was well known had large investments in opium, probably had financial stakes in some of these contracts. Madho Singh had succeeded in getting the Company to agree to a figure that was acceptable to the Kota opium lobby, thereby softening opposition to the treaty. A similar pattern is to be seen in the case of Indore. Kota and Indore, the two major Malwa states with whom treaties were eventually signed, succeeded in pitching the contracted quantities at much higher levels than their estimated produce. This was a tactical move, as we shall see, to ensure that there was no forced reduction in the quantum of the wholesale trade in the commodity at the regional level.

The agreement worked out by Caulfield was however not acceptable in its entirety to the Board of Customs, Salt and Opium, which was responsible for the routine administration of the British Indian government's opium affairs. The board regarded some of the key provisions of the treaty as being detrimental to the Company's interests and sent in its objections to the treaty as soon as it received a copy.[32] The quantity of the drug which the Company was to purchase from Kota was declared to be disproportionately large, and the promise of a bonus to the state was interpreted as an incentive to cultivation. There would naturally be a tendency, it was observed, to maximize production. The board was also unhappy with the implied flexibility of procurement price. The close connection between the state and mercantile interests in Malwa was no secret. There was a real possibility that prices would be rigged. In a letter to the governor-general, Lord Amherst, the board expressed its apprehension that Madho Singh could 'cause a general increase in the price in the Drug' as he 'doubtlessly possesses great influence over the soucars [sahukars] at Malwa'.[33] Amherst concurred that fears of the board were not unfounded and in February 1826 Caulfield was instructed to revise the treaty.[34] This marks the beginning of serious disagreements between the Calcutta authorities on the one hand and the Company's servants in Malwa on the other.

Within a fortnight of the British Indian government's endorsement of the board's opinion on Kota, the Indore resident, Gerald Wellesley, had brought his negotiations with the Holkar durbar to a successful conclusion.[35] He had not yet learnt that Caulfield's agreement had been repudiated by Calcutta. The treaty with Indore was formally signed in February 1826.[36] Its provisions were by and large identical to those of the Kota agreement. The quantity of opium that the Company was to purchase from Indore was fixed at 5,000 *man*. This was more than double the estimated yield of the state c. 1820. The various articles pertaining to procurement price and bonus were the same as in the Kota treaty. There was one unusual provision (article 4) in Wellesley's treaty by which Indore was to receive its payment, including the bonus, on the assumption that 5,000 *man* had actually been sold to the Company even if there was a shortfall in the supply.[37] The Indore state was thus guaranteed approximately 700,000 rupees irrespective of the amount of opium supplied to the Company.

The Calcutta authorities reacted by immediately censuring Wellesley.[38] The bonus had already come in for criticism. There was now the added burden of what amounted to a subsidy to Indore. It was acknowledged that article 4 'was probably designed chiefly to save Holkar's Government from loss in the event of failure of the crops'. 'But if so', the Fort William declared, 'it has gone much beyond that purpose. Under the terms of it as it now stands, the Government of Holkar may convert the whole of the land now cultivated with the poppy to other purposes, so as not to deliver to the British agent a single seer of opium, and may yet continue to be entitled to receive the full sum (including bonus) of Rs.700,000. Such a condition appears to be manifestly unequal'.[39] Moreover, the quantities contracted for did not bear any relation to the estimated yield of the state.

Negotiating the treaties had not been an easy task. Now that there was some progress in getting the Malwa states to acquiesce in the Company's attempt to regulate the opium trade, the Calcutta authorities seemed bent upon undoing whatever had been achieved. Swinton, who had been steering the negotiations preceding the 'opium treaties', was convinced that any delay in ratifying the Kota and Indore treaties would give an opportunity to 'interested parties to make the Ryotts [peasant cultivators] dissatisfied with their rulers'.[40] He also warned that if 'agreements now made are set aside, we can never expect the cordial cooperation of native states'.[41] The Swinton-Wellesley team, stationed in Indore, had produced a workable formula to create a restrictive confederacy. It is likely that the formula was developed in consultation with Holkar's prime minister, Tatya Jog. Since Indore was the headquarters of the Malwa opium agency, Swinton could use Wellesley's local connections as the resident to push the Company's point of view. At the same time sahukars could use the Holkar durbar to undermine the Company's opium interests by influencing Swinton's decisions. It needs to be mentioned that Tatya Jog owned the leading business concern of Indore. In the 1820s opium was the most important commodity that his firm dealt in. Since the days of John Malcolm, who was the principal colonial official in Malwa in the immediate post-1818 period, the British had frequently sought the advice of Tatya Jog on crucial matters. Nevertheless, despite his cordial relations with Jog, Malcolm had warned against making Indore the headquarters of the Malwa opium agency, '... to which I have objection from its being the residence of a Court under a soukar [sahukar] minister and I am satisfied the agent if there would be surrounded with an influence and an intrigue that would not be favorable [*sic*] ...'.[42] The capacity of Tatya Jog to manipulate the assessments of the opium agent should not be underestimated. Tatya Jog's connections extended to Kota where he was closely aligned with Bahadur Mal.[43]

The formula of Swinton and Wellesley ensured that the interests of the leading opium wholesalers were not totally disregarded. Only this had made possible some headway in negotiating the treaties. Between April and June 1826 treaties were concluded with Dhar, Dewas, Ratlam, Sailana, Sitamau, Jaora and Amjhera.[44] These treaties contained more or less the same terms as those of the Indore treaty. Swinton and Wellesley were, however, going slow in confirming the agreements signed, as well as in the matter of further negotiations, due to the fate that the earlier treaties had met with at Calcutta.[45]

The main reservations of the British Indian government were spelt out in a note penned by secretary Holt Mackenzie.[46] In his note Mackenzie stated that 'the only important objections to the treaties considered generally seem to be these that they do not absolutely fix the price to be paid by Government. And that they stipulate for the payment of the full purchase money of the opium, amounting in the case of Holkar, to be six lacs [600,000] of rupees, besides the Bonus, *though not an ounce of opium should be delivered* [emphasis mine]'. The matter of the price payable could be taken care of by fixing 'absolutely' the price at Rs 30 per *panseri* which 'may be considered I imagine a remunerative price'.[47] Mackenzie ignored reports that had been coming in about Malwa peasants being coerced by sahukars and rulers to hand over their opium at unremunerative prices. For instance, in Kota the peasants were being forced by Madho Singh to sell their produce for as little as Rs 18 per *panseri* which was then sold to the Company at the rate of Rs 30.[48] After all, the Company was not purchasing opium directly from the peasants. It had not eliminated the sahukars, and the bond between the state and merchants was as strong as ever. While profit margins of big opium dealers might have been reduced marginally, peasant producers could not even recover the cost of seeds and manure.[49]

For Mackenzie it was the second objection was 'more serious'. As he put it, 'It seems to me impossible that Government can engage to pay to Holkar the sum of Rs. 7,00,000 under a treaty which may eventually enable that state to pocket the whole without supplying any opium.'[50] Wellesley had gone too far in introducing this provision. The engagement had therefore to be undone. The inflated quantities of opium entered into the treaties had also not escaped Mackenzie's notice. No satisfactory explanation had been forthcoming from Swinton regarding 'the authority on which his calculations are founded'. The secretary wished that Swinton had 'stated more fully' the basis of his figures.[51] Caulfield too came in for criticism for the same reason as he had 'yielded too readily to the desire of the Kotah state that we should take a large quantity of opium'.[52]

The note led to the governor-general's ruling in June 1826 that the treaties would have to be revised substantially.[53] Existing treaties were to be adhered to for the current season (1826–7), but were to be renegotiated for the following season.[54] It took Wellesley almost six months to revise the Indore treaty. A new agreement was signed with the state in December 1826. According to the revised agreement the quantity of opium to be bought by the Company was reduced from 5,000 to 4,000 *man*. The price was fixed at Rs 30 per *panseri*. The Indore government was to prevent export and transit of opium and to ensure that the gross yield of the state did not exceed 5,000 *man*. If the state 'faithfully observed' the conditions of the engagement it was to receive Rs 100,000 per annum from the British government as a bonus.[55] Tatya Jog having passed away in April 1826 the treaty was signed by his successor, Raoji Trimbak. Trimbak had been Jog's confidential deputy, and was an opium trader on his own account.[56] He had agreed to changes in the treaty 'after some initial show of hesitation'.[57] Jog's removal from the scene at this juncture probably made Wellesley's task easier. Whereas Jog was a formidable force, Trimbak's position was far from secure. In fact he soon left Indore and joined the Sindia durbar. All that he had sought during the discussions preceding the signing of the treaty were a few advantages for himself: 'He then asked whether we could not allow him personally the profits of about 25 chests in consideration of the blow which this ... arrangement struck at his private interests cutting off as it did the gains which under the state of things previously prevailing he was able to realize by speculating in the purchase and sale of opium. I however at once repressed all expectation of such an indulgence.'[58]

Once Indore had been brought around, the Company's political agents were asked to settle with other opium producing states.[59] The quantities of opium to be purchased by the Company were scaled down in several cases. In a few instances the amount was increased marginally (Jaora, Dhar, Narsinghgarh).[60] The readjustment was done in such a manner that the total revised quantity to be purchased (16,760 *man*) approximated to total estimated production, c. 1820, in the relevant states. But the figures were juggled to suit Kota and Indore, so that the Company committed itself to purchasing significantly larger quantities of opium from these two states than their estimated production. Kota and Indore had successfully reversed colonial priorities. The objective of the Company had initially been to curtail the production of Malwa opium. It was now undertaking to buy almost 2,000–2,500 chests from these two states alone. One might mention that in the preceding season, 1825–6, the Company had sold 3,810 chests of Bengal opium at the Calcutta auctions.[61] The strategy of Malwa sahukars appears to have been to guarantee a minimum level of procurement of opium by the Company by inserting the maximum possible procurement figure in the treaties. Since it was only the larger states that could manage this, we find the Indore and Kota durbars concentrating on the quantities to be sold to the opium agent.

To Gwalior no treaty was acceptable. This was no trifling matter since the opium produce of the state was almost equal to that of all the other states put together. A definite nexus existed between the opium lobbies of Indore, Kota and Gwalior. True, there were contradictions among the indigenous business groups of Malwa – their different perceptions are reflected in the fact that Kota and Indore signed the opium treaties, while Gwalior did not – but there was also scope for alliances. The lobbies intersected at Kota with which both Holkar and Sindia had a long historical association. Moreover, the opium producing districts of Kota had been acquired or rented from either Holkar or Sindia. Caulfield made a pointed reference to 'the secret influence of courts of Gwalior and Indore' at Kota.[62] The Company had introduced an element of uncertainty in the opium trade with its restrictive policy. If British power managed to effectively seal smuggling routes, it would be useful for merchants to keep open the option of deriving profits from supplying large quantities of the drug to the Company.

The point is that the Company was not sure about how it could resolve the dilemma of absorbing almost the entire available supply of Malwa opium while at the same time keeping its procurement at a level that would not upset the international market for Bengal opium. Perhaps Caulfield and Wellesley had a better understanding of ground realities than did the officials in Calcutta, and realized that if a large surplus remained in the hands of the Malwa wholesalers it would ultimately enter the smuggling network thereby defeating the objective of the 'opium treaties'. The treaties were designed to regulate the export of Malwa opium. Controlled exports were impossible if the thriving clandestine trade in the drug was allowed to continue. The dilemma was eventually resolved by forcing open the market in China through military intervention, the First Opium War (1839–42), so that increased quantities of both Bengal and Malwa opium could be pushed into it. Simultaneously, the annexation of Sind in 1843 effectively blocked the export of Malwa opium from Portuguese Daman by closing the Karachi route. Gwalior too was compelled to fall in line by launching a major military campaign against the state in the same year (1843).[63]

*****

As we have noted, Gwalior refused to be part of the restrictive arrangement. In 1825 the Gwalior resident had accurately predicted the outcome of consultations with the state. He wrote to the Calcutta authorities that 'discussions on the part of the Durbar have been of so vague and unsatisfactory a nature' that there was 'little prospect' of 'any arrangement being entered into with the Maharajah'. After giving a gist of the deliberations he had with the maharaja, Daulat Rao Sindia (r.1794–1827), in which most of the talking on behalf of the maharaja had been done by the representative (*vakil*) of Appa Gangadhar, the revenue-farmer of Sindia's largest opium producing districts located in Mandsaur in north-western Malwa, the resident concluded that 'the Governor-General will perceive how little probability there is of coming to any kind of agreement with this government on the subject of opium'. In sheer exasperation he stated, 'It is impossible even to obtain the requisite information on which to ground any agreement.' Finally that even if such an agreement were possible 'I should despair of any engagement being efficiently carried into effect' because of the 'scattered nature of his [Sindia's] possessions'.[64]

At one stage, in February 1826, Gwalior did hint at its willingness to accept the proposed treaty if the Company would purchase 5,000 *man* from Mandsaur alone.[65] Nothing came of this proposal. By June the authorities in Calcutta were getting worried that Sindia had not become part of the restrictive system: 'The great point that is wanting is apparently to induce Sindia.'[66] Without Sindia the system was unworkable. Not only was this state the largest producer of opium in Malwa, but it also had enough political and economic resources to defeat a policy based on the treaties. Many of the prominent figures at the durbar were openly hostile to the British. Leading bankers associated with the durbar had large investments in opium and therefore strongly resisted any kind of treaty that would act as a fetter on the enterprise. In 1823 Wellesley had identified the Gwalior sahukars as the main obstacle to British control over Malwa opium. He had even come out with the suggestion that Daulat Rao should be persuaded 'to transfer by cession all his Malwa territories to our hands for a stated annual payment from us for the whole'.[67] More extensive political control over Sindia territories was the key to establishing control over Malwa opium.

As chances of Sindia's participation in the scheme receded, colonial officials no longer had their heart in negotiating the revised treaties. By the beginning of 1827 it was apparent that Gwalior would have nothing to do with the system. The Calcutta authorities were not very happy with the delay in finalizing the treaties. Reports from Canton constantly referred to vast quantities of Malwa opium in the China market.[68] Eventually this situation forced the Company to withdraw from the Malwa opium trade altogether, and allow unrestricted export of the drug through Bombay from 1831 onwards. For the next more than one decade the Company had to be content with the relatively small revenue it earned from the moderate duty it levied on opium chests brought into Bombay for onward shipment to China. Once the smuggling route was rendered inoperative following the annexation of Sind in 1843, the Company gradually hiked the duty payable on opium chests passing through Bombay, substantially enhancing its revenue from the trade.

Nevertheless, the configuration of political power in western and central India, manifested in the presence of a large number of 'native' states over which the Company exercised varying degrees of control, placed at the disposal of indigenous business groups opportunities for capital accumulation through participation in the international opium commerce, considerably altering thereby the nature of the colonial economy of western

India. Trade in Malwa opium had a subversive dimension: it fundamentally undermined an important monopoly of the Company. Opium smuggling became the means through which indigenous merchants gate-crashed into what was supposed to be an exclusive colonial preserve and helped themselves to some of the earnings of the commerce in the drug. The question of the role played by opium smuggling in indigenous capital accumulation in nineteenth century colonial India has recently been revisited by Claude Markovits. In his historical appraisal of the impact that trade in Malwa opium had on the emergence of a capitalist class in western India, Markovits contends that the 'illegal' trade in the drug was not as critical a source of accumulation for the Indian capitalist class as has been suggested in some writings on the subject.[69]

Markovits does not entirely deny the important role of opium in indigenous capital accumulation in western India. 'A narrative of Indian capitalism that gives central place to the Malwa opium trade as a source of capital accumulation is', he remarks, 'an alluring proposition, and different authors have succumbed to the slightly perverse appeal of that tune.'[70] He candidly counts himself among those who have yielded to this attraction – referring to an earlier essay of his in which he had noted that opium profits had made the process of indigenous capital accumulation in Bombay relatively more stable as compared to Calcutta.[71] However, Markovits doubts that opium smuggling was a key factor in that process. While broadly agreeing that 'the "illegal" trade in Malwa opium ... occurred on a significant scale between 1803 and 1839', he is not certain about its worth since the economic effects of this trade 'are difficult to estimate'.[72] What is more, the 'operators' involved in smuggling were diverse, scattered, and their 'identities varied overtime'.[73] This makes it difficult to think in terms of an integrated operation. Nor would opium profits have been concentrated in the hands of a single cohesive group/section of entrepreneurs. Thus opium *smuggling* can scarcely be regarded as a major source of accumulation for the indigenous capitalist class.

We are, of course, far from having even reasonably adequate data for estimating the economic effects of the 'illegal' trade with sufficient precision. The success of the smuggling venture lay in keeping it out of view. However, the inability of the colonial state to appropriate a large share of the earnings from Malwa opium till the late 1840s made it possible for the wealth created by the drug trade to be distributed among various sections of western Indian businesspersons. The opium trade, more specifically the smuggling component of it, set in motion the integration of the transitional pre-colonial economies of western India (encompassing Malwa, Gujarat, Rajasthan, Lower Sind, Kachchh, and Konkan) with the colonial economy of Indian Ocean and the international capitalist economy. The Malwa wholesale dealers took away a fairly large chunk of profits from the international trade and continued to do so beyond the 1840s. The smuggling trade made it possible for traders in Rajasthan, and even in distant Sind, to get involved in narcotrafficking partaking of its super-profits, thereby acquiring access to a major source of capital accumulation. In his monograph on the traders of Sind, Markovits has underlined the importance of Malwa opium for the trading world of colonial western India generally, and for Sind in particular. Malwa opium, he observes, 'was one of the major sources of capital accumulation in India between 1770 and 1870, and … various merchant groups derived large profits from their participation in it'.[74]

In his recent polemic Markovits regards as 'far-fetched' the suggestion that opium smuggling represented 'a conscious political defiance of the East India Company by indigenous capitalists'.[75] For him, 'the key to their behaviour more likely resided in opportunism rather than in any "subversion"'. He goes on to state that, 'This is not to deny them agency, but "subversion" is a strong term when applied to capitalists.'[76] Subversion is not necessarily a matter of conscious political intent. As James Scott has pointed out, even 'everyday' forms of resistance, such as foot-dragging, dissimulation, false compliance, feigned ignorance, and slander can be subversive in nature. Of course what the business groups of western India were engaged in was qualitatively different from, and far more potent than, such Brechtian forms of struggle.[77] The point is that the outcome of the clandestine trade was subversive. It challenged, and effectively destabilized, the colonial narcotic undertaking in Asia. As such, opium smuggling has to be seen as a form of resistance, even in the absence of the articulation of a political agenda. Opium smuggling required contestation at the political level as well. Amiya Bagchi has pointed out that the stronger position of Indian merchants in Bombay during the early nineteenth century, as compared to Calcutta and Madras, had its roots in 'the continued resistance of Indian rulers against British conquest … and the survival, in however a truncated form, of a large number of native states in that part of the country, which provided a base of operations and a sanctuary for Indian traders and financiers'.[78]

In emphasizing the collaborative aspect of indigenous participation in the opium enterprise, Markovits extends Amalendu Guha's 1970 thesis about the 'comprador role' of the Parsis to include a large section of the incipient capitalist class of western India.[79] Various regional components of this class-in-the-making (business groups in Malwa, Rajasthan, Sind, Gujarat and Bombay, respectively) were, according to Markovits, 'content with making the best of a god-sent opportunity, but without harbouring any idea of challenging British economic domination, which would have been a dead end'. In fact, Markovits considers indigenous involvement in the 'legal' trade, especially after 1842, as being more important for capital accumulation.[80]

To underplay the very serious conflict between indigenous business groups and colonialism is to miss out on the contradictions between the two, and to leave unexplained the process whereby the terms of collaboration were worked out. The terms of collaboration were defined by the actual outcome of the tussle between indigenous enterprise and metropolitan capital. One might mention here that by the early 1980s Guha had modified his thesis on the 'comprador' character of modern Parsi business by taking into account the strong element of conflict in their relationship with the British. In his earlier articles he had spoken of their 'symbiotic patron-client relationship',[81] whereas in his later paper he perceptively observed: '[T]he Indian comprador of the coastal ports was not merely a collaborator; he was also a competitor of the foreign merchant. Both collaboration and conflict were reflected in his vacillating political stand and economic position'.[82]

The East India Company initially pursued a policy of annihilating the Malwa opium enterprise. This enterprise was the creation of indigenous initiative and was developed in opposition to the Company's policy. Eventually the Company was forced to abandon its earlier policy and had to co-opt indigenous participants, conceding to them a reasonable share of the wealth accruing from opium exports to China. Earnings from the 'legal' and 'illegal' trade *both* contributed to capital accumulation. Markovits rightly states that it is no easy task to measure profits from the 'illegal' trade, as distinct from the 'legal' trade.[83] However, this is not just about quantifying the smuggling trade. Opium smuggling brought about a qualitative change by transforming the very character of the colonial opium economy. Writing in a somewhat different context, Hira Singh has criticized 'the tendency in historical analysis to privilege the metropolis'.[84] According to him, 'The problematic assumption is that the agency of doing, or not doing, anything in India … rested exclusively with European political economy.' Such a perspective can only give us a 'one-sided view of colonial encounter in which the Indian subjects are represented as mere objects of manipulation by the colonial-capitalist forces …'.[85]

Unlike Bengal opium, which directly benefited the colonial state, earnings from Malwa opium largely represented private, mainly indigenous, profits. It was this, as Richards remarks, that gave to Malwa opium its multiplier effect.[86] Over a period of 23 years, from 1821 to 1843, the total gross revenue earned by the colonial state from Malwa opium was around 74 million rupees.[87] Of this 51 million rupees came from the Company's auctions between 1821 and 1830, an annual average of a little over five million rupees. As this included the cost price of opium, mostly retained in Malwa, the Company's share did not amount to more than two to three million rupees each year during the twenties. This was just a small fraction of the total worth of the trade which amounted to roughly 20 million rupees annually in India. The pass duty brought to the Company 22.6 million rupees from 1830 to 1843, an annual average of nearly 1.75 million rupees. This may be regarded as net revenue and denotes an even smaller share of the value of the trade, which had actually increased during the thirties.

Even at a conservative estimate then, Malwa opium generated 15 million rupees annually for private enterprise in the early nineteenth century. The value of the trade would have been lower between 1800 and 1820, but the Company received no share of it during these two decades. This cannot be regarded as an insignificant sum. It would be difficult to explain the strength of indigenous capital in western India from the mid-nineteenth century onwards, reflected in the prominent presence of Indian entrepreneurs in the textile industry of Bombay and Ahmadabad, without taking into account these earnings. We need to be a little more attentive to the histories of the princely states of western and central India for a better understanding of the manner in which their presence, and intervention, shaped the organization of the international trade in narcotics during the colonial period which in turn had a profound impact on the relationship between the metropolis and India's political economy.

Notes

1 J.H. Mills, *Cannabis Britannica: empire, trade and prohibition, 1800–1928*, Oxford: Oxford University Press, 2005, p. 4.
2 J.F. Richards, 'The opium industry in British India', *The Indian Economic and Social History Review* (henceforth, *IESHR*), 39, 2, 3, 2002, 159–61.
3 D.E. Owen, *British Opium Policy in China and India*, New Haven: Yale University Press, 1934.
4 B.B. Chaudhuri, *The Growth of Commercial Agriculture in Bengal 1757–1900*, Calcutta: Indian Studies Past and Present, 1964.
5 J.F. Richards, 'The Indian empire and peasant production of opium in the nineteenth century', *Modern Asian Studies* (hereafter, *MAS*), 15, 1, 1981, 59–82.
6 J.F. Richards, '"Cannot we induce the people of England to eat opium?" The moral economy of opium in colonial India', in J.H. Mills and P. Barton (eds) *Drugs and Empires: essays in modern imperialism and intoxication, c.1500–1930*, Basingstoke: Palgrave Macmillan, 2007, pp.73–80.
7 Ibid., pp. 73ff.
8 A. Guha, 'Parsi Seths as entrepreneurs: 1750–1850', *Economic and Political Weekly*, 5, 35, 1970, M:107–15; 'Comprador role of Parsi Seths: 1750–1850', *Economic and Political Weekly*, 5, 48, 1970, 1933–6; A. Siddiqi, 'The business world of Jamsejee Jejeebhoy', *IESHR*, 19, 3–4, 1982, reprinted in A. Siddiqi (ed.), *Trade and Finance in Colonial India*, Delhi: Oxford University Press, 1985, pp. 186–217 (all references are to the article reproduced in this volume).
9 Cf. O. Prakash, *The New Cambridge History of India*, vol. II, part 5 *European Commercial Enterprise in Pre-Colonial India*, Cambridge: Cambridge University Press, 1970, pp. 327ff; A. Farooqui, *Smuggling as Subversion: colonialism, Indian merchants and the politics of opium*, New Delhi: New Age International, 1998, pp. 12–13.
10 Government of India, 30.6.1803, National Archives of India, Home Department, Misc. Letters, vol. 271.
11 For the Company's early Malwa opium policy see *Parliamentary Papers, Select Committee on the Affairs of the East India Company*, 1831, VI, Appendix IV (no. 320 D).
12 Ujjain was located in the Sindia/Gwalior state.
13 Government of India, 18.7.1823, National Archives of India, Separate Revenue Branch Consultations (hereafter, SR), 28.8.1823:14.
14 28.9.1824, SR, 21.4.1825:14.
15 10.10.1824, SR, 21.4.1825:14.
16 F. Dangerfield's report, 3.10.1820, SR, 1.12.1820:18; 'Statement', 15.11.1823, SR, 5.12.1823:16.
17 H. Mackenzie, 8.7.1824, SR, 9.7.1824:23.
18 Government of India, 24.10.1824, SR, 24.2.1825:9.
19 Cf. 28.10.1824, SR, 24.2.1825:9.

20 25.5.1826, SR, 22.6.1826:21; 3.7.1827, SR, 1.11.1827:28; 3.8.1827, SR, 1.11.1827:28.
21 11.11.1824, SR, 24.2.1825:9.
22 Agreement with Kota dated 31.7.1825, SR, 8.9.1825:22.
23 Board of Customs, Salt and Opium (henceforth, BCSO), 23.8.1825, SR, 8.9.1825:22.
24 31.10.1825, SR, 24.11.1825:14.
25 Ibid.
26 Ibid.
27 S. Swinton, Malwa opium agent, private letter, 4.11.1825, SR, 8.12.1825:5.
28 Agreement with Kota dated 29.12.1825, SR, 2.2.1826:16.
29 In the international market opium was reckoned in 'chests', one Malwa opium chest containing about 140 lbs av. (14 *panseri*), or 3.5 *man*, of opium.
30 Dangerfield's report, 3.10.1820, SR, 1.12.1820:18.
31 Swinton, 21.2.1825, SR, 17.3.1825:13.
32 BCSO, 25.1.1826, SR, 2.2.1826:15.
33 Ibid.
34 Government of India, 2.2.1826, SR, 2.2.1826:17.
35 Swinton, 17.2.1826, SR, 16.3.1826:11; Swinton, 17.2.1826, SR, 16.3.1826:12.
36 Agreement dated 18.2.1826, SR, 16.3.1826:14.
37 Article 4 of agreement dated 18.2.1826, SR, 16.3.1826:14.
38 Government of India, 16.3.1826, SR, 16.3.1826:15.
39 Ibid.
40 Swinton, 24.4.1826, SR, 22.6.1826:11.
41 Swinton, 27.2.1826, SR, 27.3.1826:20.
42 John Malcolm, 'Memorandum', 23.11.1821, SR, 18.1.1822:19.
43 Cf. Capt. J. Caulfield, 10.11.1825, SR, 8.12.1825:5; Caulfield, 10.3.1826, SR, 22.6.1826:7.
44 Agreement with Dhar dated 17.4.1826, SR, 22.6.1826:13; agreement with Dewas dated 30.4.1826, SR, 22.6.1826:15; agreements with Ratlam and Sailana, SR, 22.6.1826:17, enclosure; agreement with Sitamau, SR, 22.6.1826:21, enclosure; agreement with Jaora, SR, 29.6.1826:27, enclosure; agreement with Amjhera dated 5.6.1826, SR, 7.9.1826:11.
45 Gerald Wellesley, Indore resident, 11.5.1826, SR, 22.6.1826:17.
46 Mackenzie, 'Note', 22.6.1826, 22.6.1826:24.
47 Ibid.
48 Caulfield, 10.3.1826, SR, 22.6.1826:7.
49 Cf. ibid.; also Raj Rana Madho Singh of Kota, 'Note', SR, 26.7.1826:10, enclosure; Swinton, 30.6.1826, SR, 26.7.1826:12.
50 Mackenzie, 'Note', 22.6.1826, 22.6.1826:24.
51 Ibid.
52 Ibid.
53 Government of India, 22.6.1826, SR, 22.6.1826:5.
54 Government of India, 22.6.1826, SR, 22.6.1826:5; 22.10.1826, SR, 11.9.1826:17.
55 Agreement dated 12.12.1826, SR, 1.2.1827:9.
56 See SR, 12.6.1822:41; W. Hamilton, *East India Gazetteer*, London: W.H. Allen, 1828, vol. II, p.12; *Madhya Pradesh Gazetteers, Indore District*, Bhopal: Government Central Press, 1971, pp. 72, 79, 82.
57 Wellesley, 15.12.1826, SR, 1.2.1827:9.
58 Ibid.
59 Wellesley, 30.11.1826, 6.12.1826, SR, 1.2.1827:9.
60 Wellesley, 15.12.1826, SR, 1.2.1827:9.
61 Government of India, 27.7.1837, SR, 9.8.1837:5.
62 Caulfield, 10.3.1826, SR, 22.6.1826:7.
63 For a major reappraisal of the historical evidence pertaining to the conquest of Sind, see J.Y. Wong, 'British annexation of Sind in 1843: an economic perspective', *MAS*, 31, 2, 1997, 226, 234–7. The 1843 military campaign against Gwalior is examined in A. Farooqui, *Sindias and the Raj: princely Gwalior, c. 1800–1850*, New Delhi: Primus Books, 2011, pp. 81–97.

64 29.10.1825, SR, 24.11.1825:14.
65 Swinton, 17.2.1826, SR, 16.3.1826:12.
66 BCSO, 6.3.1826, SR, 22.6.1826:18.
67 Wellesley, 'Minute', 20.9.1823, SR, 17.1.1824:71. By the time the Anglo-Maratha wars came to an end, Sindia territories were principally confined to two regions: Malwa (mainly in the present Madhya Pradesh districts of Mandsaaur, Nimach, Ujjain, Shajapur, and Vidisha); and the Gwalior region (in the Madhya Pradesh districts of Gwalior, Morena, Bhind, Shivpuri, Guna and Datia). The Malwa territories of the Gwalior state constituted a distinct administrative unit (*prant*) with headquarters at Ujjain. Opium production was confined to the Malwa *prant*.
68 Cf. Government of India, 8.2.1827, SR, 8.2.1827:14.
69 C. Markovits, 'The political economy of opium smuggling in early nineteenth century India: leakage or resistance?', *MAS*, 43, 1, 2009, 89–111.
70 Ibid., pp. 104–5.
71 C. Markovits, 'Bombay as a business centre in the colonial period: a comparison with Calcutta', in S. Patel and A. Thorner (eds) *Bombay: Metaphor for Modern India*, Bombay: Oxford University Press, 1995, pp. 28–30, 39.
72 Markovits, 'Political economy of opium smuggling', p. 97.
73 Ibid.
74 C. Markovits, *The Global World of Indian Merchants, 1750–1847: traders of Sind from Bukhara to Panama*, Cambridge: Cambridge University Press, 2000, p. 38.
75 Markovits, 'Political economy of opium smuggling', pp. 101–2.
76 Ibid., p. 102.
77 J.C. Scott, *Weapons of the Weak: everyday forms of peasant resistance*, Indian edn, Delhi: Oxford University Press, 1990, p. 29.
78 A.K. Bagchi, 'Transition to British Indian systems of money and banking, 1800–1850', *MAS*, 19, 3, 1985, 511.
79 Guha, 'Parsi Seths as entrepreneurs', pp. M:107–15; 'Comprador role of Parsi Seths', pp. 1933ff.
80 Markovits, 'Political economy of opium smuggling', pp. 110–11.
81 Guha, 'Parsi Seths as entrepreneurs', p. M:115.
82 Guha, 'More about Parsi Seths: their roots, entrepreneurship and comprador role, 1650–1918', Mimeo, Centre for Studies in Social Sciences, Occasional Paper 50, 1982, p. 12.
83 Cf. Markovits, 'Political economy of opium smuggling', p. 103.
84 H. Singh, 'Colonial and postcolonial historiography and the princely states: relations of power and rituals of legitimation', in W. Ernst and B. Pati (eds) *India's Princely States: People, Princes and Colonialism*, London: Routledge, 2007, p. 18.
85 Ibid., p. 19.
86 Richards, 'Opium industry in British India', p. 173.
87 Calculated from SR, Consultations; Maharashtra State Archives, Mumbai, Revenue Department Consultations.

Part II

Cultural encounters: European alcohol and drug consumption in the *situation coloniale*

3 'What shall become of the mission when we have such incompetent missionaries there?': Drunkenness and mission in eighteenth century Danish East India

Tobias Delfs

I

The rather desperate-sounding question in the title of this chapter[1] was raised in a letter that Georg Christian Knapp (1753–1825), director of the Francke Foundations in Halle, wrote on 13 June 1800 to the secretary of the Mission Board in Copenhagen.[2] Supported by the Danish King Frederick IV (1671–1730) and his Mission Board, the German-Lutheran-Pietist Francke Foundations and the Anglican Society for Promoting Christian Knowledge (SPCK) had established a royal mission enterprise from 1706 to 1710, beginning in the Danish settlement of Tranquebar in the subcontinental Coromandel Coast near Madras. The mission began to expand into other regions within a short period of time.[3] In the aforementioned letter Georg Knapp referred to cases of alcohol-induced 'misbehaviour' amongst his missionaries and linked them to fears of the decay of the Danish-English-Halle Mission (DEHM)[4] in East India more generally.

As the editors of this volume persuasively argue in their introduction, compared to the history of other drugs, the role of alcohol in British India has been somewhat neglected by historians.[5] Perhaps unsurprisingly, the same holds true particularly for the few small Danish settlements in the subcontinent: neither alcohol abuse in the Danish military, nor the Danish alcohol trading activities at large have been analyzed as yet.[6] Though there are large inventories hidden in different archives relevant to the topic (for instance customs accounts, council protocols, account books of the trading companies, travelogues and diaries, court reporting or auction protocols), there is a striking lack of historical research on alcohol consumption in the everyday life of several sections of the 'white' colonial society in Tranquebar.[7] The mission archives in particular have been neglected, even by historians interested in missionary history, despite being rich in archival records dealing with the moral evaluation of the behaviour of indigenous peoples, Europeans, and missionaries, and the 'misbehaviour' related to alcohol.[8] This neglect has led to the false assumption that 'the breath of scandal has touched none' of the Danish-English-Halle missionaries.[9]

The bulk of the scant literature dealing with historical problems related to the trade and consumption of alcohol in South Asia focuses mainly on nineteenth and twentieth century British India,[10] and on the alcohol consumption of the military or native people. This chapter, however, will concentrate on the early or pre-colonial phases in the comparatively small territories controlled by the Danish East India Company, and the protestant missionaries in particular. Because of their drinking practices, these missionaries sometimes became marginalized 'white subalterns'[11] although they generally located themselves amongst the upper-classes of the 'white' social ranks. This chapter will closely scrutinize the drop-outs, mavericks and losers amongst the missionaries. The focus on these historical actors and their misconducts will challenge a linear and teleological view of European expansion in Asia in favour of a more nuanced understanding that takes into account the diversity and inconsistency of the 'rulers' and their secular and spiritual institutions. The existence of marginalized individuals within these institutions reminds us of the fragility as well as of the internal diversity of an expanding Europe. It puts existing hierarchies of social stratification and distinctions into stark relief and renders visible the broad variety of discursive and normative conditions that defined their attitudes.[12]

As the Danish kings not only encouraged missionaries of the DEHM but also of the German Moravian brethren from Herrnhut to work in missions in the Indian subcontinent,[13] the latter will also form a part of the analysis. Our main sources will be letters, reports and diaries written by the missionaries, their mission centres in Europe, and the colonial authorities.[14] As the missionaries are commonly associated with the Christian revival movement known as Pietism, the article begins with a brief discussion of this movement and a summary of the general values prevalent in eighteenth century Germany regarding the consumption of alcohol. This first section provides important background knowledge for the subsequent parts in that it reconstructs the contemporary discourses on alcohol that would also play an important role in the colony. Next, the missionary attitudes towards the intoxication of Europeans and indigenous people in South Asia will be considered before focusing on such 'misbehaviour' inside the Protestant mission itself. Finally, I will focus on the reactions of the local colonial authorities and the European mission centres to these incidents and analyze the debates that they triggered.

II

The *Großes vollständiges Universal-Lexicon aller Wissenschafften und Künste* was published between 1732 and 1754 by the German publisher Johann Heinrich Zedler (1706–51). It became perhaps the most extensive encyclopaedia in Europe, and undoubtedly the most important one of eighteenth century Germany.[15] The work contains several articles dealing with the problem of drunkenness ('Trunckenheit'[16]) and related topics such as intoxication ('Rausch'[17]) and drunkards ('Zech-Brüder'[18]). These entries offer valuable insights into the seventeenth and eighteenth century German discourses on alcohol and morality, as well as the general level of knowledge on alcohol and its effects. Drunkenness is described in the encyclopaedia as the worst form of intoxication and a vice that solely affects human beings as a consequence of the excessive consumption of 'strong drinks', unsettling the 'noble' and 'rational executions' of the brain in favour of the 'animal activities' of the human body.[19] Hence the Bible – as well as deontology and natural law – made an argument for the moderate consumption of alcohol, which was depicted as legitimate only for social purposes and reasons of health.[20] Though the entry dealing with spirits ('Brandtwein'[21]) points to its use as a home remedy with several medicinal benefits such as warming, digestive, refreshing, cleansing, and expectorant effects,[22] all of these benefits were entirely dependent on moderation, without which the opposite effect would result: 'all abundance and crapulence is deleterious and can easily make out of a water of life a water of death'.[23] On the other hand, the 'wine-like' (*Wein-artig*) beer and wine itself were perceived more as 'indispensable' (*unentbehrlich*) drinks because of their low alcohol concentration, and considered a substitute for foul water rather than as intoxicants in themselves.[24]

The entry on drunkards defined the term as a person who neglected his real responsibilities in order to visit taverns or engage in drinking bouts daily, who never recovered from his chronic excesses and thus damaged society. Serious criminal acts committed under the influence of alcohol could not be excused by alcohol consumption anymore: a drunkard rightly had to be – and indeed was – punished severely by the civil authorities.[25] Of all members of society, a teacher or clergyman benefitted the least by getting drunk in public.[26] This is mentioned specifically in the entry and agrees with accounts of the frequently occurring 'misbehaviour' of clergymen and their congregations criticized heavily by the Pietists. Of course, evidence of frequent complaints does not necessarily prove that alcohol abuse was suddenly increasing: Alexandra Lutz, for example, refers to the frequently occurring mentions of drunkenness in the divorce proceedings and visitations beginning in the 1720s and 1730s in her work on married couples in the courts of Northern Germany, which pointed to a 'culminating contemporary discourse' and a more sensitive 'changing social perception of drinking'.[27]

In some parts of the German-speaking regions of Europe at least, Pietism may have played an influential role in stimulating these developments. For instance, August Hermann Francke (1663–1727), one of the main protagonists of Pietism and founder of the Francke Foundations in Halle, began his sacerdotal work in 1691/92 in Glaucha, a poor suburb of Halle that was essentially sustained by the production of spirits. All in all, Glaucha at that time consisted of 200 houses, 37 of which were taverns. Francke tried to force through Pietist reforms on the largely passive orthodoxy in order to eliminate the increasingly prevalent alcohol-induced grievances in Glaucha.[28] Whereas the Lutheran orthodox clergy (apart from some reformist elements) differentiated between the excessive *ebriositas* and the singular or casual *ebrietas* and held the former as being more sinful than the latter,[29] the Pietists increasingly called for complete abstinence and openly criticized the orthodoxy for its lax attitude towards drink.[30] The Pietists made the fight against alcohol consumption and dancing 'a transnational and trans-denominational aim of Pietism'.[31] Pietists demanded of the individual believer the self-discipline to reject mundane pleasures in favour of the celestial, and considered the fight against worldly lures a permanent struggle. Indeed, in the view of some Pietists the believer needed such a temptation to find his God. It is perhaps for this reason that, although the ascetic and sober Pietists increasingly condemned the consumption of alcoholic substances as a whole, most of them would at the same time also forgive a drunkard when the latter fell back on divine assistance.[32]

In Europe there were mainly two professional groups that were particularly known for their intoxicated excesses: soldiers and sailors.[33] Both received daily supplies of spirits, wine and beer as steepening incentive, medicinal remedy, or adrenalizer. Alcohol also was used as a tool in the recruitment of new soldiers.[34] Writing about the eighteenth century British Army, Paul E. Kopperman even finds it 'probable that [...] the amount of liquor distributed in the form of a ration increased markedly at large'. This 'ready availability [...] naturally promoted drunkenness',[35] which in the case of both sailors and soldiers resulted in severe punishments for violations of discipline.[36]

III

In pre-colonial and early colonial times, the majority of the few Europeans living overseas were seamen and soldiers,[37] who – not only because of their drinking behaviour, as the contemporary discourse suggests, but also due to the climate, deficient sanitation, and diseases – had the highest mortality rates amongst Europeans.[38] During their voyages and in port, the Moravian brethren frequently reported alcohol-related incidents involving sailors or soldiers. One such incident occurred on a journey from Serampore to Tranquebar in 1781, when the spirits on board were in short supply because of a pilot who 'loved this drink so much that he nearly drank all of the spirits, which were supposed to last for the whole journey'.[39] Another diary in 1783 tells of two seamen who were punished severely by the captain due to their excesses on land and their late arrival on the vessel.[40] This episode was in line with the Danish ship's articles (1639) under King Christian IV (1577–1648) for the regulation of behaviour on board, which already pointed to the significance of alcohol-related offences: 'If any man gets drunk he shall each time be punished by the loss of a month's wages and further punishment as the circumstances warrant'.[41] Further, one missionary in 1786 mentioned a Bengali woman who came to him because she had been beaten by some English sailors.[42] From time to time the missionaries also used strong alcohol as a method of payment during their journey in exchange for the washing of their laundry or simply to get rid of sailors who became a nuisance.[43] Several disagreeable and even frightening encounters have been noted in their diaries, when for instance drunken soldiers or sailors late at night besieged their house in Serampore and violently tried to force entry.[44] Again in 1786, the DEHM reported that young British recruits initially showed promise, but 'within one month' would get 'corrupted by the old soldiers', having been taken along to the 'arak houses' where they then would become 'as bad as their supervisors'.[45]

Conversely, the captains of the vessels and other members of the colonial establishment seem to have been regarded with great importance by the missionaries. As Charles Cornwallis (1738–1805), governor-general and commander-in-chief in British India, made his inaugural visit in 1788, the Moravians seem to have been quite disappointed that everybody in Serampore was invited except themselves.[46] The missionaries proudly reported almost daily in their diaries on amicable relations with them and other upper- or middle-class people such as the local authority members and physicians,[47] for 'most of the captains, who come here, are friends of the brothers and would like to transport the brethren without any costs to Copenhagen'.[48] These relationships could thus prove beneficial for the brethren for communication and low priced voyages, and in return the missionaries would function as talismans for a smooth passage.[49]

The missionaries of the DEHM soon corresponded with the 'natives' in and around Tranquebar and published the letters in their missionary reports.[50] In one of these letters (published 1717) they asked a South Indian about the greatest sins of the Europeans.[51] He answered that Europeans were often drinking, 'whoring', gambling, fighting, and even killing each other. In short, he criticized them heavily for not conforming to their own religious beliefs and moral standards. Evidently, this perception entailed a problem of credibility for the missionaries, which could endanger the success of their proselytizing projects.[52] The Moravian brethren even warned each other repeatedly not to have too close contact with 'Europeans'[53], meaning in particular (but not only) the 'white subaltern' sailors and soldiers.[54]

The contemporary DEHM commentary on the letter of the Tamil confirmed these statements: Together with 'whoring', the immoderate consumption of alcohol and, to a lesser degree, overeating (*Völlerey*) were identified as the 'contagions that send most Europeans in place to the grave'.[55] This was a popular trope that can already be found in earlier European travel accounts and other sources.[56] This view of alcohol as a contagion was different from that of other contemporary authors who discussed the constitutional effects of alcohol.[57] The Moravian physician in Tranquebar Johann Andreas Betschler (1727–84), for example, ordered for his work in addition to opium 'as much Bengal spirits as you can'[58] from his colleagues in the north of the subcontinent.

Since water often was contaminated, wine was considered to be necessary for the maintenance of a good health by a discourse that was prevalent in Europe well into the nineteenth century. It was for this reason in the first place that even the missionaries themselves could purchase imported wine from Europe free of duty.[59] Accordingly, various forms of wine were the most important alcoholic trading goods in the Danish seafaring customs accounts ('Søtoldbøger') for the years 1797 and 1798.[60] Two of the earliest Danish East India ships leaving for Tranquebar, the *St Anna* and the *St Jakob*, transported 14,450 litres of wine and 1,313 litres of brandy as trading goods as early as 1635; furthermore, the *St Anna* alone carried 15,766 litres of French and 30,219 litres of Spanish wine for its crew of 140 men in addition to brandy.[61] The popularity of wine is confirmed by a look at the auction records of some households in Tranquebar: the high number of wine glasses and wine bottles listed is extraordinary.[62] Additionally, the first missionary Bartholomäus Ziegenbalg (1682–1719) reported in 1709 on 'thousands of talers' that were spent yearly by Europeans to buy wine, explained by the high prices of 'good' water and the scarcity of wells. Also in widespread use seems to have been a mixture of one spoon of the beer Brunswick Mum (*Braunschweiger Mumme*) and a mixture of water and sugar to dilute it. In this way, one could make 20 bottles of 'fresh' beer out of one bottle Brunswick Mum. If drunk in moderate amounts, even the 'expensive' and strong rubbing alcohol (*spriritus vini gallici*) was considered a way to stay healthy by the mission.[63] Hence, Ziegenbalg, although a Pietist, did not call for complete abstinence in this early phase of the mission but only for moderation in the consumption of alcohol. It was widely believed that the perceived adverse living conditions in the subcontinent required temperate alcohol consumption to prevent health problems.

The above quoted commentary on 'European sins' also refers to the consumption patterns of Europeans in the subcontinent, which had to be assigned to the different segments of colonial society. Low Europeans (*Geringe*) would 'get plastered' (*sauffen sich voll*) with 'Fincken'[64] brewed out of rice, 'middle-class Europeans' (*mittleren Standes*) would drink 'Arack'[65] for the same purpose and the nobility (*die Vornehmen*) would excessively consume 'European beer, wine and rubbing alcohol (*Frantz Brandtwein*)'.[66] Clearly, alcohol served as an agent of classification and created (or reproduced) difference and social hierarchies. This early taxonomy already points to the importance of the social stratifications imported from Europe,[67] hinted at by the Moravian reports and warnings quoted above. Furthermore, it suggests by imputing European drinks to the upper-classes of society that, compared to indigenous drinks, European drinks were of a better quality and generally superior.[68] This might be why Ziegenbalg felt impelled to state explicitly as early as 1709 that he had never touched the indigenous 'Fincken' or 'Areck', while the following comments indicate his regular consumption of European varieties of alcohol.[69]

Nonetheless, the commentary from 1717 argues that the 'natives' did not drink at all, whereas Europeans from all walks of life were consumers.[70] The missionaries in 1778 asserted that it was the Europeans who brought vices such as avarice and overindulgence with them from Europe.[71] Moreover, the same Europeans would tempt the 'natives' to consume alcoholic drinks.[72]

This reflects early European upper-class ideas of the 'civilizing' mission, and the 'orientalist' image of the generally weak, malleable, naïve, or ignorant 'native' who needed to be protected by a thus legitimized colonial empire or mission.[73] It is interesting to note, however, that a conflation of racial and class categories allows the 'native' to be seen on a level comparable to the allegedly likewise ignorant European 'white subaltern'.[74] Accordingly, in 1797 the DEHM affirmed that a 'white subaltern' soldier's chronic drunkenness was healed after just one conversation with a missionary.[75] It is obvious that through his putative moral inferiority *vis-à-vis* the indigenous population, the 'white subaltern' also tended to undermine European 'superiority'.[76]

However, contrasting the ignorant but debauched white subaltern with the ignorant but virtuous 'native' entirely disregards the alcohol consumption of the indigenous people, which mostly seems to have taken place in private, whereas European drinking was more apparent in the public sphere.[77] However, there also were cases of alcohol abuse among congregants and even among the indigenous staff of the DEHM. For some time within the missionary jurisdiction, such abuse could attract severe penalties such as a prison stay (for Titus and Timotheus in 1720 in consequence of drunkenness and brawling), transfer (for the catechist Rajanayakkan), reduction of salary, and suspension or corporal punishment.[78] The sentence, as for other deeds, was dependent on the severity of the case and on the opinion of the particular missionary in charge. What is noteworthy when considering these punishments is the fact that amongst the missionaries themselves, the sentences for 'misbehaviour' were normally less severe.[79]

IV

Since the beginning of the DEHM's enterprise, the missionaries repeatedly had to grapple with a variety of problems, ranging from encounters with the local authorities, internal quarrels, concerns about their finances, the absence of arriving vessels, and political insecurities. In the literature, the period between 1780 and 1845 especially is described as a general phase of decline for the DEHM in the subcontinent.[80] This period was critical for the mission as a whole. For some time the most important Danish establishments Tranquebar and Serampore were occupied by the British; Danish trade after the *florissante Periode* shifted more and more to Serampore, leading to fewer opportunities for the missionaries in Tranquebar to communicate with Europe in the absence of visiting ships[81] (although the total number of vessels to Asia continued to increase for some time[82]). In the trading centres of Calcutta and Madras, inflation was extremely high while at the same time donations to the mission decreased, which entailed serious financial problems for the missionaries.[83] Things got even worse in 1777 when the administrative status of the Danish establishments changed, from that of trading companies to state administration.[84]

In addition to these increasing political, economic, and administrative pressures, the mission headquarters in Europe had problems finding suitable candidates for employment in East India. A significant percentage of those who did embark on the journey died just after their arrival,[85] while the mission as a whole was aging. Accordingly, the expectations of the missionaries for new candidates were very high,[86] yet difficulties concerning 'misbehaving' missionaries seemed to occur ever more frequently. Johann Philipp Fabricius (1711–91), for instance, was arrested because of his ruinous debts.[87] Johann Zacharias Kiernander (1710–99), a Swedish missionary residing in Calcutta, was criticized, first for additional earnings out of money transactions and smuggling that made him rich, and then for his large debts.[88] Others like Fabricius, the earlier Martin Bosse (1695–1756), and Christoph Theodosius Walther (1699–1741) had embezzled or gambled away money belonging to the mission.[89] In part these specific misdemeanours expressed the financial difficulties that confronted the missionaries. Most of these misdeeds were denounced vehemently, but several incidents had to be tolerated. Kiernander's casual earnings, for example, were accepted, since a sufficient income was held to be '*strategically essential for the mission's survival*'.[90] As Peter Robb has demonstrated for Calcutta in the 1790s, 'where there was an acute shortage of cash', venturesome financial affairs spread widely at the time.[91] Men like Kiernander only adapted to the situation. The missionary Christoph Samuel John in 1778 is another case in point. Bedevilled by his own debts, he resorted to the 'sideways of mercantile activity' (*Abweg der Kaufmannschaft*) 'to protect oneself from distress' (*sich vor dem Mangel zu schützen*), distress that had already affected some of his colleagues.[92] It was even said of his earlier colleague Benjamin Schultze (1689–1760) that he illegally traded beer, wine and spirits, and that he distilled his own liquor.[93] According to Jon Miller, who referred to similar cases in the nineteenth century African Basel Mission, which was another Pietist undertaking supported by the Danish Crown, Kiernander, John, Schultze and others could be called 'norm-breakers' as well as 'creative problem-solvers' or 'strategic deviants'.[94] Young newcomers especially were criticized for wasting money and for their arrogant behaviour.[95] Besides, quite a few missionaries got into trouble because of relationships with 'native' women.[96] Other common criticisms related to the alleged laziness of fellow missionaries, some of whom, for instance, refused to learn local languages.[97] The most serious problems, however, emanated from the popularity of drink among the brethren. By the end of the 1790s alone, there were three known cases of alcohol abuse in the DEHM out of a total of ten missionaries. As these cases occurred at the same time and therefore can be considered together, we will concentrate on the most extreme case of this kind, which will be considered in the broader context of other missionary 'misbehaviour' related to the consumption of alcohol. The excesses of Lambert Christian Früchtenicht (1772–1806?) were seen as so utterly appalling that the authorities were afraid they would endanger the mission as a whole.[98]

The trouble with Früchtenicht began immediately upon his arrival in Serampore in 1799. In their letters, his missionary colleagues described him in very harsh terms, and the choir of negative voices was unprecedentedly large. The choice of terms used to describe him included 'good-for-nothing', 'rowdy' (*Schläger*),[99] 'possessed by the devil', 'miscreant' (*Bösewicht*),[100] 'pest' (*Plagegeist*), 'raised in the tavern' (*in der Schenke [...] erzogen*),[101] 'eyesore of the mission' (*Schandfleck der Mission*),[102] and most frequently 'drunkard' (*Säuffer*).[103] It is interesting to note that he was not accused of being a drunkard before he reached the subcontinent, apart from some criticism garnered in Cape Town in South Africa,[104] which at that time was primarily populated by sailors and unqualified soldiers often 'drawn from the lowest ranks of European society',[105] and where Früchtenicht had to make a stopover for some weeks on his way to the subcontinent. Contact with the riff-raff of the Cape colony would have been likely, if not inevitable. Criticisms of his behaviour before Cape Town did not mention alcohol although his stay in Copenhagen for interviews already hinted at an excessive lifestyle. The pastor Johann Hieronymus Chemnitz (1730–1800), for instance, wrote a letter from Copenhagen in August 1798 to the director of the Francke Foundations in Halle. Chemnitz wanted to visit Früchtenicht on a Sunday at 11 o'clock in the morning because the latter had not appeared at the service. However, Chemnitz was not allowed by the innkeeper to enter the room because Früchtenicht was – as per his daily habit, according to what the pastor was told – still asleep and his room in a mess. Chemnitz admonished the director that, given the 'ruinous circumstances of the mission' (*die verfallenen Umstände der Mission*), Schulze ought to have selected a more suitable person for the job.[106]

After his arrival in India, things got worse. The catechist Schawrirajen (1755–1817), who was supposed to teach Früchtenicht Tamil in Tranquebar, refused to teach him after a short trial period and referred to the unreliability of the 'drunkard'.[107] More than once it was reported by Früchtenicht's colleagues that the drunken missionary (usually in the company of a group of equally intoxicated soldiers) disrupted the holy service, and tried to give a sermon himself.[108] Furthermore, in Tranquebar he went from house to house in order to start brawls, threatening the missionaries and other residents with murder and suicide.[109] In other letters Früchtenicht was criticized for his insulting behaviour towards his colleagues as well as against the 'natives',[110] his pursuit of additional income sources,[111] for gambling and wasting the money of the mission, for his large debts, and, last but not least, for his general laziness and stubbornness.[112] All these letters reflected the high expectations that were very much let down by his failure. Moreover, the missionaries were afraid that the situation would further harm the already tainted reputation of the mission in Europe, and put off potential converts.[113] This was also the reason why the missionary Carl Wilhelm Päzold (1764–1817) wrote a letter to Knapp in Halle, insistently asking him not to publish the particulars of the case in the missionary accounts 'for this would easily cast a damning light on *the whole* mission'.[114]

Früchtenicht himself reacted to these accusations with denial and contempt. He sometimes referred to his own inexperience, and at others, accused his colleagues of slander.[115] He also wrote that he was simply not as gifted with flattery as others and that he had a lot of enemies talking badly about him as a result. The deviant missionary wrote in 1799 that though he had a 'grog or a glass of wine' more 'than appropriate for me [...]' from time to time, he never 'abandoned himself to drinking'. Such an accusation was 'deeply untrue and lying'.[116] Despite this declaration, he continued his moral misconduct and even demanded a substantial betterment[117] and was soon excluded from the regular meetings of the missionaries. The mission authorities withheld his earnings, and demanded his suspension and return to Europe.[118] Finally, they suspended him, which he did not accept. They argued their case very rationally, not only with reference to the mission's reputation, but also to the funds that appeared wasted on Früchtenicht.[119] The latter defended himself by claiming to have been afflicted by a mysterious mental disease since his arrival in Bengal. To prove this, he presented certificates composed by some of his sailor acquaintances (*Schiffer und Steuerleute*). These 'entirely fake' (*höchst falsche*) certificates were contrary to the medical opinion prepared by the missionary physician,[120] who 'as physician and eye witness' attested that Früchtenicht's excesses 'had to be ascribed to drunkenness alone'.[121]

Though nearly all of these accusations can also be found in other cases, their combined weight made the case of Früchtenicht a special and extreme one. The contemporary missionary Päzold noted this fact: 'there is virtually [...] no vice in which Früchtenicht has not indulged in!'[122] Although Päzold was very active in accusing the deviant and did so using high language, he himself was accused several times of being a drunkard, just like his colleague Immanuel Gottfried Holzberg (1770–1824) (also a target of his attacks).[123] There had been other cases in the immediate environment of the mission previous to these three: for instance, the missionary Martin Bosse in 1749 had to return to Europe because of his alcohol-induced 'misbehaviour',[124] and mission schoolmaster Christian Daniel Klein (1768–?), son of the missionary Jacob Klein (1721–90), and the former soldier and then mission schoolmaster Johann Heinrich Hutter (1712–?) were also accused of being drunkards.[125] The same would appear to be true for the mission printer Johann Gottlieb Adler (?–1723).[126] Another extreme case was that of the Moravian missionary Christian Renatus Beck in Bengal, who could only prevent his exclusion from the Brethren by his voluntary withdrawal.[127]

All these cases of alcoholism cannot be explained by one simple cause. The prevalent unavailability of clean water, closely linked to contemporary health discourses, seems to have played a significant role. In addition, Douglas M. Peers considers the 'boredom' of the soldiers in their barracks the 'principle cause of drunkenness' among the British-Indian troops.[128] The records of the Moravian Brethren indicate that this might have been a factor in their case too, combined with loneliness and monotony: in a letter written in 1782, the missionary Schmidt wrote that he longed to visit his brothers but that there was currently no possibility of doing so. The only work he felt he could do was the arduous learning of the indigenous language.[129]

The Moravian Staal in turn felt hurt 'that his post as a warden did not keep him occupied and he therefore at times was exposed to some allegations'.[130] In the DEHM, John also mentioned the constraining effects of his loneliness.[131] The vibrant drinking culture that prevailed in the colonial enclaves and the easy availability of alcohol might also have been important factors, as the diaries of the missionaries are full of descriptions of social occasions such as funerals, balls, lunches, dinners, teas, and breakfasts with captains, pastors, physicians, other missionaries, or even the governor.

V

In 1784, the Moravian mission centre in Herrnhut warned its missionaries in the subcontinent about the 'consumption of strong drinks', which the Brothers 'took to heart' though such an 'abuse has not occurred among ourselves so far'.[132] Similarly, the DEHM introduced an instruction for missionary candidates in 1798, applied for the first time in the case of Früchtenicht, in which it explicitly condemned alcohol abuse, selfish dispositions (*eigennützige Gesinnung*), and greed for money (*Geldbegierde*), all of which would drive people into corruption and illegal trading activities. Moreover, it demanded from the candidates that they learn South Asian languages and that they obey the instructions given to them by the established missionaries, who due to their length of service in the mission were also privileged in financial terms. In addition, the instruction referred to the mission as a lifelong task.[133]

The concept for such an instruction originated from the missionaries themselves and was revised by the centre in Halle.[134] It reflected in part the problems of laziness, financial mismanagement, affairs, and debts that have been described above, as also the doubts that the centres had. It seems as if Früchtenicht expected to stay only four or five years in the subcontinent when he applied for the job in 1797. After this short time he wanted to go back to Europe and be promoted to a better position. In Europe this was one of the main reasons for criticizing him before he was ordained.[135] The director of the Francke Foundations in Halle Schulze subsequently wrote a letter to Früchtenicht, sharing his experience with other missionaries and reminding him that the profession was a challenging occupation for a lifetime and not only for a few years, that it was dangerous to go, and that he had to be entirely committed to the mission. Both Früchtenicht's critics and the director were convinced that such a letter would act as a deterrent.[136] But Früchtenicht nevertheless came to Halle at his own expense and was examined by Schulze; to the director's surprise he appeared to be suitable for the job.[137]

Although most of the missionaries indeed stayed the rest of their life in the subcontinent,[138] the demanded lifelong residence was not satisfying for them. In 1797, recovery stays in Europe were recommended, as well as a minimum mission duration of 12 years.[139] Similar motives can be seen in the writings of the Moravian missionaries: in 1789 Grasmann wrote about how hard it was for a missionary to stay in the subcontinent for 20 years or longer without any success, and in the company of 'misbehaving' colleagues. In the same resigned-sounding letter he asked for the permission to go back to Europe, pleading for the granting of a general permission to do so.[140] The centres in Europe, however, had their own views and their own criteria. Given that the mission was over-aged, that donations were decreasing, that it was difficult to find fresh candidates, and that travel time and travel expenses were considerable, a lifelong engagement of its missionaries was an important condition for the centres.

The warnings were repeated before the big scandals involving Früchtenicht and the other 'unruly' brethren became known. Here the discourses and events in the subcontinent as well as in Europe and other (perhaps unknown and/or less severe) cases seem to have played a major role. As the instruction explicitly referred to alcohol abuse (along with other forms of behaviour) as misconduct (*Trunk oder einem andern Laster*), these apparently were the most important rules to which strict adherence was demanded. However, concurrent jurisdiction, the existence of legal grey areas and contradictions within the regulations complicated the enforcement of regulations. The distance to Europe and associated difficulties in communication exacerbated these difficulties.

There was a special clause (§8) in the instruction that proved to be highly problematic, in particular in the case of Früchtenicht. The other missionaries could deplore a missionary who turned out to be dishonourable, but the final decision on a suspension would be left to the Mission Board in Copenhagen.[141] When his colleagues suspended Früchtenicht, he promptly referred to §8 of the instruction and the legal authority of the Mission Board.[142] Such a decision would have taken a long time to obtain – too long' for the missionaries – even more so as his house is located quite close to the church, and even peace is disturbed'.[143]

As the conflict escalated further, the missionaries asked the local authority several times for support,[144] but the government was very reluctant to interfere, even though the Danish governor in Tranquebar, Peter Anker (1744–1832), had also clashed with Früchtenicht. The latter had apparently paid him a personal visit, drunken, in missionary dress, and taunted him: 'Bring me to the fortress in this robe, which was given to me by the king'.[145] It is worth noting that Früchtenicht often wore his robe in a provocative manner while he was misbehaving, apparently well aware of the importance of the dress for the missionaries and the concurrent jurisdictions. His colleagues interpreted the symbolism and the perceived image of this act accurately and referred again in their criticism to the missionary's function as a moral role-model for the Indian converts as well as the European residents of the Danish enclaves.[146]

Even though the Danish colonies were under the state administration of the Board of Commerce since 1777, the missionaries still insisted on their own jurisdiction within their congregation, their direct subordination to the Danish King's Mission Board, and thereby on their traditional special status as 'state within a state'.[147] The missionaries' attitude towards Früchtenicht brought them in conflict with §8 of the instruction. By giving the Mission Board the authority to settle conflicts among the missionaries, the instruction contributed to the escalation of the specific conflict at hand: without the permission of the Mission Board, Früchtenicht could not be suspended or even deprived of his salary to prevent him from further building up debts. Several such attempts had been prohibited by the local government, always with reference to a missing order by the Mission Board and to the fact that the mission did not want to obey the local authorities' rule.[148] Früchtenicht ignored his suspension, and the local government was not formally allowed to intervene. Here the institutional and normative structure in connection with the distance to Europe clearly constricted the agency of the missionaries. Even informal conversations with the members of the local government did not help.

In many desperate letters, the missionaries accused the local government of being responsible for the fact that such a missionary still had to be supported.[149] Moreover, they criticized director Schulze for his 'distrust' and his decision of adding 'that unfortunate clause' (*jene unglückl[iche] Clausel*) to the instruction on his own accord.[150] Schulze may have done so in reaction to the case of Martin Bosse, who in 1749, without such a regulating instruction was recalled by the Mission Board because of his repeated drunkenness and who had many objections against his suspension.[151] As the situation deteriorated, Anker eventually confirmed the suspension of Früchtenicht. In a report to the Board of Commerce he justified the illegal procedure with reference to the severity of the case and the breach of peace and public order.[152] Obviously, the governor at that time was more concerned about the situation in Tranquebar than about the potential legal consequences for him which would be meted out by the distant centre. In any case, the conflict had to intensify to a certain point for him to arrive at this assessment of the situation. Predictably, Anker did not encounter any legal problems later on. On the contrary, his relations with the Mission Board only improved in the aftermath.[153] Doubtless, these circumstances constricted Früchtenicht's room for manoeuvre and the experience of Anker's reconsideration of his case must have totally destroyed his expectations.

In the meantime Früchtenicht seems to have been quite isolated in Tranquebar with the exception of some European 'white subaltern' soldiers and sailors, who were his drinking mates and who, as noted earlier, sometimes helped him in disrupting the holy service or in writing fake certificates. According to the missionaries, other inhabitants were either afraid of him or observed his behaviour with amusement. By this point, he must have realized that a further career, which was one of his reasons to go to East India, was no longer a realistic prospect; even §8 could not help him anymore. Together with his extreme drinking habits, the utter hopelessness of the situation might explain his decision to embrace the last resort of first threatening and then actually trying to commit suicide.[154]

In a farewell letter, addressed to his family, he wrote that Tranquebar was full of bad fellows and that he did not want to live with such people, meaning in particular his colleague John.[155] The letter was delivered to the colonial police. When the policemen came to his room on 23 February 1801, Früchtenicht was standing on his bed, again wearing the robe, in the one hand a knife, in the other a bottle. After he had insulted and even attacked the policemen, he was imprisoned in the Danish fortress Dansborg and later examined by a physician, who could not find any evidence of a mental illness. Instead, the doctor certified that Früchtenicht would be a danger to society, if he were released from prison.[156] It is interesting to note that the missionaries in their letters here, and similarly in the letter following his suicide attempt did not so much argue by reference to moral or theological condemnations, which one might have expected from religious men of the period; instead their reports and explanations appeared quite rational or physical. This would corroborate the assumption that suicide even in the clergy at that time was perceived in more secular terms that also apply to the perception of drunkenness: 'from sin to insanity'.[157] The more so as both sides – Früchtenicht and his colleagues – used medical certificates in their judicial argumentations. The former even argued using illnesses and later on in 1803 back in Copenhagen even the 'climate in East India, which was such a detrimental factor on my body and mind that I had to fear an outright insanity, if I dared to stay longer'.[158] But neither in the writings of his missionary colleagues nor in those by the centres or the local authority was the climate explicitly used as explanation for his behaviour. The same is true regarding the case of the Moravian drunkard Beck, in whose case also very rational appeals for moderate consumption appeared, for instance, that 'he was not a child anymore and was well able to know, when he had enough' alcohol.[159] However, unlike Früchtenicht, Beck several times was gripped by melancholy and religious self-doubts,[160] an important attribute of Pietism as a part of atonement.[161] In his case, religious motives still were present but attended by secular arguments.

The whole episode of Früchtenicht's first suicide attempt was conveyed to the local government in Tranquebar before the examination in Copenhagen. Finally, Anker gave him a passport to Madras, from where he was supposed to travel home. Earlier, Früchtenicht had demanded money and assured the missionaries in written form that he would not claim anything else from the mission. This episode once more showed the legal uncertainty in this case. His colleagues agreed to this deal and Früchtenicht reached Europe in 1802, where he had to explain himself in front of the Mission Board.[162]

The 1806 records in Halle reveal that in 1805, Früchtenicht travelled to Philadelphia,[163] where the Foundations had helped to build up a congregation for German-Lutheran immigrants since 1741.[164] It is understandable that he travelled to distant America: in Europe and India his story may have been too well known. Regardless of this fact, he was apparently beyond the point of no return and could not gain a foothold in his new environment. He came several times to church drunk in his robe, and requested the right to preach. This was refused. He even was caught up in contradictions as he talked in very different versions about 'misunderstandings' with the missionaries that had forced him to leave India and to look for help from the Mission Board. The Mission Board had conceded that he was right but also stated that he ought to comply and apply for his demission 'for the sake of peace',[165] which seems to be plausible due to the legal uncertainty regarding the mission and local authority in East India and the Mission Board and Board of Commerce in Denmark. The fact that he also received money from the Mission Board also supports such a view. Another confirmation may be that the SPCK had become more and more doubtful as to whether it should continue its cooperation with Halle missionaries like Früchtenicht, about whom several reports had reached London in contrast to the lack of reports about the 'misbehaving' English missionaries Holzberg and Päzold. Within the Halle mission there were discussions on whether it would be better to keep all incidents confidential to prevent an examination by the SPCK and an 'extensive defence' (*weitläufige Vertheidigung*), which 'inevitably would put both the accused and the mission as a whole at a big disadvantage'.[166]

As soon as the 'misunderstandings' were overcome, Früchtenicht, who was still in America, announced that he would travel back to Tranquebar as a missionary. Later he confirmed that he had an offer to go to Ceylon as a missionary. Eventually however, he admitted that he did not have any such offers and wanted to travel to East India at his own expense, which because of his debts and the entire history of the case also seems totally out of touch with reality. Consequently, another pastor reported of Früchtenicht's next suicide attempt on 1 February 1806. This time Früchtenicht tried to hang himself but the rope was cut before he died. Afterwards he was brought to the Philadelphia alms house and recovered sufficiently to be sent back to Denmark eventually. A Danish newspaper from the same year carried an account of a young former missionary who killed himself in Copenhagen.[167] It seems rather likely that the man in question was Lambert Christian Früchtenicht. At least he left no further traces.

VI

In contrast to the Pietist discourses on alcohol consumption in Europe, the missionaries in the subcontinent tended to prefer moderate consumption to complete abstinence, and light alcohol to strong alcohol. As such, they were more in line with the secular discourses, reflected for instance in the *Universal-Lexicon*. This can also be seen in their rational and medical arguments against the drunkenness of Früchtenicht and others, which expressed contemporary discourses on health and subcontinental problems related to contaminated water. Accordingly, the consumption of wine prevailed in Danish East India, at any rate among the upper-classes to which the missionaries wanted to belong. The pattern of internal social stratification that was imported from Europe also involved 'inferior' indigenous forms of alcohol and the 'natives' themselves, who in the view of the missionaries originally did not drink alcohol (in contrast to the 'excessive' Europeans) and thus had to be protected against such Europeans and proselytized. However, as has been shown, there *were* cases of indigenous alcohol abuse even within the mission, and in contrast to missionary 'misbehaviour', the 'natives' were punished more severely.

Although the case of the drunken missionary Früchtenicht was most definitely an exceptional case, it casts light on the normality of a large variety of 'misbehaviour' patterns, also sometimes linked to alcohol and drunkenness, within the eighteenth century Protestant undertakings of the Moravians and the DEHM in Danish East India. The cases of alcohol-induced 'misbehaviour' moreover show that not only soldiers and sailors were affected by drunkenness,[168] but even the clergy, who therefore can also be considered 'white subalterns'.[169] Furthermore, these cases showcase the different perceptions, reactions, and 'contradictions' regarding the incidents that were dependent on diverse conditions.[170] Missionaries and mission centres were primarily concerned about their public image and reputation amongst European donors, mission partners, the 'natives', and the Europeans abroad. Whereas the distant centres above all had to bear in mind their financial situation, the missionaries on site were more concerned with their own living conditions. As a result, their interest in suspending a 'misbehaving' missionary could be more tangible than that of the centre, even apart from any prevailing double moral standards. In short, they had to be flexible. 'Useful misbehaviour' which could help the mission had to be widely tolerated, as were less severe or casual incidents. As can be seen in §8 of the instruction by the DEHM for missionary candidates, differing perceptions could lead to severe discrepancies, especially in a confused legal situation with a lot of involved parties as in Danish East India in the time of Früchtenicht.

Notes

1 This article emerged from research on my doctoral thesis at the University of Zurich in the *University Research Priority Program 'Asia and Europe'* and from a recently undertaken research project at Kiel University on alcohol in Danish East India, which is funded by the German Research Foundation (DFG) and conducted by Martin Krieger (Chair of Northern European History). Each of the archival documents, quoted in this essay, was translated from German by the author.

2 'Was will aus der Mission werden, wenn wir solche schlechte Missionare dort haben?', Knapp to Gude, 13.06.1800, Archives of the Francke Foundations, Mission Archive (AFSt/M) 4 E 5: 63.

3 On the interrelations between these groups see D.L. Brunner, *Halle Pietists in England. Anthony William Boehm and the Society for Promoting Christian Knowledge*, Göttingen: Vandenhoeck & Ruprecht, 1993; A. Gross, Y.V. Kumaradoss and H. Liebau (eds), *Halle and the Beginning of Protestant Christianity in India*, Halle: Franckesche Stiftungen, 2006, vols I–III.

4 In this article the term 'Danish-English-Halle Mission' (DEHM) is preferred to other variations like 'Danish-Halle Mission' or 'Tranquebarmission' because of the 'transnational' character of the mission network. Cf. H. Liebau, 'Das Hallesche Waisenhaus und die Tranquebarmission', in M. Mann (ed.) *Europäische Aufklärung und protestantische Mission in Indien*, Heidelberg: Draupadi Verlag, 2006, pp. 125–42, especially p. 127.

5 Cf. J. Tschurenev and H. Fischer-Tiné's introduction in this volume.

6 Some hints can be found in O. Feldbæk, *India Trade under the Danish Flag 1772–1808. European enterprise and Anglo-Indian remittance and trade*, Odense: Studentlitteratur, 1969, p. 14, and M. Krieger, *Kaufleute, Seeräuber und Diplomaten. Der dänische Handel auf dem Indischen Ozean (1620–1868)*, Köln etc.: Böhlau Verlag, 1998, pp. 114, 130, 142.

7 Martin Krieger offers a few examples of the richness of auction protocols and estates in this regard, cf. 'Some observations on life and death at Tranquebar around 1800', in E. Heinzelmann, S. Robl and T. Riis (eds) *The Oldenburg Monarchy. An underestimated empire?*, Kiel: Verlag Ludwig, 2006, pp. 111–25, especially p. 116, and the same author's 'Wohnkultur in Tranquebar um 1800. Auf Spurensuche in den Tamil Nadu State Archives', in S. Conermann and J. Kusber (eds) *Studia Eurasiatica. Kieler Festschrift für Hermann Kulke zum 65. Geburtstag*, Schenefeld: EB-Verlag, 2003, pp. 175–88, especially p. 184.

8 See the various archive record examples in T. Delfs, 'Ein Missionar auf Abwegen in Dänisch-Ostindien. Der Fall des Lambert Christian Früchtenicht', in M. Krieger and K. Leineweber (eds) *Deutschland und der Norden in der Neuzeit. Forschungserträge des Kieler Lehrstuhls für Nordeuropäische Geschichte 2009–2010*, Frankfurt/M. etc.: Peter Lang Verlag, forthcoming. For some exceptions with references on alcohol consumption in the mission mentioned in passing, cf. also J.F. Fenger, *History of the Tranquebar Mission. Worked out from the original papers*, Tranquebar: Evangelical Lutheran Mission Press, 1863 [1st edn 1843 in Danish, 1845 translated into German], pp. 137, 145, 147–50, 296–7 (without references); H. Römer, *Geschichte der Brüdermission auf den Nikobaren und des Brüdergartens bei Trankebar: auf Grunde des handschriftlichen Materials im Unitäts-Archiv zu Herrnhut*, Herrnhut: Verlag der Missionsbuchhandlung, 1921, pp. 64, 68–9 (without references); H. Liebau, *Die indischen Mitarbeiter der Tranquebarmission (1706–1845). Katecheten, Schulmeister, Übersetzer*, Tübingen: Verlag der Franckeschen Stiftungen Halle im Max Niemeyer Verlag, 2008, pp. 63, 154, 156, 171–2 and A. Nørgaard, *Mission und Obrigkeit. Die Dänisch-hallische Mission in Tranquebar 1706–1845*, Gütersloh: Verlags-Haus Mohn, 1988, pp. 138–40, 172–4. Based on personal experience, without references and only very general on alcohol in the later Asiatic mission context: H. Anstein, *Mission und Alkohol. Asiatischer und europäischer Alkoholismus*, Berlin: Neuland Verlag, 1931.

9 Cf. P. Spear, *The Nabobs. A study of the social life of the English in 18th century India*, London: Oxford University Press, 1963 [1st edn 1932], pp. 117–25, here especially p. 119.

10 An exception to this is P. Chatterjee, 'The lives of alcohol in pre-colonial India', *The Medieval History Journal* 8, 1, 2005, 189–225 with a focal point on the seventeenth century.

11 On his conception of 'white subalternity' and the classification of missionaries therein see H. Fischer-Tiné, *Low and Licentious Europeans. Race, class and 'white subalternity' in colonial India*, New Delhi: Orient Blackswan, 2009, especially pp. 1–18, 58.

12 Cf. already T. Delfs, 'Missionar auf Abwegen', in Krieger and Leineweber, *Deutschland und der Norden in der Neuzeit.*

13 On the Moravian activities in South Asia cf. for instance T. Ruhland, 'The Moravian Brethren and the Danish-Halle Mission in Tranquebar. The "Garden of the Brothers" at the centre of a European conflict', in A. Gross, Y.V. Kumaradoss and H. Liebau (eds) *Halle and the Beginning of Protestant Christianity in India, vol. II Christian Mission in the Indian Context*, Halle: Franckesche Stiftungen, 2006, pp. 743–66 and M. Krieger, 'Vom "Brüdergarten" zu den Nikobaren. Die Herrnhuter Brüder in Südasien', in S. Conermann (ed.) *Der Indische Ozean in historischer Perspektive*, Hamburg: EB-Verlag, 1998, pp. 209–44.

14 These useful sources can be found in the Archives of the Francke Foundations in Halle (AFSt/M and ALMW/DHM), the Moravian Unity Archives in Herrnhut (UAH) and the Danish National Archives in Copenhagen (RAK).

15 J.H. Zedler, *Großes vollständiges Universal-Lexicon aller Wissenschafften und Künste*, 64 vols, 4 supplements, Halle, Leipzig 1732–54. The whole encyclopaedia has been digitized by the Bavarian State Library and the German Research Foundation. Cf. Online. Available HTTP: <http://www.zedler-lexikon.de> (last accessed 5 May 2011), in the following references cited as *Universal-Lexicon* and translated from German by the author of this essay.

16 *Universal-Lexicon*, vol. 45, pp. 1293–1326.
17 *Universal-Lexicon*, vol. 30, pp. 1143–7.
18 *Universal-Lexicon*, vol. 61, pp. 276–7.
19 Cf. Art. 'Trunckenheit', *Universal-Lexicon*, vol. 45, p. 1293.
20 Cf. ibid., pp. 1293–1303.
21 *Universal-Lexicon*, vol. 4, pp. 1082–91.
22 Cf. Art. 'Brandtwein', *Universal-Lexicon*, vol. 4, pp. 1083–5.
23 Ibid., p. 1085: 'aller Ueberfluß und Unmäßigkeit ist schädlich, und kan aus einem Lebens-Wasser leichtlich ein Wasser des Todes werden'.
24 Cf. Art. 'Bier', *Universal-Lexicon*, vol. 3, pp. 1789–94, here p. 1789.
25 Cf. Art. 'Zech-Brüder', *Universal-Lexicon*, vol. 61, p. 277. On social consequences and harsh punishments cf. Art. 'Trunckenheit', *Universal-Lexicon*, vol. 45, p. 1304 and K. Wassenberg, 'Die historischen Wurzeln der Deutschen Mäßigkeitsbewegung', in K. Wassenberg and S. Schaller (eds) *Der Geist der Deutschen Mäßigkeitsbewegung. Debatten um Alkohol und Trinken in Vergangenheit und Gegenwart*, Halle: Mitteldeutscher Verlag, 2010, pp. 12–37, especially p. 19.
26 Cf. Art. 'Trunckenheit', *Universal-Lexicon*, vol. 45, p. 1301.
27 Cf. A. Lutz, *Ehepaare vor Gericht. Konflikte und Lebenswelten in der Frühen Neuzeit*, Frankfurt: Campus Verlag, 2006, p. 245 (my translation).
28 Cf. H. Obst, *A. H. Francke und die Franckeschen Stiftungen in Halle*, Göttingen: Vandenhoeck & Ruprecht, 2002, pp. 17–20.
29 Cf. K.D. Schmidt, *Die Alkoholfrage in Orthodoxie, Pietismus und Rationalismus*, Berlin: Neuland-Verlag, 1927, p. 10.
30 Cf. ibid., pp. 12–17; M. Frank, 'Trunkene Männer und nüchterne Frauen. Zur Gefährdung von Geschlechterrollen durch Alkohol in der Frühen Neuzeit', in M. Dinges (ed.) *Hausväter, Priester, Kastraten. Zur Konstruktion von Männlichkeit in Spätmittelalter und Früher Neuzeit*, Göttingen: Vandenhoeck & Ruprecht, 1998, pp. 187–212, 192; Lutz, *Ehepaare*, pp. 84–6, 245.
31 A. Gestrich, 'Pietistisches Weltverständnis und Handeln in der Welt', in Hartmut Lehmann (ed.) *Geschichte des Pietismus, Bd. 4: Glaubenswelt und Lebenswelten*, Göttingen: Vandenhoeck & Ruprecht, 2004, pp. 556–83, 575: 'Der Kampf gegen Alkohol und Tanz kann als ein nations- und denominationsübergreifendes Ziel des Pietismus angesehen werden' (my translation).
32 Cf. K. Wassenberg, 'Wurzeln der Deutschen Mäßigkeitsbewegung', in Wassenberg and Schaller, *Geist der deutschen Mässigkeitsbewegung*, p. 33 and Schmidt, *Alkoholfrage*, p. 17.
33 Cf. D. Furrer, *Zechen und Bechern. Eine Kulturgeschichte des Trinkens und Betrinkens*, Darmstadt: Primus Verlag, 2006, pp. 115–20. On excesses of soldiers see also Art. 'Privilegien der Soldaten', *Universal-Lexicon*, vol. 29, pp. 599–607, here p. 599 and P.E. Kopperman, '"The cheapest pay": alcohol abuse in the eighteenth century British army', *The Journal of Military History* 60, July 1996, pp. 445–70.
34 Cf. Furrer, *Zechen*, pp. 115–16, 119.
35 Kopperman, 'The cheapest pay', pp. 446, 449.
36 Cf. ibid., p. 457 and Furrer, *Zechen*, p. 116.
37 In the late eighteenth century there were about 90 Danish soldiers and 400 *sepoys* (employed Indian soldiers) in Tranquebar. Cf. A. Rasch, *Dansk Ostindien, 1777–1845. Storhedstid og hensygnen*, Copenhagen: Fremad, 1967, p. 88. The census of 1790 in turn showed that the total number of inhabitants in Tranquebar reached 3,721, of which 94 per cent were 'natives'. Soldiers without household were not included in the census. Cf. K.P. Pedersen, 'Tranquebars Historie', *Architectura. Arkitekturhistorisk Årsskrift* 9, 1987, pp. 11–49, especially pp. 33–4. See also M. Krieger, 'Material culture, knowledge, and European society in colonial India around 1800: Danish Tranquebar', in M. North (ed.) *Artistic and Cultural Exchanges between Europe and Asia, 1400–1900. Rethinking markets, workshops and collections*, Farnham: Ashgate, 2010, pp. 53–72, especially p. 55 and RAK, Det kgl. Ostindiske Guvernement, 1747a: *Mandtal over Indbyggerne i Tranquebar og Landsbyerne*, 1790.

38 Cf. D. Arnold, *The Tropics and the Traveling Gaze. India, landscape, and science, 1800–1856*, Seattle and London: University of Washington Press, 2006, pp. 43–4, D.M. Peers, 'Imperial vice: sex, drink and the health of British troops in North Indian cantonments, 1800–1858', in D. Killingray and D. Omissi (eds) *Guardians of Empire. The armed forces of the colonial powers c. 1700–1964*, Manchester, New York: Manchester University Press, 1999, pp. 25–53 and M. Mann, 'Indien ist eine Karriere. Biographische Skizzen deutscher Söldner, Ratsherren und Mediziner in Südasien, 1500–1800', in M.A. Denzel (ed.) *Deutsche Eliten in Übersee (16. bis frühes 20. Jahrhundert)*, St. Katharinen: Scripta Mercaturae Verlag, 2006, pp. 249–90, especially p. 251. Cf. on the Danish sailors in particular F.E. Eliassen, 'Peter Dahl (1747–1789) in the Oldenburg Empire. The life, career and interests of a Norwegian shipmaster and merchant in the 1770s and 1780s', in Heinzelmann, Robl and Riis, *The Oldenburg Monarchy*, pp. 50–71, especially p. 54.

39 *Reise Diarium der Brr Blaschke und Staal von Serampore in Bengalen bis Tranquebar d. 27. Decb 1781*, UAH R 15 Ta 101 (entry from 15 December 1781).

40 Cf. *Reise des Br. Joh Sam Voigt nach Bengalen 1783*, UAH R 15 Ta 10o (entry from 6 April 1783).

41 Quoted after A. Bredsdorff, *The Trials and Travels of Willem Leyel. An account of the Danish East India Company in Tranquebar, 1639–48*, Copenhagen: Museum Tusculanum Press, 2009, p. 40.

42 Cf. *Diarien von Bengalen 1776–92*, UAH R 15 Tb 3 (entry from 10 February 1786).

43 Cf. *Diarien von Bengalen 1776–92*, UAH R 15 Tb 3 (entries from 26 February and 9 March 1792). In these two cases they 'paid' with a bottle of *arak* and then with a bottle of gin.

44 Cf. for instance, *Diarien von Bengalen 1776–92*, UAH R 15 Tb 3 (entries from 4 January and 18 March 1789).

45 *Neuere Geschichte der evangelischen Missionsanstalten zu Bekehrung der Heiden in Ost-Indien*, 3, 36. Stück (Halle: 1790), pp. 1353–4 (my translation).

46 Cf. *Diarien von Bengalen 1776–92*, UAH R 15 Tb 3 (entry from 5 August 1788): 'wozu alle hiesige im Settlement angeseßnen, außer wir, invitiert wurden'. Another reason for mentioning this might have been that evangelizing on British territory at that time was officially forbidden. Cf. A. Porter, *Religion versus Empire? British protestant missionaries and overseas expansion, 1700–1914*, Manchester etc.: Manchester University Press, 2004, pp. 68–75.

47 Cf. also M. Krieger, 'Brüdergarten', in S. Conermann, *Der Indische Ozean in historischer Perspektive*, pp. 226–7. The same seems to be true for the DEHM, cf. Nørgaard, *Mission*, pp. 154–5.

48 Grasmann to Reichel, 05.11.1789, UAH R 15 Tb 9, 60.

49 Cf. Grasmann to Reichel, 05.02.1790, UAH R 15 Tb 9, 61. Cf. T. Delfs, 'Missionar auf Abwegen', in Krieger and Leineweber, *Deutschland und der Norden in der Neuzeit.*

50 These letters should be regarded with suspicion as they served not only as appeals for money, but also serviced specific 'oriental' images. Cf. J. Osterhammel, *Die Entzauberung Asiens. Europa und die asiatischen Reiche im 18. Jahrhundert*, München: Beck, 1998, pp. 79–80. On the question of credibility of the missionary reports, cf. G. Dharampal-Frick, *Indien im Spiegel deutscher Quellen der frühen Neuzeit (1500–1750). Studien zu einer interkulturellen Konstellation*, Tübingen: Niemeyer, 1994, p. 87.

51 Cf. *Der Königl. Dänischen Missionarien aus Ost-Indien eingesandter Ausführlichen Berichten, Von dem Werck ihres Amts unter den Heyden, angerichteten Schulen, ereigneten Hindernissen und schweren Umständen; Beschaffenheit des Malabarischen Heydenthums, gepflogenen brieflichen Correspondentz und mündlichen Unterredungen mit selbigen Heyden [...]*, 11. Continuation, pp. 942–5.

52 Cf. Liebau, *Mitarbeiter*, p. 63. Cf. also D.D. Hudson, *Protestant Origins in India: Tamil evangelical Christians, 1706–1835*, Grand Rapids and Cambridge: Wm. B. Eerdmans Publishing, 2000, pp. 92–3 on '"pariah-like"' behaviour of Europeans in the view of the Tamils.

53 For instance, Grasmann to Reichel, 05.11.1789, UAH R 15 Tb 9, 60 and Schmidt to Grasmann, 22.05.1782, UAH R 15 Tb 12. Schmidt wrote from Patna, where the Moravians wanted to build

a new station, that the chosen parcel of land was 'far from all Europeans' and a 'lonely place', which for him seems to have been a very positive criterion for the establishment of such a station.

54 Cf. T. Delfs, 'Missionar auf Abwegen', in Krieger and Leineweber, *Deutschland und der Norden in der Neuzeit.*

55 *Der Königl. Dänischen Missionarien aus Ost-Indien eingesandter Ausführlichen Berichten*, 11. Cont., p. 944: 'Seuchen, die die meisten der Europäer hier zu Grabe bringen' (my translation).

56 Cf. M. Harrison, *Climates and Constitutions. Health, race, environment and British imperialism in India 1600–1850*, New Delhi: Oxford University Press, 1999, pp. 50–2 and Chatterjee, 'Lives of alcohol', pp. 216–19.

57 Cf. Chatterjee, 'Lives of alcohol', p. 218.

58 Schmidt to Grasmann, 22.05.1782, UAH R 15 Tb 12.

59 Cf. Nørgaard, *Mission*, pp. 172–3. On the exceptional status of wine even in the early modern religious criticism of alcohol consumption see B.A. Tlusty, *Bacchus und die bürgerliche Ordnung. Die Kultur des Trinkens im frühneuzeitlichen Augsburg*, Augsburg: Wißner, 2005, p. 92.

60 They are followed by *jenever*, beer, *arak* and other spirits. Cf. RAK, Det kgl. ostindiske Guvernement, Kolonien Trankebar, *Søtoldbøger*, 1793–1798. On the importance of wine in the Danish trade, see also Krieger, *Kaufleute*, pp. 114, 130 and Feldbæk, *India Trade*, p. 14.

61 Cf. Bredsdorff, *Trials and Travels*, pp. 27–8.

62 Cf. M. Krieger, 'Observations on life and death', in Heinzelmann, Robl and Riis, *Oldenburg Monarchy*, p. 116.

63 Cf. *Der Königl. Dänischen Missionarien aus Ost-Indien eingesandter Ausführlichen Berichten*, 3. Continuation, pp. 122–3 (my translation).

64 This word derives from the colloquial Danish 'Finkel' which meant something like 'bottom shelf liquor' or 'bad spirits'. Cf. Det Danske Sprog- og Litteraturselskab (ed.), *Ordbog over det Danske Sprog.* 4. Bind, Døbe-Flytte, Copenhagen: Gyldendal, 1981, pp. 1013–14.

65 *Arak* could refer to different types of strong drinks, for instance, in this case, that extracted from the sap of a coconut palm. Cf. also Chatterjee, 'Lives of alcohol', p. 192.

66 Cf. *Der Königl. Dänischen Missionarien aus Ost-Indien eingesandter Ausführlichen Berichten*, 11. Cont., p. 944 (my translation). Cf. T. Delfs, 'Missionar auf Abwegen', in Krieger and Leineweber, *Deutschland und der Norden in der Neuzeit.*

67 See D. Arnold, 'Poor Europeans in India, 1750–1947', *Current Anthropology*, 20, 2, 1979, 454–5 and Fischer-Tiné, *Low and Licentious Europeans*, pp. 57–60 on such stratifications in the subcontinent.

68 Cf. also Chatterjee, 'Lives of alcohol', pp. 205–7, 210–12 and for later times Fischer-Tiné, *Low and Licentious Europeans*, pp. 113–14.

69 Cf. *Der Königl. Dänischen Missionarien aus Ost-Indien eingesandter Ausführlichen Berichten*, 3. Continuation, p. 122.

70 Cf. *Der Königl. Dänischen Missionarien aus Ost-Indien eingesandter Ausführlichen Berichten*, 11. Cont., p. 944. Cf. T. Delfs, 'Missionar auf Abwegen', in Krieger and Leineweber, *Deutschland und der Norden in der Neuzeit.*

71 Cf. *Neuere Geschichte der evangelischen Missionsanstalten zu Bekehrung der Heiden in Ost-Indien*, 2, 21. Stück (Halle: 1783), p. 1134. The missionary Nicolaus Dal in 1741 also 'sought to put such books as were directed against drunkenness, cursing and swearing, into the hands of his countrymen, and exerted himself [...] to distribute such books', Fenger, *History of the Tranquebar Mission*, p. 146.

72 Cf. *Der Königl. Dänischen Missionarien aus Ost-Indien eingesandter Ausführlichen Berichten*, 11. Cont., p. 944.

73 This can also be found in other thematic fields like hygiene. Cf. for an example within the Protestant mission in early twentieth century Egypt, S. Boulos, '"A clean heart likes clean clothes": cleanliness customs and conversion in Egypt (1900–1956)', *Islam and Christian-Muslim Relations* 21, 4, 2010, 315–30.

74 Cf. Fischer-Tiné, *Low and Licentious Europeans*, p. 114.

75 Cf. *Neuere Geschichte der evangelischen Missionsanstalten zu Bekehrung der Heiden in Ost-Indien*, 5, 55. Stück (Halle: 1804), pp. 631–2.

76 Cf. for later times Fischer-Tiné, *Low and Licentious Europeans*, pp. 113–14. See also on later mission enterprises in Africa and the Pacific Islands, J. Barker, 'Where the missionary ran ahead of empire', in N. Etherington (ed.) *Missions and Empire*, Oxford etc.: Oxford University Press, 2007, pp. 86–106, here pp. 100–2.

77 Cf. on this and the aforementioned aspects J.H. Mills and P. Barton, 'Introduction', in idem (eds) *Drugs and Empires. Essays in modern imperialism and intoxication, c. 1500-c. 1930*, Houndmills etc.: Palgrave MacMillan, 2007, pp. 1–16, especially pp. 1, 7, 11 and Chatterjee, 'Lives of alcohol', p. 210. For an example of apparent 'Indo-Muslim' spirits consumption on occasion of new moon, described quite neutral by the Moravian brethren, see *Reise Diarium der Brr Blaschke und Staal von Serampore in Bengalen bis Tranquebar d. 27. Decb 1781*, UAH R 15 Ta 10l (entry from 15 December 1781).

78 Cf. Liebau, *Mitarbeiter*, p. 154 and Nørgaard, *Mission*, p. 193.

79 Cf. Liebau, *Mitarbeiter*, p. 152. This corresponds to the common impunity of 'white' violence in British India. Cf. E. Kolsky, *Colonial Justice in British India. White violence and the rule of law*, Cambridge: Cambridge University Press, 2010.

80 Cf. Nørgaard, *Mission*, pp. 189–243; Liebau, *Mitarbeiter*, pp. 83–4 .

81 Cf. for instance, Missionaries to Knapp, 16.07.1802, AFSt/M 1 C 43b: 62.

82 Cf. E. Gøbel, 'Danish shipping and trade with Asia around 1800', in Heinzelmann, Robl and Riis, *Oldenburg Monarchy*, pp. 72–86, especially p. 76.

83 Cf. for instance Kiernander to Broughton, 29.12.1758, AFSt/M 1 B 48: 24; Schulze to Mission Board, 23.08.1785, AFSt/M 4 E 3: 5; Gude to Knapp, 27.01.1801, AFSt/M 4 E 5: 68; John to Freylinghausen, 18.10.1784, AFSt/M 1 B 75: 18 and in earlier times Ziegenbalg to Gründler, Plütschau, 16.12.1713, ALMW/DHM 10/21: 52. Cf. also Liebau, *Mitarbeiter*, pp. 156–65. The Moravians had similar problems, cf. UAH R 15 Ta 10r, *Reise der 2 Brr Urban und Beck von Tranquebar nach Bengalen vom 15. März bis 29. April 1784*, entry from 19 March 1784.

84 Cf. with more literature on these problems and their interdependency Nørgaard, *Mission*.

85 These were Lorentz Friedrich Rulfsen (1780), Johann Jakob Schöllkopf (1777) and Wilhelm Jakob Müller (1771).

86 Cf. John to Freylinghausen, 10.10.1778, AFSt/M 1 B 69: 24.

87 Cf. Breithaupt to Freylinghausen, 03.01.1781, AFSt/M 3 B 2: 30.

88 Cf. Becker to Fabricius, 13.10.1778, AFSt/M 1 B 69: 30, John to Freylinghausen, 06.07.1779, AFSt/M 1 B 69: 24 and Nørgaard, *Mission*, p. 155.

89 Cämmerer to Nebe, 23.10.1799, AFSt/M 1 C 40b: 29; Freylinghausen to Missionaries, 08.11.1779, AFSt/M 1 B 69: 92; Dal to Francke, Ziegenhagen, Mission Board, 07.09.1738, AFSt/M 1 G 2: 1-1a; Kohlhoff to Francke, 20.01.1739, AFSt/M 1 G 2: 4-4a.

90 J. Miller, *Missionary Zeal and Institutional Control. Organizational contradictions in the Basel Mission on the Gold Coast, 1828–1917*, Grand Rapids and Cambridge: Wm. B. Eerdmans Publishing, 2003, p. 128 (quotation, original emphasis), see also pp. 162, 172–3.

91 Cf. P. Robb, 'Credit, work and race in 1790s Calcutta. Early colonialism through a contemporary European view', *The Indian Economic and Social History Review*, 37, 1, 2000, pp. 1–25, especially pp. 3–4.

92 Cf. John to Freylinghausen, 10.10.1778, AFSt/M 1 B 69: 24. Cf. also John to Freylinghausen, 18.10.1784, AFSt/M 1 B 75: 18.

93 Cf. Liebau, *Mitarbeiter*, p. 156 (note 49) and Nørgaard, *Mission*, pp. 138–9. Cf. also his defence, Schultze to Francke, 21.01.1737, AFSt/M 2 G 15: 8.

94 Miller, *Missionary Zeal*, p. 128. The Basel Mission began its work in the Danish settlement Christiansborg on the Gold Coast in 1828.

95 Cf. Cämmerer to Nebe, 23.10.1799, AFSt/M 1 C 40b: 29. Cämmerer here in particular referred to the 'native' Jan Gilbert, who went to the royal boarding school in the orphanage of the Francke Foundations and who in 1798 together with his brother travelled back to Tranquebar. In Cämmerer's view the younger would 'always put on airs' ('spielen immer gleich große Herren').

96 Cf. Nørgaard, *Mission*, pp. 71–2. The Moravian Raabs even deserted the Brethren to find a woman in the orphan house of Calcutta. Cf. *Diarien von Bengalen 1776–92*, UAH R 15 Tb 3 (entries from 19 November, 1 and 2 December 1788).

97 Cf. for instance John to Knapp, 27.03.1800, AFSt/M 1 C 41: 94; John to Freylinghausen, 10.10.1778, AFSt/M 1 B 69: 24.

98 See on this case extensively T. Delfs, 'Missionar auf Abwegen', in Krieger and Leineweber, *Deutschland und der Norden in der Neuzeit*. Cf. also Nørgaard, *Mission*, pp. 206–8.

99 Pohle to Schulze, 17.10.1799, AFSt/M 1 C 40b: 16.

100 Päzold to Nebe, 26.05.1801, AFSt/M 1 C 42b: 74.

101 John to Knapp, 27.03.1800, AFSt/M 1 C 41: 94.

102 Missionaries to Früchtenicht, 21.06.1800, RAK, Kommercekollegiets Ostindiske Sager 1777–1848: *Ostindisk Journalsager 1777–1845*, Appendix to Anker to Board of Commerce, 12.02.1802.

103 Pohle to Schulze, 17.10.1799, AFSt/M 1 C 40b: 16; Cämmerer to Nebe, 23.10.1799, AFSt/M 1 C 40b: 29 ('drunkenness'); John to Knapp, 27.03.1800, AFSt/M 1 C 41: 94 ('not even devoid of drinking' - 'nicht einmal vom Trunke frei').

104 Cf. Früchtenicht to Missionaries, 09.10.1799, RAK, Missionskollegiet og Direktionen for Vajsenhuset, 1738–1808: *Indkomne Sager ang. den Ostindiske Mission, 1800–1808*, where he gainsays such accusations.

105 Cf. N. Worden, E. van Heyningen and V. Bickford-Smith, *Cape Town. The making of a city. An illustrated social history*, Claremont: Philip, 1998, pp. 49–70. On the difficult living conditions of the soldiers and sailors in eighteenth century Cape Town, see especially pp. 49–55, 51 (quotation) and on the perceived interrelations of social stratification and alcohol, which seems to have been quite similar to East India, cf. pp. 78–9. Many of the European soldiers and sailors went abroad to climb the social ladder and to escape their hopeless economic situations at home. Cf. M. Mann, 'Indien ist eine Karriere', in Denzel, *Deutsche Eliten*, p. 289.

106 Chemnitz to Schulze, 01.08.1798, AFSt/M 4 E 5: 35.

107 Cf. John, Rottler, Cämmerer to Mission Board, 06.08.1800, RAK, Missionskollegiet og Direktionen for Vajsenhuset, *Indkomne Sager ang. den ostindiske Mission 1738–1808*, 1800. Cf. also Liebau, *Mitarbeiter*, pp. 171–2.

108 Cf. Gude an Knapp, 17.01.1801, AFSt/M 4 E 5: 67.

109 Cf. Missionaries to Unknown, 23.01.1801, RAK, Missionskollegiet og Direktionen for Vajsenhuset, 1738–1808: *Indkomne Sager ang. den Ostindiske Mission*, 1800–1808, 1801 and John to Knapp, 23.03.1801, AFSt/M 1 C 42a: 8.

110 Cf. Cämmerer, John, Rottler to Mission Board, 18.03.1801, AFSt/M 1 C 42a: 11; Gericke to Nebe, 18.10.1799, AFSt/M 1 C 40b: 15.

111 Cf. Cämmerer to Schulze, 20.04.1799, AFSt/M 1 C 40a: 33.

112 Cf. Cämmerer to Nebe, 23.10.1799, AFSt/M 1 C 40b: 29.

113 Cf. Gude to Knapp, 03.03.1801, AFSt/M 4 E 5: 69.

114 Päzold to Knapp, 24.09.1800, AFSt/M 1 C 41: 35 (original emphasis).

115 Cf. Früchtenicht to Missionaries, 22.06.1800, RAK, Kommercekollegiets Ostindiske Sager 1777–1848: *Ostindisk Journalsager 1777–1845*, Appendix to Anker to Board of Commerce, 12.02.1802; Früchtenicht to Missionaries, 09.10.1799, RAK, Missionskollegiet og Direktionen for Vajsenhuset, 1738–1808: *Indkomne Sager ang. den Ostindiske Mission, 1800–1808*. Gude to Knapp, 17.01.1801, AFSt/M 4 E 5: 67.

116 Früchtenicht to Missionaries, 09.10.1799, RAK, Missionskollegiet og Direktionen for Vajsenhuset, 1738–1808: *Indkomne Sager ang. den Ostindiske Mission, 1800–1808*.

117 Früchtenicht to Missionaries, 28.02.1800, RAK, Missionskollegiet og Direktionen for Vajsenhuset, 1738–1808: *Indkomne Sager ang. den Ostindiske Mission, 1800–1808*.

118 Cf. Gude to Knapp, 27.01.1801, AFSt/M 4 E 5: 68.

119 Cf. Cämmerer, John, Rottler to Mission Board, 18.03.1801, AFSt/M 1 C 42a: 11.

120 Cf. Gude to Knapp, 27.01.1801, AFSt/M 4 E 5: 68.

121 Klein to Mission Board, 25.08.1800, RAK, Missionskollegiet og Direktionen for Vajsenhuset, 1738–1808: *Indkomne Sager ang. den Ostindiske Mission*, 1800–1808, 1801.

122 Päzold to Knapp, 20.09.1800, AFSt/M 1 C 41: 35.

123 Cf. John to Knapp, 27.03.1800, AFSt/M 1 C 41: 94. On Päzold's double moral standards, cf. also his harsh criticism on his colleagues Holzberg, John and Rottler: Päzold to Nebe, 26.05.1801, AFSt/M 1 C 42b: 74; Päzold to Holzberg, 11.03.1806, AFSt/M 1 C 47: 100a.

124 Cf. Kohlhoff to Francke, 24.09.1739, AFSt/M 1 B 26: 28. Cf. also Fenger, *History of the Tranquebar Mission*, pp. 147–50.

125 Cf. Rottler to Schulze, 20.01.1798, AFSt/M 1 C 39a: 8 and Missionaries to Francke, 30.12.1750, AFSt/M 1 B 40: 10.

126 Cf. the biographical database of the Francke Foundations. Online. Available HTTP: <http://192.124.243.55/cgi-bin/gkdb.pl> (last accessed 19 May 2011).

127 Cf. for instance UAH R 15 A 65 I, *Protocoll des Missions-Departements in der Unitäts-Ältesten-Conferenz*, 125, entry from 20 May 1790.

128 Cf. D.M. Peers, 'Imperial Vice', in Killingray and Omissi, *Guardians of Empire*, p. 41.

129 Cf. Schmidt to Grasmann, 22.05.1782, UAH R 15 Tb 12.

130 UAH R 15 A 65 I, *Protocoll des Missions-Departements in der Unitäts-Ältesten-Conferenz*, 257–8., entry from 4 February 1791: 'daß er, da ihn sein Vorsteheramt nicht hinlänglich beschäftigt zuweilen darüber einige Vorwürfe hören muß'.

131 Cf. John to Freylinghausen, 10.10.1778, AFSt/M 1 B 69: 24.

132 *Diarien von Bengalen 1776–92*, UAH R 15 Tb 3 (entry from 1 August 1784).

133 Cf. *Instruction für einen angehenden Missionarium zu Trankenbar*, RAK, Missionskollegiet og Direktionen for Vajsenhuset, 1738–1808: *Indkomne Sager ang. den Ostindiske Mission*, 1793–1799, 1798. Cf. Liebau, *Mitarbeiter*, pp. 148–50.

134 Cf. Schulze to Gude, 05.04.1798, AFSt/M 4 E 5: 20, 21, 21a. Cf. also Liebau, *Mitarbeiter*, p. 148.

135 Cf. Chemnitz to Schulze, 9.01.1798, AFSt/M 4 E 5: 8; Chemnitz to Schulze, 1.08.1798, AFSt/M 4 E 5: 35.

136 Cf. Schulze to Früchtenicht, 20.01.1798, AFSt/M 4 E 5: 9; Schulze to Chemnitz, 25.01.1798, AFSt/M 4 E 5: 4b.

137 Cf. Schulze to Valentin Früchtenicht, 20.02.1798, AFSt/M 4 E 5: 15; Schulze to Gude, 20.02.1798, AFSt/M 4 E 5: 10; Schulze to Stegmann, 27.02.1798, AFSt/M 4 E 5: 14; Schulze to Chemnitz, 27.02.1798, AFSt/M 4 E 5: 18.

138 Between 1706 and 1826, out of a total number of 57 missionaries of the DEHM 44 died in South Asia, on their way there or on their way back to Europe. Cf. the biographies in J. Gröschl, 'Missionaries of the Danish-Halle and English-Halle Mission in India 1706–1844', in A. Gross, Y.V. Kumaradoss and H. Liebau (eds) *Halle and the Beginning of Protestant Christianity in India, vol. III: Communication between India and Europe*, Halle: Franckesche Stiftungen, 2006, pp. 1497–1528; A. Gross, 'Missionaries of the Danish-Halle Mission', in ibid., pp. 1571–2 and A. Gross, 'Missionaries of the English-Halle Mission', in ibid., pp. 1573–4. The same is true regarding the Moravian Brethren: Out of a total number of 73 missionaries only 20 came back to Europe. Cf. H. Beck, *Brüder in vielen Völkern. 250 Jahre Mission der Brüdergemeine*, Erlangen: Verlag der Evang.-Luth. Mission, 1981, p. 143.

139 Cf. Liebau, *Mitarbeiter*, p. 149.

140 Grasmann to Reichel, 05.11.1789, UAH R 15 Tb 9 Nr. 60.

141 Cf. *Instruction für einen angehenden Missionarium zu Trankenbar*, RAK, Missionskollegiet og Direktionen for Vajsenhuset, 1738–1808: *Indkomne Sager ang. den Ostindiske Mission*, 1793–1799, 1798. Cf. also Nørgaard, *Mission*, p. 206.

142 Cf. Cämmerer, John, Rottler to Mission Board, 18.03.1801, AFSt/M 1 C 42a: 11.

143 Missionaries to Anker, 21.06.1800, RAK, Kommercekollegiets Ostindiske Sager 1777–1848: *Ostindisk Journalsager 1777–1845,* Appendix to Anker to Board of Commerce, 12.02.1802: 'sonderlich da sein Haus so nahe an der Kirche lieget, und sogar die öffentliche Ruhe dadurch gestöret wird'.

144 Cf. Missionaries to Anker, 21.06.1800, RAK, Kommercekollegiets Ostindiske Sager 1777–1848: *Ostindisk Journalsager 1777–1845,* Appendix to Anker to Board of Commerce, 12.02.1802.

145 Cf. Cämmerer, John, Rottler to Mission Board, 18.03.1801, AFSt/M 1 C 42a: 11: 'Man bringe mich auf die Festung in diesem Rock, den mir der König gegeben'. Cf. also Nørgaard, *Mission*, p. 207.

146 On the importance of the missionary dress in general, cf. Liebau, *Mitarbeiter*, pp. 172–3.

147 Cf. Nørgaard, *Mission*, pp. 204–7.

148 Cf. ibid., pp. 206–7.

149 Cf. for instance Cämmerer, John, Rottler to Mission Board, 18.03.1801, AFSt/M 1 C 42a: 11.

150 Cf. John to Knapp, 27.03.1800, AFSt/M 1 C 41: 94; John to Knapp, 28.02.1801, AFSt/M 1 C 42a: 29; John to Knapp, 23.03.1801, AFSt/M 1 C 42a: 8 (quotation).

151 Cf. Fenger, *History of the Tranquebar Mission*, p. 150.

152 Cf. Anker to Board of Commerce, 12.02.1802, RAK, Kommercekollegiets Ostindiske Sager 1777–1848: *Ostindisk Journalsager 1777–1845*, 1802.

153 On Anker and the mission in general cf. Nørgaard, *Mission*, pp. 202–9.

154 Cf. Cämmerer, John, Rottler to Mission Board, 18.03.1801, AFSt/M 1 C 42a: 11.

155 Cf. suicide note Früchtenicht, misdated 23.02.1810 (23.02.1801), RAK, Missionskollegiet og Direktionen for Vajsenhuset, 1738–1808: *Indkomne Sager ang. den Ostindiske Mission*, 1800–1808, 1801.

156 Cf. Cämmerer, John, Rottler to Mission Board, 18.03.1801, AFSt/M 1 C 42a: 11.

157 J.R. Watt (ed.), *From Sin to Insanity. Suicide in early modern Europe*, Ithaca: Cornell University Press, 2004.

158 Früchtenicht to Mission Board, 11.03.1803, RAK, Missionskollegiet og Direktionen for Vajsenhuset, 1738–1808: *Indkomne Sager ang. den Ostindiske Mission*, 1800–1808, 1803: 'das Clima in Ost-Indien äusserte auf meinem Körper und Geist einen so nachtheiligen Einfluß, daß ich eine gänzliche Verstandes-Verrückung befürchten mußte, wenn ich es wagen wollte, länger dort zu verweilen'.

159 *Diarien von Bengalen 1776–92*, UAH R 15 Tb 3 (entry from 9 January 1789): 'er sey ja kein Kind mehr u. könne wißen, wenn er genug habe'.

160 *Diarien von Bengalen 1776–92*, UAH R 15 Tb 3 (entry from 22 February 1789): He 'said to me that he also had to leave the Brethren; he could not bear the name of a Brother and had no belief'. See also the entries from 16 March and 9 April 1789.

161 On suicide and 'religious melancholy' in Pietism, cf. V. Lind, *Selbstmord in der Frühen Neuzeit. Diskurs, Lebenswelt und kultureller Wandel am Beispiel der Herzogtümer Schleswig und Holstein*, Göttingen: Vandenhoeck & Ruprecht, 1999, pp. 170–81.

162 Cf. John, Rottler, Cämmerer to Mission Board, 5.01.1802, ALMW/DHM 12/26b: 1f and Gude to Knapp, 10.07.1802, AFSt/M 1 C 43b: 72.

163 Cf. Knapp to John, 16.09.1806, AFSt/M 1 C 47: 78.

164 Cf. H. Wellenreuther, 'Heinrich Melchior Mühlenberg and the Pietisms in colonial America', in J.N. Strom, H. Lehmann and J. van Horn Melton (eds) *Pietism in Germany and North America 1680–1820*, Farnham: Ashgate, 2009, pp. 127–32 and H.-J. Grabbe (ed.), *Halle Pietism, Colonial North America and the Young United States*, Stuttgart: Steiner Verlag, 2008.

165 Cf. Früchtenicht to Missionskollegium, 11.03.1803 and 19.01.1803, RAK Missionskollegiet og Direktionen for Vajsenhuset, 1738–1808: Indkomne Sager ang. den Ostindiske Mission, 1800–1808, 1803. Knapp to John, 16.09.1806, AFSt/M 1 C 47: 78 (quotation).

166 Ubele to Knapp, 05.03.1802 AFSt/M 1 C 43a: 66 (SPCK); Knapp to Gericke, 04.04.1802, AFSt/M 1 C 43b: 28a (quotation): 'die nothwendig so wohl den Angeklagten selbst, als auch der ganzen Mission zum großen Nachtheil gereichen müßte'.

167 Cf. Knapp to John, 16.09.1806, AFSt/M 1 C 47: 78.

168 Cf. also Harald Fischer-Tiné's chapter in this volume.

169 Two earlier and very extreme cases of drunkenness within the orthodox clergy in Tranquebar are described in Bredsdorff, *Trials and Travels*, pp. 106–20.

170 On similar 'contradictions' in the Basel Mission, that sometimes even were 'institutionalized', cf. Miller, *Missionary Zeal*, pp. 162–8.

4 Liquid boundaries: Race, class, and alcohol in colonial India[1]

Harald Fischer-Tiné

[T]he drinking habits of our countrymen of all classes, are making a very injurious impression on the natives of India.

Reverend H. Jeffreys, Bombay 1834

Than the loafer, the vagrant, the drunken uneducated or debased European, whose passions are under no control, and who is amenable to no public opinion, nothing can be more sad to the Christian and more alarming to the statesman.

The Friend of India, 8 November 1860

Western Civilization, the greatest blot on which has been its drinking proclivities, has risen to condemn the habit on social and political grounds; and […] social workers in India and Calcutta may seek illumination from the Temperance events transpiring in Europe and America.

Herbert Anderson, *Calcutta Gazette*, October 1916

I

This chapter aims to extend our knowledge of the effects that European alcohol consumption had on both colonial ideologies as well as actual governance by examining the problems arising from the drinking practices of the middle and lower ranks of the non-official community in British India. It is my contention, that this focus on the 'white' lower middle and working classes in Britain's most important colony, not only provides a helpful correction to received interpretations of the Europeans in India as a homogeneous ruling elite, but is also an important addition to the existing research on the history of alcohol at large. Although some scholars have recently highlighted the importance of drinking in colonial contexts,[2] the focus so far has almost exclusively been on the impact of Western drinks on colonized societies, thus completely neglecting the European side of the colonial equation.

The chapter starts with a brief section providing information on the evolution of a European drinking problem in the Company era and the emergence of moral and medical discourses on alcohol (and abstinence) among the colonial elites. The subsequent parts focus on particular communities that were often discussed with respect to the 'liquor question'. The first group under scrutiny are European sailors and pilots. Similar to 'white' soldiers, the representatives of maritime professions were not only mainstays of the colonial projects of expansion, control and exploitation; they were also regarded as 'naturally' prone to the temptations of drink. The next section looks at the 'wrong sorts' of the non-official European community that transcended the maritime periphery of the subcontinent: European planters and vagrants. Planters, although not part of the lower classes according to economic criteria, possessed a reputation for being intemperate, violent and troublesome among colonial authorities throughout the nineteenth century. The vagrant or, in the parlance of the time, 'loafer' community, by contrast, were clearly 'low class' by any definition of the term. These peripatetic 'white subalterns'[3] came to be seen as fundamentally dangerous to colonial self-legitimizing ideologies through their mere existence. As was the case with the planters, part of their negative image, too, derived from their drinking culture and the implications of their 'drunk and disorderly behaviour' and particularly their propensity of uncontrolled aggression and violence against the 'natives' when 'under the influence'.[4] As will be demonstrated in the case studies below, this perceived link between alcohol consumption and violence was regarded as one of the main reasons why the colonial government should regulate the alcohol consumption of certain segments of the European population in British India.

Since European intoxication in colonial India was most conspicuous in the urban centres, the case studies will largely concentrate on Calcutta and Bombay, although occasional excursions to the *mofussil*[5] proved necessary. In terms of the time frame, the focus lies on the period of the 'imperial heyday', i.e. the years between the suppression of the Great Rebellion 1857–9 and the outbreak of the First World War. I submit that it was during this period, when British rule had acquired an official character and the 'politics of colonial difference'[6] was most pronounced, that the undisciplined drinking behaviour of members of the 'ruling race' became most perilous for colonial officials. However, in order to understand the particular social and political configurations in that phase, it is helpful to first have a brief look at the historical roots of the European alcohol problem in India. Before I start this historical sketch, let me try to develop my argument further while situating it in the existing historiography on colonial South Asia.

The history of drugs in British India has recently received a great deal of attention from historians. As a result, we now possess a fairly sophisticated and nuanced literature on the economic and political consequences of the production and trade of mood-altering substances like cannabis[7] and opium[8] as well as of the social, cultural and political implications of their consumption. Although no less enmeshed with the economy and politics of the Raj than these exotic stimulants, alcohol still belongs to the psychoactive commodities that are profoundly under-researched by scholars of modern South Asian history. The best part of the small body of literature that is engaging with the alcohol problem at all, examines the British politics of gaining control over the liquor revenue by enforcing a standardized variety of drinks and taxation[9] as well as (proto-)nationalistic efforts to resist such attempts.[10] While the existing literature sheds some light on Indian drinking customs and indigenous reactions to colonial alcohol policies, we know much less about the flip side of the coin: the role played by alcohol in the 'white' colonial society. This is surprising, given the fact that social and cultural historians have long pointed to the fact that regulation of the access to alcohol and the control of the actual drinking behaviour are crucial elements in the constitution of authority and the fixation of difference. As Prasun Chatterjee has observed, 'The social hierarchies of class, caste and gender as well as differences across culture and religious affiliation manifest themselves around consumption patterns and cultural attitudes to alcohol.'[11] Although the analysis of colonial drinking cultures thus promises to provide insights into processes that are crucial for the imperial politics of difference, the picture we possess is still one-sided. The few existing studies addressing the issue of the colonizers' drinking habits concentrate almost exclusively on its military dimension. Thus, some proponents of military history of South Asia have recently attended to the problem of excessive consumption of liquor in the European regiments of the British Indian Army and analyzed official strategies to curb it.[12] Douglas Peers in particular has reminded us that the efficacy of the armed forces was perceived as vital for the survival of the Indian dominion. Since alcoholism was undeniably a serious problem in the 'white' detachments, the colonial state felt a pressure to control and curtail the soldiers' access to alcoholic beverages in order to safeguard the most fundamental imperial interests.[13]

Important as such insights are, they should not mislead one into believing that the perils arising from immoderate drinking among Europeans for the colonial rulers were restricted to the misbehaviour of the notoriously 'drunk and riotous' 'Tommy'.[14] The three quotes given above indicate that, over almost a century, the containment of alcohol abuse by Europeans *in general* was regarded as central to the maintenance of power in Britain's most important colony. For one thing, they suggest that binge drinking was not restricted to the barracks and cantonments: it was prevalent in other segments of 'white' colonial society, too. Second, they point to the fact that – apart from the obvious threat emanating from a colonial army that had become dysfunctional on account of the constant intoxication of its soldiers – there was another, more subtle menace at work. The very existence of an alcohol problem among the members of the self-styled 'ruling race' called into question the legitimizing myth of an alleged civilizational superiority that was undergirding the colonial 'rule' or, rather, 'politics of difference'.[15] Especially in the late Victorian era, when alcoholism was increasingly construed as a 'disease of the will'[16] in the West, the presence of white drunkards in Britain's colonies could be easily read as symbolizing the loss of imperial 'pluck' and self-control.

Third, the middle quote above, from the *Friend of India*, implies that, though the popularity of alcoholic beverages was apparently characteristic of 'countrymen of all classes',[17] it was particularly the drinking habits of the lower orders that caused the greatest concern of colonial officials and temperance activists alike. To some extent, this attitude certainly reflects the metropolitan elite discourses of the time that posited an innate affinity between the lower classes and intemperance. Fuelled by social Darwinism, they viewed the drinking practices of the degenerated denizens of 'darkest England'[18] as a burning political issue affecting society as a whole rather than as a moral concern for the individual conscience.[19] At the same time, however, it might be safe to assume that colonial administrators, missionaries and representatives of the medical profession targeted the lower segments of Anglo-Indian society, on the grounds that they were more visible for the colonized population. There was a widespread fear that European soldiers drunk on parade, gangs of intoxicated white sailors touring the port towns in search of amusement or European vagrants lying around in the bazaars after collapsing 'under the influence', 'exhibit[ed] to the natives of India, a disgusting specimen of the European character, – the Christian character, and even of human nature itself'.[20] Although this anxiety flourished fully in the last third of the nineteenth century its roots can be traced back to a much earlier period.

II

The gradual expansion of the East India Company (EIC) from the early seventeenth century went hand in hand with an equally steady growth of the European population in the subcontinent. Even in this pioneering phase, when the number of Europeans living in the Company's possessions barely surpassed 1,000, the directors were perfectly aware of the problems arising out of the high levels of alcohol consumption prevalent in all segments of Anglo-Indian[21] society. It is well documented that the upper echelons of the Company hierarchy (councillors, merchants, factors etc.) indulged in drinking astounding amounts of equally astonishing varieties of imported alcoholic beverages. An inventory dating from 1717, for instance, lists the range of brews regularly imported into Madras as 'Mountain Wine, Rhenish, Syder, Galicia, Florence, Hock, Canary, Brandy, Claret, Ale, Beer, Shyrash Wine'.[22] From various autobiographical accounts, we know that these items were consumed by Europeans 'of class' in generous quantities during and especially after the two main meals of the day.[23] The reasons for the popularity of strong drinks in this early period were manifold and cannot be reduced simply to the boredom of 'life in the station'. Thus, very often the poor quality of the local drinking water made imported alcoholic drinks seem to be the healthier alternative for many Britons in the Company's Eastern possessions. Moreover, liquor survived the long voyage from Europe much better than beer and it was only with the success of Hodgson's Indian Pale Ale in the first decades of the nineteenth century, that beer was available in decent quality, large quantities and at an affordable price.[24]

That said, it is hard to disagree with the contemporary observers who speculated as early as the late seventeenth century that the popularity of drink combined with a heavy meat biased diet was partly responsible for the short average life expectancy of the Company's servants in this period.[25] Even though it took some time for the majority of Anglo-Indians to realize that there was a 'connexion between drink and mortality bills',[26] by the early decades of the nineteenth century this had become common knowledge. In addition, medical experts were convinced that over-drinking was also often responsible for the growing number of Europeans that had to be sent to the newly created lunatic asylums.[27] That the old India hands on the spot and the EIC authorities back in London were concerned with the problem is reflected by the lengthy passages warning of the social ostracism and physical deterioration resulting from overindulgence in 'spirits' in the most widespread advice manual for Europeans in India.[28] The 'griffins'[29] were made aware that: '[…] if habitual inebriation be in question, the unhappy man pursues his career, either until the grave may receive his dropsical remains, or the Invalid Establishment affords him asylum against the mortifying neglect of his late associates'.[30]

In line with a gradual paradigm shift in the global discourse on alcohol,[31] medical arguments clearly outweighed moral ones during the second half of the nineteenth century. Accordingly, Britons preparing their voyage to India in the 1870s were warned that, while a glass of beer and claret were acceptable, 'any […] ardent spirit must be shunned as poison and, like all other poison, should be taken only under medical advice'.[32] The longevity of the official anti-alcohol discourse should not distract from the fact that not many among the male members of the Anglo-Indian elite appear to have taken such warnings seriously. As we know from a broad array of Raj memoirs and other sources, collective as well individual drinking of 'ardent spirits' remained widespread among army officers, colonial administrators and non-officials, although it rarely took place in public.[33]

Right from the outset, problems emanating from the alcohol consumption of the European community's less privileged segments were still more unsettling for the EIC authorities than the drinking proclivities of wayward Company servants. Chief amongst the reasons for this drinking double standard was the fact that soldiers and sailors, who formed the bulk of the white underclass, could not afford the imported drinks so popular among the elites. They therefore frequently turned to Indian spirits and most notably to *arrack,*[34] or *punch*,[35] the colonial cocktail *par excellence*.[36] If contemporary sources are to be trusted, these drinks were not only much cheaper than their imported equivalents but often also of dubious quality. Emanating, as they did, from an Oriental environment that, from the early nineteenth century, was increasingly construed as hostile and dangerous,[37] they were held as threatening both the health and morality of the European consumer and simultaneously reducing the distance to the life-world of the 'natives'. Thus, the author of the 1825 edition of the *East India Guide and Vademecum* cautioned his readers that 'such beverages are deleterious, rarely failing, in the first instance to injure and ultimately disgracing all who yield to the temptation'.[38] Due to their financial situation, however, soldiers and sailors especially had few alternatives to the 'country' liquor and consequently most of them 'yielded to the temptation' on a regular basis.

The results could be devastating for the ruling power: intoxicated by local drinks, the very troops that had been recruited to impose law and order, frequently caused order problems themselves, through 'wanton and cruel assaults'[39] on Indians, by 'lying drunk and naked by the roadside'[40] or engaging, as they sometimes did, 'in a little amateur highway robbery'.[41] Given these obnoxious side-effects of the availability of cheap local brews, it is hardly surprising that already by the 1760s attempts were being made to curtail the European community's access to Indian liquor stores.[42] However, even a century later such efforts were carried out half-heartedly at best, since they were hampered by a 'constant struggle between the *Abkarry* [i.e. excise] Authorities and the Police, the former endeavouring to increase by every possible means the number of shops, and consequently their revenue, and the latter to keep them out'.[43] It goes without saying, that this kind of 'drug *realpolitik*'[44] was a standard problem that advocates of temperance or prohibition had to cope with in a wide variety of settings during the course of the nineteenth century.

Apart from the regimental canteens and the shops of native liquor vendors – who were in need of a license granted by the EIC – , the centres of plebeian conviviality were the infamous urban taverns and 'punch houses', the highest concentration of which could be found in Calcutta, Bombay and Madras.[45] They were often owned by time-expired soldiers (many of whom were apparently Irish) or Eurasian 'half-castes' – a growing community that was in search of new sources of income ever since they had been barred from army service in early nineteenth century – , as is reflected by their eclectic names such as 'Paddy Goose' or 'Portuguese George'.[46]

Once Company rule was firmly established and the adventurers and nabobs of the eighteenth century were gradually replaced by a new generation of administrators of the bureaucratic type, the punch houses came to be regarded as no-go areas for members of the respectable sections of white society. Thus, the 1810 edition of the *East India Vademecum* warned that 'should [a gentleman] so far lower himself as to associate with the ordinary company of the common drinking-room he is irretrievably gone'.[47] In like vein, reputable citizens (both European and Indian) often complained about the proliferation of 'punch houses' in the port cities. An anonymous writer to the editor of the *Bengal Hurkaru*, for instance, considered it a 'great shame' that the police tolerated the spread of these establishments, resulting in the 'utmost annoyance' of the families living nearby. The disgust of the European elite was only partly provoked by the 'bustling noise kept up in these houses during the night'.[48] More important was the fact that punch houses were associated with 'evils' – or 'social diseases' as the late nineteenth century parlance had it – that were viewed as being closely related, indeed inseparable from 'intemperance', namely gambling and prostitution.[49]

Already, decades before the middle of the nineteenth century, there was widespread unease with the presence of low-class Europeans in India, an unease that was, in turn, interrelated to the uncontrolled drinking ascribed to their class. The problem became particularly pressing after the licence system that restricted the immigration of Europeans into India was finally abolished in 1833 and the non-official population grew almost five-fold within a few decades. The major influx of non-official Europeans from a working class background began in the early 1850s mainly in connection with the construction of the Indian railways and telegraphs and gained in intensity during the last quarter of the century.[50]

However, the mere increase in numbers cannot explain the dwindling tolerance of the ruling elite with the plebeian drinking culture. It is important to bear in mind that, roughly between 1830 and 1860, an ideological shift in the self-identity of the colonizers had taken place. As in other parts of the British Empire, so in India, too, the growing 'race consciousness' that was characteristic of the late Victorian era encouraged aggressive self-assertion *vis-à-vis* the 'native' population throughout the spectrum of European colonial society.[51] It is hardly surprising, then, that in the context of this new self-perception of the British as 'lords of humankind'[52] chosen by providence to carry out a civilizing mission in a hostile environment, the existence of a 'residuum' of 'European [...] slaves to the bottle'[53] was much more disturbing than before and an urgent need to deal with the problem began to be felt among a colonial elite fond of 'maintaining its high refinement and asserting its dignified purity'.[54] It is to the culmination of the contestations over low-class drinking during the high noon of the empire that we are now going to turn.

III

Similar to the contemporary perception in Europe, in British India, too, port cities were seen as the sites where drinking caused the greatest problems. This has partly to do with the image of the maritime professions that were strongly represented in these places. Although situated on the middle rungs of colonial society, and at times described as 'intelligent, skilful, and gentlemanly men',[55] the Europeans in the Bengal Pilot Service acquired particular notoriety for being drunk on duty in the 1860s. The service, whose task it was to guide the ships through the Hooghly to Calcutta was founded in the seventeenth century and employed around 150 Europeans by the mid-century.[56] In the early 1860s, a number of serious incidents brought the prevalence of heavy drinking among the European pilots to the notice of the Government of Bengal. Thus, in December 1861 Master Pilot W.T. Long and Mate Pilot E. Cole were convicted of neglect of duty after having grounded the French steamship *Ephrem* because they had been 'perfectly drunk' on the job.[57] How ugly the face of European alcohol abuse could be is also evident from the case of Licensed Mate H. Williams who was dismissed from the service in 1863 on the same grounds. The statement of a witness before the committee of enquiry gives a vivid impression of the annoyance which the excessive drinking of individual Europeans caused both for compatriots and 'natives':

> At 1 a.m. I observed Mr. Williams fall off the couch and lay upon the deck until the end of my watch, that was at 2 a.m. I observed a stream of water running from Mr. Williams person as if he had wet himself. [...]
>
> I again went below, but was roused by a Lascar calling out – 'Sahib panne ma geer jatta'.[58] [sic.] I ran on deck again, found Mr. Williams on the hen-coop leeward with Mr. Beale, holding him down by his legs. The rain was pouring down this time in torrents but Mr. Williams insisted that he wanted to bathe. [...] I saw nothing of Mr. Williams until 7 a.m. when he was dancing a jig in the between deck. He continued very noisy all day and asking officers if they would not drink with him [...] and at 5 p.m. Mr Stout put him below under arrest.[59]

That these were not singular cases is demonstrated by a number of similar files in the Marine records of the Government of Bengal. The alcohol abuse prevailing among the pilots in Bengal thus certainly posed a very palpable danger to the colonial state, as it affected a service that was crucial for the economic exploitation and military domination of India. Nonetheless, European prestige among the colonized was hardly at stake here, because the incidents happened on the river and the ensuing law cases rarely made it to the public. Things were utterly different in the case of ordinary European sailors who were not only much more numerous but also highly visible for the Indian population while they were ashore.[60]

The first reliable census of Calcutta's European population dating from 1866 lists the total number of permanent European inhabitants at about 11,000 against more than 2,000 sailors who were 'transient members of white Calcutta'.[61] According to other sources, this number could even double during seasonal peak times.[62] Thus, it seems reasonable to assume that the average sailor population must have been around 3,000. 300–500 of them were unemployed or 'distressed' seamen, sailors without affiliation to one of the ships lying in harbour who would stay for several months or even longer in the city.[63] Jobless seamen not confined to jail were usually residing either in the Sailors' Home or private boarding houses concentrated in the 'grey area' between 'White Town' and 'Black Town',[64] and namely around Lal Bazar Street (popularly known as 'Flag Street' because of the string of flags across the street showing the way to punch-houses, cheap eating-places and brothels).[65] There were also a noteworthy number of seamen being compelled to extend their sojourn in Calcutta as they were lying ill in one of the city's hospitals or had been taken to the lunatic asylum.

That the presence of such a large community of sailors was suffered by the city's respectable white citizens as a necessary evil only is evident from government records[66] and English newspapers dating back to the 1780s. Complaints against the sailor population and their drinking habits continued to appear occasionally in the press throughout the early nineteenth century,[67] but it was only in the 1860s that the problem took on so threatening a dimension as to call for massive government intervention.

In early October 1864 the coastal areas lining the Bay of Bengal were hit by a cyclone, which proved devastating for the capital of British India.[68] The port area was affected considerably. As many as 36 vessels were completely destroyed and 96 severely damaged by the storm.[69] Hundreds of seamen lost their ships and their numbers added to the usual pool of those kept on reserve to replace incapacitated seamen, casualties and deserters. Within a couple of days the total number of unemployed and shipwrecked European sailors in the 'city of palaces' rose to more than 1,000, many of whom came in conflict with the police, after random attacks on Indians, drunken punch-ups in the city's taverns or robbing their own compatriots.[70]

As a result of the constant trouble caused by the city's distressed sailor population, the Lieutenant-Governor of Bengal eventually requested the Sanitary Commission in August 1865 to produce a report on the 'State of the Sailors in Calcutta'.[71] The Commission, it was hoped, would not only find out the causes of the high unemployment rates but also provide information on their actual living conditions. Major Malleson, who headed the working group, submitted the results of his detailed enquiry to the Government of Bengal in February 1866.[72]

The first issue touched upon in the Malleson Report was the health of the sailors. The high mortality prevailing among this group had been a major concern for the colonial authorities for some time. Now the appalling housing conditions of the sailors as well as their alleged lack of hygiene and cleanliness were largely blamed for the frightening death rate. The discovery of enclaves of dirt and disease in areas of the colonial metropolis that were predominantly inhabited by Europeans was more than disconcerting for the colonial authorities, who had always tended to associate these features with the densely populated 'Black Town' inhabited by Indians.[73]

An even greater blow to claims of moral superiority of the 'imperial race' resulted from Malleson's description of the seamen's drinking habits which were also believed to contribute to increasing sailor mortality. The excessive consumption of alcohol had been a problem in the British navy and merchant marine for a long time[74] and the propensity to drink was certainly part of the image of the sailor current in contemporary elite discourse, where he was usually portrayed as morally weak and easily influenced by all sorts of temptations.[75] In a colonial setting, his alleged lack of self-restraint rendered 'Jack Tar' (as the British seaman was popularly known) very similar to the 'natives' in the eyes of many upper-class observers. This trope of racial boundary-crossing is also important in a more direct sense: Once more, it was widely assumed that the worst effects of alcohol abuse did not arise from the consumption of 'pure and sound European brandy' – sailors were given their daily rations of rum or grog on board ships as part of their regular diet[76] – but of poisonous 'country liquor'. It was understood that liquor sold in native shops was not only 'drugged with several powerful narcotics' but also 'doctored to the point of giving cholera to him who swallows it almost as certainly as a pistol fired into the mouth blows the head off'.[77] Hence several medical experts proposed to prohibit the selling of 'that most intoxicating and deleterious of all drinks, the native Rum or "Doasta"'[78] to Europeans. *Doasta* was the cheapest variety of Indian spirits. It is hard to establish how exactly it was produced, but according to a contemporary dictionary of the sailors' slang it was 'an inferior spirit, often drugged or doctored for unwary sailors in the pestiferous dens of filthy Calcutta and other sea-ports in India'.[79] That the bad image of Indian liquor was not limited to Calcutta becomes evident though in the account of the 'sailor question' in Bombay, written by Michael Joyce, a former police officer. Having described at length the degree of 'intemperance' prevalent among European sailors in Bombay, Joyce mentions that Indian liquor shop owners had reacted to the strong demand by offering a cheap brand of *arrack* mixed with chillies and opium under the label 'Sailor Jack'.[80]

However, this line of argument did not remain uncontested. Some critics soon pointed to the results of an official enquiry conducted in 1858 where it had been 'conclusively prov[en] that the excessive drunkenness and its results' among Europeans resorting to the native shops 'was due rather to the quantity than the quality of the liquor drunk in them'.[81] Accordingly, official endeavours to remedy this evil pursued a double strategy. On the one hand, the authorities tried to control the quality of alcoholic beverages and regulate the access to liquor stores (particularly the 'native' ones) by granting fewer licenses and restricting the opening hours.[82] On the other hand, attempts to educate seamen, to persuade them to be 'moral and religious' and abstain from heavy drinking were encouraged.[83] The new moralizing agenda found a very practical expression in the relocation of Calcutta's Sailor's Home. The Home was shifted to a new location, partly because the building had become too small to accommodate the ever-growing number of distressed seamen and partly because it was situated 'in the very centre of the touters' hell'[84] which had provoked constant criticism both from medical officers and missionaries. The medical expert and evangelical preacher Norman Chevers tried to convince an audience of white sailors of the advantages of temperance by invoking their 'manly pride' as well as their fear of God:

> You are not poor men: you are, as a body, rich in health and in an amount of strength and manly beauty such as is granted by Providence to scarcely any other race under the sun. Your Father, who made you in His image cares for and loves you in that equal measure in which he cares for and loves all His children; and you violate his law and hopelessly separate yourselves from him when you deface His image in this abominable disease and death which drunkenness engenders.[85]

As Chevers' warning clearly demonstrates, the official concern about the sailors' drinking habits was linked to anxieties about the spread of venereal

Figure 4.1 'Two dishevelled sailors', in Lal Bazar Calcutta (1860s). By permission of the British Library, London.

Source: 'Two dishevelled sailors, in "Lal Bazar", Calcutta'. Pencil, pen-and-ink drawing, c. 1860s. British Library London, BL WD 4336.

diseases.[86] In the vein of metropolitan discourses on the lower classes, drunkenness was seen as 'engendering lust' which could not but result in the infection with sexually transmitted diseases. Such fears were additionally fed by the first results of the emerging scientific interest in the 'sailor class'. A medical officer, who accompanied a large party of sailors from Calcutta to Assam in 1863, discovered that 90 per cent of them had contracted syphilis during their stay in the port.[87] Here again, the close physical involvement with 'natives' was held largely responsible for the contamination of the seamen as the majority of them visited Indian prostitutes, rather than the few and expensive European and 'Eurasian' sex workers available.[88] As Philippa Levine and others have shown, the concept of venereal diseases was, much like the discourse on alcohol, intensely affected by racial ideology. Analogous to the unfavourable effects ascribed to various varieties of 'country liquor', it was not only widely held that 'native' women were the main carriers of syphilis and gonorrhoea because of their low standards of hygiene, it was also supposed that such diseases were much more dreadful if they were contracted not from European but from 'Oriental' women.[89]

Seamen's health was not the only concern of the colonial authorities. Even before the official interest in the sailor population had led to an increased effort in data collection about drunkenness, disease and debauchery, another facet of the seafarers' behaviour had been the object of statistics compiled by the colonial government: their 'disorderly' or even criminal conduct. As far as Calcutta is concerned, the sources leave no doubt that the sailors' unenviable notoriety in this regard was not completely unfounded. They were indeed largely responsible for the high crime rates among Europeans. In 1855, for instance, the magistrate tried more than 500 cases in which seamen were involved. Next to the more obvious breaches of marine law like 'wilful neglect of duty',[90] 'disobedience' or 'desertion', there were 248 sailors involved in violent assaults, several of them resulting in loss of life. The Police Commissioner of Calcutta observed 'that in four of the nine manslaughters, and five of the eight cases of cutting and wounding, the offenders were sailors sojourning at this port'.[91] It is also remarkable that in 1864 as many as 12 out of 21 inmates of the prison in Ootacamund – one of the few jails that had been especially constructed to accommodate European long-term convicts[92] – were former sailors, sent over from Calcutta.[93]

The frequent occurrence of crime soon resulted in special police controls with the aim of disarming sailors of their 'clasp knives and other offensive weapons'.[94] Nevertheless, drunken brawls in the 'Punch houses' remained quite common, as did disputes over money in the brothels, which were also often the causes for quarrels and punch-ups, sometimes even for murder. The evidence cited in the police records clearly suggests that most criminal offences went hand in hand with excessive drinking[95] and not seldom the taverns, punch houses and native liquor shops were the sites where the severest felonies were committed. Thus, in 1858, a party of sailors lynched a Bengali tavern keeper whom they suspected of selling poisonous liquor by hanging him from Kidderpore Bridge.[96] The violence was often completely arbitrary. The following is a rather typical example:

> On the 18th of February [1855] a party of sailors, ripe for mischief, were parading a part of town most infrequently visited by persons of their class, and were amusing themselves by striking more or less every person passing them, or destroying the articles (water jars &c.) they carried. At length they entered a liquor shop and called for liquor, which on getting they refused to pay for, at the same time destroying the bottle it was served in, by throwing it at the vendor and decamping.[97]

There are dozens of references to similar cases of random attacks on the Indian population in the police reports and in almost all of them the perpetrators were in a state of intoxication. This particular excursion, it ought to be added, ended in a clash with Malayan seamen and the murder of an Indian *chaukidar* (watchman) who had dared to interfere to end the dispute.

The question almost inevitably arises as to how the indigenous population reacted to such incidents? Was the official *angst*, that the 'disorderly' behaviour of the seafaring specimens of the ruling race might endanger the slender basis of British power, a mere product of colonial imagination? There are at least some indications that this was not the case. As far as we can judge from articles in the 'native' press,[98] the elite section of the Indian population in the seaport towns affected by the problem was well aware of the misdemeanours committed by intoxicated European seamen and condemned them in the strongest terms. Describing the 'broils and mischievous frolics of drunken sailors in the Native quarters' of Bombay, a Gujarati newspaper states in 1868 that Europeans of this kind had become 'a curse to the native inhabitants of the town by their rude and lawless pranks'.[99]

Already decades before unemployment had become a mass phenomenon in Indian ports, the British had realized what an effect the presence of 'drunk and disorderly' Europeans could have for their missionary aspirations. The account of one Reverend Wilson, a clergyman living in Bombay during the 1830s and 1840s, marvellously illustrates this point:

> In the discharge of my duties as a Missionary to the heathen, I go to the high-ways and hedges to invite sinners to come to the marriage supper of the Son of God; I announce the glad tidings of Salvation through our crucified Redeemer, and I speak of the sanctifying influence of his gospel. As I proceed in my discourse my attention is frequently directed to a gang of drunken sailors or soldiers, bearing the Christian name, staggering along the streets in a state of intoxication; and I am sneeringly asked by the natives: 'Would you like to become us like these your kindred'? I need not to tell you [...] what my answer is. [...] The unbelievers triumph; and it is the promise of God alone, which can sustain me and enable me to repeat my message.[100]

IV

It goes without saying that European alcohol abuse was not restricted to the maritime professions, nor was it confined to the large seaport towns in the subcontinent. Other sections of 'white' society caused similar anxieties among the gentlemanly elite of the Raj. Particularly the members of the planter community must be mentioned in this respect, not least because they mostly lived in remote areas at the frontiers of the colonial territory, removed from the direct control of the government. On account of their distance from the large Presidency towns, which were often perceived as bridgeheads of Western civilization,[101] as well as the constant exposure to 'native society', they were seen as rather dubious figures by the colonial authorities. Moreover, the sight of a European drew much more attention from the local population in rural areas than in the cosmopolitan port cities, and cases of 'European misconduct' hence seriously threatened to undermine the civilizing ambitions of the colonial state. And the colonial anxieties were not unfounded. Throughout the nineteenth century the indigo and later tea planters were watched with suspicion by the administrative elites,[102] not only because they were notoriously violent against their Indian 'coolies',[103] but also because of their alleged proclivity to heavy drinking. This became particularly disturbing when the consumption of liquor did not take place in the privacy of their homes but in public, thus exposing the 'depravity of the European character' to the native gaze. In the early 1880s, Colonel Henry S. Olcott, the American founder of the Theosophical Society, was touring Northern India. The account he gives of one of his public lectures in a small *mofussil* station in Bihar is most instructive in this regard. Even Olcott, who had a very particular background and certainly did not belong to the colonial establishment, felt offended by the uncivilized behaviour of the 'rowdy element' within the European population:

> A most unpleasant and to me as an European mortifying thing happened at the Dumraon lecture. A drunken, foul-mouthed indigo planter came with a bottle of brandy and a basket of soda water bottles, and while I was lecturing kept drinking pegs. Fancy what was the impression made upon the audience of sober, self-respectful and intelligent Hindus by this misconduct. Can anyone be surprised by the contempt in which they hold the dominant race whose social habits are so different from their own standard of propriety?[104]

It was precisely the occurrence of this type of 'mortifying' event and the fear of alienating the 'sober and self-respectful' Indian elites which influenced the legislation introduced around a decade earlier to check European 'loaferism'. Unlike planters, who were certainly troublesome but at least economically independent from the colonial state, the lowest segment of the Europeans in India lived in truly precarious conditions and not infrequently offered a sad spectacle to the Indian population. Although 'mean whites' had caused trouble time and again, legislative measures were not regarded as necessary, as long as the overall number of 'black sheep' belonging to the 'dangerous classes' outside the confining garrisons or remote up-country plantations had been relatively small.[105] It was only in the 1860s that white vagrancy became a pressing problem for the colonial authorities. Several thousand of the so-called European 'loafers' – most of them ex-soldiers, stranded sailors or unemployed railwaymen – criss-crossed the subcontinent in the early 1860s, making a living from begging, extortion and petty crime.[106] The Government of India reacted with the promulgation of the European Vagrancy Act of 1869, which made it an offence for Europeans to loiter around without any visible means of subsistence and provided for the erection of workhouses for Europeans, which were built in the capitals of all the presidencies of British India.[107]

It is noteworthy that drinking in public was one of the facets of the 'loafer' problem that was regularly mentioned, with particular contempt, in official or semi-official reports. Alcoholism was a major problem among the European and Eurasian loafer population, especially in the urban centres. A police report from Bombay shows, for example, that of the 3,869 people who had been arrested in 1867 for being 'drunk and incapable' more than a quarter were Europeans or 'Hindoo-Britons' (Eurasians), even though these communities made up for less than 5 per cent of the city's population.[108] Such behaviour was hardly tolerable even in the Presidency towns with their fairly large European population living for the most part in clearly segregated areas (or in Army barracks). Their presence was a still greater nuisance in the *bazaar*s of smaller *mofussil* towns where the sight of helplessly drunk Europeans tended to 'create disturbances'[109] and thus inflicted further damage on the official policy of maintaining the social distance between rulers and ruled. In villages, the locals seem to have been mostly so intimidated by the presence of a 'sahib' that, as far as the scarce evidence goes, they often supported him with their modest means – a situation that many loafers apparently exploited to stay in a village for several days extorting food, tobacco or even drink from the villagers.[110] Thus it was the uncontrolled mobility of the loafers, their peripatetic or 'bohemian'[111] lifestyle, which made them particularly dangerous for the colonial state. While the planters' radius was largely confined to the vicinity of their plantation, even the remotest villager could now potentially realize through the presence of a drunken white hobo that the claims to racial superiority of the ruling power were ridiculous.

According to the popular Victorian theory alluded to above, the Indian climate considerably aggravated the effects of alcohol addiction[112] and hence accelerated a man's 'descent from honest industry and independence to ruinous idleness' as the director of a European Strangers' Home in Allahabad put it.[113] To stop this fatal process, he suggested that the inebriates should be reclaimed by placing them under strict supervision and administering them a special medicine 'for the cure of that internal craving for drink'.[114] Interestingly, the remedy against the 'internal craving' that was now tested on the 'white' flotsam and jetsam in Allahabad had originally been developed to combat the alcohol problem in the United States.[115] This single case does certainly not allow to draw safe conclusions, but it could be read as an early example of the medicalization of the liquor problem in British India reflecting the increasing convergence of the global discourse on alcohol. Especially in North America representatives of the medical professions were ever more successfully appropriating the authority to solve the 'alcohol problem' at around the same time,[116] and it would certainly be a rewarding task for future research to find out if there indeed existed a transfer of their ideas to the British Empire, for instance via articles in medical journals.

At any rate, the Reverend's views were not uncontested. Most colonial officials in British India seem to have been less optimistic as to the chances for successful rehabilitation of 'confirmed drunkards' through special medication imported from the United States and some of them suggested much harsher measures. Thus, the Commissioner of Police, Bombay, reported in 1868:

> There are in Bombay at the present time about a score of this class whose normal state is that of helpless incapacity from drink, and who are as familiar with the House of Correction as with the Back Street Grog Shop and from this state of vicious lethargy there is at present no means of reclaiming these miserable men, who are no sooner released from prison than they beg or extort a few Annas which is immediately spent in drink [...] The Magistrates being empowered to flog such men might diminish the evil.[117]

Just how closely intertwined the problems of alcoholism and 'loaferism' were in official eyes is also evident from a statement by the Bombay Police Magistrate. Asked his opinion of the planned vagrancy legislation, he declared that 'greater surveillance over the numerous dens of intemperance and debauchery' (the grog shops and brothels) would probably have a greater effect in checking 'loaferism' than the erection of workhouses.[118]

Public drunkenness of Europeans was particularly disturbing for the colonial elites when women were involved. Although the group of 'confirmed drunkards' among European females in India was not large in number, their symbolic significance can hardly be overestimated. The workhouse reports provide us with the details of some of these female vagrants' life stories. To be sure, the majority of European women who fell on black days in British India were soldiers' wives,[119] who had gained a reputation for being 'greater drunkards than the men'[120] at an early stage. But there were women from other backgrounds as well. Rather untypical for the career of a female vagrant, but nevertheless a proof that the boundary between female vagrancy and prostitution was difficult to establish, is the case of one Mrs Mahon. The daughter of a timber merchant from North Shields in north-eastern England, she had met her future Anglo-Indian husband in her home town, while he was training for a career in engineering. She followed him to Calcutta, where they got married in 1905. Mahon was employed by the East India Railway and they lived together for some years in Jamalpur 'where they drank heavily'.[121] When her husband left her in 1911, she had to face the difficulties of a single European woman's life in the colony:

> After his departure, the woman lived with another Anglo-Indian for about three years, but in 1914 she was rescued by the Oxford Mission and sent to their Home at Barisal, where she remained for ten months. She then returned to Calcutta where she gave a good deal of trouble owing to her dissolute habits. She was again rescued and sent to a Roman Catholic Home at Bangalore. Here, her behaviour was so scandalous that it was impossible to retain her, and she was sent back to Calcutta in August 1916.

> She was arrested for disorderly conduct in September 1916 and declared a vagrant and sent to the workhouse. On her release she again gave trouble and was sent back to the workhouse.[122]

Clearly, alcohol addiction is seen here as the root cause of female 'downfall',[123] not least because in Victorian middle and upper-class circles, 'the debauching impact of alcoholic excess on the female frame'[124] was generally regarded as much more pronounced than on the male. Such double transgressions of gender as well as racial norms made female vagrancy an extremely disturbing phenomenon.[125]

For the male vagrants, too, excessive drinking in itself was often not seen as the only transgressive act. Strikingly similar to the arguments made about the 'distressed sailors' we have discussed earlier, begging and crime were likewise regarded as natural results of the vagrants' drinking habits. According to a widely spread view, alcohol catalyzed a process of degeneration that turned the white riff-raff of the Raj into a threat for their own fellow countrymen on more than a symbolic level. Thus, a writer in an Anglo-Indian newspaper complained in 1866 that it was no longer possible even in the remotest up-country station to leave an English lady alone in a house or keep the doors unlocked during the day as the loafers were 'increasing in shamelessness' every year.[126] Sharing this view, the Bombay Magistrate warned the government that 'the lives and property of the [European] community of Bombay are endangered by the great number of European vagrants (or loafers) who appear to have spread themselves over the whole Island' and mentioned several cases of 'impudent robbery in pure daylight'.[127]

Since plebeian drinking practices were regarded as the root of crime, indecency and various other kinds of evil[128] by 'respectable' Anglo-Indians, colonial administrators and missionaries alike, it was only logical that the inculcation of temperate habits was also at the heart of the process of reclamation that ought to be realized in the newly opened Government Workhouses. The temperance agenda was hence clearly reflected in the workhouse regime.[129] In Bombay, for instance, alcohol was strictly prohibited on the premises of the institution and it was hoped that constant surveillance and strict enforcement of a rigorous daily routine would eventually break even the 'hardened loafers' who were generally believed to have 'an intense dislike [for] the regularity, and [...] the painful sobriety which obtain in the Workhouse'.[130] However, an examination of the copious workhouse records collected by the Judicial Department would suggest that the institutions apparently more often than not failed in 'making better men' of their inmates by curing them of their alcohol addiction. The following report by Captain Walshe, governor of the workhouse in Bombay, is not untypical. Referring to the case of an inmate named John Smith, who was declared a vagrant in 1884, Walshe remarks, somewhat disillusioned:

> For a few days he behaved himself well and worked. Wanting something for maintenance and clothing, the Officer gave him a few rupees. For a

> couple of days after this he went on all right and then absented himself from his work and was found drunk on several occasions on the public roads and was prosecuted for that offence. He was then turned away as every means to make a better man of him failed and he would not leave off drinking. [...] I myself tried all I could to reclaim him, but I fear that there is not the least possible chance to keep him from drink and to make a better man of him. If allowed to be free from the Workhouse he will only again go about (as often he has done before) to beg and drink.[131]

V

The present chapter, it is hoped, has helped to substantiate the hypothesis that, in more ways than one, intoxicating substances 'were at the heart of empires'[132] and that alcohol is no exception in this regard. More specifically, it has demonstrated that the study of alcohol in a colonial context can offer valuable insights into the social history of imperialism and colonialism that are otherwise difficult to get at. A closer look at the moral economy of alcohol in colonial India in general and the official policies of dealing with European consumption of liquor in the age of high imperialism in particular lay bare many of the contradictions and ambivalences that are characteristic of the wider imperial project. The most striking observation, perhaps, is that the question was apparently less *if* drinking was acceptable for Europeans in a colonial setting but rather *who* drank *what* and *where*. The multi-layered drinking codes that existed in colonial India thus point to deep internal fissures within the European community, which was certainly not the homogeneous 'middle-class aristocracy' some historians want us to believe.[133] Most of the pre-assumptions and ascriptions underlying the internal stratification of the 'men (and, for that matter, women) who ruled India'[134] were imported from the metropole and decisively affected the colonial debate on the liquor question. As was the case with the lower elements of the working classes back home, the excessive consumption of alcohol by white underlings in India was particularly shocking for the colonial elites for it 'exemplified the responsibility of the poor for their failings and dramatized the threat they posed to the rest of society'.[135] In both arenas the middle and upper-class segments of European society pointed to their own habits of discipline and self-control which, besides other things, entitled them to drink 'in a civilized manner' in the anonymity of a bungalow or club. The examples of pilots and planters, however, have indicated that such moral ascriptions on the basis of class identity can be misleading since these groups cannot be ranked among the lower class Europeans in India and yet had acquired a reputation for drunkenness in public. Although it is open to debate if 'booze' was in fact 'what ke[pt] the machine going' and acted as 'the cement of empire',[136] as Mr Flory, the protagonist in George Orwell's novel *Burmese Days* famously claimed, there can hardly be a doubt that alcohol did play an important role in the social life of the Raj, by 'strengthening the masculine ties'[137] in virtually all segments of colonial society.

It has further been argued that, apart from reinforcing the internal class divide imported from the 'motherland', undue alcohol consumption by both elite and non-elite Europeans in India posed a threat to the ruling power on two accounts. On a very obvious level, the functioning of key institutions of the colonial regime like the army, navy and merchant marine, pilot service (one might as well add the railways) were adversely affected by the prevalence of binge drinking among whites of various social backgrounds. Secondly, and equally importantly, the symbolic menace deriving from the public demonstration that British rule was not inevitably linked with 'moral progress' – a message that was not least conveyed through the numerous incidents of alcohol-induced violence towards 'natives' – turned white drunkards into a political danger. In addition, especially sailors and 'loafers' physically transgressed the boundaries of 'white' respectability by imbibing not only imported European brews like their middle and upper-class compatriots, but 'native liquor', thus corrupting, as it were, their European identities and blurring the bounds of race. Although altruistic and humanitarian motives ought not to be denied, it was partly also for *these* reasons, that both colonial administrators and a broad array of civil society agents who were advocating a moralization of the British Empire launched crusades to change the 'drinking habits of their countrymen' from the mid-nineteenth century onwards.

Notes

1 This chapter is a slightly modified version of an article that has been published earlier as H. Fischer-Tiné, '"The drinking habits of our countrymen": European alcohol consumption and colonial power in British India', *Journal of Imperial and Commonwealth History*, 40, 3, 2012, 383–408.

2 Cf., for instance, D. van den Bersselaar, *The King of Drinks: schnapps gin from modernity to tradition*, Leiden: Brill, 2007; E.K. Akyeampong, 'What's in a drink? Class struggle, popular culture and the politics of *akpeteshie* (local gin) in Ghana, 1930–67', *Journal of African History* 37, 2, 1996, 215–36; C.H. Ambler, 'Alcohol, racial segregation and popular politics in northern Rhodesia', *Journal of African History* 31, 2, 1990, 295–313; S. Diduk, 'European alcohol, history, and the state of Cameroon', *African Studies Review* 36, 1, 1993, 1–42; C. van Onselen, *Studies in the Social and Economic History of the Witwatersrand 1886–1914, vol. I New Babylon*, Harlow, New York: 1982, pp. 44–102; P. Chatterjee, 'An empire of drink: gender, labor and the historical economies of alcohol', *Journal of Historical Sociology* 16, 2, 2003, 183–208; I. Munshi Saldanha, 'On drinking and "drunkenness": history of liquor in colonial India', *Economic and Political Weekly*, 30, 37, 1995, 2323–31; and N. Varma, 'For the drink of the nation: drink, labour and plantation capitalism in the colonial tea gardens of Assam in the late nineteenth and early twentieth century', in M. van der Linden and P. Mohapatra (eds) *Labour Matters. Towards global histories. Studies in honour of Sabyasachi Bhattacharya*, New Delhi: Tulika, 2009, pp. 295–318.

3 The concept is introduced in H. Fischer-Tiné, *Low and Licentious Europeans: race, class and white subalternity in colonial India*, New Delhi: Orient Blackswan, 2009, see especially pp. 5–18.

4 For ample examples of alcohol-induced 'white violence' targeted at various segments of the Indian population see, for instance, J. Bailkin, '"The boot and the spleen": when was

murder possible in British India?', *Comparative Studies in Society and History* 48, 2, 2006, 462–93.

5 *Mofussil*, provincial town or 'up-country station' in the hinterland.

6 Cf. J. Burbank and F. Cooper, *Empires in World History. Power and the politics of difference*, Princeton, Oxford: Princeton University Press, 2010, pp. 11–13.

7 Cf., for instance, J.H. Mills, *Cannabis Britannica: trade and prohibition*, Oxford: Oxford University Press, 2003; R. Shamir and D. Hacker, 'Colonialism's civilizing mission: the case of the Indian Hemp Drug Commission', *Law & Social Inquiry* 26, 2, 2001, 435–61; J.H. Mills, *Madness, Cannabis and Colonialism: the 'native only' lunatic asylums of British India 1857–1900*, Houndmills, Basingstoke: Palgrave Macmillan, 2000, pp. 43–65.

8 Cf., for instance, C. Markovits, 'The political economy of opium smuggling in early 19th century India: leakage or resistance?', *Modern Asian Studies* 43, 1, 2002, 89–111; A. Farooqui, *Opium City : the making of early Victorian Bombay*, New Delhi: Three Essays Collection, 2006; P.C. Winter, *Anglo-European Science and the Rhetoric of Empire: malaria, opium and British rule in India, 1756–1895*, Lanham Md: Lexington Books, 2003; J.F. Richards, 'The opium industry in British India', *Indian Economic and Social History Review* 39, 2–3, 2003, 149–80; the same author's 'Opium and the British Empire: The Royal Commission of 1895', *Modern Asian Studies* 36, 2, 2002, 375–420; and C.A. Trocki, *Opium, Empire and Global Political Economy. A study of the Asian opium trade 1750–1950*, London, New York: Routledge, 1999. The only work to date that provides a comprehensive overview of a broad variety of psychoactive substances in an empire context is the extremely helpful J.H. Mills and P. Barton, 'Introduction', in idem (eds) *Drugs and Empires: essays in modern imperialism and intoxication, c.1500-c.1930*, Basingstoke, New York: Palgrave Macmillan, 2007.

9 D. Hardiman, 'From custom to crime: the politics of drinking in colonial south Gujarat', in R. Guha (ed.) *Subaltern Studies IV*, New Delhi: Oxford University Press, 1985; and M.J. Gilbert, 'Empire and excise: drugs and drink revenue and the fate of states in South Asia', in Mills and Barton, *Drugs and Empires*, pp. 375–420.

10 D. Fahey and P. Manian, 'Poverty and purification: the politics of Gandhi's campaign for prohibition', *Historian* 67, 3, 2005, 489–506; K. Palaniappan, 'Temperance movement and excise policy of the British in the Madras Presidency (up to 1920)', *Quarterly Journal of the Mythic Society* 92, 3–4, 2001, 133–61; L. Carroll, 'The temperance movement in India: politics and social reform', *Modern Asian Studies* 10, 3, 1976, 417–80; and the same author's 'Origins of the Kayastha temperance movement', *Indian Economic and Social History Review* 11, 1974, 432–47.

11 P. Chatterjee, 'The lives of alcohol in pre-colonial India', *The Medieval History Journal* 8, 1, 2005, 206.

12 Cf., for instance, E. Wald, 'Health, discipline and appropriate behaviour: the body of the soldier and the space of the cantonment', *Modern Asian Studies*, 46, 4, 2012, 815–56; R. Holmes, *Sahib: the British soldier in India, 1750–1914*, London: Harper Collins: 2005, pp. 415–25, D. Peers, 'Imperial vice: sex, drink and the health of British troops in north Indian cantonments, 1800–1858', in D. Killingray and D. Omissi (eds) *Guardians of Empire*, Manchester: Manchester University Press, 1999, pp. 25–52; P. Stanley, *White Mutiny: British military culture in India 1825–1875*, London: Hurst, 1998; D. Peers, 'Sepoys, Soldiers and the Lash: race, caste and army discipline in India, 1820–1850', *The Journal of Imperial and Commonwealth History* 2, 23, 1995, 211–47.

13 D. Peers, 'Imperial vice', in Killingray and Omissi, *Guardians of Empire*, pp. 43–6.

14 On the widespread trope presenting British soldiers as inveterate drunkards see also B. Harrison, *Drink and the Victorians: the temperance question in England, 1815–1872*, Pittsburgh: University of Pittsburgh Press, 1971, p. 332.

15 The concept of 'rule of difference' has very successfully been introduced by Partha Chatterjee in P. Chatterjee, *The Nation and Its Fragments: colonial and postcolonial histories*, Princeton: Princeton University Press, 1993. I prefer Burbank/Coopers notion of the 'politics of difference', because it rightly stresses the fragile and precarious character of the colonial divide. Burbank and Cooper, *Empires in World History*, pp. 11–13.

16 See also M. Valverde, *Diseases of the Will: alcohol and the dilemmas of freedom*, Cambridge: Cambridge University Press, 1998.

17 *Proceedings of a Meeting for forming a Temperance Society, held in the Town Hall of Bombay etc.*, Bombay: Courier Press, 1834.

18 The term 'darkest England' was introduced by Salvation Army founder William Booth in 1890 to describe the life-world of the inhabitants of Britain's urban slums. Cf. W. Booth, *In Darkest England and the Way Out*, London: International Headquarters of the Salvation Army, 1890.

19 A. White, *Efficiency and Empire*, London: Methuen & Co., 1901, p. 98. Cf. also J. Greenaway, *Drink and British Politics since 1830: a study in policy-making*, chapter 2.

20 M. Monier-Williams, *A few Remarks on the Use of Spirituous Liquors among the European Soldiers; and on the Punishment of Flogging in the Native Army of the Honourable East India Company*, London: D.S. Maurice, s.a. [1823?], p. 6.

21 Until it became the official term for the Indo-British 'mixed race' population in 1911, 'Anglo-Indian' was used to refer to the British (or more broadly: Europeans) living in India. It is used in this sense throughout the present article whereas the term 'Eurasian' is reserved for people of mixed parentage.

22 H.D. Love (ed.), *Vestiges of Old Madras, 1640–1800: traced from the East India Company's records preserved at Fort St. George and the India Office, and from other sources*, vol. II, s. l. [London]: John Murray, s.a., p. 71.

23 S.C. Ghosh, *The Social Condition of the British Community in Bengal*, Leiden: E.J. Brill, 1970, pp. 122–6.

24 A. Pryor, 'Indian pale ale: an icon of Empire', *Commodities of Empire, Working Paper No. 13*, November 2009. Online. Available HTTP: http://www.open.ac.uk/Arts/ferguson-centre/commodities-of-empire/working-papers/WP13.pdf (accessed 23 June 2010); and P. Mathias, *The Brewing Industry in England, 1700–1830*, Cambridge: Cambridge University Press, 1959.

25 M. Harrison, *Climates and Constitutions: health, race, environment and British imperialism in India 1600–1850*, New Delhi: Oxford University Press, 1999, pp. 50–2. On European mortality rates see also R. Travers, 'Death and the nabob: imperialism and commemoration in eighteenth-century India', *Past and Present* 196, 2007, 87–9.

26 P. Spear, *The Nabobs: a study of the social life of the English in eighteenth century India*, London, Dublin: Curzon, 1980 [first ed. 1932], p. 17.

27 W. Ernst, *Mad Tales from the Raj: the European insane in British India, 1800–1858*, Delhi: Oxford University Press, 1990, p. 41.

28 J.B. Gilchrist, *The General East India Guide and Vade Mecum*, London, 1825, pp. 116–24 and 151–4.

29 'Griffin' was a term used in Company jargon for the inexperienced newcomers to India.

30 Ibid., p. 125.

31 H.G. Levine, 'The discovery of addiction: changing conceptions of habitual drunkenness in America', *Journal of Studies on Alcohol and Drugs*, 39, 1, 1978, 143–74.

32 R.S. Mair, *Medical Guide for Anglo-Indians* (part of E.C.P. Hull, *The European in India, or, Anglo-Indian's vade-mecum: a handbook of useful and practical information*, London, 1871), p. 238.

33 Cf. for instance R.V. Vernède, *British Life in India*, Delhi: Oxford University Press, 1995, pp. 163–73; H. Hobbs, *John Barleycorn Bahadur: old time taverns in India*, Calcutta: H. Hobbs, 1943; H. Hobbs, *It was like this!*, Calcutta: Thacker, Spink & Co., 1918; D. Gilmour, *The Ruling Caste: imperial lives in the Victorian Raj*, London: John Murray, 2005, pp. 135–7 and L.H. Thornton, *Light and Shade in Bygone India: a study of the soldier in India at the end of the eighteenth and beginning of the nineteenth centuries*, London: John Murray, 1927, pp. 30–1.

34 *Arrack* was an umbrella term used for a variety of local brews. In Southern India it mostly referred to spirits distilled from the fermented sap of palms, whereas in Bengal it generally denoted a liquor made out of sugar cane molasse.

35 *Punch* (from Persian *panj* = five) was a less fiery drink consisting of the following five ingredients: *arrack*, sugar, lime juice, spices and water). Cf. also H. Yule and A.C. Burnell,

Hobson-Jobson: a dictionary of Anglo-Indian words and phrases, repr., Calcutta: Rupa, 1986, pp. 737–8.

36 Cf. also Chatterjee, 'The lives of alcohol', pp. 192–5.

37 D. Arnold, 'Deathscapes: India in an age of Romanticism and Empire, 1800–1856', *Nineteenth-Century Contexts* 26, 4, 2004, 339–53.

38 Gilchrist, *The General East India Guide and Vade Mecum,* pp. 125–6. It is interesting to note how this contrast between the varieties of drink consumed by the lower classes and those preferred by the elites mirrors the metropolitan discourse. Cf. T.G. Coffey, 'Beer Street: Gin Lane. Some views of 18th-century drinking', *Quarterly Journal of Studies on Alcohol* 27, 1966, 669–92.

39 'Europeans in India 1800–1803', Bengal Law Consultations, 24 August 1800; Govt. Magistrate of Calcutta to Henry Barlow, Chief Secy., IOR: O/5/6, Asia, Pacific and Africa Collection, British Library (henceforth: APAC).

40 Letter by an anonymous traveller to the editor of the *Calcutta Gazette* dated 10 June 1837, in R. Raychoudhury (ed.), *Calcutta, a Hundred Years Ago*, Calcutta: Nachiketa Publications, 1978, pp. 20–1.

41 D. Kincaid, *British Social Life in India 1608–1937*, London: Routledge and Kegan Paul, 1973 [first ed. 1938], p. 36.

42 Ghosh, *The Social Condition of the British Community,* p. 123. Cf. also W.S. Seton-Karr, *Selections from the Calcutta Gazettes of the Years 1789, 1790, 1791, 1792, 1793, 1794, 1795, 1796 and 1797, Showing the Political and Social Condition of the English in India Seventy Years ago*, vol. II, no. 5, Calcutta: O.T. Cutter, 1865, pp. 68–9.

43 *Report on the State of the Police of the Town of Calcutta and its Suburbs for 1862–63*, Calcutta: Military Orphan Press, 1863, p. 4.

44 D. Courtwright, *Forces of Habit: drugs and the making of the modern world*, Cambridge MA, London: Harvard University Press, 2001, pp. 190–3.

45 Cf. also T. Williamson, *The East India Vade-Mecum: or complete guide to gentlemen intended for the civil, military or naval service of the Hon. East India Company*, 2 vols, London, 1810, vol. I, pp. 162 and 165, on the 'Punch Houses' as institutions corrupting the morals of Europeans and Spear, *The Nabobs*, p. 45.

46 Hobbs, *John Barleycorn Bahadur*, p. 44.

47 Williamson, *The East India Vade-Mecum*, p. 165.

48 Letter by one 'Positive Fact' to the editor of the *Bengal Hurkaru* dated 10 June 1837, in: Raychoudhury, *Calcutta*, pp. 20–1. See also *Bengal Hukaru* 22 September 1842.

49 For the entanglement of the temperance and 'sexual purity' movements see also A. Hunt, *Governing Morals: a social history of moral regulation*, Cambridge: Cambridge University Press, 1999, pp. 94–103.

50 For an exhaustive account see S. De, *Marginal Europeans in Colonial India, 1860–1920*, Calcutta: Thema, 2008, pp. 63–73. Cf. also Fischer-Tiné, *Low and Licentious Europeans*, pp. 50–4; I. Kerr, *Building the Railways of the Raj 1850–1900*, Delhi: Oxford University Press, 1997, pp. 149–50 and 198–200; and D. Arnold, 'European orphans and vagrants in India in the nineteenth century', *The Journal of Imperial and Commonwealth History* 7, 2, 1979, pp. 114–15.

51 T. Ballantyne, *Orientalism and Race: Aryanism in the British Empire*, Houndmills, New York: Palgrave Macmillan, 2002, pp. 44–8; E.M. Collingham, *Imperial Bodies: the physical experience of the Raj*, Cambridge: Polity Press, 2001, pp. 121–4 and R. Hyam, *Britain's Imperial Century, 1815–1914: a study of empire and expansion*, 3rd edn, Houndmills, Basingstoke: Palgrave Macmillan, 2002, pp. 155–66.

52 Cf. C. Hall, 'The lords of humankind revisited', *Bulletin of the School of Oriental and African* Studies 66, 3, 2003, 473–4. See also the by now classical V.G. Kiernan, *The Lords of Human Kind: European attitudes towards the outside world in the Imperial Age*, London: Weidenfeld & Nicholson, 1969.

53 *The Friend of India*, 2 June 1871, p. 628.

54 *The Friend of India*, 8 November 1860, p. 1060.

55 R.M. Martin, *Statistics of the Colonies of the British Empire in the West Indies, South America, North America, Asia, Austral-Asia, Africa, and Europe etc.*, London: W.H. Allen & Co., 1839, p. 330.

56 On the history of the Bengal Pilot Service Cf. also M.H. Beattie, *On The Hooghly*, London: Philip Allan & Co. Ltd., 1935.

57 GoBeng, Marine Department Proceedings 1861, Sept. 1861, A – Nos. 56–59, IOR: P/173/8, APAC. For similar cases see also GoBeng, Marine Department Proceedings, 1862, May 1862, A – Nos. 66–68, IOR: P/173/9, APAC.

58 *Sāhib pānī men ghīr jātā*; Hindi, can be roughly translated as: 'The Sahib falls overboard.'

59 GoI, Home Department Proceedings, Marine, 1865, February 1865, A – Nos. 1&2: 'Report regarding late Licensed mate Pilot H. Williams', Letter No. 1416: J. G. Reddie, Master Attendant at Calcutta, to A. Eden, Secretary to GoBeng, 8 July 1863, IOR: P/213/57, APAC.

60 The following section draws heavily on Fischer-Tiné, *Low and Licentious Europeans*, chapter 2.

61 P. Marshall, 'The White Town of Calcutta under the rule of the East India Company', *Modern Asian Studies* 34, 2, 2000, 307–31, especially 309. To put these figures into perspective, it is helpful to recall that the overall population of the city exceeded 300,000 at this point.

62 N. Chevers, *On the Preservation of the Health of Seamen, especially those frequenting Calcutta and the other Indian Ports etc.*, Calcutta: Military Orphan Press, 1864, p. 39.

63 Anonymous, 'Sailor Life in Calcutta', *The Friend of India*, 14 April 1864, pp. 461–3.

64 For the politics of segregation in colonial Calcutta see also S. Chattopadhyay, 'Blurring boundaries: the limits of "White Town" in colonial Calcutta', *Journal of the Society of Architectural Historians* 59, 2, 2000, 154–79.

65 P.T. Nair, *A History of Calcutta's Streets*, Calcutta: Firma KLM, 1987, p. 501. The atmosphere of these boarding-houses has been captured in Kipling's famous 'Ballad of Fulta Fisher's Boarding House'. Cf. R. Kipling, *The Collected Poems of Rudyard Kipling*, Ware: Wordsworth Editions, 2001, pp. 43–4.

66 Europeans in India 1787–1792, 11–13, (Bengal Consultations, 23 January 1788), Superintendent of Police to Governor-General Cornwallis, 22 January 1788, IOR: O/5/2, APAC.

67 See for instance letter by 'Aclaus' to the editor of the *Calcutta Journal*, 27 April 1820, in S. Das (comp.), *Selections from the Indian Journals, Vol. II Calcutta Journal*, Calcutta: Firma K.L. Mukhopadhyay, 1965, pp. 169–70 and R. Raychoudhury (ed.), *Glimpses of Old Calcutta (Period 1836–50)*, Bombay: Nachiketa Publications, 1978, pp. 14, 68 and 106.

68 *A Brief History of the Cyclone at Calcutta and Vicinity, 5th October1864*, unknown ed., Calcutta: Cutter, 1865, p. 3. Cf. also P. Ghose, 'Scientific study in Calcutta: the colonial period', in S. Chaudhuri (ed.) *Calcutta. The Living City, Vol I The Past*, Calcutta: Oxford University Press, p. 199. For a detailed survey of the effects of the cyclone cf. also J.E. Gastrell and H.F. Blanford, *Report on the Calcutta Cyclone on the 5th of October 1864*, Calcutta: Military Orphan Press, 1866, and GoBeng, Marine Dept. Progs., 1864, A–13–43, November 1864, IOR: P/173/, APAC.

69 *A Brief History of the Cyclone at Calcutta*, p. 12. See also J.G. Reddie, *Annual Report of the Marine Department and Dockyard under the Government of Bengal for 1864–65*, Calcutta: Military Orphan Press, 1865.

70 For a detailed account see H. Fischer-Tiné, 'Flotsam and jetsam of the Empire? – European seamen and spaces of disease and disorder in mid-nineteenth-century Calcutta', in H. Fischer-Tiné and A. Tambe (eds) *The Limits of British Colonial Control: spaces of disorder in the Indian Ocean region*, London, New York: Routledge, 2009, pp. 116–49.

71 GoI, Home Dept. Progs., Marine, 1866, No. 18, May 1861, G.B. Malleson, 'The State of Sailors in Calcutta', IOR: P/437/29; No. 18, February 1866, IOR: P/437/29, APAC.

72 G.B. Malleson, 'The State of Sailors in Calcutta', IOR: P/437/29; No. 18, APAC.

73 Cf. also Harrison, *Climates and Constitutions*, pp. 153–203.

74 See, for instance, M.A. Conley, *From Jack Tar to Union Jack: representing naval manhood in the British Empire, 1870–1918*, Manchester, New York: Manchester University Press, 2009, pp. 77–8; I. Land, 'Flogging, empire, and the 'true British seaman' 1770 to 1870', *Interventions: International Journal of Postcolonial Studies*, 3, 2, 2001, 169–85; C. Lloyd, *The British Seaman, 1200–1860: a social survey*, London: Paladin, 1968, pp. 254–6.

75 That this trope was not restricted to the British discourse on seamen is evident from T. Heimerdinger, *Der Seemann: Ein Berufsstand und seine kulturelle Inszenierung, 1844–2003*, Köln etc.: Böhlau Verlag, 2005, which analyzes a strikingly similar discourse in the German context.
76 Cf. also Conley, *From Jack Tar to Union Jack*, p. 77.
77 Chevers, *On the Preservation of the Health of Seamen*, p. 37. Cf. also L. Sykes, *Calcutta Through British Eyes, 1690–1990*, Delhi: Oxford University Press, 1992, pp. 47–8.
78 Malleson, 'The State of Sailors', p. 3. Cf. also Chevers, *On the Preservation of the Health of Seamen*, Appendix B, 'Adulterated Liquor sold to Sailors and Soldiers in the Bazars of Calcutta', pp. 62–4.
79 W.H. Smyth, *The Sailor's Word-Book: an alphabetical digest of nautical terms, including some more especially military and scientific, but useful to seamen; as well as archaisms of early voyagers, etc.*, London: Blackie and Son, p. 253.
80 M.K. Joyce, *An Exposure of the Haunts of Infamy and Dens of Vice in Bombay. Collected from facts*, Bombay: published by the author, 1854, p. 3.
81 Ibid., p. 2.
82 This decision was disputed as the 366 licensed liquor shops which existed in the city in 1862 were an important source of income for the government. *Report on the State of the Police of the Town of Calcutta 1862–63*, p. 4. Cf. also W.S. Meyer (ed.), *Memorandum on excise administration in India, so far as it is concerned with intoxicating liquors*, fourth ed., Simla: Manager of Publications, 1906 for definitions and details on the exact distribution of European and 'native' liquor stores.
83 For a helpful discussion of similar endeavours back in Britain see Conley, *From Jack Tar to Union Jack,* pp. 66–98.
84 *The Friend of India*, 6 April 1865, p. 393.
85 Chevers, *On the Preservation of the Health of Seamen*, p. 38.
86 P. Levine, *Prostitution, Race and Politics: policing venereal disease in the British Empire*, London, New York: Routledge, 2003, pp. 285–6.
87 Chevers, *On the Preservation of the health of Seamen*, Appendix C, 'The Dangers to which Soldiers and Sailors are exposed in the Bazars of Calcutta', p. 68. See also GoBeng, Judl. Dept. Progs., 1862, A–74, March 1865, Letter No. 1666, 15 February 1864, A. Turnbull, Secy. to the Justices of Peace of Calcutta, to S.C. Bailey, Secy. to GoBeng, IOR: P/173/9, APAC.
88 Cf. Fischer-Tiné, *Low and Licentious Europeans*, p. 212.
89 Levine, *Prostitution, Race and Politics,* pp. 85–6 and J. Whitehead, 'Bodies clean and unclean: prostitution, sanitary legislation and respectable femininity in colonial North India', *Gender and History* 7, 1, 1995, 41–2. See also A. Tambe, *Codes of Misconduct: regulating prostitution in late colonial Bombay*, Minneapolis, London: University of Minnesota Press, 2009, pp. 34–5.
90 In the five years from 1856 to 1861 altogether 1,522 seamen were sentenced to imprisonment in the Calcutta House of Correction for 'refusal of duty' alone. Cf. GoBeng, Judl. Dept. Progs., 1862, A–77, IOR: P/173/9, APAC.
91 *Report on the State of the Police of the Town of Calcutta for 1855. (With figured statements and comparative statements for 1854 and 1855)*, Calcutta: Military Orphan Press, 1856, p. 3.
92 The issue of special penitentiaries for Europeans is dealt with in-depth in H. Fischer-Tiné, 'Hierarchies of crime and punishment? European convicts in colonial India and the racial dividend', in H. Fischer-Tiné and S. Gehrmann (eds) *Empires and Boundaries: rethinking race, class and gender in colonial settings*, London, New York: Routledge, 2009, pp. 41–65.
93 APAC, IOR: P/147/4; GoBeng, Jail Dept. Progs., Nov. 1864, No. 82, 'Statement of Prisoners in the European Jail Ootacamund'.
94 *Report on the State of the Police of the Town of Calcutta For 1861–62. (With figured statements and comparative statements for 1860–61 and 1861–62)*, Calcutta: Military Orphan Press, 1862, p. 3. See also GoBeng, Judl Dept. Progs, No. A–113–7, 6 January 1859 'Prevention of Sailors from going out with their knives', No.113–7, 6 January 1859, WBSA.
95 For a more general discussion of Victorian perceptions of the interrelations between alcohol intoxication and violence see also J. Rowbotham, 'Only when drunk: the stereotyping of

violence in England, c. 1850–1900', in S. D'Cruze (ed.) *Everyday Violence in Britain, 1850–1950*, Harlow: Pearson Education, 2000, pp. 155–69.

96 H.E.A. Cotton. *Calcutta Old and New. A historical and descriptive handbook to the city*, Calcutta: W. Newman & Co., 1907, p. 222.

97 *Report on the State of the Police of the Town of Calcutta for 1855*, p. 16.

98 S. Banerjee, *Dangerous Outcast: the prostitute in nineteenth century Bengal*, Calcutta: Seagull, 2000, p. 52. For an example from Bombay see *Bombay Samachar,* 9 June 1868, in *Report on Native Papers Published in the Bombay Presidency* [cited as *RNPBom*], 1868.

99 *Bombay Samachar,* 9 June 1868, in *RNPBom*, 1868.

100 *Proceedings of a Meeting for forming a Temperance Society, held in the Town Hall of Bombay etc.*, p. 10. Cf. also Spear, *The Nabobs*, pp. 59–60 and T. Raychaudhury, 'Transformation of Indian sensibilities: the West as catalyst', in idem, *Perceptions, Emotions, Sensibilities. Essays on India's colonial and post-colonial experiences*, New Delhi: Oxford University Press, 1999, p. 7.

101 Cf., for instance, H. Fischer-Tiné, 'Stadt der Paläste? Europäische Lebenswelten im kolonialen Calcutta', in R. Ahuja and C. Brosius (eds) *Mumbai - Delhi - Kolkata: Annäherungen and Indiens Megastädte*, Heidelberg: Draupadi, 2006, pp. 241–2.

102 Anonymous, *Brahmins and Pariahs: an appeal by the indigo manufacturers of Bengal to the British government, parliament and people, for protection against the Lieut.-Governor of Bengal etc.*, London: James Ridgway, 1861. The conflicts between the European planter community and colonial administrators came to a head in the wake of the so-called 'Blue Mutiny' in the early 1860s. Cf. B.B. Kling, *Blue Mutiny: indigo disturbances in Bengal, 1859–1862*, Philadelphia: University of Pennsylvania Press, 1967.

103 E. Kolsky, *Colonial Justice in British India: white violence and the rule of law*, Cambridge: Cambridge University Press, 2010, pp. 57–63 and E. Kolsky, 'Crime and punishment on the tea plantations of British India', in M.D. Dubber and L. Farmer (eds) *Modern Histories of Crime and Punishment*, Stanford CA: Stanford University Press, 2007, pp. 272–98.

104 H.S. Olcott (ed.), *Old Diary Leaves: the history of the Theosophical Society, 2nd series, 1878–83*, Adyar: Theosophical Publishing House, 2002, p. 420. I should like to thank Maria Moritz for providing me with this extremely interesting source.

105 An EIC record compiled in 1827/28 meticulously lists all cases of misconduct by non-licensed Europeans or ex-soldiers which had occurred in the previous decades. In the thirty years from 1793 to 1823 it relates a total of 532 cases, or an annual average of about 18. Most of the misdemeanours were committed by European soldiers. Cf. APAC, IOR: O/5/25, vol. 24. See also Kolsky, *Colonial Justice in British India*, chapter 1.

106 Cf. for instance, *Jam-e-Jamsed*, 19 June 1868, in *RNPBom*, 1868 and *Bombay Samachar*, 23 June 1868, and *Rast Goftar* 21 June 1868, ibid.

107 See also De, *Marginal Europeans in Colonial India*, pp. 109–14 and Fischer-Tiné, *Low and Licentious Europeans*, pp. 163–5.

108 Government of Bombay, 'Annual Police Return showing the State of Crime in the Town and Island of Bombay during the year 1866–67', Bombay: Government Central Press, 1867, p. 8.

109 GoMad, Publ. Progs., 1900, No. 861, August 1900, Letter No. 1626, 18 August 1900, H. Dobbs, Secy. to the Chief Comm. of Coorg to GoMad, IOR: P/5990, APAC.

110 H. Hervey, *The European in India*, London: Stanley Paul & Co., 1913, p. 97 and T.C. Arthur, *Reminiscences of an Indian Police Official*, London: Sampson Low & Co., 1894, pp. 229–33.

111 Arthur, *Reminiscences of an Indian Police Official*, p. 235.

112 J.D. Packman, *Remarks on some affections of the Liver and Bowels: Being an enquiry into their principal causes, and suggestions for avoiding their influence, with a few practical observations regarding what should be the conduct and habits of Europeans in India with reference to health*, Madras: Pharoah &Co, 1850, p. 3.

113 GoI, Home Dept., Legisl. Progs., No. 9, October 1868, Letter No. 867, 4 February 1868, J.R. Baldwin, Secy. to Allahabad District Charitable Organisation, to E.C. Bailey, Secy. to GoI., IOR: P/436/55, APAC.

114 Ibid. The prescription consisted of 5 grains of sulphate of iron, 10 grains magnesia, 11 drachms of peppermint and one drachm of spirit of nutmeg. The mixture was to be given twice a day.

115 Ibid.
116 Cf. also C. Heron, *Booze: a distilled history*, Toronto: Between the Lines, 2003, pp. 139–45.
117 MSA, GoBom, Judl. Dept. Progs., Vol. 25, 1868, Letter No. 4, Comm. of Police, Bombay to GoBom, Judl. Dept., 23 July 1868.
118 MSA, GoBom, Judl. Dept. Progs., Vol. 25, 1868, Letter No. 423, J. Connor, Senior Mag. of Police, Bombay to the GoBom, Jud. Dept., 17 September 1868.
119 For a rather typical example, see the case of one Mrs Mac Erlane, a woman of Irish origin 30 years of age, admitted in Bombay's female workhouse in late 1885. 'Born in Dublin, Ireland, 25 March 1855. Married to Gunner James Mac Erlane on 25th Nov. 1870. She has three children who are in charge of her husband who is still in India with his Battery. Came to India with her husband's Battery in May 1880; was removed from the married establishment of the Battery for misconduct and deported by Government in March 1884. Returned to India at her own expense in June 1884 has lived in Bombay since that date. Obtained shortly after arrival a situation as "bar maid" in the Grant Road hotel, which she quitted in August 1885 being ill from the effects of drink. She was received to the J. J. Hospital, has twice suffered from delirium tremens.' MSA GoBom, Judicial Department Proceedings, vol. 47, 1886, Letter no. WF 15, P. Cooper, Governor, Government Female WHBom, to GoBom Judicial Department, 10 March 1886.
120 Monier-Williams, *A Few Remarks on the Use of Spirituous Liquors*, p. 12.
121 GoI, Home Department Proceedings, Public, A–303–306, August 1917, National Archives of India, [NAI], 'Grant of Rs 120 per mensem for the upkeep of a European Vagrant named Elizabeth Mahon still pending the ultimate disposal'.
122 Ibid.
123 For insightful observations on the popular Victorian discourse on 'fallen women' see also D.A. Logan, *Fallenness in Victorian Women's Writing: marry, stitch, die or do worse*, Columbia-London: University of Missouri Press, 1998.
124 J. Rowbotham, 'Only when drunk', in D'Cruze, *Everyday Violence in Britain*, p. 165.
125 See also Fischer-Tiné, *Low and Licentious Europeans*, chapter 3.
126 *The Friend of India*, 24 May 1866, p. 607.
127 MSA, GoBom, Judl. Dept. Progs., Vol. 13, 1867, Letter No. 419, R. B. Barton, Chief Mag. of Police to C. Gonne, Secy. to GoBom, Judl. Dept, 10 December 1866.
128 Thus, a temperance activist touring the British empire declared in a speech he gave in 1864: 'Drink is the source of all crimes; it fills the prison cells; it loads the convict ship, it throngs the workhouse, it crowds the lunatic asylum it guides the footsteps of the robber; it nerves the red hand of the murderer, and peoples the scaffold with haggard victims of despair'. Edward Chapple, *Temperance. Five addresses delivered to the members of the Total Abstinence Society Aden* etc., Bombay, 1864.
129 For a detailed description of the workhouse regime see also H. Fischer-Tiné, 'Britain's other civilising mission: class-prejudice, European "loaferism" and the workhouse-system in colonial India', *Indian Economic and Social History Review* 42, 3, 2005, 316–26.
130 MSA, GoBom, Judicial Department Proceedings, vol. 59, 1874, 'Report of the Working of the European Vagrancy Act for 1873'. Letter no. 4/48, Captain Walshe, Governor GWHBom, to the President of the Committee of Management, 18 February 1874.
131 MSA, GoBom, Judl. Dept. Progs. Vol. 59, 1884, Letter No. W. 34, Captain W. P. Walshe, Governor, GWHBom to GoBom Judicial Dept., 21 February 1884.
132 J.H. Mills and P. Barton, 'Introduction', in idem, *Drugs and Empire*, p. 1.
133 This argument has been most strongly made in F.G. Hutchins, *The Illusion of Permanence. British imperialism in India*, Princeton: Princeton University Press, 1967.
134 This was the title of a somewhat outdated account of the European elite. P. Mason, *The Men Who Ruled India*, Calcutta: Cape, 1992 [first ed. 1952/53].
135 J. Briggs et al., *Crime and Punishment in England: an introductory history*, London: UCL Press, 1996, p. 194.

136 Cf. G. Orwell [i.e. Eric A. Blair], *Burmese Days*, London: Secker and Warburg, 1997 (= vol. II of *The Complete Works of George Orwell*, ed. P. Davison), p. 37. Orwell's marvellous novel is full of references to the drinking culture of the white community in a rural outpost in British Burma.

137 N. Jayasena, *Contested Masculinities: crises in colonial male identity from Joseph Conrad to Satyajit Ray*, London, New York: Routledge, 2007, p. 112.

5 Looking for spirituality in India: A German theosophist's experiments with *ganja* (1894–1896)

Maria Moritz

References to Hippie counterculture of the late twentieth century conjures up drug experiments of Euro-American seekers guided by South Asian 'gurus'. It evokes images of Western youth journeying to places like Goa and Rishikesh to experiment with cannabis, free love and the so-called 'Indian spirituality'. This article is concerned with one such individual's journey to India in a countercultural context; it also attempts to historicize these pilgrimages by analyzing the case of the German theosophist Wilhelm Hübbe-Schleiden (1846–1916) at the end of nineteenth century. His experiments with cannabis and the suppression of his sexuality in order to attain a 'spiritual state of mind', however, rendered results that differed considerably from the average Hippie experience.

The focus on a specific case of drug tourism *avant la lettre* is significant not only because it is embedded in an often forgotten countercultural milieu but also because it provides a window into major globalizing processes such as the rise of tourism or the integration of international markets, which accelerated in the final decade of the nineteenth century. Wilhelm Hübbe-Schleiden's journey to India in 1894–6 is thus meaningful in three major inextricably linked contexts that mutually reinforce one another. Globalization is understood here as both an actual process of accelerated exchange and mobility as well as a change in perspective. While the processes of increased commodity exchange, international migration, and the development of modern telecommunication have been much studied,[1] globalization as a perspective entails first and foremost the evolvement of a global awareness that understands cultural differences not as backwardness but as an alternative to Eurocentric concepts.[2]

The present case study is useful in grasping a phenomenon that British historian David Courtwright has called the 'psychoactive revolution' as both a further popularization of drugs and their increased global circulation around the turn to the twentieth century. This process 'had its roots in the transoceanic commerce and empire building of the early modern period'.[3] Though the consumption of drugs has been central to various cultures, the 'psychoactive revolution' made drugs more easily available for ordinary people. The term 'drug' kept its connotation of abuse and addiction even though its rise to a global commodity was supported by major global players such as the British colonial government.[4] However, recreational consumption became a popular means to counteract the tensions of modern lifestyle and investigate the newly discovered realm of the subconscious. Alcohol, tobacco and caffeine – 'the big three'[5] – were consumed and traded by Europeans on a large scale around 1900 and thus had become global commodities. Resistance to the spread of 'the big three' was equally global, with prohibition activists all over the world linking it to their respective political, social or religious agendas. In contrast, Europeans encountered 'the little three' – opium, cannabis, and coca(ine) – only in very restricted circles while cultures such as India or China had customarily benefited from their psychoactive properties. These 'little three' that are usually associated with the otherwise neutral term 'drugs' were introduced into global markets during the 'psychoactive revolution'.

Secondly, Hübbe-Schleiden's diaries and the correspondence with his Indian guru reflect the increasing exchange of spiritual ideas and concepts between Euro-America and Asia around the turn of the century. This phenomenon is best illustrated by the astonishing global success of the Theosophical Society as the forerunner of the twentieth century New Age Movement. The society relied on and contributed to the information explosion around the turn of the century through its massive diffusion of magazines, letters, books and pamphlets, all of which supplied its swelling audiences with 'wisdom from the mystic East'. Informed by the wider 'affirmative Orientalist' discourse the Theosophical Society privileged Asia as the supposed repository of global spirituality as opposed to an assumedly materialist West, thus pioneering a stereotyping discourse still in full swing today.[6]

Apart from the media and technological innovations that allowed for discursive activity between continents, the period around 1900 saw an increase in travel. India, the so-called 'mystic East', 'had become the principal reference point for a vast array of non-Christian spiritualities and spiritualists'.[7] Germany in particular had a long tradition of a fascination with India starting with eighteenth century philosophers such as Arthur Schopenhauer (1788–1860)[8] and Johann Gottfried Herder (1744–1803)[9]. This fascination had encouraged an increasing number of travelling German literati such as Max Dauthendey (1867–1918), Waldemar Bonsels (1880–1952), Herman Graf Keyserling (1880–1946) or Hermann Hesse (1877–1962) to visit South Asia.[10,11] Since the Theosophical Society most successfully catered 'Indian spirituality' to German intellectual centres,[12] it is not surprising that in addition to the protagonist of this study, theosophy also inspired Herman Graf Keyserling's and Hermann Hesse's journeys to India. Indeed, a considerable portion of Keyserling's reminiscences of his 1911 trip to India deal with his visit to Adyar, the international headquarters of the Theosophical Society[13] followed by a critical evaluation of theosophy in *Some Suggestions concerning Theosophy* (1912).[14] In the case of Hermann Hesse, a reawakened interest in Arthur Schopenhauer from 1904 drew his 'attention to theosophy, and theosophy, in turn took him back to India'.[15] The translation and (theosophical) interpretation of German theosophist Franz Hartmann's (1838–1912) *Bhagavad Gita* in 1905/1906 was Hesse's access point to an intense reading of literature on 'Indian spirituality'[16] which eventually led to his Indian journey in 1911 in 'a vague hope that he might encounter the living spirit of India, might find a more innocent community of man, and perhaps even some answers to personal problems'.[17] Thus, both Hübbe-Schleiden's transnational biography and his trip to India are testimony to this major trend. Historically, he represented a new type of German traveller on the subcontinent, one who was not a missionary, colonial officer, merchant, explorer or scholar but rather exclusively on a quest for spiritual insight.[18]

Hübbe-Schleiden's actual physical journey to India for the sake of an 'inner trip' at the intersection of drug consumption, spiritual quest, and explorations of sexual fantasies and the subconscious links his experience with central aspects of the Hippie movement in the 1960s and 1970s as well as more recent varieties of counterculture. This combination associated with 'spiritual tourists' to India has been convincingly captured by Anita Desai in her novel *Journey to Ithaca*, in which the young bourgeois Italian couple browses various Indian ashrams only to find that the journey itself was the answer to their questions.[19] In the 1960s and 1970s, young people, especially students, were prone to both countercultural cannabis consumption and extensive travelling in non-western countries as a result of parental affluence and increasingly cheap fares.[20] The nexus of travelling and transportation that we see are 'crucial variables in drug history, just as they are in the history of infectious diseases'[21] argues Courtwright.

Apart from increasing opportunities to travel, a pervasive cultural stereotype and the well-established indigenous market for cannabis in India, the relative laxity of the law to effectively control cannabis added to the attraction of India as a space for countercultural experiments. James Mills has convincingly argued that this official attitude had a tradition since the colonial government had already surveyed the indigenous cannabis market but considered it too tightly controlled to be profitable and too well-established in everyday culture to effectively ban cannabis without provoking aggressive opposition from their colonial subjects. In the famous Indian Hemp Drug Commission report of 1894 the colonial government opted against strict regulations as the report shows 'most clearly how little injury society has hitherto sustained from hemp drugs'.[22] The smoking of cannabis in *chillums* (pipes), for example, was a widespread practice of Shiva worshippers in India. The appropriation of *chillums* by Hippies and beatniks in the 60s 'represents the most widespread and consistent borrowing from Indian culture among freaks'.[23] Geographer Arun Saldanha even goes so far as to claim that 'What most enthused hippies was the extremely low prices of cannabis; the Asian hippie trail of the late sixties was first and foremost a pot trail.'[24]

This essay will examine the impact of global changes on the thinking and activities of a globalized individual such as Wilhelm Hübbe-Schleiden.

In doing so, I will attempt to show how the increasing interconnection experienced in British India during this period led this historical actor to closely interact with his guru and thus firmly establish a transnational identity. Against this backdrop, the analysis of Hübbe-Schleiden's consumption of cannabis under the guidance of his Indian guru can help understand countercultural practices around 1900 that merged into the mainstream of today's culture. The case study thereby reflects the increased ability and demand of the modern subject to transcend (or escape? That is a matter of interpretation and discussion) geographical, cultural and psychological constraints by travelling both inwardly and outwardly.

Wilhelm Hübbe-Schleiden visited India for a mystical experience that would at once bring about a complete change in his life both by relieving him from his suffering and opening his eyes for the spiritual. In short, like spiritual travellers of all cultures and of all times, he wanted to free himself from himself, and drug consumption was one means to achieve this goal. Religious travels to holy places, on the other hand, are as such not a new phenomenon.[25] They are usually considered the 'oldest form of non-economic travel'[26] and multi-religious India has a vibrant pilgrimage scene.[27] Scholars of tourism, however, have detected a form of 'religiously motivated travels' to contemporary Goa on India's south-western coast that combines 'New Age spirituality with pilgrimage travel'.[28] In a micro-study of this milieu in Goa, American anthropologist Anthony D'Andrea has analyzed the drug practices, sexual identities and spiritual orientations of those he labels 'Global Nomads' due to their hypermobile lifestyles.[29] Their New Age spirituality derives 'from the early 1970s counterculture, [and] its ethno-ecological, parascientific and psychospiritual syncretisms reflect social diffusion of a reflexive mysticism formerly confined within erudite circles of Romanticism'.[30] One of the major institutions within these 'erudite circles of Romanticism' was the Theosophical Society, a forerunner of New Age spirituality.[31]

The Theosophical Society

A prominent member of the German section of the Theosophical Society, Hübbe-Schleiden's openness towards new experiences and readiness to embrace unknown situations during his journey was facilitated by both the infrastructure and the ideology of the Theosophical Society. Around the turn of the century, the Theosophical Society, originally founded in New York in 1875, was the single most important spiritual organization in the West seeking spiritual insight in Asia by popularizing esoteric knowledge in Europe and North America and supporting its paradigmatic shift towards the 'mystic East'.[32] Based on what has been called 'affirmative orientalism'[33] and 'loyal opposition',[34] this influential though highly understudied discourse[35] interpreted South Asian cultures as predominantly religious and thus imagined the subcontinent as an ideal space for a spiritual search.[36] Consequently, the founders of the Theosophical Society Helena Blavatsky and Henry Steel

Olcott moved its international headquarters from New York to Bombay in 1879 and developed a close network of branches not just in India but on a global scale.[37] The Theosophical Society became a far-from-marginal movement between 1891 and 1935, by the end of which period it had established 45 branches in countries as disparate as Great Britain, Holland, India, Ireland, the United States, Ceylon, Australia, Vietnam, Indonesia and several countries in Africa and Latin America. 'This is evidenced by the fact that Annie Besant's[38] lectures at the Sorbonne were attracting audiences of over 4,000 people at a time.'[39]

While the Theosophical Society was partly built on imperial connections, its network transcended the boundaries of the British Empire. Hübbe-Schleiden's home country Germany, for example, was foremost in diffusing 'affirmative orientalism' and subsequently became an important member of the theosophical network that promoted an eastward turn that was reflected by an increasing popularity of meditation, the *Bhagavad Gita*[40] or Yoga practices.[41] This theosophical intervention has played a considerable role in making these practices central elements of the New Age spirituality and lifestyle.

The transnational Wilhelm Hübbe-Schleiden

The combination of frequent international travels, countercultural practices, and openness towards new experiences in 'exotic countries' mark Wilhelm Hübbe-Schleiden (1846–1916) as a transnational actor on the stage of political, economic and cultural integration around 1900. The multitude of educational centres Hübbe-Schleiden attended within Germany – Göttingen, Heidelberg, Munich and Leipzig – while training as a lawyer, indicate his early restlessness.[42] Instead of applying his legal skills either in his native town Hamburg or any other of his many residences, however, he actively participated in the integration of markets. He initially joined the trading company *Kleinwort Cohen & Co.* in London in the early 1870s and then went on to establish his own trading company *Bolton & Schleiden* with his companion Augustus Bolton 1875 in Gabun, a part of the French West African colonies. However, the complete plundering of his stores forced Hübbe-Schleiden to close his company down by 1877. The thieves were caught and Hübbe-Schleiden was officially accused in a colonial court in Senegalese St Louis of complicity in the killing of two of the thieves and was sentenced to five years in prison. Diplomatic negotiations, however, saved him from the penalty and allowed him to sail home. Though he denied any complicity in Senegal, his diary entry of 25 November 1895 in India revealed that Hübbe-Schleiden still struggled after 18 years with his involvement as he interpreted his difficulties in the north-Indian hill-station Almora as an atonement for his deeds in Gabun.[43]

Because global political visions of the late nineteenth century were predominantly expressed in the form of imperialism, scholars such as Arif Dirlik label the accelerated integration of the world around 1900 a Euro-American centred globalization as distinct from contemporary global modernity.[44] From

Hübbe-Schleiden's point of view, globalization certainly centred around Euro-America not only economically but also politically and culturally. As a result, Hübbe-Schleiden embarked on a colonial expansionist project back in Hamburg by publicly campaigning for the German colonial political movement.[45] Like the Christian missionary and 'godfather of German colonial expansionism' Friedrich Fabri (1824–91), Hübbe-Schleiden agitated for German overseas expansion to West Africa and South America so as to combine economic and 'civilizational' interests. German colonialism overseas would help to 'uplift' the colonies by infusing 'culture' and the German homeland in turn would be helped by the establishment of new, profitable markets.[46] His most influential and well-received work on West Africa reflects his practical experiences and expansionist ideas.[47]

For his promotion of cultural integration Hübbe-Schleiden relied on the Theosophical Society. Establishing the Theosophical Society in Germany in 1884 was Hübbe-Schleiden's most noteworthy contribution to German theosophy. However, this contribution is almost forgotten today and suppressed by the contribution of the more influential and charismatic Rudolf Steiner (1861–1925) to both theosophy and German anthroposophy. Hübbe-Schleiden was not only acquainted with Germany's most famous theosophist[48] but supported both Steiner's election as general secretary of the German section in 1902 as well as the break with Steiner in 1912–13 that resulted in the founding of the Anthroposophical Society.[49]

As a prominent member of the German section of the Theosophical Society, Hübbe-Schleiden travelled in India using the pan-Indian theosophical network where he met other German theosophists such as his rival Dr Franz Hartmann and also important theosophical figures such as Annie Besant and Anagarika Dharmapala. Hübbe-Schleiden used the society's India-wide infrastructure, but he looked for spiritual insight at the margins of the organization as he considered the leading theosophist Helena Blavatsky 'irreligious'[50] and its president Annie Besant 'undiscriminating' and 'weak'.[51] Although he remained in constant contact with theosophical branches in Bombay, Calcutta and Madras, Hübbe-Schleiden – perhaps owing to these personal animosities – approached spirituality independently with the help of a native guru, Pasupati Deva and the support of Ras Bihari Mukherjee. It has proved to be impossible to reconstruct the exact biographical details of Pasupati Deva, Hübbe-Schleiden's 'main guru'; however, the available records make clear that he was certainly a brahmin and from the Calcutta area. His 'assistant', Ras Bihari Mukherjee, was a Bengali scholar who translated the *Philosophical Dialogues and Fragments* of French scholar Ernest Renan (1823–93) into English in 1883[52] and who thus contributed to the circulation of Renan's philosophical ideas in the English speaking world. As both Wilhelm Hübbe-Schleiden and Ras Bihari Mukherjee were close friends of Anagarika Dharmapala (1864–1933), the founder of the Buddhist Mahabodhi Society who frequently interacted with the Bengali *bhadralok* in Calcutta, the arrangement might have been initiated by him.[53]

The Indian guru and his German disciple

The events that lie at the heart of this study took place in Uttarpara near Calcutta and Almora, a small town and religious center in the north-eastern foothills of the Himalayas between the end of 1895 and beginning of 1896. I reconstructed the events from Hübbe-Schleiden's correspondence and diaries[54] he kept for the entirety of his Indian journey from October 1894 to April 1896.[55,56]

Though his experiments with *ganja* are by far not the only topic taken up in Hübbe-Schleiden's diaries and are certainly not as detailed as Thomas De Quincey's famous 'Confessions of an English Opium-Eater' (1821), they contain a wealth of valuable source material for scholars focusing on the history of travelling, the apprehension of 'Eastern cultural practices' such as Yoga or meditation by an increasing number of people in the West, the history of sexuality, psychoanalysis and much more. Moreover, they allow an unfiltered insight into his bodily practices and mental experiments as the diaries were not meant for publication and thus are rich in intimate details. Whereas the vast majority of the existing historical literature on drugs in the *fin de siècle* focuses on civil society campaigning and state politics concerning drug traffic and regulation, the present study seeks to reintroduce the consumer perspective to studies on the history of drugs and travelling.

The transcultural encounter with his Indian guru defines the mode of Hübbe-Schleiden's spiritual quest for which he used a mix of 'traditional' and 'modern' techniques in his religiously motivated ascetic practice:

1. Interaction with a guru,
2. Regular meditation and Yoga practice,
3. Celibacy,
4. Analysis of dreams, and
5. Consumption of drugs.

While celibacy or devotion towards a guru certainly belonged to the 'classical repertoire' of spiritual searchers in order to attain a body prepared for the reception of spiritual knowledge[57] the interpretation of dreams, experiments with drugs, and Yoga by other than indigenous people reflected a trend in transcultural interaction. For Westerners, these techniques provided new elements for spiritual search and wellbeing. At the same time, practices such as Yoga or meditation were transformed and integrated as central elements of the global physical culture movement.[58] The close analysis of the interaction between Hübbe-Schleiden and his Indian guru reveals how concepts travelled from the 'classic' country through ascetics and mendicants.[59]

For example, Hübbe-Schleiden was introduced by his Indian gurus to the indigenous differentiation of food into 'hot' and 'cold' items. According to this concept, 'hot' food consists of deep-fried items, sweets, meat, eggs, onions and garlic.[60] This indigenous concept associates 'hot food' with desire and aggression, thereby linking certain psychological or emotional qualities with specific substances. This classification system applies to drugs as well. Psychoactive substances are similarly classified according to their influence on the psyche of the consumer. Using the same logic, Hübbe-Schleiden immediately supposes that an unusual activity of his 'reproductive system' must be a result of his recent albuminous diet of 'meat' and 'eggs' or alternatively the discussion of sexual matters with his guru Ras Bihari.[61] Subsequently, he tries to restrict his diet to 'cold food' such as fruits, rice or lentils that are classically associated with 'brahmanical' qualities such as austerity and gentleness.[62]

At the beginning of 1895, Hübbe-Schleiden asks Pasupati Deva for spiritual guidance as a necessary prerequisite for any spiritual progress:

> My thoughts would then be directed towards yourself, because in this life I have never seen anyone realizing my ideal of 'Christ' more than you – and such living example works further with me than any ideal which is to me hitherto only a theoretical hypothesis in the thought world. Oh, if I could live for some time in your presence, I think the goodness and holiness of your spiritual aura might do the miracle to change me altogether! But I never felt so much in a spiritual desert and in such a deadening hell as here in this spot on earth which is to all external appearance a perfect paradise.[63]

This quote reveals that Hübbe-Schleiden's journey to India is designed as the discovery of a new geographical as well as psychological space even though he feels that these levels contradict one another: while he considered the geographical space a 'perfect paradise', he found his inner landscape a 'spiritual desert'. Nevertheless, he sets out to confront his inner reality in exotic lands.

This discrepancy is also implicit in his conception of his guru and his motives for approaching him. He called Pasupati Deva not just a 'living example' but an ideal embodiment of 'Christ'. Paradoxically, though Hübbe-Schleiden searched for spirituality in India, he was apparently not interested in a specifically 'Indian spirituality'. He much rather wanted to realize an esoteric interpretation of Christ through 'indigenous methods' in India and receive a spiritual training that would authorize him for spiritual leadership in Germany.[64]

Pasupati Deva was ready to admit that Hübbe-Schleiden 'has parts which can only be properly developed, in the spiritual land of Bharat'[65] and therefore asked his friend Ras Bihari Mukherjee to receive him as he possessed better 'spirituality than the ordinary rim of German savants (best thinkers though they are in the European world) or majority of the self-styled "Theosophists" of Europe and America'.[66] Deva considered the teachings of the Theosophical Society not only overseas but also within India 'a failure' as the 'Higher class of Hindus are natural Theosophists; to them Theosophy is not an intellectual feast, as it is now getting in Europe and America'.[67] Confronted with this outspoken criticism, Hübbe-Schleiden was quick in assuring him that he had 'always been absolutely independent from the Theosophists'.[68]

However, the Theosophical Society itself operated within the wider milieu of the highly competitive religious movements of which Pasupati Deva is similarly critical as he calls them 'Religious Insurance Companies of the world':

> All these Insurance companies which are now in existence, and all those which existed before, are always vying with each other (and ever ready to cut each other's throat, in the very name of religion, which preaches nothing but love and self-sacrifice) to insure cheapest salvation with the least personal sacrifice and the greatest amount of personal comforts, even in this contemptible period of a hundred year's life, in the history of Eternity. Some of these companies are ready to insure 'Eternal Happiness' to their own customers, on swallowing some pills and certain 'articles of faith'; and Eternal damnation to those who would patronize other companies.[69]

On his journey Hübbe-Schleiden moves within the vibrant religious milieu and personally interacts with its eminent spokesmen like Anagarika Dharmapala, Abhedananda, and followers of Swami Vivekananda and members of the Brahmo Samaj in Calcutta.[70] Despite being aware of the existing alternatives, Hübbe-Schleiden keeps a firm distance not only from religious reformers but also from local religious practices and festivals such as the Bengali Durga Puja even though he calls himself a 'European sannyasi' throughout.[71]

This contradictory approach to India is a central element in 'affirmative orientalism'[72] that 'owes much to Europeans like the vegetarian Henry Salt, the Theosophist Annie Besant, the Hindu convert Sister Nivedita, the simplifier Edward Carpenter, and the champion of spiritual non-violence, Tolstoy, all of whom employed these positive stereotypes against a modernist, aggressive, capitalist, materialistic, and carnivorous Europe for which they bore little love.'[73]

The Theosophical Society as an institution is thus responsible for much of the New Age obsession with the 'orient', which for many 'functioned mainly as a *symbol* of "true spirituality" and as a repository of exotic terminology'.[74] However, recent scholarship has also emphasized that 'affirmative orientalism' has been equally shaped, influenced and promoted by prominent Indian reformers such as Swami Vivekananda[75] and M.K. Gandhi who effectively used this argumentative pattern to combat British colonialism.[76] In short, scholars are sensitive to the entanglement of discourses and the agency of indigenous actors and aim at transcending simplistic binaries between East and West.[77]

Pasupati Deva's appropriation of the 'affirmative' orientalist rhetoric brilliantly illustrates this entanglement. Referring to the popular nineteenth century discourse that brought Hübbe-Schleiden to India in the first place, Pasupati Deva claimed that 'Europeans and Americans' are as 'yet barbarians or mlecchas' and it 'would take them ages of evolution, before they can come to the same stage of spiritual evolution, which the higher class of Hindus are using just now'.[78] However, Deva abhorred massive conversion of Westerners to Hinduism as fostered by the Theosophical Society since 'Christ is the only Ideal son in the recorded history of the European world' and 'The duty of a son or sonhood stage, is simply to obey the Father's command and not to ask Him questions' while the 'Ideals of Krishna and Shiva are too sublime, too much complicated, to be grasped by people, who are spiritually in sonhood stage."[79]

Consequently and in the fashion of famous twentieth century New Age 'reluctant gurus' such as Jiddu Krishnamurti[80] or Bhagwan Shree Rajneesh, he warned Hübbe-Schleiden:

> One thing more I should tell you, you must not take me as your guru. I have neither the ambition, far less the power, to be of anybody's guru or guide. I can scarcely with the utmost difficulty guide my own self; I falter at every step, almost at every breath. [...] It would be unpardonable sin to presume to guide others, when scarcely I can guide myself.[81]

Hübbe-Schleiden himself aspired to becoming a guru thus constantly reminding Deva that a mystical experience in India would not only boost his reputation in Germany but would similarly add credibility to his claim to becoming the German guru of the 'hundreds and thousands' in the German Theosophical Society eagerly awaiting inspiration from the mystic East.[82]

Experiments with *ganja*

Unfortunately, however, neither the four to five hour morning Yoga practice and *pranayams* (breathing exercises) nor the mantra meditation seemed to entail spiritual progress. Therefore, in August 1895 Hübbe-Schleiden declared them 'futile child's-play' and concluded: 'It appears laughable if not mad, that an otherwise sensible man like I perhaps am considered to be, should waste three months of his remaining 4 years of life in his present body, on such unsuccessful practise all its best hours of his days and nights.'[83] Hübbe-Schleiden's recklessness in experimenting with mind-altering substances was partly based on his conviction that he would only live for four more years. It is almost ironic that he actually died not four but 21 years later in 1916.

Hübbe-Schleiden interpreted the constant 'excitement of the sexual sphere of [his] physical body'[84] the main hindrance to any further advancement in the 'occult training' but like ascetics generally, he attempted not only to control the 'physical body' but also sexual visions, fantasies and dreams.[85] He therefore complained that while 'sleeping' his 'physical body escapes any conscious control', a 'grievance' he was not able to get rid of for the 'last 20 years'.[86] Hübbe-Schleiden's desperation is best seen when he even considered 'falling into a (married) family life the very last eventuality to which [he] would recur' if he had to give up 'all hopes of "seeing God"' in this present 'physical life'.[87]

Celibacy has in many cultures been considered a prerequisite for spiritual aspirations most prominently in the Catholic church and various ascetic practices. Hübbe-Schleiden combined both discourses as he searched for a spiritual Christian vision with Indian methods such as Yoga and meditation. He attempted to combat the sexual desire that was constantly threatening his spiritual exercises with a *langota*, a cotton underwear that some Indian *sadhus* wear in order to suppress erection. However, throughout the diaries he confirmed his weakness with the succinct note: 'wet dream'.[88,89]

On 15 January 1896 at the suggestion of Ras Bihari Mukherjee Hübbe-Schleiden decided to 'seek refuge in Ganja (Hashish)' in order to help check the 'physical excitement of the sexual sphere' that had recently become 'unbearable'.[90] For a period of about two weeks from 16 to 28 January 1895 he experimented with both *ganja* and *bhang*. He started with *bhang*, a light liquid preparation of cannabis[91] that yielded no results even though it made it difficult to concentrate on reading a theosophical publication by Annie Besant. However, he positively noted its laxative effects.[92]

As his first experiment with *bhang* failed to uplift him spiritually, Hübbe-Schleiden turned to stronger preparations. On 16 January 1896 at 9 p.m. Ras Bihari showed him how to prepare *ganja* using the 'necessary utensils and tobacco' but 'eventually brought Asthma Cigarettes by Grimault & Cie. from Paris' as he feared that smoking of a 'chillum from a hookah' might be too strong for a beginner.[93]

While in India cannabis consumption is and has been an integral part of both spiritual and public culture, the focus in the West around 1900 was typically on its medical properties. Medical preparations of cannabis were popularly available in the West, while only 'isolated individuals in most tiny groups that moved in restricted circles'[94] like the *fin de siècle* literati consumed it for its recreational effects. The Parisian *Club des Hachichins* in the 1840s inspired only a chosen few intellectuals such as Baudelaire but from the 1940s onwards it became a fashionable commodity for the global Hippie counterculture when marijuana entered the mainstream.[95]

In contrast to Europe, cannabis was widely consumed in India, labelled the first 'cannabis oriented culture'[96] by Courtwright. Consumption here for both spiritual and recreational purposes[97] cut through all social classes and has been prominently associated with religious groups like the Shaivites.[98] The Indian working class used it as a combination of intoxicant and medicine in order to cope with their harsh lives,[99] and it was primarily through the informal interactions of working immigrants in the colonies that cannabis spread to Africa and subsequently became globalized.[100] The French asthma cigarettes that the German Hübbe-Schleiden smoked in British colonial Bengal for 'spiritual purposes' are thus a perfect example of the changing meaning of psychoactive substances in varying cultural settings as well as the circulation of cannabis preparations not just from the East to the West but also vice versa. They also illustrate the typical career of drugs. Around 1900, medical preparations of cannabis secured their status as a licit drug in Europe while recreational consumption was associated with addiction, ruin, and filth needing to be checked by national governments, and therefore labelled as illicit.[101] David Courtwright argues that this pattern is universally applicable to drugs: they typically began their international career as exotic medicines but escaped the medical sphere when they became widely used in nonmedical contexts and eventually entered the larger realm of popular and global consumption.[102] According to Courtwright, the popularization and globalization of drugs included the element of westernization since only drugs that were sought after by western consumers became global commodities.

Hübbe-Schleiden emphasized the nexus between drug consumption and psychoanalytical exploration of the subconscious by describing his *ganja* experiments predominantly in a dream-mode, a connection popularly associated with the founder of modern psychoanalysis Sigmund Freud. In Hübbe-Schleiden's 'intoxicated dreams', drug use and abuse were an issue of reflection. For example, he feared 'get[ting] used to the medical usage of *bhang*' and was afraid that despite his 'respectability[, he] might abuse the poison as a drug'.[103] In another 'intoxicated dream' he felt that he was followed by an equestrian, whom he tried 'to confuse by smoking'. However, in the same dream 'after having been busy with killing mosquitoes' he dreamed that smoking *ganja* in a chillum had helped him to concentrate on the image of Christ and thus served religious purposes.[104] In another remarkable 'intoxicated dream' Hübbe-Schleiden discussed the weak effects of *ganja* with the German Kaiser Wilhelm I. He described the Kaiser's astonishment when Hübbe-Schleiden insisted on 'never' having 'narcotic substances' despite 'coffee in the morning and tea in the afternoon'.[105]

In contrast to the rather unglamorous realities of Hübbe-Schleiden's experiments with *ganja*, both Deva and Hübbe-Schleiden render the desperately desired mystical experience in 'psychoactive terms', calling it 'God intoxicatedness'.[106] Though Hübbe-Schleiden's cannabis consumption generated no 'God intoxicatedness' whatsoever, it created conflicting loyalties between his affiliation with the Theosophical Society and his Indian gurus.

Loyalty conflict between theosophy and a 'native approach'

Through prominent theosophists such as Annie Besant[107] and even more so the Buddhist reformer and nationalist Anagarika Dharmapala,[108] the 'sober' Theosophical Society supported the transnational Temperance Movement which was as globally organized as drug trafficking by 1900.[109] The pamphlet *The Influence of Alcohol* that the president of the Theosophical Society Annie Besant originally delivered at the Livesey Central Temperance Hall, London, on 7 February 1892 under the presidency of George Ling saw three reprints in 1892, 1912 and 1930, illustrating the lasting engagement of the society in the global prohibition movement.[110] Annie Besant added her efforts to those of the wider Temperance Movement in order to 'combat this great enemy of our race'[111] by pointing to the 'spiritual effects' of 'strong drink' rather than repeating temperance activists' favourite argument about 'the misery it spreads throughout the country'. She stated: 'I am a Teetotaler because I am a Theosophist'.[112] Besant promoted 'absolute cessation of the drink-habit'[113] because it negatively affects not only the 'economy of the human body'[114] but prevents spiritual progress. She thus held the opposing position to Hübbe-Schleiden's Indian gurus as she considered psychoactive substances a hindrance rather than a trigger to spiritual aspirations.

Though the damnation of alcohol was and is often considered consistent with the consumption of 'exotic drugs' such as cannabis or opium in countercultural circles, this particular historical actor did become involved in a loyalty conflict between his Indian gurus and the Theosophical Society. Despite his critique of both policy and personnel of the Theosophical Society, Hübbe-Schleiden considered joining the inner circle of the movement called Esoteric Section in which all 'intoxicating drugs',[115] not just alcohol, were strictly prohibited. Driven by a vague loyalty towards his Indian guru Pasupati Deva, he assured himself that 'you have to carry out your Ischtadeva's [sic!][116] order even if he suggests Ganja'[117] in his private diary.

The political implications of temperance

Apart from cultural meanings, Hübbe-Schleiden's drug experiments also had important political connotations in India. Western reformers like Besant and nationalists such as Dharmapala[118] belonged to an array of activists who emphasized their anti-colonialist agenda by supporting the temperance movement.[119] They accused 'British greed' of 'spread[ing] alcoholism among the poor'.[120] British historian Mark Frost has recently illustrated the nexus between nationalist aspirations and international concerns through the example of the Temperance Movement in the case of Ceylon (Sri Lanka).[121] In India, political reformer M.K. Gandhi even argued that alcohol consumption undermined the cause of national independence as the taxes subsidized the British government and weakened the people.[122] A glance at the global proliferation of wine production shows that viticulture was indeed most effectively spread by Europeans, often colonial powers or Christian missionaries.[123] Thus the stereotypical association of alcohol consumption and distribution with Christian Europeans bears an element of truth, although the full story is of course more complicated. Nevertheless, as British historian Andrew Sheratt argues, this stereotyping of certain drugs and their association with specific ethnic groups increased as a result of the accelerated world integration around 1900, when increased mobility led to more direct contact.[124] Opium, for example, was associated with Chinese immigrants in Britain while cannabis was linked with Indians. Hübbe-Schleiden's guru Pasupati Deva shared the established stereotypes and associated the detrimental results of habitual alcohol consumption with the influx of 'Christian civilization' in India. At the same time he expressed his anti-colonial attitude through a critique of British alcohol policies in India, reflecting the anti-colonial temperance agitation in India:

> As for 'drinking'? Well, this is the result of your Christian civilization, the fruit of the 'benign' rule of your 'most Christian government', the government of the 'defenders of faith', who have given to the 'heathen Hindus' and other 'heathens' of the world, every Christian privilege, to worship the modern trinity – wine, women and wealth![125]

Final disillusionment

Though Hübbe-Schleiden concurred with his Indian guru and Theosophists in interpreting alcohol consumption as a hindrance to spiritual progress,[126] he eventually had to admit that his *ganja* experiments had also failed to elevate him spiritually. By March 1896 he had become disillusioned and was ready to leave India 'without the slightest feeling of holiness of either the country or the relationships'.[127] He explained the disenchantment with both country and people as follows:

> Instead of real brotherhood you only find courtesy here. There is a lack of trust and openness in a mutual understanding, as it is generally between European friends. Both cultural levels are too different. Aesthetically and socially the Hindu is on the level of our middle ages. [...] I have never been so sick of a country, as I am of India now. I would be really surprised if I would come back soon.[128]

The failure of his spiritual search aside, the two years in India obviously did not lead to a deeper cultural understanding of India and its people. Hübbe-Schleiden eventually sailed back to Germany in April 1896. Hübbe-Schleiden's final disappointment, distrust, and lack of understanding corresponds with his lack of success during the journey in achieving spiritual progress. On the ship back to Germany, he grudgingly admitted the failure of the *langota* to prevent ejaculation, as the journey reminded him that he was still the same miserable human being that had left Europe two years earlier.[129] Having said that, it is also interesting to note that Hübbe-Schleiden continued to wear his *langota* and adhere to an ascetic program of morning, noon, and evening meditation, dream analysis, and an austere diet during the ship's passage.[130] Other passengers might have concluded from either his intense spiritual training in India or his impressive ascetic practice that Hübbe-Schleiden was an authority in spiritual matters. It seems more likely, however, that he presented himself as a spiritual guide who authoritatively advised his fellow passengers that 'withdrawal from alcohol is the first and most essential prerequisite for obtaining a higher stadium from which it becomes possible to understand and solve highest metaphysical problems'.[131]

His advice concluded with the prophetic words and an optimistic attitude towards his immediate future in Germany as a guru:

> 'In the evening: chiromancy
>
> I felt assured that through my altruistic tendencies I will be able to help others, many others.'[132]

Conclusion

In Romantic imaginaries, the journey to the East is a mythical ritual in which the traveller transforms herself in the process of discovering the Other, more fundamentally expressing the wish to overcome the spiritual malaises of modern civilization. The further and the longer a trip is, the more charisma it grants to the traveller. Along with the status to be enjoyed back at home, the traveller invigorates herself, even at the price of an existential exile, since such a prolonged absence fosters utter individuation. In other words, rather than a mere spatial displacement for entertainment, travelling is framed as a veritable practice of self-formation.[133]

The motivations and hopes of 'Global Nomads' in travelling to contemporary Goa are thus described by D'Andrea. The above analysis shows that these words are equally true for Wilhelm Hübbe-Schleiden's spiritual search and drug experiments in British India, allowing us to detect a new type of traveller on the subcontinent that interpreted India as the 'sacred space' *par excellence*, an imaginary landscape that could free one from all restrictions. The emergence of this new type of traveller was informed by his attempt to cope with the forces of economic, political and cultural globalization and to make use of its opportunities. Thus his journey and his countercultural drug practices were partly rooted in the wider theosophical network and ideology, and embedded in structural changes within the global sphere such as the acceleration of long-distance travel, the intensification of information exchange, and the growing circulation of drugs as global commodities. In his transcultural quest for spiritual insight in India, Hübbe-Schleiden operated at the intersection of licit and illicit drugs, between cannabis and alcohol consumption, pointing not only to differing meanings of drugs in different cultural settings but also illustrating the dynamics of transcultural exchange. However, the issue of temperance illustrated that drug consumption was not only a matter of cultural difference or private negotiations but also provided arguments in wider political contexts thereby linking nationalist concerns with international aspirations.[134]

For Hübbe-Schleiden himself, drug consumption was only a byproduct of his 'spiritual travel' while the spiritual search within Hippie counterculture and the 'Global Nomads' in Goa's 'psychedelic paradise'[135] seem to have become a byproduct of the consumption of psychoactive substances. Drug tourism has long since caused serious problems in Goa and is thus a subject of heated debate among politicians, activists, and residents in the region.[136]

Hübbe-Schleiden's journey at the nexus of spiritual questing, fascination with the Orient, and drug consumption in a countercultural milieu demonstrates that western drug tourism in India has a rather long history.

Notes

1 S. Conrad and A. Eckert, 'Globalgeschichte, Globalisierung, multiple Modernen: Zur Geschichtsschreibung der modernen Welt', in S. Conrad (ed.) *Globalgeschichte: Theorien, Ansätze, Themen*, Frankfurt: Campus-Verlag, 2007, p. 20.

2 Ibid., p. 21.

3 D.T. Courtwright, *Forces of Habit: drugs and the making of the modern world*, Cambridge Mass. etc.: Harvard University Press, 2001, p. 2.

4 J.H. Mills, *Cannabis Britannica: empire, trade, and prohibition 1800–1928*, Oxford: Oxford University Press, 2003.

5 Courtwright, *Forces of Habit*, p. 9.

6 R. King, *Orientalism and Religion: postcolonial theory, India and 'the mystic East'*, repr., London: Routledge, 2005, p. 141.

7 L. Gandhi, *Affective Communities: anticolonial thought, fin-de-siècle radicalism, and the politics of friendship*, Durham, London, 2006, p. 115.

8 M. Kossler, *Arthur Schopenhauer und die Philosophien Asiens*, Wiesbaden: O. Harrassowitz, 2008.

9 A. Frank, *Sanftes Gefühl und stille Tiefe der Seele: Herders Indien*, Würzburg: Königshausen & Neumann, 2009.

10 V. Ganeshan, *Das Indienbild deutscher Dichter um 1900: Dauthendey, Bonsels, Mauthner, Gjellerup, Hermann Keyserling und Stefan Zweig: ein Kapitel deutsch-indischer Geistesbeziehungen im frühen 20. Jahrhundert*, Bonn: Bouvier, 1975.

11 V. Kade-Luthra, *Sehnsucht nach Indien: Ein Lesebuch von Goethe bis Grass*, orig. ed., München: Beck, 1991.

12 Ganeshan, *Das Indienbild deutscher Dichter um 1900*, p. 47.

13 Ibid., p. 245.

14 H. von Keyserling, *Some Suggestions concerning Theosophy*, Madras, 1912.

15 J. Mileck, *Hermann Hesse: between the perils of politics and the allure of the Orient*, New York: Peter Lang, 2003, p. 128.

16 Ibid., p. 130.

17 Ibid., p. 136.

18 W. Hübbe-Schleiden, *Indisches Tagebuch 1894/1896*, ed. Norbert Klatt, Göttingen: Norbert Klatt Verlag, 2009, pp. 18–19. Online. Available HTTP: <http://www.klatt-verlag.de/images/stories/downloads/Huebbe-Tagebuch.PDF> (last accessed 3 July 2011).

19 A. Desai, *Journey to Ithaca*, repr., Noida: Random House India, 2009.

20 Courtwright, *Forces of Habit*, pp. 44–5.

21 Ibid., p. 46.

22 J.H. Mills, 'Cannabis in the commons: colonial networks, missionary politics and the origins of the Indian Hemp Drugs Commission 1893–4', *Journal of Colonialism and Colonial History* 6, 1, 2005, 44.

23 A. Saldanha, *Psychedelic White: Goa trance and the viscosity of race*, Minneapolis: University of Minnesota Press, 2007, p. 66.

24 Ibid., pp. 28–9.

25 D.J. Timothy and D.H. Olsen, 'Tourism and religious journeys', in idem (ed.) *Tourism, Religion and Spiritual Journeys*, Oxon: Routledge, 2006, pp. 1–21.

26 Ibid.

27 See for example: A. Feldhaus, *Connected Places: region, pilgrimage, and geographical imagination in India*, 1st ed., New York: Palgrave Macmillan, 2003.

28 D.J. Timothy and D.H. Olsen, 'Tourism and religious journeys', in idem, *Tourism*, p. 4.

29 A. D'Andrea, *Global Nomads: techno and New Age as transnational countercultures in Ibiza and Goa*, New York: Routledge, 2007, p. 9.

30 Ibid., p. 21.

31 W.J. Hanegraaff, *New Age Religion and Western Culture: esotericism in the mirror of secular thought*, Leiden: Brill, 1985, p. 443.

32 M. Bevir, 'The West turns eastward: Madame Blavatsky and the transformation of occult tradition', *Journal of the American Academy of Religion* 62, 3, 1994, 747–67.

33 G.R. Fox, 'East of Said', in M. Sprinker (ed.) *Edward Said: A critical reader*, Oxford: Blackwell, 1992, p. 152.

34 R.B. Inden, *Imagining India*, London: C. Hurst, 2000, p. 73.

35 D. Vidal, 'Max Müller and the theosophists or the other half of Victorian orientalism', in J. Assayag, R. Lardinois and D. Vidal (eds) *Orientalism and Anthropology: from Max Müller to Louis Dumont*, 2nd edn, Pondicherry: Institut Français de Pondicherry, 2001, p. 18.

36 P. van der Veer, *Imperial Encounters: religion and modernity in India and Britain*, Princeton: Princeton University Press, 2001, p. 4.

37 Pasupati Deva, letter to Hübbe-Schleiden, 28 January 1896, letter no. 35, Cod MS W. Hübbe-Schleiden 221, Niedersächsische Staats-und Universitätsbibliothek, Göttingen (NSUG).

38 Annie Besant was the international president of the Theosophical Society from 1907 to 1933. For a detailed biography see: A. Taylor, *Annie Besant. A biography*, Oxford: Oxford University Press, 1992.

39 C. Risseuw, 'Thinking culture through counter-culture: the case of theosophists in India and Ceylon and their ideas on race and hierarchy (1875–1947)', in A.R.H. Copley (ed.) *Gurus and their Followers. New religious reform movements in colonial India*, New Delhi: Oxford University Press, 2000, p. 183.

40 M. Bergunder, 'Die Bhagavadgita im 19. Jahrhundert. Hinduismus, Esoterik und Kolonialismus', in idem (ed.) *Westliche Formen des Hinduismus in Deutschland. Eine Übersicht*, Halle: Verlag der Franckeschen Stiftungen zu Halle, 2006, pp. 187–216.

41 C. Fuchs, *Yoga in Deutschland: Rezeption, Organisation, Typologie*, Stuttgart: W. Kohlhammer, 1990.

42 N. Klatt, *Theosophie und Anthroposophie: Neue Aspekte zu ihrer Geschichte aus dem Nachlass von Wilhelm Hübbe-Schleiden (1846–1916)*, Göttingen: Klatt, 1993, p. 15.

43 Ibid., p. 16.

44 A. Dirlik, 'Globalisierung heute und gestern: Widersprüchliche Implikationen eines Paradigmas' in Conrad, *Globalgeschichte*, p. 163.

45 K.J. Bade, 'Friedrich Fabri: Missionsleiter und "Vater der deutschen Kolonialbewegung": Expansionspublizistik und Organisation der Kolonialbewegung', in idem (ed.) *Imperialismus und Kolonialmission: Kaiserliches Deutschland und koloniales Imperium*, Wiesbaden: Steiner, 1982, pp. 104–5.

46 K.J. Bade, *Friedrich Fabri und der Imperialismus in der Bismarckzeit: Revolution, Depression, Expansion*, Freiburg i. Br.: Atlantis, 1975, pp. 173–9.

47 W. Hübbe-Schleiden, *Ethiopien: Studien über West Afrika mit einer neu entworfenen Special Karte*, Hamburg: Friederichsen, 1879.

48 Due to the 150th anniversary of Rudolf Steiner's birth several new biographies attempt to throw fresh light on him, for example: H. Zander, *Rudolf Steiner: Die Biografie*, München: Piper, 2011.

49 For further details on the German section and its transformation into the still influential Anthroposophical Society, see: H. Zander, *Anthroposophie in Deutschland. Theosophische Weltanschauung und gesellschaftliche Praxis 1884–1945*, Göttingen: Vandenhoeck & Ruprecht, 2007.

50 Hübbe-Schleiden, *Indisches Tagebuch*, pp. 580–1.

51 Ibid.

52 E. Renan, *Philosophical Dialogues and Fragments. From the French by Ras Bihari Mukharji*, London: Trübner & Co., 1883.

53 S. Amunugama, 'A Sinhala Buddhist "Babu": Anagarika Dharmapala (1864–1933) and the Bengal connection', *Social Science Information* 30, 3, 1991, 555–91.
54 As the correspondence between Hübbe-Schleiden, Pasupati Deva and Ras Bihari Mukherjee was in English I stayed with the original. The diaries, however, are in German and I translated the quotes myself. Any mistakes are therefore entirely mine.
55 Hübbe-Schleiden, *Indisches Tagebuch.*
56 I am deeply indebted to Norbert Klatt (Göttingen) for transcribing the diaries from old German script and publishing them online on my request.
57 A.-B. Renger and A. Stellmacher, 'Der Asketen- als Wissenskörper. Zum verkörperlichten Wissen des Simeon Stylites in ausgewählten Texten der Spätantike', *Zeitschrift für Religions- und Geistesgeschichte* 62, 4, 2010, 313–38.
58 M. Singleton, *Yoga Body: the origins of modern posture practice*, Oxford, New York: Oxford University Press, 2010.
59 A. Michaels, *Die Kunst des einfachen Lebens: Eine Kulturgeschichte der Askese*, orig. ed., München: C.H. Beck, 2004, p. 9.
60 Ibid., p. 23.
61 Hübbe-Schleiden, *Indisches Tagebuch*, p. 530.
62 Michaels, *Die Kunst des einfachen Lebens*, p. 23.
63 Wilhelm Hübbe-Schleiden, letter to Pasupati Deva, 25 July 1895, Cod MS W. Hübbe-Schleiden 221, NSUG.
64 Hübbe-Schleiden, *Indisches Tagebuch*, p. 523.
65 *Bharat* is the Sanskrit term for India.
66 Pasupati Deva, letter to Rasbihari Mukerji, 15 Mai 1895, Cod MS W. Hübbe-Schleiden 221, NSUG, 1.
67 Pasupati Deva, letter to HS, 5 August 1895, letter no. 21, Cod MS W. Hübbe-Schleiden 221, NSUG.
68 Wilhelm Hübbe-Schleiden, letter to PD, 6 July 1895, letter no. 10, Cod MS W. Hübbe-Schleiden 221, NSUG.
69 Pasupati Deva, 5 August 1895, letter no. 21, Cod MS W. Hübbe-Schleiden 221, NSUG.
70 Hübbe-Schleiden, *Indisches Tagebuch*, pp. 34–5.
71 Ibid., p. 361.
72 G.R. Fox, 'East of Said', in Sprinker, *Edward Said*, p. 152.
73 Ibid.
74 W.J. Hanegraaff, *New Age Religion and Western Culture: esotericism in the mirror of secular thought*, Leiden: Brill, 1985, p. 517.
75 H. Fischer-Tiné, '"Deep Occidentalism"? Europa und "der Westen" in der Wahrnehmung indischer Intellektueller und Reformer ca. 1890–1930', *Journal of Modern European History*, 4, 2006, 189.
76 G.R. Fox, 'East of Said', in Sprinker, *Edward Said*, p. 152.
77 Fischer-Tiné, '"Deep Occidentalism"?', p. 175.
78 Pasupati Deva, letter to HS, 5 August 1895, letter no. 21, Cod MS W. Hübbe-Schleiden 221, NSUG.
79 Pasupati Deva, letter to HS, 4 July 1895, letter no. 8, Cod MS W. Hübbe-Schleiden 221, NSUG, 2.
80 S. Field, *The Reluctant Messiah*, New York: Paragon House, 1989.
81 Pasupati Deva, letter to HS, 17 August 1895, letter no. 24, Cod MS W. Hübbe-Schleiden 221, NSUG.
82 Hübbe-Schleiden, *Indisches Tagebuch*, p. 379.
83 Hübbe-Schleiden, letter to PD, 2 August 1895, letter no. 20, Cod MS W. Hübbe-Schleiden 221, NSUG.
84 Hübbe-Schleiden, *Indisches Tagebuch*, p. 630.
85 Michaels, *Die Kunst des einfachen Lebens*, p. 35.
86 Hübbe-Schleiden, *Indisches Tagebuch*, p. 630.
87 Hübbe-Schleiden, letter to PD, 2 August 1895, Cod MS W. Hübbe-Schleiden 221, NSUG.

88 Hübbe-Schleiden, *Indisches Tagebuch*, p. 530.
89 Ibid., p. 551.
90 Ibid., p. 569.
91 *Bhang* is still firmly established in Indian everyday culture as it is consumed at the spring festival of *Holi* in order to relax and cheer up the festive crowd.
92 Hübbe-Schleiden, *Indisches Tagebuch*, pp. 589–90.
93 Ibid., pp. 574–5.
94 Mills, *Cannabis Britannica*, p. 150.
95 Courtwright, *Forces of Habit*, p. 44.
96 Ibid., p. 40.
97 J.H. Mills, 'Globalizing Ganja. The British Empire and international cannabis traffic c.1834 to c.1939', in J. Goodman, P.E. Lovejoy and A. Sherratt (eds) *Consuming Habits: global and historical perspectives on how cultures define drugs*, 2nd edn, London: Routledge, 2007, p. 180.
98 Courtwright, *Forces of Habit*, p. 169.
99 J.H. Mills, 'Globalizing ganja', in Goodman, Lovejoy and Sherratt, *Consuming Habits*, p. 180.
100 Ibid., p. 181.
101 J. Goodman and P.E. Lovejoy, 'Afterword', in Goodman, Lovejoy and Sherratt, *Consuming Habits*, p. 258.
102 Courtwright, *Forces of Habit*, p. 69.
103 Hübbe-Schleiden, *Indisches Tagebuch*, pp. 592–3.
104 Ibid., pp. 581–2.
105 Ibid., p. 582
106 Ibid., p. 529.
107 To my knowledge thorough accounts of the theosophical engagement in the global Temperance Movement are not yet available.
108 M.R. Frost, '"Wider opportunities": religious revival, nationalist awakening and the global dimension in Colombo, 1870–1920', *Modern Asian Studies* 36, 4, 2002, 964.
109 M.L. Shrad, *The Political Power of Bad Ideas: networks, institutions, and the global prohibition wave*, Oxford: Oxford University Press, 2010, p. 47.
110 A. Besant, 'The influence of alcohol', *Adyar Pamphlets*, no.138 (1892, 1912, 1930).
111 Ibid., p. 2.
112 Ibid.
113 Ibid., p. 3.
114 Ibid.
115 Hübbe-Schleiden, *Indisches Tagebuch*, pp. 592–3.
116 The Sanskrit term *Ishtadeva* means god. Hübbe-Schleiden used it to designate his guru.
117 Hübbe-Schleiden, *Indisches Tagebuch*, p. 594.
118 Frost, 'Wider opportunities', p. 964.
119 L. Carroll, 'The Temperance Movement in India: politics and social reform', *Modern Asian Studies* 10, 3, 1976, 417–47; J.D. Rogers, 'Cultural nationalism and social reform. The 1904 Temperance Movement in Sri Lanka', *Indian Economic and Social History Review* 26, 3, 1989, 319–41 and P.T.M. Fernando, 'Arrack, toddy, and Ceylonese nationalism. Some observations on the Temperance Movement, 1912–1921', *Modern Ceylon Studies*, 2, 1971, 123–50.
120 Courtwright, *Forces of Habit*, p. 156.
121 Frost, 'Wider opportunities', p. 964.
122 D.M. Fahey and P. Manian, 'Poverty and purification. The politics of Gandhi's campaign for prohibition', *The Historian* 67, 3, 2005, 489–506. Cf. also the chapter by Robert Eric Colvard in the present volume.
123 Courtwright, *Forces of Habit*, p. 10.
124 A. Sherratt, 'Peculiar substances', in Goodman, Lovejoy and Sherratt, *Consuming Habits*, p. 5.
125 Pasupati Deva, letter to HS, 27 August 1895, letter no. 29, Cod MS W. Hübbe-Schleiden 221, NSUG.

126 Hübbe-Schleiden, *Indisches Tagebuch*, p. 669.
127 Ibid., p. 661.
128 Hübbe-Schleiden, *Indisches Tagebuch*, pp. 661–2.
129 Ibid., pp. 669–70.
130 Ibid., p. 667.
131 Ibid., p. 669.
132 Chiromancy is palm reading.
133 D'Andrea, *Global Nomads*, p. 175.
134 Frost, 'Wider opportunities', p. 964.
135 Saldanha, *Psychedelic White*, p. 59.
136 One example for the intense debate about drug tourism in Goa is: F. Noronha, 'Goa: fighting the bane of tourism', *Economic and Political Weekly*, 32, 51, 1997, 3253–6.

Part III

Nationalism and Internationalism: Contested regulatory regimes

6 The opium question in colonial Assam

Kawal Deep Kour

Introduction

Scholars investigating mankind's long and complex relationship with 'mind altering' substances have agreed that drug[1] use is a 'culturally universal' phenomenon, i.e. consumption of 'mind altering' substances seems to have been ubiquitous in human history.[2] In different regions of the world psychoactive substances have not only been acceptable but often also an integral part of religious practices, social and cultural life. They were sometimes viewed as 'sacred', 'curative', 'stimulant', and 'aphrodisiac', and often encoded meanings that had spiritual and metaphysical, moral and transmutative effects.

The use of drugs within different geographical and social settings was facilitated by their inclusion in the global stream of commerce, setting in motion what David Courtwright called a 'psychoactive revolution'.[3] This process, which can be roughly situated between 1500 and 1789, has brought about the confluence of 'psychoactive resources' into the stream of international commerce. The commodification of drugs thus became the basis for a promising profiteering trade. Global trading systems created a supply-chain network, generating profits through the circulation of capital and commodities while also facilitating the exchange of new ideas. As two leading American anthropologists, Sidney Mintz and Eric Wolf, have showed, modern commerce in commodities resulted in more than mere economic exchange. These have redefined global politics, culture, and social structure in fundamental ways.[4] Mintz concludes his study of sugar's modern history with the comment that 'the first sweetened cup of hot tea to be drunk by an English was a significant historical event, because it prefigured the transformation of an entire society, a total re-making of its economic and social basis'.[5] Similarly, from the late eighteenth century onwards, opium became a key commodity in the expanding commerce between a number of regions in Asia and the Atlantic and thereby making a deep economic and cultural impact in these regions.

The Sumerians are said to have been the earliest users of the opium poppy (*Papaver somniferum*) in around 3400 BCE. They called it *Hul-Gil*, the 'joy plant'. Alexander the Great is believed to have introduced opium to the people of Persia and India around 330 BCE. The Arab traders carried them from the Egyptian fields into China. Indian medical treatises written around 1200 CE like the *Shodal Gadanigrah*, *Sharanngdhar Samhita* and the *Dhanvantari Nighantu* describe the medical properties and uses of opium.[6] Gradually, opium came to fulfil a variety of purposes that endowed its consumption generally with positive meanings – it was a 'medical product', a sign of hospitality, a recreational item, a badge of social distinction, and a symbol of 'elite' culture.[7]

References to the use of poppy in Assam date back to the time of the Ahom-Mughal conflicts in the seventeenth century.[8] The *Baharistan-i-Ghaibi*[9] refers to the Mughal general, Raja Ram Singh, who sent a packet of *aphu-guti* (poppy seeds) to the Ahom general Lachit Barphukan – the number of seeds was to indicate the great number of Mughal soldiers under his command. Barphukan retorted by sending a piece of pestle and mortar with which the seeds could be easily reduced to powder.[10] According to Assamese historian S.K. Bhuyan, the practice of poppy cultivation and consumption in Assam was possibly borrowed from the bordering tribes of China.[11] However, Maniram Dewan records that poppy seeds were brought from Bengal and cultivated at Beltola during the reign of Lakshmi Singha (1769–80).[12] Opium was believed to have been consumed only by the royal house and the aristocratic families around the eighteenth century. Opium consumption consisted of either eating it (*kanikhowa*) or smoking it (*kanipankhowa*).[13] 'When opium is eaten in smallpillules [sic!], or made into a decoction by mixing it with water, the process is known as *kanikhowa* or *kanimolikhowa*. When it is smoked after mixing the opium decoction with dried betel leaves, the process is known as *kanipankhowa*.'[14] The use of a *hoka* (hookah) is said to have popularized the habit of smoking; however, as the preparation of opium for smoking takes a considerable amount of time, opium eating has been the preferred mode of consumption in the initial stages.

This paper attempts to understand the far-reaching investigation of the opium problem in colonial Assam, the results of which are stated in the *Report on the Assam Opium Enquiry Committee, 1933*. The paper explores the various dimensions of the opium narrative, including opium control and revenues, opium suppression, reforms, and treaties. In doing so, it examines the intellectual underpinnings of this narrative within the colonial framework and at the international level, and ultimately facilitates an exhaustive analysis of a document that traces the trajectory of an important phase of the opium question in colonial Assam.

The emergence of an anti-opium reformist discourse in Assam

The Anglo-Burman Treaty of Yandaboo signed in 1826 resulted in the expulsion of the rulers of Burma from Assam and the concession of the sexagenarian dynasty of the Ahoms to the colonial apparatus of the British East Indian Company. The colonial encounter not only transformed the economy but also facilitated a cultural metamorphosis. This was a direct outcome of the implementation of the colonial apparatus of administration, under which the evolution of new land laws, trade and property relations fostered a major restructuring of the agrarian landscape. The forces of 'westernization' and 'modernization', which had so long eluded the province, unlike Calcutta, gradually set at work, altering the basic economic and social structure and fostering the emergence of a new class, the English-educated Assamese intelligentsia. Through literary contributions to the *Samachar Darpan*, *Samachar Chandrika* and the *Hindu Patriot* new ideas and discussions emerged. Publications such as *Orunodoi*, *Jonaki*, *Bijulee*, *Banhi* and *Asam Bandhu* enabled the dissemination of reformist ideals. There was no major social reform movement in nineteenth century Assam. It was through the *Orunodoi (New Dawn)* – the mouthpiece of the Baptist Missionary Society of Assam, founded in 1846 – that attempts were made to create awareness about prominent social evils like *kanikhowa* (opium eating) and *kanipankhowa* (opium smoking). The campaign proliferated the number of articles on opium consumption and its aftermaths. The first one appeared in the inaugural issue of the *Orunodoi*, called 'Evils of Opium' (January 1846), followed by 'The Death of an Opium-eater' (May 1846), 'Kani lukor Katha' (June 1860) and 'Kani Erabor Katha' (June 1861).[15]

Awareness of the evils of opium eating also echoed in literary contributions of the nineteenth century, which addressed the need for reform presented through the garb of satire and wit, for example Hemchandra Barua's 'Kaniar Kirtan' (1861) and Dutiram Hazarika's 'Rasik Puran' (1877), which had some innovative reform agenda. Both the literary compositions were written in the language of the masses, and were filled with satire and humour, so as to create awareness against the evils of opium consumption, prevalent in the Assamese society. Conversely, Anandaram Dhekial Phukan depicted opium consumption as a very serious social ill in his memorandum[16] to A.J.M. Moffat Mills, who was deputed to investigate into the conditions of the province of Assam in 1853: '… the universal use of opium has converted the Assamese, once a hardy, industrious and enterprising race, into an effeminate, weak, indolent and a degraded people …'.[17]

The period of government monopoly: 'Maximum revenue from the minimum consumption'

This section explores the colonial state's policy towards opium consumption and production in Assam. Following a vigorous anti-opium propaganda by the Assamese gentry and the Baptist missionaries, opium use was declared 'problematic'. In 1861, private cultivation of poppy was prohibited. Opium distribution henceforth became a government monopoly. In 1874, the 'Fixed License Fee System' was initiated, which was then replaced by the so-called 'Mahal System',[18] all in accord with the professed colonial policy of 'righteousness before revenue'. The colonial government declared that it would 'countenance only to the narrowest extent a habit which it finds impossible to eradicate'. The colonial administrators viewed opium as a medical necessity and a stimulant which would only lead into abuse and addiction under conditions of unrestrained consumption. They strongly contested the proposition that the presence of opium in Assam was a 'vice', a view echoed by the report of the Royal Commission on Opium (1895).

The Royal Commission on Opium (henceforth RCO) which visited India in 1894 was aware of the efforts of the aforementioned Hemchandra Barua, and he was asked to appear before the Commission in Calcutta which he was unable to do for health reasons. However, he got his 'Kaniyar Kirtan' translated into English through Upendranath Barua, one of his ardent supporters, and sent it to H.J. Wilson, a member of the Commission.[19] Hemchandra Barua's written statement to the Commission, however, exposed the ambivalent attitude of the newly emerging intelligentsia, itself a product of 'Western' thought and self-professed loyal collaborators of the Empire in its 'civilizing mission':

> [T]he people of Assam are naturally disposed to use opium for non-medicinal purposes and are not, I believe, willing to bear any part of the cost of prohibitive measures, nor can they afford to do so … [The sale] of opium by the Government should not, I think, be prohibited for non-medicinal purposes. Such prohibition is not, in my opinion, practicable.[20]

The members of the *Jorhat Sarbajanik Sabha*, a large number of whom were tea-planters, 'wanted to prove that the Assamese people were opium eaters from the remotest times and the hard-working classes in the malarious plains of Assam require some stimulant to keep up their powers'.[21]

Although opium consumption was often proclaimed an evil which needed immediate eradication, the colonial policy always stopped short of prohibition. One explanation lies with the large opium revenues of the colonial government. It might be argued that the Assamese middle class at large remained loyal to the colonial enterprise and would only hesitantly campaign against such a large – to borrow from Courtwright – financial prop of the regime. Nevertheless, individual actors were very active in the propagation of their anti-opium ideas. Hemchandra Barua is a bright example for being such a campaigner and it might be argued that his absence in the campaigns against consumption of opium was felt intensely after his death in 1896.

The RCO 1893 was convinced that the great mass of Indian opinion was opposed to the proposal of prohibition that had been on the agenda of the RCO. A prospective prohibition of the use of opium poppy was seen as an unnecessary restriction on the individual and an interference with established customs and habits. Statistics for the period 1873–4 to 1890–1 reveal that there was no significant decline in consumption[22]; instead, there were considerable flows of revenue into the government coffers. The consumption levels declined from 1,837 *maunds* in 1874–5 to 1,494 *maunds* in 1889–90, while the duty on opium per *seer* increased from Rs 23 in 1874–5 to Rs 37 in 1890–1.[23] However, the report of the Botham Committee – which will be introduced below – attested to a sudden upsurge in consumption of opium and *ganja* (cannabis) from 1900 onwards that became a source of serious concern to the government.

The anti-opium rhetoric in twentieth-century Assam

From 1900 to 1921, dramatic developments in Assam led to a redefinition of the political identity of the province and added a new dimension to the anti-opium discourse. With the formation of the 'Assam Association'[24] in 1903, the Assamese elite, although not necessarily anti-colonial, entered a more organized and assertive phase.

A number of temperance and anti-opium societies sprang up in Assam at the initiative of the *sattradhikars*[25] between 1907 and 1912, spurred on by the increasing international criticism of Britain's opium trade. With the formation of legislative councils, the anti-opium discourse entered a new phase. Phanidhar Chaliha (1854–1923) and Ghanashyam Barua (1867–1923), both members of the legislative council, spoke against the abuse of opium in the Provincial Councils. In 1918, Chaliha recommended the introduction of the prohibition of opium. Raising the issue before the Council in its budget session on 6 April 1918, he said, 'The pernicious habit of opium eating of the Assamese is greatly responsible for the poverty of the people.'[26] Ghanshyam Barua exposed the hollowness of the government policy on opium and pushed for drastic measures against it, but the government refused to concede anything. Meanwhile, members of the Assam Association including Ghanashyam Barua and Rai Bahadur Nilambar Datta suggested that the organization of Temperance Societies be at the top of their agenda. However, by 1920, the anti-opium crusade in Assam acquired national recognition along with a new crusader and a new dimension.

The internationalization of the opium question and its repercussions in Assam

The growing recognition of addiction as a social phenomenon in almost all parts of the world displayed global concerns over the threat to public health and the need for institutions and laws to fight against such threats.[27] It was assumed that an international policy enforced by national governments would remedy this situation. The anti-opium movement was internationalized by the crusade in the Chinese Empire against the growth of poppy and the production and use of opium, prohibitionist voices at home, and the American appreciation of the magnitude of the opium problem following the Philippine Opium Committee. Hamilton Wright argued in his article on the International Opium Conference about how international action against opium had revitalized domestic activism.[28]

The International Opium Conference at Shanghai in 1909 was the result of the common apprehension that addiction to manufactured drugs threatened the welfare of humanity and signified the worldwide determination to get rid of the opium evil. The Hague Opium Convention of 1912 attempted to suppress opium abuse by inciting public opinion worldwide against the practice of smoking opium and against the traffic in opium. Accordingly, the Assam administration was advised to impose restrictions on opium smoking, but the situation remained far from satisfactory. After a brief drop in consumption levels, an upward trend was registered. Consumption levels shot up to 1,557 *maunds* in 1912–13 from 1,227 *maunds* in 1901–2 and revenue from opium increased from Rs 17,23,238 to around Rs 27,38,307 in 1912–13, even though population figures were constant at 5,759,444 from 1901–2 to 1911–12.[29]

The Government of Assam conceded to the 'native' demand for an enquiry into the opium situation amidst the growing local concerns over the continuous upward trend of consumption in spite of the global resolutions at Hague where India formally committed to suppressing opium in all its provinces. The Botham Committee was appointed in December 1912 with A.W. Botham as chairman and Kaliprasad Chaliha, Kutubbuddin Ahmed, and Radhanath Phukan as members. It submitted its report in 1913 though this report was made public only in June 1925. Interestingly, a major finding of the Botham Committee was that smoking *madak* – a mixture of opium and tobacco – was widely prevalent, and that there had actually been an increase in the habit since the prohibition of poppy cultivation in 1860. It authenticated the government's contention that further restrictions on the sale of opium would risk the consumption of more deleterious stimulants such as *ganja*, and expressed its apprehension that the 'younger generation is taking to *ganja* instead of taking to opium.' Apprehending the smuggling of cocaine and morphia from Burma into Assam, the Committee advocated caution and was against prohibition or any other stringent restriction on opium.

From 1919, the opium policy of the provinces was a so-called 'transferred subject' over which each province had full control. However, in Assam, it remained a reserved subject till 1928.

Gandhi's campaign against Assam opium

Council politics in Assam voiced strong opinions against downplaying the extent of opium smoking and came down heavily on the Government of Assam for its complacency about the 'opium menace' in the province. The legislative council members in Assam continued to protest against the ambiguous policies of the Government of India and to petition for the immediate redressal of the opium menace. The Assam Association (formed in 1903) spearheaded the movement in pronouncing the grievances and aspirations of the people of Assam. It was a result of the vigorous propaganda that was carried out by members of the Assam Association that at the Nagpur session of the Indian National Congress (INC) in December 1920, Assam was virtually recognized as a separate Congress Province.[30] An opium restriction campaign was included in the agenda of the Non-Cooperation Movement (1919–21), which was a major boost to the anti-opium agitation in the province. At the height of the Non-Cooperation Movement, Mahatma Gandhi toured the interior villages, resulting supposedly in a 26 per cent drop in opium consumption within six months, to which Gandhi's close comrade, the temperance campaigner C.F. Andrews asserted, 'Assam is no longer the "black spot of India" that it was in the previous years.'[31]

The years preceding the campaign, from 1913–14 to 1918–19, showed a fluctuating trend in opium consumption. Ultimately, the decrease in the number of shops, the rise in the price of opium, and the change in the method of licensing had no appreciable effect on the consumption of opium in the Assam villages and among the hill tribes. It was asserted, however, that there was a marked reduction following Gandhi's visit to Assam and the launch of the temperance movement in 1921, which included a strong case against opium. Certainly, in 1921–2, the consumption of opium dropped from 1,614 *maunds* to 1,013 *maunds*, a reduction of 601 *maunds* within 12 months.[32] A similar reduction was also noticed in the consumption of *ganja* and country liquor.

The promotion of temperance as part of the Non-Cooperation Movement followed the declaration of the All-India Congress Committee that:

> the [opium] policy of the Government of India is altogether contrary to the moral welfare of the people in India and other countries. The AICC is further of the opinion that the people of India would welcome the total abolition of the opium traffic for purposes of revenue and is also of the opinion that the production of opium is out of all proportions to the medical requirements of India.[33]

The All-India Congress Committee (AICC) appointed C.F. Andrews to conduct an enquiry in collaboration with the Assam Provincial Congress Committee into the 'opium habits' of the people of Assam and the effect of the government's opium policy upon them.[34] This Opium Resolution was necessary for two reasons, as Mahatma Gandhi expressed. According to Gandhi, C.F. Andrews

> … has shown [that] the Government of India made itself responsible for changing at the Opium Convention, the word 'medical' to 'legitimate' in describing people's requirements. It therefore became necessary in view of the approaching convention for the A.I.C.C. to say what the nation thinks of the Government of India policy. It had become equally necessary to investigate the conditions of the Assamese under the opium habit. A fine body of men and women are undergoing a process of decay under the cursed opium habit. The Assam Provincial Congress Committee is

> ready to inquire into the matter. The A.I.C.C. has therefore, thought it desirable to appoint Mr. Andrews to conduct the inquiry in cooperation with the Provincial Committee.[35]

The Enquiry's report charged the Indian government's representative at Geneva, Mr Walton, of having misled the international community about the extent to which opium smoking constituted a problem in India. A far-reaching investigation of a non-official character, it declared that if opium was regarded as a dangerous drug in the West, it should equally be regarded as a dangerous drug in the East.[36]

The Assam Congress Committee's Report, however, revealed the inefficacy of the government's policy of 'maximum revenue and minimum consumption'. While the retail price of opium increased year by year, consumption showed no material reduction.[37] The report suggested drastic steps to eradicate the evil. Its major recommendations included limiting opium use to medical and scientific needs, registration of addicts above the age of forty, and treating opium addiction as a medical problem. The Assam Legislative Council passed a resolution in its March 1921 session to the effect that opium consumers should be registered and each consumer should be given a definite ration of the drug. It further proposed that rations be reduced by 10 per cent annually so that in 10 years users would be entitled to no rations beyond what might be used on medical grounds. In 1919, the system of registering opium addicts was introduced as an experimental measure in the Sadiya Frontier Tract. The system was gradually extended to the whole of Kamrup district in Lower Assam by 1925 and then to the remainder of the province with effect from 1 April 1926. By this time, the Bengal Government in the Calcutta Gazette drafted the Indian Poisons Act of 1926 for the control of particular poisons. Opium and its derivatives were listed in Schedule A as being dangerous poisons. Interestingly, the law made no mention of 'excise opium'.[38] Multilateral efforts spearheaded by the League of Nations to address concerns about the global proliferation of opium strengthened domestic enforcement efforts. Following the withdrawal of the Non-Cooperation Movement in 1922, the Indian legislature was employed by the local elites as a powerful platform for propaganda and influence. Already, the self-purification movement launched as a part of constructive programme of the Non-Cooperation at the initiative of M.K. Gandhi had amply demonstrated the strength of voluntary effort and moral suasion, 'themselves vital springs of reform'.[39]

The Assam Opium Enquiry Committee report, 1933

The members of the councils raised demands for sincere efforts on the part of the government to step up measures towards a successful implementation of the opium curtailment policy. Nevertheless the policy of rationing and registration in effect from 1919, including the intensive temperance campaign of 1921, had resulted in a significant decline in consumption. The annual consumption amounted to 64,000 *seers* per year in 1920, to 28,000 *seers* per year in 1927, and further down to 16,000 *seers* per year in 1932.[40] On 6 March 1933, the Assam Legislative Council voted, to institute a seven member non-official committee with a mandate of reviewing the government's opium policy and advising on the future policy to be adopted in the light of conclusions of a global enquiry made by the League of Nations.[41] In addition, it was inspired by an apprehension expressed by excise prevention that 'very great quantities of opium are being smuggled in'. That smuggling was threatening to swallow the positive effects that the reduction was expected to bring in, along with revenue considerations, demanded an investigation.

The document is an indispensable source to those who wish to study the problem extensively. It is an exhaustive survey of the opium problem in Assam, and presents an in-depth study of the underlying causes of the prevalence of the habit, and the consumption patterns since the formation of the province of Assam in the year 1874. It is further an analysis of the opium policies pursued so far as well as a survey into the problem of opium contraband and the related questions of the effectiveness of the detection and preventive staff. For a comprehensive understanding of the various aspects of the opium problem and the policies adopted, it had included the recommendations of the Botham Committee (1913), the conclusions of the Assam Congress Opium Enquiry Committee (1925) and the findings of the Ekstrand Commission (1931). Considering that the government was seriously apprehensive about smuggling and the problem of short-weight sales, it entails a detailed study of the various facets of contraband opium in Assam. It is the first report of its kind to have taken up the issue of opium smuggling as a constraint to the effective implementation of opium policies.

The Council chose the following members of the committee through a vote: J.J. Nichols Roy, as chairman, Brindaban Chandra Goswami, Nilambar Dutta, Mahendra Nath Gohain, Abdur Rahim Chaudhari, E.S. Roffey and Rohini Kumar Chaudhary. The Commissioner of Excise was appointed by the government as a member and secretary of the committee. During the proceedings, 134 witnesses were examined, including some 35 opium eaters, six civil surgeons, five European medical officers of tea gardens, a retired civil surgeon who had served in Burma and one private practitioner. The committee focused on a review of the 'present' opium policy, to identify the extent of threat posed by the existence of contraband opium, including the prevalence of short weight, an assessment of the prospective results of total prohibition, which was yet to receive acceptance as a government policy. It also attempted to explore effective instruments for eradicating opium consumption, including the registration of addicts and influencing public opinion and called for the strengthening of control and regulatory mechanisms.

The report, out of many important guidelines, strongly recommended a major reformation of opium legislation and policy. While being treated as a non-official document, the report was, however, acknowledged as a reflection of public opinion. The spontaneous social response represented by the government and the 'native' opinions greatly surprised the committee.

The committee had, for the first time, attempted to create a comprehensive understanding of the cause and effects of the opium problem in outlining government policy, the consumption pattern, and international treaty obligations on reduction and suppression of the ill-practices. In comprehending the issues of demand and supply, and the possibility of reducing opium consumption by legal means to control the corresponding offences, it recommended an effective opium eradication policy.

Although medical opinion did play an important role in the deliberations, the report was highly reflective of the major international interventions, for instance the efforts of the League of Nations, with a growing sense of concern for the global proliferation of drugs and the need to regulate their trafficking. The moral, political and economic contours had undergone enormous transmutations since 1895, the year in which the report of the RCO came out. The rising tide of nationalism, diplomacy, the changing nature of trade, the 'globalization' of the 'drug-ism', all led to the institutionalization of enforcement mechanisms. Global collaborative efforts reiterated through conventions and treaties the need to stem the tide of the growing 'psychoactive revolution'. The Shanghai Conference of 1909, the Hague Convention held in 1912, the International Opium Convention of 1925, and the Convention for Limiting the Manufacture and Regulating the Distribution of Narcotic Drugs in 1931 all provided a basis for containing the damaging effects of the use, abuse and trade in psychoactive substances. International efforts strengthened domestic enforcement efforts. In Assam, the Assam Congress Opium Enquiry Committee, 1925, the promulgation of the Assam Opium Smoking (Prohibition) Act, 1927, the 'Black Spots' Conference of 1930, and the appointment of the Assam Opium Enquiry Committee, 1933, are but the visible manifestations of the multilateral efforts, at an international, national and local level.

The Assam Opium Enquiry Committee clearly repudiates the scientific validation of the 'colonial rhetoric' that claimed that opium was a prophylactic and a curative drug. It presents a detailed analysis of the nature, extent and effects of the opium use and abuse in Assam. The pamphlet on 'the present position of the opium habit in India', published in 1928 by Colonel Chopra of the Calcutta Tropical School of Medicine, contains an analytical study of the opium habit. Another publication, a brochure on the 'the action of opium and nicotine in malaria', that came out in 1930 and was written by Colonel Chopra and Colonel Knowles, had greatly assisted the Committee, as was acknowledged by it, in its understanding of the progression of the opium habit in Assam. The findings attest to the opium habit rapidly disappearing from amongst the educated and the middle classes, although still widely prevalent amongst the ordinary cultivators, mostly plantation workers, small income groups, and less educated people who supposedly could not apprehend the malicious consequences of the habit.

The Committee understood addiction as a medical problem which could be cured. Although it lamented the lack of necessary infrastructure for the treatment of addicts, it suggested that 'Dr Modino's cure' – a serum method originating in Alexandria in the early 1920s, widely believed to cure opium addiction at the time – could be given a trial in the jails of Assam. Reiterating the 'nationalist stand' adopted by C.F. Andrews, in the Assam Congress Opium Enquiry Committee, the report argued that opium's classification as a poison in Britain showed that the drug demanded the greatest care and discrimination. As already mentioned, the Bengal Government had already listed opium and its derivatives in the Indian Poisons Act under Schedule A as being dangerous poisons. On the other hand, the rules excluded 'excise opium'. The findings of the Ekstrand Commission of 1931 form one of the most authoritative statements and are central to the conclusions arrived at by the Committee. The Committee suggested deterrents to contain smuggling and short-weight. It proposed the strict enforcement of the Assam Opium (Amendment) Act of 1933 and the Deportation Act III of 1864. In appraising the government policy of 10 per cent cut, the Committee acknowledged rationing to be a major factor in restraining consumption. Undeniably the policy had an influence, yet the major upheavals in the economic and political contours added new dimensions to the opium rhetoric.

Aftermath

The economic depression of the 1930s and the phased Civil Disobedience Movement tended to encourage an anti-imperialist mass revolt. This phase saw the resurgence and institutionalization of peasant movements under the aegis of the All Assam Ryot Sabha in 1933. In the second phase of the Civil Disobedience Movement, reeling under the impact of the Great Depression (1929–32), the *ryots* in Assam (as elsewhere) were in a pitiable condition. The cumulative arrears of land revenue increased from Rs 2 lakhs in 1928 to Rs 37 lakhs in 1933.[42] Again, there was a heavy decline in the revenue collections from land, excise, and forests. The Provincial Excise Revenue was down from 6.5 million in 1929–30 to 3.4 million by 1933–4. A finance committee visiting the province in the second half of 1933 had already declared Assam to be a 'deficit province'. The revenue collection from opium showed a progressive decrease during the period 1925 to 1931, down from Rs 35,54,870 in 1925 to Rs 21,82,601 in 1931. The loss of revenue reverberated in the House of Commons in London, where the issue was highlighted:

> [I]n view of the fact that Assam is a deficit province now with an additional prospective loss of 15 lakhs per annum from opium revenue, we will take all possible steps to make the Excise duty on motor spirit and on kerosene a provincial source of revenue ...[43]

The heightened legislative intervention in major issues concerning the province is worth mentioning. After 1919, the Legislature became the mouthpiece for voicing concerns over vital issues including the opium question. The councils carried on an unceasing struggle against the official opium policy. The Committee's recommendations assessed the drug problems as 'broadly apolitical and philosophical in nature'. The Assam Opium Enquiry Committee dismissed the idea of prohibition arguing that drugs did not disappear as a result of a ban. Instead, it endorsed the recommendations of the Assam Congress Opium Enquiry Report of 1925 regarding its propaganda, the organization of anti-opium societies, and the perpetuation of the temperance movement initiated by Mahatma Gandhi.

On 3 December 1934, an important resolution was issued by the local government that published its observations in the report of the Assam Opium Enquiry Committee and laid down detailed instructions for the future working of the policy of reducing rations to persons 'under 50 years of age' by 10 per cent annually. According to this resolution, no new pass for the consumption of opium was to be granted merely on the grounds of addiction without the production of a medical certificate from a recognized medical practitioner. No monthly allowance exceeding 2½ *tolas* was permissible in any case without the sanction of the local government. In order to stop the system of short-weight of opium, an experimental project for the manufacturing of opium in a pill form through a private chemist was carried out.[44] The first attempts at the legal prohibition of opium were initiated in Assam in 1937 following the Government of India Act of 1935. Though the Act of 1935 made no explicit reference to prohibition, it empowered the provincial governments to 'legislate' with respect of 'narcotic drugs and intoxicating liquors'.

In 1937, an Excise Committee consisting of 14 members of the Provincial Legislative Assembly was constituted and the last percentage cut was carried out in the plains district in 1938–9. In 1939, Assam's coalition government finally implemented the measures in the Dibrugarh subdivision and Lakhimpur Frontier Tract, with Omeo Kumar Das as the Honorary Prohibition Commissioner. Work was organized at three levels, *viz.* propaganda, relief, and vigilance through the non-official agency. Arrangements were made to organize treatment in special treatment centres that were to be opened and to train doctors to take charge in these institutions. The training was carried out at Dibrugarh and Sibsagar and was conducted by Dr G.S. Chopra of the School of Tropical Medicine, Bengal. With a view to effect the necessary legislation, a prohibition bill was passed by the Assam Legislative Council and introduced in the Assembly after necessary modifications to the Opium Act. The Assam Opium Prohibition Act was passed in 1947. The Act gave legal sanction to the non-official organizations, and provided for exorbitant fines and imprisonment, enhanced sentences for habitual offenders, and restricted the movement of offenders and those involved in smuggling. The Constitution of independent India made specific provisions for prohibition in the Directive Principles of State Policy (Article 47): '[T]he State shall endeavour to bring about prohibition of the consumption except for medicinal purposes, intoxicating drinks and of drugs which are injurious to health.'

In the September 1948 session of the Assam Legislative Assembly, Bijay Chandra Bhagabati, M.L.A., moved the following resolution, which was subsequently adopted:

> That this assembly is of the opinion that the Government of Assam do move the Government of India to help in making the Opium Prohibition Campaign in Assam a success by making poppy cultivation and traffic in opium illegal and punishable in law all over India, including the states, and to take such effective steps as to stop smuggling of opium into Assam from other provinces and countries.[45]

Elucidating the Congress government's policy on opium and liquor, Bhagabati called for the cooperation of the Government of India to ensure success in a 'stupendous task'. It was insisted that prohibition would be successful only if the Government of India would cooperate to limit the production of opium. This was an important point of discussion at the All-India Opium Conference of 1949. It was unanimously agreed that 'within a maximum period of 10 years, the use of opium for other than scientific and medicinal purposes should be totally prohibited'. It however added that the province/state/union of states was free to achieve the objective within a shorter period. It was recommended that total prohibition of opium should be achieved within 10 years, and subsequently the Narcotics Commissioner declared Assam's quota of opium to be 'NIL' by 31 March 1959.[46]

Notes

1 Commonly understood, a 'drug' is a substance that produces significant physiological and psychological changes. Drugs can be sedatives, analgesics and stimulants, and put to both therapeutic and non-therapeutic use.
2 J. Goodman, P. Lovejoy and A. Sheratt (eds), *Consuming Habits. drugs in history and anthropology*, London: Routledge, 1995.
3 D.T. Courtwright, *Forces of Habit: drugs and the making of the modern world*, Cambridge Mass. etc.: Harvard University Press, 2001.
4 A.W. McCoy, *Interim Draft Final Report on Historical Review of Opium Production.* Online. Available HTTP: <http://www.druglibrary.org/schaffer/heroin/historic.htm> (accessed 27 September 2009).
5 Ibid.
6 R.N. Chopra, I.C. Chopra, K.L. Handa and L.D. Kapur, *Indigenous Drugs of India*, 3rd edn, Kolkata: Academic Publishers, 1993, pp. 204–5.
7 Ibid., p. 7.
8 The seventeenth century incursions of the Mughal emperors into Assam it is believed were prompted by the quest for territorial expansion and also for trade routes into Tibet and China. H.K. Barpujari, *Comprehensive History of Assam*, vol. II, Guwahati: Publication Board Assam, 1992.
9 For details, see *Baharistan-i-Ghaibi*, trans. M.I. Bora, Guwahati: Department of Historical and Antiquarian Studies, 1992.

10 H.K. Barpujari, *A Comprehensive History of Assam*, vol. III, Guwahati: Publication Board Assam, 1994, p. 110.
11 S.K. Bhuyan, *Asamar Buranji Katha*, Guwahati: Department of Historical and Antiquarian Studies, 1989.
12 A. Guha, *Medieval and Early Colonial Assam*, Calcutta: K.P. Bagchi, 1991, pp. 281–96.
13 *Report of the Assam Congress Opium Enquiry Committee 1925*, Calcutta: N. Mukherjee, 1925 (henceforth ACOECR 1925), p. 37.
14 Ibid., p. 38.
15 See notes in T. Misra, 'Social criticism in nineteenth century Assamese writing – The Orunodoi', *Economic and Political Weekly*, 20, 37, 1985, 1558–66.
16 For details, see Appendix 'J', 'Observations on the administration of the province of Assam by Baboo Annundurum Dekial Phookan', in A.J.M. Moffat Mills, *Report on the Province of Assam*, repr., Guwahati: Publication Board Assam, 1984 [1854].
17 Ibid.
18. ACOECR 1925, p. 3.
19 R. Saikia, *Economic and Social History of Assam, 1853–1921*, New Delhi: Manohar Publishers and Distributors, 2000, p. 218.
20 Written testimony of Hemchandra Barua to the Royal Commission on Opium 1893. For details, see Appendix XXXIV, 'To the Secretary to the Government of Madras, Revenue Department, Calcutta, December 1893', in *Report on the Royal Commission on Opium 1893*, vol. IV, 29 January-22 February 1894, p. 372, Central Secretariat Library, Delhi.
21 From the President and Secretary, Jorhat Sarbajanik Sabha to William Erskine Ward, Chief Commissioner of Assam. *Report on the Royal Commission on Opium, 1893*, vol. II, Appendix XXXVI, p. 462, Assam State Archives (henceforth ASA).
22 We learn from excise reports that the slight variable decrease in consumption between 1881 and 1901 was due to the many disasters – disease, famine and earthquake – that caused a decline in the indigenous population (ACOECR 1925, p. 23).
23 Report on the Royal Commission on Opium, 1893, vol. II, Appendix XXXXV.
24 The Assam Association can be regarded as the first 'broad based provincial organization' formed by the elites aimed at better representation of the political aspirations of the province. It was formed in Guwahati in 1903 by Manik Chandra Barua, leading Assamese entrepreneur and later an eminent figure in Assam politics. H.K. Barpujari and A.C. Bhuyan, *Political History of Assam, 1826–1919*, Guwahati: Publication Board Assam, 1992.
25 *Sattradhikar* is a term used to designate the head of a *sattra* (Vaishnavite monastery) in Assam. In 1907, an anti-opium conference was held at Dibrugarh urging upon the government to check the opium menace, and call out for a formation of the Assam Temperance Association. In 1912, an anti-opium conference was summoned at Dibrugarh, with the *sattradhikar* of Dinjay Sattra in the chair, where a temperance society was formed. It recommended the opening of a public register of opium eaters, as had been successfully done in Burma, with a view to check the further progress of the habit. Saikia, *Social and Economic History of Assam*.
26 Assam Legislative Council (ALC) debates, April 1918, ASA.
27 J. Buxton, *The Historical Foundations of the Narcotic Drug Control Regime*, World Bank Development Research Group, 2008. Online. Available HTTP: <http://www-wds.worldbank.org/servlet/WDSContentServer/WDSP/IB/2008/03/12/000158349_20080312084905/Rendered/PDF/wps4553.pdf> (accessed 23 January 2010).
28 H. Wright, 'The International Opium Conference', *The American Journal of International Law*, 6, 1912, 865–89.
29 ACOECR 1925, Appendix X, pp. 90–1.
30 P. Girin, *Assam: attitude towards federalism*, Kolkata: Allied Publishers, 1984, p. 3.
31 The consumption of opium in Assam was much higher than the standard that was set by the League of Nations which was 6 *seers* per 10,000 of population. 'Black spots' were identified as those areas where the consumption was around 30 *seers* per 10,000 of population. In Assam, as of 1920–1 when consumption was at its highest, it was 229 *seers* per 10,000 of

population. Government of Assam, *The Assam Opium Enquiry Committee 1933*, Shillong: Assam Government Press, 1933, ASA (henceforth AOECR 1933).

32 AOECR 1933, p. 28

33 Resolution no. VI (Opium Policy) adopted at the A.I.C.C. annual session in Ahmedabad (published on 6 July 1924 in the newspaper *Navjivan*); cf. also M.H. Desai, *Day to Day with Gandhi (Secretary's diary)*, vol. IV (28 January-8 November 1924).

34 For this purpose, it authorized the Working Committee to sanction a sum of Rs 1,000 for the Assam Opium Enquiry Committee, subject to the Assam Provincial Congress Committee collecting Rs 2,000 for the same purpose. For details, see R. Bakshi, *Gandhi and the Congress*, New Delhi: Sarup & Sons, 1996, p. 48.

35 Resolution no. VI (Opium Policy) adopted at the A.I.C.C. annual session in Ahmedabad (published on 6 July 1924 in the newspaper *Navjivan*); cf. also M.H. Desai, *Day to Day with Gandhi (Secretary's diary)*, vol. IV (28 January-8 November 1924).

36 T. Brook and B.T. Wakabayashi, *Opium Regimes – China, Britain, and Japan 1839–1952*, California: University of California Press, 2000, p. 44.

37 For example, the price of opium in 1874 was 22 rupees per *seer*, which increased to 65 rupees per *seer* by 1924. At the same time, opium consumption in Assam was 1,874 *maunds* in 1875 and 1,614 *maunds* in 1920–1.

38 Excise opium referred to the opium that was supplied from the government-controlled factories at Ghazipur in the present day north Indian state of Uttar Pradesh. From the treasuries of the state governments it was supplied to the vendors who had bid for the lease of the opium vends. No other opium except excise opium was allowed to be sold. The other opium was the Provision Opium which was the opium of high purity meant for export.

39 E.S. Reddy (ed.), *Heartbeats of India: C.F. Andrew's debates in foreign periodicals*, New Delhi: Konark Publishers in association with National Gandhi Museum, 2005, pp. 67–9.

40 AOECR 1933, p.1.

41 For a discussion of the interaction between Indian governmental and civil society actors with the League of Nations cf. Maria Framke's chapter in this volume.

42 A. Guha, Planter-Raj to Swaraj: freedom struggle and electoral politics in Assam 1826–1947, New Delhi: ICHR, 1977, p. 177.

43 Cf. Parliamentary Debates (Hansard), House of Commons, 1803–2005, Vol. 278, 24 May 1933.

44 Government of India, Memorandum on CISE (Opium) Administration in India, 1934–35, ASA.

45 Assam Legislative Assembly (ALA) debates, September 1948, Assam Secretariat Library.

46 E.H. Pakyntein, 'Opium prohibition campaign in Assam', *UNODC Bulletin on Narcotics*, 4, 1958, 12–14.

7 Internationalizing the Indian War on Opium: Colonial policy, the nationalist movement and the League of Nations

Maria Framke

Introduction

In December 1924 at the annual meeting of the Indian National Congress in Belgaum the following resolution was adopted:

> The Congress is of opinion that the policy of the Government of India in using the drink and drug habit of the people as a source of revenue is detrimental to the moral welfare of the people of India and would therefore welcome its abolition. The Congress is further of opinion that the regulation by the Government of India of the opium traffic is detrimental not only to the moral welfare of India but of the whole world, and that the cultivation of opium in India which is out of all proportion to medical and scientific requirements should be restricted to such requirements.[1]

This resolution clearly revealed the Indian National Congress' dismissal of the official opium policy of the British Indian government. In addition it touched upon several globally discussed issues in regard to opium consumption such as the medical usage of the drug, ethical questions of opium abuse as well as the financial side of any curtailment of opium production and distribution. While the Congress reference to the question of restricting opium cultivation to medical and scientific requirements demonstrates the organization's knowledge of contemporary global debates taking place in the League of Nations, the resolution remained silent about the institution's responsibility for framing international drug control initiatives in the interwar period.

International negotiations to regulate opium production and trade had taken place before the 1920s, although these were initiated by civil society actors or single governments. In the interwar period, a new intergovernmental actor became active in the field for the first time with the establishment of the League of Nations. In recent years, research on the League of Nations' so-called non-political work has substantially increased, bringing to the forefront the work of the League's non-European members as well as lesser examined themes such as the traffic in drugs and women, health issues and intellectual cooperation.[2] This paper contributes to this recent trend by analyzing the relationship of India and the League of Nations in regard to the opium problem. Even more importantly, when looking at the history of opium and more precisely at conflicts regarding its production and distribution in British India in the twentieth century, the role of international actors such as the League of Nations has so far been ignored. With the emergence of the Genevan body as a global drug regulating institution, the British Indian government was confronted with opposition on two fronts, the international level and at home from the Indian national movement. The work at these two levels, but also existing linkages between national and international actors and differences in approaches and goals in the different arenas are examined in the paper.

At the outset, the article gives a short outline of India in the League of Nations, focusing on the public perceptions of the country's status and representation in Geneva. Subsequently, the paper presents an overview of the international dimension of the opium question and the work of the official Indian delegation in the League. This will be followed by a discussion about the nature and aims of responses in the Indian National Congress and the Indian nationalist press as well as within British-Indian government circles including the Indian establishment press[3] before, during, and after the League's opium conference of 1924/25.

India in the League of Nations – Public perceptions of its status and representation

Owing to its participation and major military contribution to the First World War, but also because the public in British India was observing quite closely the fate of the Caliphate, India was not only allowed to participate in the Paris Peace Conference in 1919 but also to sign the Peace Treaties along with the representatives of other sovereign states on the basis of legal equality of status.[4] After long discussions, India was also admitted to the League of Nations. What is striking about this fact is that India was a non-sovereign state, and became therefore the only non-self-governing colonial member of the League of Nations.[5] This anomaly – the fact that the country officially enjoyed sovereign rights in external matters in the League of Nations while being neither autonomous nor having any substantial power in internal affairs – became one of the major themes of public debate in India.[6]

However, the anomalous status of India was not the only aspect that was widely debated amongst Indian politicians and in Indian newspapers and journals. The issue of representation in Geneva, the precise status of India within the League of Nations, the activities of the League with regard to the mandates and the arrangement of international cooperation within the organization evoked further discussions.[7] The nature and mode of selecting the delegates who went to the annual Assembly meetings in Geneva was also widely questioned by Indian public opinion. The Indian delegation consisted of three people, who were neither elected nor nominated by the Indian population but were instead appointed by the Secretary of State for

India in consultation with the Government in India.[8] This procedure, together with the fact that a British person usually led the delegation until 1928,[9] was resented by the majority of the Indian nationalists. Critics felt that the selected delegates, British as well as Indian, would work along the prescribed official lines of the British Government and would therefore not represent India's real wishes and ambitions.[10] After continuing protests and nationalist agitations, the Government of India agreed that from 1929 onwards an Indian would usually assume the leadership of the delegation.[11] However, it did not revise either the policy of nomination or the inclusion of British members, which remained a cause of great complaint in Indian public opinion.

International efforts to regulate the opium traffic in the 1910s and 1920s: From the Shanghai Opium Commission to the League of Nations

In his dissertation on 'India's role in the League of Nations' the American scholar Karl Schmidt examines the Indian responses to the League of Nations' work to limit opium production and consumption. Schmidt argues that 'the Government of India was able to adopt an independent line in the League of Nations' non-political, or functional work. India's participation in these activities did not affect the Empire or its security; thus, the Indian delegation was able to pursue policies which were more in keeping with India's interests and would, at least partly, satisfy educated Indian opinion'.[12] Schmidt's argument is largely based on the analysis of Indian National Congress activities and debates in the Legislative Assembly. The basic validity of Schmidt's argument – that parts of India's intelligentsia felt satisfied with both the League of Nations' non-political work including the suppression of the opium trade and with the activities of the official Indian delegation in Geneva – is not denied here. This paper, however, would like to question if this statement can be maintained when looking at nationalist newspaper discourses about and responses of the Indian National Congress toward the opium question as debated in the League of Nations.

Problems associated with the opium trade were of global concern long before the advent of the League of Nations and had been the cause of conflicts and wars, for instance between China and Britain.[13] The first international meeting that considered the problem of how to regulate the production and distribution of drugs was the Shanghai Opium Commission, which gathered in 1909. Initiated by the Anglican Bishop Charles Henry Brent, the Commission consisted of 13 countries, including China, Siam, Britain, America, France, Italy and Japan among others. The achievements of the meeting, however, were few and despite the passing of some idealistic resolutions like the one calling for the suppression of the illicit opium trade, the latter continued unchanged.[14] Highly unsatisfied with the results, Bishop Brent together with the American physician Hamilton Wright proposed to call for an international gathering to address the issue again. Supported by the government of the United States, both men lobbied reluctant governments with the result that an international conference took place in The Hague in December 1911. The conference adopted the 'International Opium Convention'. The document, however, did not contain comprehensive and generally accepted regulations that would suppress the use of opium and other manufactured drugs such as morphine, heroin, codeine and cocaine. Although the Convention included in its first and second chapters the demand to control the production and distribution of raw and prepared opium for internal purposes, it focused more on the restriction of the international opium traffic.[15] The envisaged control in the international sphere, however, proved to be of a limited nature as in the end each country maintained the right to pursue the trade as it thought appropriate. Notwithstanding, some clauses in regard to the export of raw and prepared opium proved to be achievements, such as the agreement to proscribe the export of raw and prepared opium to such countries that had not explicitly allowed any import.[16] However, before the International Opium Convention could be ratified by all signatory powers, the First World War broke out and delayed any implementation.[17] After the end of the First World War the opium issue was discussed again during the Paris Peace Conferences and subsequently in the League of Nations, which became an important factor in the field of global drug regulation.

In 1920, during its first sessions, the League of Nation took up the question of opium trade and created an Advisory Committee on the Traffic in Opium and Other Dangerous Drugs (OAC) on which India was represented.[18] The committee that met for the first time in May 1921 brought forth a series of recommendations suggesting, for instance, that there should be an enquiry about the global need for opium for 'medical and other legitimate purposes'.[19] This question of whether the League of Nations should have requirements about raw and prepared opium for medical and scientific purposes in different countries became a major point of difference as it opened up questions of the legal sphere of the League and touched upon the sovereignty of its member states.[20] Representing the view of the Government of India, the appointed official Indian delegates to the League dismissed this proposal on the grounds that it would interfere with India's domestic policy. The use of opium in India was defended by V.S. Srinivasa Sastri in 1921 and by the Maharaja of Nawanagar in 1922, on the basis that it served as local medicine in wide parts of society and had supposedly recreational value when eaten in limited dosage.[21] The latter elucidated in his speech before the Assembly of the League of Nations that there was no misuse of opium in India and pointed out that in the general public, for instance amongst soldiers, labourers or old people, 'opium may be regarded as the Indian parallel to wine and beer in Europe and America'.[22] The comparison with the 'Western' world was even taken further by the Maharaja of Nawanagar, who explained that the consumption of opium in the United States was twice as much as India,[23] thereby referring to the very country that acted as one of the toughest opponents in regard to the opium policy over the next few years.

In 1923 the controversy reached its first climax. Already in January, and again in May and June, the delegation of the United States pressed for limiting opium production in order to prevent any surplus for non-medical and non-scientific use.[24] Although one of the delegates for India, John Campbell, accepted the proposal, he insisted on adding the reservation that the raw opium that was used domestically in India would be still legitimate. This reservation was accepted by the OAC after much debate.[25]

International help for nationalist Indian demands? British India, the League of Nations and the opium question until 1925

Let's now turn our attention to the Indian nationalists and the opium question. In India, the government's opium policy was determined by the findings of the Royal Opium Commission that had visited India in 1893–4. Indian opium was produced under the government's monopoly and any suggestion of prohibiting the crop was dismissed due to financial considerations.[26] While the rules of production and distribution of opium in India remained unchanged up to the mid-1920s, India's opium traffic to China experienced some alterations in 1907. In this year, the British government signed an agreement with China to reduce the annual Indian export by 10 per cent on the condition that China would decrease its domestic production at the same rate. It was hoped that after 10 years the opium consumption in China would be abandoned.[27] The British Indian government adhered to the treaty and eliminated its opium export to China on a decreasing annual basis. Nonetheless the agreement did not mark a general change in India's opium policy or bring about far-reaching changes as it still shipped opium to other Asian destinations. Furthermore, the treaty did not influence the issue of internal Indian consumption, and its clauses also did not deal with the drug trade between or with other states such as Turkey or Persia.[28] Yet, the British Indian government, its delegates to the League of Nations, and British government representatives and pro-British newspapers like *The Times of India* referred repeatedly to the advanced stance of India's opium policy by pointing to the country's adherence to the treaty.[29] Thus, *The Times of India* for instance wrote in its editorial on the speech of the Maharaja of Nawanagar:

> And as for the export to China, he [the Maharaja of Nawanagar, M.F.] laid his finger on the point which is well understood in India but rarely or never grasped in Europe, namely, that while the Indian Government have sacrificed millions of revenue and while the Indian cultivators have surrendered more millions of income by the suppression of opium cultivation out of feelings of humanity towards China the net result has been so far too great an extent merely to transfer their sacrificed profits into the pockets of other opium growers, mainly Turks and Persians besides the Chinese themselves.[30]

By pointing to India's model character, the supporters of the British Indian opium policy did not want only to counter European notions about

India's responsibility for China's condition. They also felt the need to point to other important, and often less publicly accused, players in the game that according to their understanding had done hardly anything to curb the opium problem. Moreover, in arguing along these lines, they emphasized the international dimension of the opium problem.[31] To enlighten the European and American public about India's 'advanced stance' and to explain the country's adherence to the production and distribution of opium within India, the representatives of the British Indian government used diverse opportunities. Besides the speeches before the League of Nations, meetings in the House of Commons in London and addresses at the Imperial Conferences were utilized to publicize Delhi's standpoint.[32] This publicity strategy became even more important when the government's depiction of the opium problem was severely questioned by Indian nationalists in the mid-1920s.

In contrast to the colonial government's view, the British opium policy was critically assessed by eminent Congress politicians, intellectuals and in nationalist newspapers in the 1920s, especially in regard to China and to the issue of internal consumption in India. Although there also had been deprecating Indian voices such as Keshab Chandra Sen, Rabindranath Tagore, Romesh Dutta, Gopal Krishna Gokhale or Taraknath Das[33] in the late nineteenth and early twentieth centuries, early Indian nationalists did not necessarily object to the government policy as they did in the case of alcohol. One of the reasons seems to have been that a significant section of Indian businessmen had made their fortune by participating in the opium trade – similar to their participation in alcohol production and trade[34] – and continued to play a role in it during the second half of the nineteenth century; another one was that opium was regarded as an important medicine by parts of the Indian general public.[35] The Indian nationalist opposition, therefore, evolved slowly and came to the forefront only after the end of the First World War.

In the wake of the non-cooperation movement, the Indian National Congress became interested in the promotion of abstinence in regard to opium consumption. A comprehensive campaign to restrict the opium habit in Assam was started in 1920/21.[36] Furthermore, Mohandas K. Gandhi and his close friend, the English missionary and educator, Charles F. Andrews began to publish several articles on the opium question in Gandhi's journals *Young India* and *Navajivan*.[37] Although during the non-cooperation movement Gandhi made the prohibition of alcohol a far more prominent theme[38] than the restriction of opium, he repeatedly reported in the columns of the journals about the successes of the Congress campaign in Assam.[39] Moreover, Gandhi stated clearly that when India would have won *swaraj*, i.e. when the country would have become independent, the new Indian government would abandon the opium trade altogether.[40] While Gandhi displayed some interest in the opium question, Charles F. Andrews, who also supported strongly the temperance of alcohol, emerged as the far more active proponent of the anti-opium struggle in the Indian national movement in the early 1920s.[41]

Andrews, who had lived since 1904 in India, was deeply involved in the Indian independence movement, which he considered a justified endeavour.[42] Besides the abolition of opium and India's right to freedom,[43] the Reverend campaigned for the rights of Indians in Africa and wrote about the problem of Indian indentured labour in Fiji.[44] With his publications, Andrews aimed at both Indian and international readers whose moral and material support he deemed important for the different causes. This applied in particular to the opium question. The Reverend did not only write a number of articles on this theme in Gandhi's newspapers. He also published widely in Indian and foreign dailies and journals such as *The Hindustan Review*, *The Modern Review*, *The Mahratta, The Bombay Chronicle* and *The Contemporary Review*,[45] and authored several books on opium in the 1920s.[46] Andrews also was appointed by the All India Congress Committee to lead an Enquiry Commission on the opium habits in Assam in 1924 (see the chapter of Kawal Kour in this volume).

Initially, the Indian National Congress did not link its anti-opium stance with the discussions going on in the League of Nations. For instance, Gandhi did not refer to the Genevan institution in his early writings on the restriction of opium. This changed in 1924 after the publication of an article by Andrews in *Young India,* in which the latter claimed that the Indian delegate in Geneva, John Campbell, had used Gandhi's name in defence of the British Indian government's opium policy.[47] Referring to his rather cursory knowledge about the opium question, Gandhi repudiated the governmental opium policy.[48] Soon afterwards, the problem of opium production, distribution and trade became again an internationally disputed theme. In the fall and early winter of 1924/25, a number of opium conferences took place in Geneva with the object to review the Hague Convention and to address debated questions in regard to the opium traffic.[49] Although the conferences were partly successful, for instance in setting up a Permanent Central Opium Board, one major issue arose again in connection with India's internal consumption and the continued external opium traffic.[50] The United States delegation pressed for the redrafting of Article 1 of the Hague Convention and demanded that, at the international level, only the production and distribution of opium and coca for strictly medical and scientific purposes should be allowed in future. This proposal was utterly rejected by the appointed delegation of the British Indian government. On the internal consumption of opium, the Government of India perceived the American proposal as an unacceptable intrusion into the domestic jurisdiction of India. The issue of exporting opium initially left room for debate. In the end, however, since no agreement could be reached on this issue, the American delegation withdrew from the conferences without signing the Convention, as did China. The remaining countries agreed upon the introduction of a certificate system for the international trade.[51]

Before the upcoming opium meetings in autumn 1924 in Geneva, the Indian National Congress decided to approach the League of Nations directly 'to say what the nation thinks of the Government of India policy'.[52] For this purpose, Gandhi and the well-known poet Rabindranath Tagore sent a message to the International Opium Conference in Geneva in which they petitioned it 'to adopt measures adequate for total extirpation of the plants from which these drugs originate, except as found necessary for medicine and science'.[53] While the Indian National Congress presented India's case at the international stage by approaching the League of Nations and adopting a resolution against opium traffic in December 1924,[54] nationalist Indian newspapers also took up the issue. *The Modern Review*, for instance, praised Gandhi's message as an 'invaluable service to humanity'.[55] The authors, furthermore, discussed the fact that the Opium Advisory Committee had accepted the Indian government's reservation on the domestic use of raw opium. In a 1924 article published in the *Bombay Chronicle*, a writer asked if this claimed 'legitimate' use of opium would also include the drugging of babies. He reported about this habit amongst working class mothers in industrial areas and pointed to the easiness with which these mothers could procure the drug. The writer questioned the legitimacy of British rule in India by stating that the policy of the government was repudiated by the Indian nation. With his critique of British rule, however, he did not exclusively aim to reach an Indian audience. The article concluded with the request that 'the Geneva Convention would do well, to note this fact'.[56] It seems that the author wished to repeat his repudiation of any legitimate foundation of British rule at the international level.

While touching on the question of domestic use of opium in India, one author in *The Modern Review* not only reversed the government's argument but also used it as a rhetorical device to prove India's readiness to gain freedom. First, the author rejected the government's objections to reform the internal opium policy in India by taking up the discussion about the medical situation of the country. One governmental argument against reform was that opium constituted an important medical necessity due to the fact that there were not enough medical practitioners working in India. The author, however, repudiated the governmental argument by pointing out that the government was itself responsible for the medical conditions in the country. Secondly, he stated that the government was completely aware that opium was mainly taken in non-medical circumstances and therefore constituted a source of harm. According to him the sufficient British knowledge about the dangers of opium was evident when looking at the opium policy in England itself. There even consumption for medical uses was limited and only possible when prescribed by a doctor. The contrast between a strong control in the metropolis and rather weak regulations in India was explained in the article by the government's assumption that the Indian people 'possess sufficient intelligence, general knowledge, medical and physiological knowledge as to diagnosis and dosage etc., and sufficient moral control over themselves and sense of responsibility to be able to use opium or its preparations only for medical purposes'.[57] All these qualities, the author summarized, showed that

Indians 'are fitter for exercising civil and political freedom than Englishmen'.[58] The opium policy of the British Indian government served as proof that India was not less advanced than other so-called civilized nations and deserved political freedom. The latter theme occurred repeatedly, albeit in a less obvious manner, in articles discussing the opium problem and more specifically in the question of representation to the League of Nations. Authors in *The Modern Review*, *Hindusthan* and the *Sindh Observer* complained that the appointed delegates of the British Indian government for the opium conferences did not represent real Indian opinion.[59]

Consequently, the Indian nationalist press followed closely the proceedings in Geneva in 1925. The rejection of the American proposals by the Indian government delegation was described in several articles as diametrically opposite to India's 'true' interests.[60] Pointing to the humiliating effects of the official representation policy of the British Indian government in the League, C.F. Andrews, for instance, claimed that 'Never perhaps before in recent times has the complete political subjection of India been so shamefully exposed before the civilised world as at Geneva.'[61] According to his note that was published in the journal *Young India*, the American proposal was supported by resolutions of several Indian organizations such as the Indian National Congress, the National Liberal Federation, the National Christian Council and the All-India Social Conference, all of which expressed, according to Andrews, the true Indian public opinion.[62] In Geneva, Mr. Dukes, a member of the Society of the Oppression of Opium, drew the attention of the delegates to the objections of Indian nationalists by reading out Gandhi's message. This direct representation of nationalist criticism was viewed in the newspapers as moral vindication for India, since it made obvious that the British rulers controlled and determined India's opium policy without Indian consent.[63] At the same time, many articles did not mention the efforts to present another non-official Indian view before the League. The authors rather pointed to the 'disgrace' that the official government delegation in pursuing their politics had brought on India in front of the world.[64] Yet, they stated time and again that these delegates were not the true voices of India, which would demand a complete cessation of the opium production.[65] Against this background, both lines of argument – moral vindication and disgrace – seemed to have aimed at drawing international attention to India's subordinate political status within the British Empire. Similar efforts to interest international civil society actors and pressure groups in the Indian opium problem were also carried out by Indians living abroad. Especially in the United States, eminent nationalists like Sudhindra Bose and Taraknath Das explained nationalist demands and challenged the official depiction of the British Indian government that opium was not harmful to Indians.[66] Their efforts were supported by and linked to political and highly public and influential American anti-opium crusaders such as Ellen LaMotte,[67] a connection that could pose a severe challenge to Britain's public image.[68]

The critical assessment of the British Indian government's policy during the opium conferences in Geneva also had severe repercussions on the perception of the League of Nations amongst educated nationalist Indians. Journalists for nationalist papers began to question the League's utility by describing the outcome of the opium conferences as a failure.[69] The author of an article published in February 1925 in the daily *Saurashtra*, even denied any positive value that the League had for India. Therefore he asked his fellow countrymen not to rely on this body any longer for India's deliverance, but rather to recognize their own determination and moral force.[70]

While the nationalist stance on opium aimed at the abolition of both external trade and internal use of opium, for the time being the British Indian government adhered to its traditional policy by reiterating its arguments about India's model character in regard to its export politics and the necessity of opium in the domestic realm. Both lines of argument were put forth in Geneva and in British newspapers[71] and also in the Indian Legislative Assembly, where Indian members raised critical questions.[72] One answer of the government representatives to these critical questions involved the problem of constitutionality. As explained in the Legislative Assembly in January 1925: 'Excise is in Governors' provinces a provincial transferred subject and it is for Ministers in consultation with their Legislative Councils to determine the policy. Then there are the Indian States, the rulers of which have to settle their own internal policy.'[73] According to the Government of India Act of 1919 excise and thus opium belonged to the provincial 'transferred' subjects[74] and therefore did not come under the responsibility of the central British Indian government, an argument highlighted by British officials. Another argument brought forward in defence of the official opium policy dealt with the limited public objection towards opium in India.[75] Thus, the British representative of the government declared in the Legislative Assembly in March 1925 'that except for a few social workers like Mr. Andrews there had been very little of public opinion expressed on this matter [the internal use of opium, M.F.]. The Indian National Congress discovered this opium question only last year'.[76] Although the opium issue did not feature prominently before the 1920s and produced diverse Indian opinions, such statements did not present a realistic view about the publicity and urgency of the question at the time, as the analysis of nationalist Indian newspapers and journals have shown.

In contrast, the Indian establishment press rather followed the government standpoint on the opium question. *The Times of India*, for instance, underscored repeatedly India's pioneering role as the only one of the supplying countries that would follow international rules, thereby criticizing the unwillingness of Turkey and Persia to limit their opium production and trade.[77] Furthermore, the daily dismissed the American proposals during the opium conferences in Geneva as well as the public opinion in the United States as ill-informed and sentimental.[78]

Outlook and conclusion: Indian debates on opium and the League of Nations after 1925

Though during and in the immediate aftermath of the Geneva opium conferences of 1924/25 the Indian government adhered to its opium policy, a few months later it started to revise it. This change of mind was far from solely motivated by the constant nationalist anti-opium propaganda: it was also connected with the anxiety that political costs at the international level would be too high.[79] To improve its reputation and the relationships with the United States and the London Home Office, the Government of India announced that it would gradually decrease all non-medicinal opium exports in 1926, and implemented this policy successfully in the following years.[80] In regard to the question of internal consumption, however, changes in policy took time. In March 1926, during a debate on opium in the Legislative Assembly, the government representative stated that letters had been sent to the local governments asking them to re-examine if there was the necessity for a general new inquiry on opium in India. Although not all answers had been received, the speaker felt that the local governments did not see the need for such an overall inquiry.[81] Over the next years some provincial governments, for instance in Bengal, Bombay and Assam, took steps to collect data about the non-medical use of opium and to restrict its consumption, but a uniform policy applicable to all provinces and the princely states was not established.[82]

The responsibility for the continuing internal production, traffic and use of opium was mostly attributed to the government in nationalist debates. Delhi was charged with neglecting the health of the Indian nation[83] in return for sufficient revenue.[84] Therefore the debates focused on two arguments brought forward by British officials in defence of their policy: one, the assertion that there was no widespread and serious abuse of opium in India, and, two, that the moderate use of opium did not lead to any harm.[85] Both claims were repudiated in the nationalist press.[86] Authors pointed time and again to the amount of opium consumption in different parts of India that exceeded by a large amount the average quantity recommended by the League of Nations.[87] These figures were an important point of reference not only in the press but also for opium enquiries that were conducted in India, for instance on behalf of the Indian National Congress.[88]

While the League figures remained in use in India, it seems that the League of Nations' activities to control and restrict the opium trade and its consumption became a less debated subject in the nationalist press from the late 1920s, although it presumably continued to be an important theme in the British Indian press. When going through the Collected Works of Mahatma Gandhi, it becomes obvious that the Indian National Congress still addressed the topic and included opium prohibition in its constructive programs and in the civil disobedience movement.[89] Yet, the Congress did not deal with the League of Nations' policy on opium anymore. This silence, which was unfortunately not explained, seems to be connected to a feeling of disappointment with the League's actual potential to achieve a globally accepted opium control regime.

The opium question was a widely debated theme in British India that had repercussions at the international and national level. While the revision of the Government's international opium policy in 1926 was acknowledged in nationalist circles on the subcontinent and described as an important achievement of the Geneva opium conference in 1924/25, questions like the continuation of the internal opium policy and India's representation and its status at the League of Nations were overall perceived critically.

The non-political work of the League of Nations, therefore, did not satisfy the members of the Indian National Congress and the larger part of the nationalist press. As a result, not only did the League of Nations' authority as a supranational organization dwindle, but its utility in improving India's situation was also repudiated in nationalist circles. Thereby, a large part of the criticism brought forth by the Indian public in regard to question of opium production and distribution was less connected with the League itself, but rather associated with the perception of Great Britain as ruler of India. The British Indian government, in the prevalent view, did not act in accordance with the 'real' wishes of the country. The sober conclusion drawn by many was that the Indian people must not rely on the League but on their own efforts to free India from the opium evil. Anti-opium activism in India was therefore linked with efforts for political emancipation and led to a reinforcement of nationalist ideas.

Notes

1 Jawaharlal Nehru, 'To A.C. Wilson (09.01.1925)', in *Selected Works of Jawaharlal Nehru*, vol. 2, ed. S. Gopal, New Delhi: Orient Longman Ltd., 1972, p. 168.

2 See for instance: H. Goto-Shibata, 'The International Opium Conference of 1924–25 and Japan', *Modern Asian Studies* 36, 4, 2002, 969–91; L. Kozma, 'The League of Nations and the debate over cannabis prohibition', *History Compass* 9, 1, 2011, 61–70; D. Laqua, 'Transnational intellectual cooperation, the League of Nations, and the problem of order', *Journal of Global History* 6, 2011, 223–47; I. Borowy, *Coming to Terms With World Health: the League of Nations Health Organisation 1921–1946*, Frankfurt: Peter Lang, 2009; B. Metzger, 'Towards an international human rights regime during the interwar years: the League of Nations' combat of traffic in women and children', in K. Grant et al. (eds) *Beyond Sovereignty: Britain, Empire and transnationalism, c. 1880–1950*, Basingstoke: Palgrave Macmillan, 2007, pp. 54–79.

3 The Indian media landscape can be divided in three broad categories for the first decades of the twentieth century: in the English-language media either (1) in British or in (2) Indian possession and in (3) Indian-language newspapers and journals. While the English-language dailies and journals in British possession, called the establishment press, mainly supported the politics of British colonial rule, the media belonging to the other two categories often took a nationalist view and were close to the independence movement or were published by Congress politicians (N.-C. Schneider, *Zur Darstellung von 'Kultur' und 'kultureller Differenz' im indischen Mediensystem: Die indische Presse und die Repräsentation des Islams im Rahmen der Zivilrechtsdebatte, 1985–87 und 2003*, Berlin: Logos Verlag, 2005, pp. 89–90).

4 Due to its war contributions the British Indian Government was allowed to send three representatives to the Imperial War Cabinet and the Imperial War Conference in 1917. Subsequently, India became a permanent member of the latter and endeavoured to obtain the same powers and privileges in international politics as were granted to the British Dominions. When the Dominions were admitted to the Paris Peace Conference, India was also allowed to

participate owing to its membership of the Imperial Conference (D.N. Verma, *India and the League of Nations*, Patna: Bharati Bhawan, 1968, pp. 1–13).

5 Ibid., pp. 14–24; J.C. Coyajee, *India and the League of Nations*, Madras: Waltair, 1932, pp. 20–3.

6 M. Framke, 'India's opinion and the League of Nations: the case of India's freedom', paper presented at the symposium 'Asia after Versailles, 1919–1933' at Japan Centre, Ludwig-Maximilians-University Munich, June 2009. See for the question of political self-determination, the League of Nations and India: E. Manela, *The Wilsonian Moment. Self-determination and the international origins of anticolonial nationalism*, New York: Oxford University Press, 2007, pp. 77–97 and 159–75.

7 Verma, *India*, pp. 270–302; K. Grant and L. Trivedi, 'A question of trust: the Government of India, the League of Nations, and Mohandas Gandhi', in R.M. Douglas, M.D. Callahan and E. Bishop (eds) *Imperialism on Trial. International oversight of colonial rule in historical perspective*, Oxford: Lexington, 2006, pp. 21–43.

8 Verma, *India*, p. 46.

9 The English leader was normally joined by two Indian representatives, of whom one was a public figure of British India and the other a ruling prince of an Indian state.

10 Verma, *India*, pp. 58–9; *Paisa Akbar*, 30 October 1920; *Punjab Press Abstract [hereafter cited as INR Punjab; the name for the Punjab Press Abstracts changed in the 1920s to Note on the Punjab Press]*, 33, 1920, 443; *Andra Patrika*, 16 July 1924; *Report on English papers examined by the criminal investigation department, Madras, and on vernacular papers examined by the translators to the Government of Madras [hereafter cited as INR Madras]*, 30, 1924, 957; *Swarajya*, 30 November 1929; *INR Madras* 49, 1929, 1675; Anon., 'Inadequate representation of India at Geneva', *The Modern Review*, 40, 2, 1926, 221.

11 Verma, *India*, pp. 51 and 65–75; Anon., 'Leader of Indian delegation to League of Nations', *The Modern Review* 45, 4, 1929, 530; *Tribune*, 19 July 1924; *INR Punjab*, 29, 1924, 243; *Bombay Samachar*, 10 May 1928; *Report on Newspapers published in the Bombay Presidency [hereafter cited as INR Bombay]*, 19, 1928, 508. The question of the leadership of the delegation troubled politically-minded Indians in a way that they tried persistently to convince the government to appoint an Indian. Especially P.C. Sethna fought intensively for this matter and moved several resolutions in the Council of State demanding an Indian leading the delegation. The agitation and the efforts of P.C. Sethna and his nationalist colleagues were supported largely by the press and were finally crowned with success in 1929.

12 K.J. Schmidt, 'India's role in the League of Nations, 1919–1939', unpublished thesis, The Florida State University, 1994, p. 191.

13 J. Lovell, *The Opium War: drugs, dreams and the making of China*, London: Picador, 2011; H.G. Gelber, *Opium, Soldiers and Evangelicals: Britain's 1840–42 war with China, and its aftermath*, Basingstoke, Hampshire: Palgrave Macmillan, 2004; W.T. Hanes and F. Sanello, *The Opium Wars: the addiction of one empire and the corruption of another*, Naperville, Illinois: Sourcebooks, 2002.

14 W.B. McAllister, *Drug Diplomacy in the Twentieth Century: an international history*, London et al.: Routledge, 2000, pp. 27–30; K. Meyer and T.M. Parssinen, *Webs of Smoke: smugglers, warlords, spies, and the history of the international drug trade*, Lanham, Maryland et al.: Rowman & Littlefield Publishers, 1998, p. 22.

15 'International Opium Convention. Signed at The Hague, January 23rd, 1912'. Online. Available HTTP: <http://treaties.un.org/doc/Treaties/1922/01/19220123%2006-31%20AM/Ch_VI_2p.pdf.> (accessed 20 March 2013).

16 Meyer and Parssinen, *Webs of Smoke*, p. 23; McAllister, *Drug Diplomacy*, pp. 30–5. The international conference at The Hague also considered the problem of manufactured drugs such as morphine, heroin, codeine, and cocaine. This was a highly contested issue and all provisions laid down in the Convention in regard to manufactured drugs remained vague and no substantive control was established (McAllister, *Drug Diplomacy*, p. 34).

17 Before the outbreak of the First World War, two more conferences were held with the objective to invite other countries that had not been present at the first conference at The Hague to

sign the Convention. This move did not prove successful. Q. Wright, 'The opium question', *The American Journal of International Law* 18, 2, 1924, 284.

18 McAllister, *Drug Diplomacy*, p. 44.

19 Schmidt, 'India's role', pp. 194–5. Furthermore, the OAC suggested that every member state of the League should adopt the Hague Convention of 1912 and made several recommendations to limit the consumption of opium in China. In this regard it was suggested to implement measures to prevent the smuggling of the drug into Chinese territory and to ban the cultivation of the poppies.

20 Aside from the fact that this issue was contested among the representatives of the different countries in the League of Nations, the question of defining the parameters of 'legitimate' demands also led to conflict between different League bodies. For instance, the Mixed Sub-Committee, which included members of the League Health Committee and the OAC, was dominated by the rather liberal stance of the latter and proposed different standards of legitimate need than the League Health Committee. These standards, however, were seen as being applicable only for countries with advanced medical systems and therefore not for the most states of South America, Africa and Asia (McAllister, *Drug Diplomacy*, pp. 46–9).

21 Schmidt, 'India's role', pp. 196ff.; w.a., 'The world and India. Speeches by the Jam Saheb', *The Times of India*, 17 November 1922, p. 11.

22 W.a., 'The world and India. Speeches by the Jam Saheb', p. 11. The Maharaja also equated the 'Western' use of tea, coffee and cocoa as recreational products with the consumption of opium.

23 Ibid.

24 McAllister, *Drug Diplomacy*, pp. 53–6.

25 W.a., 'Opium control. Discussions at Geneva', *The Times of India*, 4 June 1923, p. 10; w.a., 'Opium control. No ban on usage in India', *The Times of India*, 5 June 1923, p. 7; w.a., 'Opium control. U.S. objection to Indian usage', *The Times of India*, 7 June 1923, p. 9; w.a., 'Article One amended', *The Times of India*, 7 June 1923, p. 9.

26 Schmidt, 'India's role', pp. 193–4.

27 McAllister, *Drug Diplomacy*, pp. 24–5; R.K. Newman, 'India and the Anglo-Chinese opium agreements, 1907–14', *Modern Asian Studies* 23, 3, 1989, 525–60. In the first three years after signing the treaty China was able to reduce its opium production. Due to political turmoil resulting in the disintegration of the central authority, the production and consumption of opium was not abandoned completely, but China experienced an opium revival from the mid-1910s.

28 McAllister, *Drug Diplomacy*, p. 26.

29 Editorial, 'Indian opium', *The Times of India*, 20 April 1922, p. 6; w.a., 'India and opium. Lord Peel replies to the critics', *The Times of India*, 15 October 1923, p. 12; From a correspondent, 'The opium problem. International settlement', *The Times of India*, 27 February 1923, p. 8. Often these statements pointed in a wider sense to India's responsible behaviour in regard to the opium traffic by describing the country as a faithful proponent of the opium provisions of the League such as the certificate system (w.a., 'India and opium. Lord Peel replies to the critics', p. 12; Editorial, 'Indian opium', p. 6).

30 Editorial, 'Indian problems abroad', *The Times of India*, 17 November 1922, p. 6.

31 Ibid.

32 W.a., 'India's opium policy. Unjustified attacks', *The Times of India*, 14 June 1923, p. 7; w.a., 'India and opium. Lord Peel replies to the critics', p. 12; w.a., 'A harmful drug. Indians' knowledge', *The Times of India*, 21 September 1922, p. 10.

33 C. Lin, 'Friendship-in-need between Chinese and Indian people in modern times', in C. Tan (ed.) *In the Footsteps of Xuanzang: Tan Yun-Shan and India*, New Delhi: Indira Gandhi National Centre, 1999, p. 154; P. Biswas, 'Colonial displacements. Nationalist longing and identity among early Indian intellectuals in the United States', unpublished thesis, University of California, 2008, pp. 48–9.

34 D. Hardiman, 'From custom to crime: the politics of drinking in colonial South Gujarat', in R. Guha (ed.) *Subaltern Studies IV. Writings on South Asian History and Society*, New Delhi: Oxford University Press, 1985, pp. 165–228.

35 J.F. Richards, 'Opium and the British Indian Empire: the Royal Commission of 1895', *Modern Asian Studies* 36, 2, 2002, 380–2; P. Chakrabarti, 'The empire of trade and the morality of science', June 2004, review of P.C. Winther, *Anglo-European Science and the Rhetoric of Empire: malaria, opium, and British rule in India, 1756-1895*, New York, Oxford: Lexington Books, 2003. Online. Available HTTP: <http://www.h-net.org/reviews/showrev.php?id=9508> (accessed 16 November 2012); J.S. Palsetia, 'The Parsis of India and the opium trade in China', *Contemporary Drug Problems* 35, Winter 2008, 647–78; R. Chandavarkar, *The Origins of Industrial Capitalism in India: business strategies and the working classes in Bombay, 1900–1940*, Cambridge: Cambridge University Press, 2002, pp. 60–2; A. Deshpande, 'An historical overview of opium cultivation and changing state attitudes towards the crop in India, 1878–2000 A.D.', *Studies in History* 25, 1, 2009, 111, fn 11.

36 T. Brook and B.T. Wakabayashi, *Opium Regimes: China, Britain and Japan, 1839–1952*, Berkeley, Calif. et al.: University of California Press, 2000. See also the chapter of Kawal Deep Kour in the present volume.

37 C.F. Andrews, 'The opium poison I', *Young India*, 11 May 1921, p. 147; idem, 'The opium poison II', *Young India*, 18 May 1921, pp. 157–8; idem, 'The opium traffic', *Young India*, 18 August 1921, pp. 258–60.

38 See for Gandhi's work in regard to alcohol prohibition: D.M. Fahey and P. Manian, 'Poverty and purification: the politics of Gandhi's campaign for prohibition', *The Historian* 67, 3, 2005, 489–506.

39 M.K. Gandhi, 'Experiences of Assam - I (04.09.1921 rep. from Navajivan)', in *Collected Works of Mahatma Gandhi*, vol. 21, New Delhi: The Publication Division, Ministry of Information, 1966, pp. 53–8; idem, 'Notes: Lovely Assam', *Young India*, 1 September 1921, p. 273.

40 M.K. Gandhi, 'Definitions of swaraj (14.08.1921 rep. from Navajivan)', in *Collected Works of Mahatma Gandhi*, vol. 20, New Delhi: The Publication Division, Ministry of Information, 1979 rep., pp. 506–7.

41 L. Carroll, 'The temperance movement in India: politics and social reform', *Modern Asian Studies*, 10, 3, 1976, 423.

42 P.C. Roy Chaudhury, *C.F. Andrews: his life and times*, Bombay: Somaiya Publications, 1971; D. O'Connor, *Gospel, Raj and Swaraj: the missionary years of C.F. Andrews, 1904–14*, Frankfurt am Main: Peter Lang, 1990.

43 C.F. Andrews, *India and the Simon Report*, London: George Allen & Unwin Ltd., 1930; idem, 'What next in India?', *The New Republic*, 26 February 1930, pp. 41–3.

44 C.F. Andrews, *India and the Pacific*, London: George Allen & Unwin Ltd., 1937; idem, *Indians in South Africa*, Madras: Ganesh, 1922; idem, *The Indian Question in East Africa*, Nairobi: Swift Press, 1921; C.F. Andrews and W.A. Pearson, *Report on Indentured Labour in Fiji: an independent enquiry*, Calcutta: Star Printing Works, 1916; w.a., 'India's opium traffic', *The Nation*, 20 May 1925, pp. 580–2.

45 C.F. Andrews, 'A memorandum on opium', *The Hindustan Review* 48, April 1925, 251–5; idem, 'Opium in India', *The Modern Review* 35, 1, 1924, 106–7; idem, 'The sin of the opium traffic', *The Mahratta*, 27 March 1921, pp. 155–6; idem, 'A new opium policy', *The Contemporary Review* 128, July/Dec. 1925, 163–9.

46 C.F. Andrews, *The drink and opium evil*, Madras: Ganesh & Co., 1921[?]; idem, *Assam Congress Opium Enquiry Report*, Cinnamara: R.K. Hatibarua, 1925; idem, *The Opium Evil in India: Britain's responsibility*, London: Student Christian Movement, 1926.

47 M.K. Gandhi, 'Opium policy and Mr. Gandhi', *Young India*, 20 March 1924, p. 95. Gandhi wrote: 'In that paragraph he [Charles F. Andrews, M.F.] quotes Mr. Campbell, the Government representative at the Geneva Conference held in May 1923. Mr. Campbell is reported to have stated that "from the beginning India had handled the opium question with perfect honesty of purpose, and not even its most ardent opponents including Mr. Gandhi had ever made any reproach in that respect".' (Ibid.).

48 Ibid.

49 Schmidt, 'India's role', p. 201.

50 During the first conference in early November 1924, a major controversy arose between Great Britain and Japan in regard to the illicit drug traffic and the certificate system. Although this dispute could be solved, the conference hardly revised the malfunctioning measures to suppress opium use in the Far East. Its missing results affected seriously the second conference (McAllister, *Drug Diplomacy*, pp. 67–9; Goto-Shibata, 'The International Opium Conference', 976–9).
51 Schmidt, 'India's role', pp. 201–2; Meyer and Parssinen, *Webs of Smoke*, pp. 29ff.; McAllister, *Drug Diplomacy*, pp. 69–78. The system of import certificates and of governmental export authorizations aimed to control the opium trade and to eliminate the diversion of drugs when exported from one country to another. To export opium one needed to possess an import certificate from the respective importing country.
52 M.K. Gandhi, 'The All-India Congress Committee', *Young India*, 3 July 1924, p. 220.
53 M.K. Gandhi and R. Tagore, 'The opium evil', *Young India*, 2 October 1924, p. 327. See for the question of medical and non-medical use of drugs: D.T. Courtwright, *Forces of Habit: drugs and the making of the modern world*, Cambridge, Mass.: Harvard University Press, 2001, pp. 69–132.
54 Nehru, 'To A.C. Wilson', p. 168.
55 W.a., 'Opium', *The Modern Review* 36, 6, 1924, 743.
56 *Bombay Chronicle*, 22 July 1924; *INR Bombay*, 30, 1924, 631.
57 W.a., 'The government's opium policy', *The Modern Review* 36, 4, 1924, 480.
58 Ibid.
59 Ibid.; *Hindusthan*, 3 November 1924; *INR Bombay*, 45, 1924, 926; *Sindh Observer*, 3 December 1924; *INR Bombay*, 49, 1924, 1002; w.a., 'Opium', p. 743–4.
60 C.F. Andrews, 'The shame of Geneva', *Young India*, 12 February 1925, p. 55; *Bombay Chronicle*, 21 January 1925; *INR Bombay*, 4, 1925, 50.
61 Andrews, 'The shame of Geneva', p. 55.
62 Ibid.
63 *Bombay Chronicle*, 21 January 1925, p. 50.
64 Ibid.; *Voice of India*, 29 January 1925; *INR Bombay*, 5, 1925, 69; *Praja Mitra and Parsi*, 3 February 1925; *INR Bombay*, 6, 1925, 90; *Bombay Samachar*, 11 February 1925; *INR Bombay*, 7, 1925, 115.
65 *Advocate of India*, 6 February 1925; *INR Bombay*, 6, 1925, 90; *Voice of India*, 29 January 1925, p. 69; *Bombay Samachar*, 11 February 1925, p. 115.
66 W.a., 'Professor from India commends Iowa students for initiative', *The Daily Iowan*, 14 November 1922, p. 1; T. Das, 'The menace of opium', *The Nation* 116, 1923, 729–30; T.K. Mukherjee, *Taraknath Das: life and letters of a revolutionary in exile*, Calcutta: National Council of Education, Bengal, 1997, pp. 32, 105–6, 167–9, 183–4. One of Das' publications, in which he wrote about the opium problem in India, was translated into German, thus reaching out internationally to a diverse readership. T. Das, *Indien in der Weltpolitik; eingeleitet von Karl Haushofer und Robert Morss Lovett*, München: Verlag Georg D.W. Callwey, 1932, pp. 177–9.
67 On the relationship between Taraknath Das and Ellen LaMotte see: Mukherjee, *Taraknath Das*, pp. 105–7, 115, 183. Ellen LaMotte published comprehensively on the opium question. Her writings were cited by Indian critics of the British-Indian opium policy or rejected by its defenders (E. LaMotte, *The Opium Monopoly*, New York: Macmillan, 1920; idem, *The Ethics of Opium*, New York, London: The Century Co., 1924; idem, *Opium at Geneva: or, how the opium problem is handled by the League of Nations*, w.p.: w.p., 1930; Schmidt, 'India's role', p. 199; Gandhi, 'The All-India Congress Committee', p. 220; Andrews, 'The opium poison II', pp. 157–8).
68 Mukherjee, *Taraknath Das*, pp. 183–5.
69 *Saurashtra*, 21 February 1925; *INR Bombay*, 8, 1925, 127–8; *Bombay Samachar*, 11 February 1925, p. 115; *Advocate of India*, 6 February 1925, p. 90; *Hindusthan*, 9 February 1925; *INR Bombay*, 7, 1925, 115.
70 *Saurashtra*, 21 February 1925; *INR Bombay*, 8, 1925, 127–8.

71 J. Campbell, 'Use of opium in India', *The Asiatic Review*, reprinted in *The Modern Review* 35, 5, 1924, 634.

72 W.a., 'The Assembly. Government Bills', *The Times of India*, 10 September 1924, p. 7; From our special correspondent, 'Opium policy. Misguided attacks on Govt.', *The Times of India*, 28 January 1925, p. 9; w.a., 'Indian opium policy. Critics answered', *The Times of India*, 29 January 1925, p. 10.

73 W.a., 'Delhi - 27 January, 1925: the opium question', in *The Indian Annual Register, 1919–1947, I (1925)*, ed. H.N. Mitra, New Delhi: Gian Publishing House 1988, p. 161.

74 The Government of India Act of 1919, also popularly known as Montagu-Chelmsford-Reforms, represented basically 'Britain's reward' to India for its efforts during the First World War. The Act, however, was also the first step in the progress towards self-government. It introduced an indigenous constitutional system, called 'dyarchy', which encompassed a central government almost completely under British control, and provincial governments responsible to provincial legislatures in which Indian ministers were allowed to take in-charge of certain areas. The excise policy belonged in the area of provincial responsibilities (B.D. Metcalf and T.R. Metcalf, *A Concise History of India*, Cambridge: Cambridge University Press, 2002, p. 166).

75 Schmidt, 'India's role', pp. 207–8.

76 W.a., 'Insurance in India. Claims settlement', *The Times of India*, 6 March 1925, p. 12.

77 Editorial, 'Opium and common sense', *The Times of India*, 19 January 1925, p. 8; Editorial, 'The international control of opium', *The Times of India*, 4 December 1925, p. 10.

78 Editorial, 'Opium and common sense', p. 8; Editorial, 'The Opium Conference', *The Times of India*, 10 February 1925, p. 8.

79 McAllister, *Drug Diplomacy*, p. 81; Schmidt, 'India's role', p. 209.

80 McAllister, *Drug Diplomacy*, p. 81.

81 W.a., 'Government's opium policy', *The Times of India*, 11 March 1926, p. 14.

82 K. Chaliha, 'Opium in Assam', *The Modern Review* 61, 1, 1937, 52–3; Editor of Prohibition, 'Prohibition on opium', *The Modern Review* 41, 2, 1927, 240; w.a., 'The Bengal Government and opium-smoking', *The Modern Review* 50, 2, 1931, 243; C.F. Andrews, 'The government opium monopoly in India', *The Modern Review* 47, 5, 1930, 614–16; w.a., 'The opium evil in India', *The Modern Review* 46, 5, 1929, 593–4; From our own correspondent, 'Bombay Council: power to prevent assembly of persons for smoking opium', *The Times of India*, 25 September 1936, p. 5.

83 *Servant of India*, 18 February 1926; *INR Bombay*, 8, 1926, 195.

84 *Bombay Chronicle*, 28 June 1926; *INR Bombay*, 27, 1926, 719; *Bombay Chronicle*, 22 June 1926; *INR Bombay*, 26, 1926, 693.

85 Editorial, 'On black spots', *The Times of India*, 19 May 1930, p. 8; Editorial, 'Opium policy', *The Times of India*, 8 August 1927, p. 10; w.a., 'Consumption of opium in India. Govt.'s steps to check it', *The Times of India*, 23 August 1930, p. 6. The Government representatives and the establishment press explained the high figures of consumed opium for instance with its veterinary usage (Editorial, 'Opium policy', p. 8).

86 *Bombay Chronicle*, 22 June 1926, p. 693; *New Times*, 19 June 1926; *INR Bombay*, 26, 1926, 694; *Social Reformer*, June 1926; *INR Bombay*, 26, 1926, 694.

87 *Bombay Chronicle*, 22 June 1926, p. 693; *Social Reformer*, June 1926, p. 694; M.K. Gandhi, 'An opium report', *Young India*, 12 November 1925, p. 391; w.a., 'Opium consumption in and about Calcutta', *The Modern Review* 41, 6, 1927, 774.

88 M.K. Gandhi, 'An opium report', *Young India*, 12 November 1925, p. 391; C.F. Andrews, 'Some alarming facts', *Young India*, 9 April 1925, p. 128; *Bombay Chronicle*, 22 June 1926, p. 693.

89 M.K. Gandhi, 'Drugs, drink and devil', *Young India*, 22 April 1926, p. 145; idem, 'Then and now', *Young India*, 17 January 1929, p. 20; idem, 'What happened in India', *Young India*, 18 April 1929, p. 121; idem, 'Speech at Borsad (18.03.1930, rep. from Navajivan)', in *Collected Works of Mahatma Gandhi*, vol. 43, New Delhi: The Publication Division, Ministry of Information, 1971, pp. 100–3.

8 'Drunkards beware!': Prohibition and nationalist politics in the 1930s

Robert Eric Colvard

> There was evidence everywhere of universal rejoicings in the city. The city's roads, bazaars, shops, markets and houses were decorated with buntings and floral arches. Two motor cars equipped with loud speakers moved from place to place announcing the programme of the Prohibition Day. Accompanied by music, a procession of motor lorries decorated with pictures, posters and placards moved through all parts of the city and suburbs. An effigy measuring 20' by 5' symbolizing the Monster of Drink was specially prepared for the occasion. [It] was mounted on a motor lorry and paraded through the city.[1]

On the morning of 20 July 1938, the people of Ahmedabad, an urban city in the Bombay Presidency, awoke to a radically altered world. Prohibition Day marked the first day of a temperate future. Minister of Health for the Bombay Presidency David Gilder and Indian National Congress leader Sardar Patel, both dedicated temperance advocates, presided over the ceremonies. Their speeches called for a celebration of Prohibition and the requisite vigilance to ensure the success of this important pilot program that would serve as a model for other Indian cities.

Ahmedabad's dry future represented the fruition of nearly 50 years of temperance activism by a wide array of social reformers including temperance workers from India and abroad, men and women, and nationalists of all classes, *jati*s, religions, and political ideologies. One might be forgiven for proclaiming, as did Kailas Nath Katju, the United Provinces Excise Minister, that 'no one [in India] is against the promotion of temperance'.[2] Temperance journals in India, Britain, and the United States breathlessly praised the actions of the Congress Ministries for setting a new standard for moral governance in the fight against demon drink. Yet beneath this veneer of unanimity a much more complicated reality threatened to undermine not only the victory against alcohol, but the very future of the nationalist coalition. The debates surrounding alcohol in colonial India reveal what Ranajit Guha calls 'very real tension between force and consent from which Indian nationalism acquired its form and substance'.[3]

This essay examines alcohol and the discourse surrounding it from the beginning of the Civil Disobedience Movement in 1930 to the end of Congress-led provincial governments in 1939. It argues that tensions between nationalists devoted to the prohibition of drink and the liquor men and their clients increased dramatically during this period. Growing anger between the nationalists and the colonial government fighting tooth and nail against them manifested itself in debates regarding access to drink. These tensions led to crisis point forcing drinkers to decide whether to support the nation or continue in their habit. When the Congress joined government in the provincial assemblies in 1938, it used the power of the state to begin the long fight of eradicating the drink menace from India. In the process, drinkers found themselves subject to moral criticism from nationalist leaders and to the full might of Congress-led provincial governments. Impending Indian freedom held out a promise but also a threat to the drinking classes. An independent India appeared poised to destroy the existing drink-producing industry and to force drinkers to conform to the social mores of the upper castes.

By 1930, India's then-50-year-old temperance movement had undergone considerable change in focus and tone, largely as a consequence of its close association with nationalism. Public activism against drink policy in colonial India dates back to the 1880s, when the drinkers of Bombay and parts of the surrounding Konkan staged a drink strike, refusing to drink highly-taxed locally-produced liquor until the authorities lowered its price.[4] In the 1880s and 1890s, British temperance workers recruited elite Indian nationalists to form hundreds of local temperance organizations within India, affiliated with the Anglo-Indian Temperance Association.[5] Beginning in 1905, the Swadeshi movement was instrumental in changing the 'nationality' of liquor, with liquor joining foreign cloth in myriad bonfires, culminating in a 'temperance riot' in Poona in 1908.[6] By the 1920s, temperance in India had been largely subsumed by a form of Indian nationalism that labelled alcohol as 'foreign' to India.[7] The 1920s also witnessed a move away from moral suasion as the ideal method of ensuring temperance towards a new goal of all-out prohibition. With the colonial state firmly siding with revenue-generating liquor producers, prohibition became a necessary aspect of non-cooperation and an important goal of the Indian National Congress.

However, despite the increasing prominence of temperance propaganda, a large drinking culture persisted in India in the 1930s. Temperance campaigns, propaganda, and picketing associated with the Civil Disobedience Movement redefined drinking as a quintessentially un-Indian habit. Temperance agitation became a key aspect of the Civil Disobedience Movement. The energy with which Congress prosecuted these campaigns provoked occasionally violent hostility from drink sellers and their patrons. Moreover, the colonial government's crackdown on nationalists during the Civil Disobedience Movement compelled leaders to entrust the stewardship of temperance organizations to non-Indians. With the 1931 Gandhi-Irwin Pact, the technical distinction between legal anti-alcohol agitation and illegal nationalist demonstrations grew in importance with the result that Congress leaders exercised control over the actions of their workers and other temperance organizations to emphasize that distinction. When the Congress used its power in Provincial Assemblies to enact prohibition, its form, the style of its implementation, and the rhetoric of its propaganda revealed elite nationalist attitudes regarding class, social status, national identity, and the use of state power to effect social change.

The drinking classes

Alcohol use in South Asia was much more widespread than commonly recognized, though both nationalists and missionaries downplayed the significance and scale of pre-colonial drinking.[8] Drinkers were legion and sometimes vocal. The drink strikes of the 1890s forced both the colonial government and befuddled European temperance advocates to acknowledge the high rates of alcohol use associated with some communities.[9] The revenue of the colonial government and of some later independent Indian state governments depended on large-scale alcohol production and consumption.[10] So widespread was the use of alcohol that its taxation provided as much as 32.4 per cent of total revenue for Madras Presidency.[11] Though many Indians conceived of their nation as abstemious, great numbers of their fellows drank quite a bit of alcohol.

Prohibition in India was as much a matter of social status as it was about drink. Despite the close relationship between temperance and the nationalist movement, many Indian drinkers persisted in their habit even during its eventual criminalization in some areas by the Congress provincial governments of 1937-9. Indian social reformers and European activists operating in India noted the traditional association of alcohol use with low social status. Middle class drinkers alarmed nationalists and temperance activists on occasion but they were not mentioned with anything approaching the frequency of lower class drinkers. Elite Indians associated with both nationalism and the temperance cause increasingly saw the drinking habits of the poor as a threat to the nation at large.[12]

Civil disobedience and drink

With the increasing violence and scale of the freedom movement and associated colonial responses, tempers flared against liquor-men and their patrons. Drinkers found themselves on the wrong side of the growing dichotomy between those who favoured British rule and those who did not. Drink increasingly represented not just social degradation but political apathy in a struggle that called for unity and sacrifice. The tone of moral suasion, essential to temperance work into the 1920s, changed by the 1930s as nationalist volunteers grew impatient with the stubborn resistance of drinkers. The colonial government had a stake in the revenue-flow from these drinkers but also found them potential allies, a low-status complement to the generally pro-British rulers of the princely states. As a result, nationalist discourse and imperial responses were marked by a struggle to determine who had the right to speak in the interests of India's subaltern, largely drinking, population.

In 1930, imperial administrators again frustrated the hopes of the Congress by allowing a December 1929 deadline to pass without pledging to award India 'dominion status' and thus effective autonomy. In response to this decision, the Congress launched the Civil Disobedience Movement, which lasted from 1930-1. A key aspect of Civil Disobedience was the picketing of liquor shops. Although such picketing was technically legal under tightly controlled circumstances, district collectors and magistrates routinely arrested picketers for violating the strict rules for picketing.[13] Thousands of Congress volunteers spoke in the bazaars, picketed, and visited the homes of drinkers in a concerted effort to rid India of drink.

In the early weeks of the Civil Disobedience campaign, picketers gathered around liquor shops in great numbers, ensuring the confrontation of all customers with their 'sinful' and pro-empire/anti-Indian behaviour. The writer Premchand, praised for the realism of his stories, described how Congress volunteers articulated these warnings in the short story *Maiku.* Approaching a toddy shop, a would-be drinker, Maiku, is met by a Congress *sevak* (volunteer) who, hands clasped together in supplication, advises him that the drinking of toddy is forbidden in his religion: 'आपके मजहब में ताडी हराम है|'.[14] Maiku responds violently to this instruction on the tenets of his own faith by striking the *sevak* bloody before his epiphany regarding the justice of the Congress cause. Nevertheless, the confrontation of would-be drinkers of low social ranking on religious grounds doubtlessly raised hackles.

After Congress ratcheted up liquor shop picketing in 1930, some of these interactions became heated, even violent. British-administered government added to the frustration of picketers by increasingly overlooking *abkari* violations.[15] A black market emerged, and sales occurred outside of licensed shops and after legal hours of operation. Some liquor sellers hired men to attack picketers who dared to disrupt illegal sales or giveaways. In July 1931, *The Hindu* reported that a liquor contractor 'announced a free distribution of toddy and hired rowdys [sic] from a neighbouring village and created a disturbance in front of the liquor shop'.[16] Such use of violence by liquor-vendors is further echoed in Premchand's *Maiku* in which a liquor vendor rewards a street-tough with free drinks for punching a *sevak*.[17] Although the wishes of the Congress in 1931 were not the law of the land, the effect of the Congress's widespread influence and enormous volunteer corps provoked liquor sellers to continue alcohol sales by hook or by crook. The Congress's assertion of hegemony and universality provoked the very resistance that belied the actualization of its claim.[18]

The problem of illegal sales was ubiquitous. Tamil Nadu's famous nationalist, C. Rajagopalachari, or Rajaji, complained that 'toddy pots are carried about on the head and sold like curds and buttermilk in the streets'.[19] Where illegal sales might once have cost government revenue, the dramatic reduction in legal alcohol sales associated with picketing changed the dynamic. Markedly lower sales left *abkari* contractors without the means to pay their annual fees to the district collectors. Illegal sales were now a lifeline for liquor dealers, one that colonial bureaucrats were only too happy to provide. One worker described to Rajaji an instance of illegality in the following manner:

> Two of the people who bought toddy were known to me and I went with them to the Sub Inspector's house and told him about the shop being opened beyond lawful hours. The Sub Inspector himself came with me to the shop to verify. The shop was open. But the vendor had concealed himself somewhere. Then a car came belonging to a big Abkari contractor. There were some gentlemen in it. One of them got out and inspected the shop. From his behaviour and from the evasive answers he gave me, I think he was a high officer of the Abkari department. The Sub Inspector told me that he will enquire into the sales outside lawful hours. I have not yet heard anything about it ...[20]

The same reporter complained of one particular sub-inspector at a shop distributing free toddy who not only allowed the illegal activity to continue but 'marched into the shop' and 'ordered' the men 'in a loud voice to get in and drink'. From that day 'a police constable and two salt peons [were] posted in front of the shop ... directly inviting people to drink and threaten the [picketing] volunteers'.[21] Rajaji explained the misguided actions of the police, writing that, 'the Indian policeman feels it is his duty to help the business of the drink shops and looks upon the place as holding the sacred Majesty of the British *Sircar* [Government] in spite of vulgar surroundings'.[22]

There were no easy solutions for the colonial government as it was true that when *abkari* taxes were too high, illicit manufacture burgeoned. Prohibition seemed likely to provoke the same response. Reducing taxes on drink produced yet another set of problems. For example, in 1935, the Excise Department of Madras cut taxes on *arrack* because 'the drinking public cannot in the prevailing economic condition afford to pay the high price for licit arrack charged by the licensed vendor', leading to illicit distillation.[23] Temperance activists saw this reduction as yet more evidence that government was more concerned with increasing sales of licit alcohol than in checking consumption, which was the stated goal of the Abkari Department.

Colonial administrators eagerly investigated all instances of alleged violence during picketing to discredit the nationalist and temperance movements more generally. Congress leaders worried particularly that administrators would arrest their volunteers on trumped up charges. Rajaji wrote of a case in September 1931 in which volunteers compelled an illegal liquor seller to report to the magistrate along with her pot of illegal toddy. She did so but Rajaji considered this a 'narrow miss' for the volunteers, who were fortunate that 'the pot was not broken and a charge brought against them under sections 143, 147 and all other sections, on the allegation that they waylaid and assaulted the renter's servants lawfully carrying a pot of toddy'.[24]

Picket organizers foresaw inevitable conflicts with drinkers. As Ambedkar put it, 'naturally, when people are denied the luxury of a vice to which they are used to indulge … they will rebel for a time'.[25] To protect the viability of picketing, the Congress issued detailed rules for volunteers. These picketing rules included an explicit disavowal of 'coercion, direct or indirect', a limit of five picketers at any one location, a proscription against the physical blocking of customers or goods going in or out of the shops, and the admonition that interventions with drinkers should be based on nothing more than 'courteous entreaty'.[26] Gandhi added to these guidelines the suggestion that picketers 'penetrate into the home[s] of the drinkers'.[27]

Drinker's agency

Despite Congress's anti-drink campaign, many Indians continued to imbibe during the Civil Disobedience Movement. Ambedkar estimated that 'almost all the castes comprising the three groups of Backward classes and more than one-fifth of the total population' continued to populate the drinking classes.[28] This estimate contrasts starkly with that of Rajaji, who asserted that 'all shades of public opinion in India (except those actually interested in drink) are agreed to the desirability of Prohibition at the earliest possible date'.[29] Ambedkar's estimate was more accurate than Rajaji's: a large segment of the Indian population necessarily opposed a key aspect of the Congress's platform and the Indians dismissed as 'those actually interested in drink' comprised a large portion of the population. The Congress elided the agency of the drinking poor, instead recasting them as put-upon 'victims' who needed to be 'kept away' from liquor shops.[30] Poor drinkers, by this logic, needed to be protected from danger as a child by her parent.

Indian temperance reformers, most of them ardent nationalists, found themselves arguing against the colonial state on the basis that it denied them their agency, even as they simultaneously sought to check the wishes of drinkers using the force of law. This discrepancy was mitigated by the repeated assertion that drinkers fundamentally could not be agents. Rather, drinkers were 'victims'. When they persisted in their stubborn resistance to righteous picketers, activists referred to them as 'hardened victims'.[31] These 'hardened victims' lacked true volition, the argument went, 'lending themselves to be used as tools' by 'interested' parties.[32] Reformers characterized the continued resistance of drinkers as an expression of the agency of anthropomorphized drink itself, or of British rule and the liquor interests. Temperance reformers and nationalists pitied drinkers, hoping that through social pressure and the physical removal of the temptation, the latter might be freed of their 'slavery' to alcohol. This was a 'difficult situation' requiring the Congress to 'start quietly and to get the other side habituated gradually to the interference on [their] part'.[33] Gandhi argued that 'drinking [was] like a disease and the sufferer must be protected against himself. It is not coercion to give him treatment for his own good nor is it coercion for the State to save its people from the disease of drink by driving it out'.[34] The drinking classes could not be allowed the right to poison the Indian nation.

Liquor men

Liquor dealers did not fare as well as their customers in the eyes of temperance activists and nationalists in the early 1930s. Dealers were traitors, not victims. Sensitive to these condemnations, one repentant liquor dealer begged Rajaji to intervene and stop the picketing of his liquor shop until the end of his annual contract when he would no longer have an interest in the business. He acknowledged that 'drink was among the five deadly sins' and that continuing in the trade would render him 'a traitor to the country'.[35] This link between drinking and treason was no accident. Teams of volunteers picketing liquor shops made the display of the national flag a key visual element of their protest.[36] In August 1931, the Bangalore district magistrate prohibited the hoisting of the national flag within 100 yards of a liquor shop in a clear attempt to drive a wedge between nationalism and temperance.[37]

Temperance activists and nationalists consistently made the link between their two causes evident by working within both camps for the realization of both ideals. As a result, colonial administrators complained of the 'increasing tendency on the part of local [temperance] bodies to indulge in activities designed to support or show sympathy with the disloyal movement promoted by the advocates of civil disobedience'.[38] The association was cemented by the use of powerful symbols such as the hoisting of the national flag to emphasize temperance as a goal of the coming sovereign state. Despite the efforts of administrators to separate the issue of Indian freedom from that of alcohol policy, it remained clear to leading nationalists that the liquor dealer took in revenue 'on behalf of the Government' and sold alcohol as 'an agent of the British *Sircar*'.[39] Rajaji argued that ostensibly well-intended arguments in favour of access to alcohol were necessarily disingenuous, as he 'has not found a single place where there has been really agitation against prohibition except when it is manufactured and financed' by outside forces.[40]

In the face of such harsh criticism for moral dissolution and treason, it is not surprising that interactions between liquor dealers and temperance men carried the threat of violence. At the commencement of the Civil Disobedience Movement in 1930, Chauri Chaura was only eight years gone and violence, even if isolated at this point, threatened to forestall picketing across India.[41] The Government of India's Home Department Secretary, H.W. Emerson, solicited reports documenting 'instances of violence, coercion, destruction of property', and other 'objectionable methods' in the picketing of shops.[42] Picketers also accused liquor dealers of violence. Reports that picketers had been assaulted with *lathi*s, kicks and 'foul abusive language' were common.[43] One volunteer in Hyderabad, Sindh reported in a telegram to Vallabhbhai Patel that 'one picketer at liquor shop Mirpurkhas followed Muslim servant Guteval carrying liquor bottle. Picketer very severely beaten with lathi by servant at lonely place outside the town. Picketers beaten six times before also. Policy of beating seems determined upon'.[44] Yet, unlike the behaviour of temperance workers, the violence of liquor-shop men was ignored by the police in all but the most egregious cases. It was due to these hostile circumstances that the Congress conducted liquor shop picketing under tightly controlled circumstances.

As a growing number of liquor men migrated from (or were forced out of) the trade, those who remained became a focal point for the disapproval of nationalists. The era of politely entreating liquor men to give up the trade ended in the 1920s, and licensees in the next decade would be spared no quarter within legal means. Rajaji admitted that despite the 'hectic activities during the auction sales', 'hardened dealers' could not be swayed from the low-hanging fruit of cut-rate licenses.[45] Even in the 1930s, the zenith of the anti-alcohol movement in India, liquor dealers continued to do a brisk trade.

Nevertheless, many liquor sellers ceased or significantly scaled back their businesses in response to losses incurred during the Civil Disobedience Movement. One liquor shop owner in the Madras Presidency petitioned the Congress to stop picketing his shop until 1 January 1932 on the grounds that his license would expire by then. However, he needed to continue selling liquor until then because he still owed the government money on the existing license, which he could only earn through sales. The seller pleaded, 'I support the Congress movement sincerely. I do not like to carry on the liquor traffic. It is due to my ignorance that I have got myself involved in this business.'[46] He added that he would not 'again take lease of any Arrack shop'.[47] Rajaji frustrated the hopes of this petitioner by releasing a press statement that said picketing would not be stopped because 'no reform is possible without this kind of suffering on the part of some people'.[48] The message was a public warning: those who placed themselves in alliance with the colonial state and the liquor upon which it depended could expect little sympathy from the Congress.

The firm link between the liquor trade and the British government pitted them against the temperance-advocating nationalists. This had nearly led to a crisis in Poona as far back as 1908,[49] and in 1931 there was a similar clash between officialdom and temperance-advocating protesters. Yet, unlike the events in Poona, this new clash revealed divisions between highly-respected Congress leaders on the one hand and Congress volunteers at the local level on the other. Nevertheless, the All-India Congress Working Committee tried to exert more control over local events than was possible with such a widespread phenomenon as liquor store picketing. The time had come for a comprehensive plan and strict hierarchy of leadership right down to the village level.

Controlling picketers

The Congress Working Committee, in conjunction with the Congress's Prohibition Committee chaired by Rajaji, established a tightly regimented system to control picketers along several fronts. One of these fronts involved coordinating picketing organizations, whether nationalist organizations or nominal temperance organizations. Picketing that involved any Congress-*walla*s required the supervision of the local Congress Committee. These local Congress Committees were supervised by Provincial Congress Committees which were, in turn, supervised by the Congress's Prohibition and Working Committees. Recognizing that with regard to the pickets, 'the stricter we are, the greater will be our prestige and strength', the Congress issued the following rules applicable to all picketers:

1 There should be no coercion, direct or indirect.
2 There should be no show of intimidation, hence not more than any five pickets should work at one and the same place at a time.
3 There should be no more than courteous entreaty and distribution of literature.
4 There should be no fine levied by Congress Committee for breach of promise.
5 There should be no hooting of purchasers.
6 There should be no cordon formed to surround the purchasers.
7 There should be no lying down to block the passage of customers or goods.[50]

The Congress anticipated continued government accusations that picketers strove to initiate violence. Rajaji consequently urged that athletic men be precluded from picketing liquor shops. Volunteers were to be 'mere lads'. 'The people that gather to drink or the men in the employ of the vendors could easily give a thorough beating to them. We have limited the lads to such small numbers that they could be attacked and badly assaulted by the liquor-shop men even if they had been big sturdy soldiers instead of being boys.'[51] Local Congress leaders made public speeches during periods of exceptional violence, the texts of which often appeared in the press and called for calm, exhorting volunteers to 'follow Mahatma's principle of non-violence and sufferance'.[52] Hoping to mitigate further violence, 'ladies and girls' volunteered to picket as well.[53]

Other methods: Auction pickets, plays, and pressure tactics

British administrators continued to sell toddy and arrack shop licenses by auctioning 'tenders', which became an important target for Congress picketers. Auctions were particularly contentious as they brought high-ranking liquor men and government officials together but once per year. They were the one yearly occasion when temperance volunteers could confront the very heart of the liquor menace in India. Since selling tenders was a major revenue source for government, even ordinarily complacent magistrates and officials were at their most severe. The Excise Commissioner of Madras made a failed attempt at outlawing auction pickets altogether.[54] Congress issued strict rules for the picketing the auction of tenders to prevent violence:

1 Picketing should be absolutely peaceful. There should be no coercion direct or indirect.
2 The most influential persons should form the picketing party.
3 Leaders may enter the compound of the offices where auctions take place. But the volunteer party shall do the picketing from outside the compound only.
4 Volunteers should be limited in number – not more than six for each entrance.
5 Picketers should not touch or obstruct or fall across the passage.
6 They will accost could-be-renters and entreat them not to participate in the auctions.
7 They will distribute hand-bills to the intending bidders.
8 As far as possible, it should be seen that crowds do not gather at the places of picketing.[55]

To this the Congress added that 'processions with suitable Anti-drink placards and *Bhajana* [hymn-singing] may be organized'.[56] Tenders thus could continue with little internal disturbance, but six picketers per entrance guaranteed that bidders would fall under the gaze of Congressmen and that the bidding might be scored by the distant notes of devotional music.[57]

The campaign against license tenders was moderately effective. By September 1931, 30 per cent of existing liquor shops in Madras Presidency had not been re-licensed for the following year.[58] Administrators were forced to hold secret tenders to avoid protesters and to accept far lower bids for the ensuing years.[59] In an ironic turn, the relative success of auction picketers meant that those who stubbornly persisted in the liquor trade despite social pressure to desist could earn more profit due to lower cost licenses. As successful bidders made yet more money, they increasingly depended on the support of administrators and police to enforce picketing rules. The result was more money, more *lathis*, more social pressure, and more anger.

Temperance workers under the direction of the Congress used pledges to further isolate those who chose the liquor trade over the vision of an independent India. Volunteers entreated Indians to sign pledges to the effect that they supported complete and immediate prohibition of alcohol.[60] Pledge books functioned as yet another form of social coercion, compelling literate Indians to firmly commit themselves on the side of prohibition.[61] Anyone approached with the pledge, whether they signed it or not, was subject to personal surveillance by temperance workers and nationalists. Pledges thus facilitated the creation of a dichotomy characterized by a strict division between those who favoured drink and empire and those who favoured temperance and the nation. Pledges had long been a key technique for American and British temperance advocates at home. In India temperance pledges took on new meaning due to the colonial context within which they were signed. Those who signed the pledges allied themselves not only with temperance, but also with the nationalist movement more generally and with high-caste social mores eschewing drink.

Picketing and pledging were tried and true forms of protest in Britain that also found great success on the subcontinent, but India's unique culture offered other means to further the goal of prohibition. For instance, caste proscriptions against the use of alcohol first enacted in the late nineteenth century (for an entirely different end) continued, and some local authorities continued to closely monitor caste organizations in the 1930s. Most local administrators wisely refrained from attacking organizations that enacted prohibitions against alcohol use. The South Indian cities of Chittoor and Salem were exceptions to this restraint. Local administrators launched prosecutions against caste leaders who proscribed the use of alcohol in Chittoor and they suspended a village *munsif* for supporting caste-based prohibition.[62] The latter case was particularly disturbing to administrators because it tied the social authority of the caste leaders to the nominal legal authority of the village *munsif*. The Indian revenue divisional officer reported that the 'munsif proclaimed in the village by the beat of tom tom to the effect that the villagers should stop drinking toddy, etc. with effect from 17-8-31 failing which they would render themselves liable to be fined Rs. 10 each by the caste Panchayat besides being deprived of the services of dobhi, barber, exc.'[63] British administrators suspended the *munsif* and rescinded the legal imprimatur given to the caste proscriptions.

The Congress-led prohibition campaign aimed at the control of both public and private spaces. In the public space, local Congress Committees organized public processions on the second Sunday of every month on thoroughfares with drink-shops.[64] These processions marked an assertion of the elite ideal regarding drink over the greater population of India. Drink stalls on and near public thoroughfares had long drawn the ire of temperance workers. Counter-attractions were also established for diverting people from the drink-habit.[65] This meant that counter-attractions specifically targeted the spaces within which drinking took place. Such processions and counter-attractions represented an overt attempt to reclaim the public space of drink shops. The chants and *bhajan*s of those marching in processions were at once both appeals and warnings, as a free India was emerging on the horizon, one that would not brook drink sellers and their patrons.

The social pressure directed at liquor men changed the economic world within which they operated. Rajaji boasted that 'tree owners in many areas have pledged themselves not to give their trees for toddy tapping'.[66] This pledge did not happen spontaneously but was the product of a concerted effort by Congress to induce anti-drink *sabhas* (societies) to 'exercise their influence to prevent landholders and lessees [from] letting out their trees for tapping'.[67] Elites who facilitated the drink trade by leasing out their toddy trees had long enjoyed a degree of separation from the socially degrading manufacture and trade. Congress and anti-drink *sabha*s worked to remove that degree of separation, painting toddy tree owners with the brush of social degradation and treason. Many owners of toddy trees who had long leased out their toddy trees to tappers simply cut them down, with Periyar being a famous example. While nationalist histories continue to treat the cutting of toddy trees as a 'popular' movement,[68] the trend certainly was not popular with those who depended on toddy trees for their livelihood.

Temples similarly changed their practice of letting out toddy trees on temple-owned land. Thus, for toddy tappers, the moral epiphany earnestly desired by activists became less important.[69] After all, without toddy trees how could there be toddy tapping?[70] Despite the legality of alcohol production during this period, the Congress pressure succeeded in making it an impossibility for many would-be brewers. Finding space for the opening of liquor shops also grew increasingly problematic. 'Many licensees in the rural area [we]re unable to start their business because people refuse to let premises for the purpose [of selling liquor.]'[71] When moral rhetoric failed to dissuade drinkers, elites simply denied access to the means to make or sell liquor.

Nationalist leaders occasionally had to check the zeal of temperance activists, discouraging them from such initiatives as the boycott of Adi-Dravida, or Dalit, women vegetable carriers 'because the money is utilized for drink later on'.[72] Congress had to tread carefully here. One local Congressman reported to Rajaji that 'officials and renters of shops are trying to organize Adi-Dravidas to oppose the Congress movement against drink'.[73] The nationalist movement simply could not afford to alienate the entire population of low-caste drinkers. They certainly did not want the caste-based and class-based aspects of the prohibition movement to come to the fore. If they could not manage to get drinking classes fully behind the movement, then at least the Congress could hope for ambivalence. The issue could not be pushed further until the creation of prohibition zones in 1939 as discussed below.

In addition to the public sphere, nationalist volunteers also brought their activism into the domestic space of the home. 'House visits' placed activists on the doorsteps of drinkers with the expressed purpose of persuasion, but it was also necessarily a form of surveillance and identification of drinkers who were in opposition to the good intentions of their fellows. During one such home visit in September 1931, volunteers discovered a woman 'in her own hut who was handed over with toddy pot to the Abkari inspector'.[74] The volunteers recounted the woman's explanation:

> At about 4 p.m. this evening at _____'s toddy shop, south of the village well, I went to redeem my jewel that I had pledged. The renter's servants told me they would give me a big pot of toddy and that I might keep it in my hut and sell it, and drink up what was left unsold. I agreed. So I was asked to stop at the well, and so-and-so and so-and-so brought and gave me a pot of toddy. They said they would give back the jewel only if I carried out these directions. I took the pot to my hut. I sold up till now 1 ½ measures.[75]

Since the words of the liquor-selling woman were mediated both by the volunteer witnessing her statements and the translations he made, the perspective of the toddy seller is obscured. That said, one could see her story as the basis for a counter-narrative. Women who engaged in the public sale of alcohol were of extremely low social status. As this was an activity almost entirely associated with men, it is a reasonable assumption that she was either widowed or otherwise unattached to a male. With few resources to meet her basic needs, she pawned her jewellery, a recourse of the unfortunate. Operating in a social space where money was hard to come by, she agreed to sell toddy. This allowed her to use her socially degraded status to her economic advantage, making money by breaking both the law and social custom to regain her jewellery. The intervention of the volunteers barred the woman from benefiting, however nominally, from her low social status.

In the above example, the woman's social status was not the concern of the volunteers who forcibly took her and her toddy pot to the *abkari* inspector. She was subjected to the humiliation of her trade being made public, particularly among those classes who did not engage in public drinking. Of greater import, no mention is made of her being remunerated for the loss of the toddy pot. As the trade was illegal, she would have lost the value of the remaining toddy. She certainly would not have expected to be aided by Congress volunteers since Rajaji had made it clear time and again that little sympathy would be spared for those who engaged in the iniquitous trade. It is a safe assumption that the jewellery she wanted to reclaim from the pawnshop was lost for the near future if not forever. No mention is made in the documents about whether she was punished by the police, although it is a distinct possibility. Excluded from the protection of both the colonial state and the freedom movement allied against it, she simply had to suffer the consequences of the subalternity predicated upon her class and gender.

Anti-alcohol volunteers applied pressure not only through focused interactions in homes and drinking dens, but also through a systematic propaganda campaign focused on public spaces. On behalf of the Indian National Congress, Rajaji implored volunteers to 'hold, not only large meetings in central places, but also and more particularly small meetings in street corners and nearer the dwellings of the people concerned so that the message may go to every corner'.[76] It could be more darkly stated that a drinker could scarcely find a corner without substantial social pressure to reform his habits.

Nationalism, temperance, and the Prohibition League of India

Due to the Government's harsh response to the Civil Disobedience Movement, nationalists found it increasingly important to distinguish between activism associated with the Congress's temperance program or the Prohibition League of India (PLI) from that of the Congress as a political organization. The close links between the PLI and Congress helped both organizations but also required PLI representatives to frequently state the divisions between them. For example, in inviting a local temperance organization to perform a Marathi-language adaptation of the temperance play, *Just a Peg*, Rajaji pointedly advised his correspondent that 'the Prohibition League of India ... is a non-Congress, non-party organization'.[77] What Rajaji wrote was technically true; but it was also technically true that the letterhead on which he often wrote was topped by information about both the Congress and the Prohibition League of India.[78] Even if the Prohibition League of India as an *institution* was 'non-party and non-political', its membership was decidedly not.[79]

The language of the Prohibition League of India's literary organ, *Prohibition*, was delicately crafted by its editors lest its strictly moral mission be obscured by nationalist politics. This is to say, although the PLI was quite nationalist in orientation, it remained important for its leadership to maintain a façade that its goal of realizing prohibition was separate from that of gaining Indian independence. Rajaji described liquor shop picketing of the Non-cooperation Movement as 'social reformation' rather than 'political change'.[80] This is a curious distinction given that the Indian nationalist movement, particularly under Gandhi's tutelage, fused the two. After all, how could nationalists campaign for true *Swaraj* while ignoring the 'father of all vice'?[81] Temperance activists, however pure their motives, could not be allowed great influence over the carefully crafted statements of the PLI.

Publishing and editing the PLI journal was a delicate task, straddling the fence between political and moral reform. When *Prohibition* appeared set to disappear in the wake of mass arrests and budgetary problems, N.S.R. Iyengar, a Bombay nationalist and temperance advocate offered to take it over 'even if it costs my life and the life of my family members ... till the last drop of all Drinks ... exists no more in my Motherland'.[82] In a rather sternly-worded reply, Rajaji admonished that 'I have no authority nor do I intend to ask you to continue the journal.'[83] He added that his correspondent had every right to start another temperance journal, but hoped that Iyengar would 'find a suitable name that will not confound it with the journal of the Prohibition League'.[84]

Divided loyalties grew increasingly problematic in the 1930s. Those Indians who chose to take up government positions prior to the 1938-9 Congress governments were suspect. The decision to cooperate with colonial rule in a nationalistic context within which non-cooperation was the ideal placed Indian bureaucrats outside of the nation. Rajaji went so far as to question the religious authenticity of those Indians who supported 'outrageous' Legislative Council decisions and who were present when the 'local option' often died a quiet death.[85] He criticized Indians in such meetings who judged prohibition impractical, saying that their arguments 'sound extremely funny from the mouths of a professing Hindu or Muslim minister'.[86]

Indian temperance activists during the Civil Disobedience period fought against drink on several fronts. They pressured governments of the Presidency to reduce public access to alcohol though a variety of measures, from expanded local option to complete prohibition. At the local level, activists fought to reduce the number of liquor shops in urban cities and rural villages. To further this goal, activists picketed liquor shops and confronted would-be customers emphasizing the evil effects of drink on the individual, the family, the village, and the nation.

The Gandhi-Irwin pact

So many participants were arrested in 1931 during the Civil Disobedience picketing that the Congress began to deploy women and children instead of men to picket the shops. This move proved somewhat effective. For instance, the Government of Bombay sent out a directive that

> 'the most satisfactory way of countering these unchivalrous tricks is to arrest the women before beginning to use force, to remove them to a police station or some other convenient spot at a distance, and to release them when the disturbance is at an end. It is not desirable from any point of view that the prisons should be filled with women'.[87]

If the larger Civil Disobedience Movement was losing energy as a consequence of mass arrest, female picketers presented the government with a new set of problems that they were keen to avoid. Children who demonstrated posed an equally vexing problem for colonial officials, some of whom recommended draconian responses such as placing them in reform schools or publically whipping them.[88] The latter course of action was dismissed in all but the 'rowdiest' of cases, implying that beating children in public in the defence of demon drink might have a detrimental effect on the government's already poor public-relations. Both the Congress and the government had their own interests in pulling back from the brink.

In March 1931, Viceroy of India Lord Irwin and Gandhi reached an accord wherein the Congress agreed to suspend the Civil Disobedience Movement in exchange for a leading role in the upcoming Round Table Conference in London. Further, the Government of India released nationalists imprisoned for non-violent offenses while the Congress agreed to curtail several forms of agitation. However, one notable exception to this new amiability was that Congress workers continued picketing liquor shops and carried on with the 'social work' of reforming drinkers.[89] The decision of the government to allow picketing to continue under the terms of the Gandhi-Irwin pact met with some rearguard resistance from British officials. This resistance caused some friction within the colonial government that did not go unobserved by nationalists. The Collector of Madras, A.R. Cox, argued against liquor-shop picketing, provoking a very public condemnation from Rajaji who reminded him that he was not the Viceroy of India but 'only the Collector of Madras'.[90]

Embarrassing exchanges such as the above notwithstanding, the colonial government proved able to use the vague language of the Gandhi-Irwin pact to its benefit. When Congress officials intermittently reported government crackdowns on peaceful picketing in violation of the pact, the Government of Madras reported to Rajaji the instructions they had issued to the police with regard to the pickets. The tone of these instructions was initially conciliatory towards the picketers: for example, an order from March 1931 stated that, 'no notice [should] be taken of picketing unless it threatens serious disorder or danger to the public peace'.[91] But more ominous warnings appeared in the summer of 1931, indicating that 'several clear breaches of the pact had been reported, particularly in rural areas'.[92] The report concluded with the assertion that all district magistrates had the authority to call upon local Congress Committees to 'suspend picketing ... if such a course is thought expedient'.[93]

The assertion that local magistrates had the authority to call on Congress to break up picketing when 'expedient' was inimical to the Congress's political strength. When the Government of Madras demanded that the Congress stop picketing on the rather loose grounds of 'expediency', Rajaji responded by immediately consulting Gandhi regarding this 'wrong interpretation of the pact by local Government'.[94] Government restrictions on picketing threatened to drive a wedge between the Congress high command and the activism of local volunteers across India.

The ability to continue anti-liquor activism despite the suspension of the Civil Disobedience Movement provided a much-needed outlet for the energies of Congress volunteers. As Rajaji told Congress leader Vallabhbhai 'Sardar' Patel, 'good work is done throughout the country and not a little of it is due to the feeling that the Truce protects Congress workers. If we break the spell, all work may get dislocated'.[95] Congress continued a robust anti-liquor campaign despite the arrest of much of its leadership in 1931.

Congress-led prohibition 1938-9

When the Gandhi-Irwin pact failed in 1932, British authorities once again rounded up and imprisoned much of the Congress leadership. Picketing continued in isolated locations but the movement had lost much of its energy. With many of the 'respectable community leaders' once involved in picketing incarcerated, Congress pickets all but ceased. Although the system of dyarchy established in 1919 was marginally improved by the 1935 Government of India Act, the Congress maintained that the new Act's limited sovereignty was insufficient for participation in a colonial government.

In 1937, the Congress reversed its position, agreeing to form ministries in the five provinces where they had won majorities. Since *abkari* administration was a 'transferred' or provincial department and thus under Indian control, the Congress endeavoured to make good on its pledge to work towards total prohibition in the Congress-controlled provinces, namely Madras, Bombay, United Provinces, Central Provinces, and Bihar. Congress had already established in 1931 that 'if and when elections to legislative councils and assemblies are held and congressmen participate in them, the introduction and active promotion of total prohibition shall be made part of the election pledge of the Congress candidates'.[96] Under Rajaji's tutelage, the Congress Government of Madras instituted a pilot prohibition program in Salem in 1937.[97] Similarly, Minister of Health and Excise for Bombay, D. Gilder, initiated a pilot program in the industrial city of Ahmedabad. Kailas Nath Katju, United Provinces Excise Secretary, began pilot programs in the villages of the Etah district. Much was at stake in these pilot programs as their success or failure would decide the ultimate fate of prohibition in India.

There were a myriad reasons to proceed slowly. America's failed experiment with prohibition had come to an end in 1933, suggesting that the evil of drink could not be dealt with by law alone. Prohibition in the United States failed because, Indian temperance advocates argued, 'there was no social backing in America'.[98] Frustrated American temperance advocates turned their eyes to the East, praising the activism of Indian nationalists in the cause of temperance but also warning them to avoid the same pitfalls. Hattie Menzies, a member of the Women's Christian Temperance Union, urged for the strong enforcement of prohibition laws in India. She wrote that 'to wink at and ignore an offense causes vice to grow and thrive and encourages crime and wantonness'.[99] Only if prohibition were enforced to the same extent as laws against violent crime could it truly be realized. She argued further that 'if the public does not back up the officials by giving truthful testimony and needed information, if they let the Traffic buy them off, if they tie the hands of those trying to get the best for their countrymen, then you might as well not have the law'.[100]

Despite the increasing certainty in the United States about the failings of prohibition, nationalists greeted reports on the subject with a great deal of suspicion until the American law was repealed in 1933. Rajaji implored his readers to 'not believe the interested writings in newspapers that total Prohibition has been a failure in America. Scarcely an American who comes to India goes away without seeing me'.[101] Rajaji's interactions with Americans sympathetic to the cause of temperance and nationalism led him to make the unfortunate observation that 'there is no public opinion in America supporting the removal of Prohibition. The Government is their own Government and the people are satisfied with the state of things there'.[102] The sanguine predictions of some Indian temperance workers for America's dry future proved ill-founded. When American prohibition suffered setbacks, Rajaji drew a key distinction between Indian and American drinkers based on an idealized past. In ancient India, he averred, 'drink was necessarily held disreputable' and complete prohibition had been achieved, at least in Bengal, 500 years ago by the fiat of the Hindu saint, Chaitanya. This fiat 'very soon solved the problem of intemperance'.[103]

An even greater threat to prohibition in India was the fact that alcohol consumption underlay the system of government funding. A large portion of state revenue came from excise taxes on intoxicants, and state services such as education and municipal drainage depended on alcohol revenue. The

Government of India had given the Congress a poison pill: it could institute prohibition only at the cost of defunding important public programs. Financial prudence alone suggested a gradual move towards prohibition, a tactic that seemed all the more important as news of the United States' woes drew the anxious attention of the world temperance community.

With the formation of provincial ministries, the Indian National Congress found itself in fairly unique circumstances. They had access to some of the levers of state power without sovereignty. This provided nationalists with the ability to use the state's powers to further the independence struggle. Indian nationalists and temperance advocates of all stripes had long cast alcohol as an alien contaminant that came to India with the empire and would doubtlessly leave along with it. Since temperance or complete abstention were tightly held values for the leading nationalist organization, using state power to move towards prohibition was an opportunity for the Congress to demonstrate that these values were not mere rhetoric. Indian freedom meant independence from both colonial administrators and the liquor they brought with them.

The decision to use state power to implement prohibition again placed Congress in conflict with a segment of the population for whom they hoped to speak, i.e. liquor sellers and a vast numbers of their customers. The recent history of half-hearted enforcement of *abkari* laws by magistrates and police during the Civil Disobedience Movement frustrated the Congress Working Committee, which had good reason to doubt the full cooperation of all bureaucrats in schemes of prohibition. Some of those officials were known to have imperial sympathies. The Working Committee therefore decided to set up a non-state bureaucracy to function much like a shadow-state that would cooperate with amenable bureaucrats and force the cooperation of recalcitrant officials. Prohibition boards were peopled by both government officials and volunteers who worked in tandem with each other. Within the Congress provinces, the new governments established official prohibition departments that would adapt the goal of prohibition to local circumstances. The Congress governments also replaced those excise ministers known to be hostile to temperance with heartfelt temperance men.

To ensure the cooperation of law enforcement and the judiciary, Congress-run non-state Prohibition Committees carefully surveilled their districts. The broad participation of non-official Indians was a fundamental aspect of prohibition. For example, Bihar's prohibition law dictated that 'Every village *chaukidar* [watchman] and *dafadar* [non-commissioned officer] shall be bound to give immediate information at the nearest police-station or to a Prohibition authority of any breach of any of the provisions of this Act which may come to his knowledge.'[104] Yet this injunction went far beyond petty officials and extended virtually to all Indians. Bihar required that:

> Every person who occupies any land or building or who is a landlord of an estate, residing in the village, or in which there shall be any tapping for tari [toddy] or manufacture of any liquor or intoxicating drug not

> authorized by a permit or license issued under this Act, shall, in the absence of reasonable excuse, be bound to give notice of the same to a Magistrate or to a Prohibition authority or to an officer of the Police as soon as such tapping or manufacture shall come to his knowledge.[105]

Bihar's prohibition law required virtually all Indians to inform on drinkers and police the moral standards of the drinking classes.

Prohibition officers also used the power of employer over employee to further their cause. In the Bombay Presidency, 'all the mill-officers co-operated with the [Prohibition] Committee in the effort to dissuade mill-workers from going for drink'.[106] This 'suasion' reinforced the patriarchal authority of mill-owners over their employees. Just as prohibition activists 'encouraged' temperance by denying producers toddy trees, mill-workers were 'encouraged' by bosses to abstain from drink with the implied threat of dismissal. Prohibition was in most, but not all, cases a top-to-bottom affair, with those on the lower rungs of the social order more or less compelled to follow the moral example of their social betters.

Surveillance by prohibition committees also included 'watching lonely paths usually taken by smugglers, checking conveyances, shadowing suspected individuals, spotting illicit distillation, checking *niro* [non-alcoholic toddy juice] for alcohol content, and keeping in touch with the taluk and village prohibition committee members and village officers'.[107] Checking *niro* for alcohol content was particularly burdensome to toddy tappers who complained of outright harassment. The *India Temperance Record and White Ribbon* reported favourably on this harassment as evidence for the vigilance of government officials:

> … a close watch is already being kept in some areas as is clear from complaints received from some toddy tappers that they have become weary of constantly climbing trees to bring down pots and show to police officers, of another complaint that persons frequently ask to see their licenses and take the opportunity of having a swig of their sweet toddy at the same time.[108]

The complaints of toddy tappers seemed well-founded. With their hereditary profession outlawed, even sweet toddy was simply being taken by 'respectable' men. Moreover the tappers were compelled to climb the trees far more than necessary to prove again and again their fidelity to the new law, no easy feat as evidenced by figure 8.1.[109]

Prohibition Committees blurred the line between government officialdom and 'leading citizens' as 'leading men' of local communities comprised approximately half of each committee with prohibition-friendly state officials filling the remaining spots. 'Respectable and well-to-do' men, in addition to the various social pressures they could already initiate, now had the expanded authority to operate as a quasi-official police force. Prohibition committees were thus authorized to impose the social values of 'leading men' on the drinking classes so as to root out 'anti-social and disgraceful acts'.[110] In Bombay

Figure 8.1 Toddy Palms.

Source: W.S. Caine, 'Letters from India', *Abkari: The Quarterly Organ of the Anglo-Indian Temperance Association I*, no. 28, 1897, 59.

City alone, 'besides the 4,000 city police, the Government draft[ed] 500 more police from the moffusil. Voluntary service [was] provided by 800 prohibition guards among whom are many students and professional men'.[111]

Prohibition departments also watched the movements of individuals who journeyed from their homes in dry districts to slake their thirst in wet districts. Since the Congress opted for a piecemeal implementation of prohibition to avoid setbacks and budget crises, prohibition areas were abutted by wet districts. Ahmedabad's prohibition department documented a significant amount of daily migration by drinkers. An inspector charged with surveilling these movements noted that 'The statistics for persons going to take their drink outside the dry area by passing various outposts has been compiled by the Excise Department ... Average number of persons coming after drinking outside the Dry Area per day: Sphijpur Outpost 144, Chandola Outpost 10, Rakhial Outpost 4, Nicol Outpost 1. Total average 159 per day'.[112] To that number, prohibition authorities added an estimated 100 other drinkers who travelled by railway, bringing the total to 259 individuals per day. Prohibition officers and volunteers 'watched the people visiting these places [drink shops] and tried to get their names and addresses'.[113] This close surveillance met with sporadic resistance by some drinkers. At least one prohibition inspector was 'assaulted by a drunken man'.[114] Prohibition officers observed drinkers and visited them individually, attempting to use every means at their disposal to root out the drink curse from every nook and corner. In one month alone, Ahmedabad's Prohibition Department received the names of 244 'drunkards'.[115] The prohibition department analyzed the names on the list to determine their 'places of occupation', adding the threat of joblessness to already stringent legal and social sanctions.[116] Inspectors also kept tabs on liquor shops *outside* the 'Dry Area' to 'get the names and information regarding the persons going there on weekends and holidays'.[117]

Although the Congress's surveillance plans were extensive and ambitious, their efficacy is debatable. Detection of illegal drinking and brewing made manifest the seriousness with which prohibition officers took their 'holy task', but it also represented a failure of moral suasion and appeals to nationalistic feeling. To take a specific case, Ahmedabad's monthly prohibition reports in 1938 show some odd numbers suggesting that the near unanimity of prohibition sentiment among Indians was illusory. In one month alone the department processed 448 applications for drinking permits and documented the daily trek of some 260 drinkers to wet areas. It is notable that these 448 applications were completed by either literate drinkers or drinkers who used the aid of literate men with at least a cursory knowledge of how to petition the bureaucracy for a drink license. Yet only 33 reports of alleged breaches of prohibition laws were reported to the Prohibition Department during the same month.[118] Of these, only nine were reported to the excise department for prosecution, and only four prosecutions were successful while five failed. If the number of wandering drinkers and drink license applicants is any indication, nationalist (and now official government) appeals to report illicit drinking inspired few Indians to inform on their kith and kin.

Invested with the power of the state and the future of the nation, Congress ministries set out to help 'poor peasants and workers and *Harijans* in very humble circumstances of life ... to make them strong in body and mind, full of self-respect and self-reliance and self-control'.[119] This installation of 'self-respect and self-control' among the masses required a great deal of disciplinary control from elites. In the United Provinces, 'warning boards' were set up on roads leading into prohibition areas, warning drinkers to 'beware'.[120] Those who illegally engaged in the drink trade, whether as sellers or their customers, were put on notice that they would be prosecuted to the fullest extent of the law and that their actions were being observed by both officers of the state and by their 'respectable' neighbours.

These regulations provoked desperate behaviour in those involved in the liquor trade and extreme measures among enforcers. In the early months of prohibition in Bihar, of an estimated 6,000 people involved in the liquor trade, 2,500 left for non-prohibition districts and 2,330 others found employment in low wage positions as vegetable *walla*s, cart-men and railway workers.[121] In Madras, some Salem district families that refused to give up the liquor trade were 'assisted to emigrate to Malaya', where they could continue their occupations.[122] Salem's prohibition committee eventually had to curtail the ambitious program of literally expatriating liquor-trading Indians due to 'depressed wages' at the new destination.[123] Those involved in the production of alcohol were stigmatized by prohibition officers who labelled them as 'unclean' and 'unfavourable elements'.[124]

Like lapses in the failed experiment of prohibition in the United States, loopholes persisted in South Asia. The decision to introduce prohibition into British India piecemeal allowed drinkers to simply walk to locations where the trade remained legal. More problematic was princely rule in the native states. The princely state of Baroda particularly benefited from prohibition in Ahmedabad, enjoying the tax revenue that came with the influx of drinkers and drink-makers from nearby prohibition areas. Ahmedabad's prohibition committee complained that liquor-men in Baroda 'are canvassing and inducing people to come to their shops where they provided them with all the necessary facilities. They are also providing motor cars for conveying customers to their shops and back. This organized move stands out as a grave danger'.[125]

Individual permits allowing the continued consumption of alcohol in prohibition areas on a limited basis were another loophole. Madras had a rather liberal policy, granting drink permits to people of all confessional groups irrespective of their country of origin. Bombay's prohibition committees were much more restrictive, granting permits only to those of 'non-Asian' extraction, based on the assumption that liquor was 'alien to Indian culture'.[126] By the early 1930s it was a long-settled 'fact' that 'Asia has always been the cradle of all the great religions of the world and nearly all of the religions that have nestled in its bosom strongly denounced the use of liquors'.[127] If Indians had never belonged an abstemious 'race', Bombay's government had every intention of making them so. Administrators from the Central Provinces and Berar followed Bombay's lead in 1939, providing special dispensations only to 'non-Asiatic' drinkers or members of the armed forces.[128] In its prohibition areas, Bihar granted permits only to 'persons other than Musalmans', making the state a guarantor of religious ethics.[129]

In the brief period from 1937-9 during which the Congress held provincial power under a still sovereign empire, Congress nationalists had the opportunity for the first time to enforce an imagined common heritage of abstention from alcohol on Indians, many of whom had long traditions of drinking. Nationalists attempting to usher in prohibition at once fought against colonial rule and for a new standard for Indian behaviour modelled upon the supposed temperate lifestyle of the upper castes. On the cusp of freedom, India was set to be an example for the world with little room for the now un-Indian habit of drinking.

As dry areas slowly spread across the Congress provinces it might have appeared that India was on the cusp of complete prohibition, but a Bombay judge in the case of *Imperator verses Sheth Chinubhai Lalbhi* suddenly cut short this progress. The judge discovered an arcane technicality that effectively halted or reversed prohibition in the presidencies.[130] This ruling coincided with the withdrawal of Congress participation in the legislative assemblies. The implications of the Bombay ruling influenced all Indian presidencies and forced an end to prohibition. India would have to wait until freedom in 1947 to attempt prohibition on a large scale again, another effort that won only mixed results.

Conclusion

The temperance movement in the 1930s was inextricably linked to nationalism and Indian freedom. Drinking became a symbol not only of personal degradation but also of disloyalty to the concept of a free India. As thousands of volunteers poured through the bazaars, narrow lanes, and even into the homes of drinkers, it became increasingly clear that a free India would make a claim on the bodies of its citizens. But in a free India, drinkers could not allow the degradation of their bodies to infect the body politic. Increasing activism (or harassment, depending on one's perspective) contributed to growing tensions between drinkers and nationalists, tensions that were never resolved in the prohibition areas of the late 1930s.

As we see, temperance as introduced to India in the late nineteenth century had changed dramatically by the 1930s. Prohibition, the stated goal of most temperance reformers of the 1930s, became indivisible from Indian freedom. High-caste Indian nationalists used temperance as a means to address the condition of the poor in a way that (they hoped) would mobilize them politically. To some extent, prohibition was successful. One of the few studies on the economic impact of prohibition areas (Salem, Madras) found that much more money was being spent by families here on food and other necessities rather than on liquor.[131] This finding echoes that of other studies on the effects of prohibition on families. But, as we have seen, the discourse surrounding alcohol far surpassed the borders of what was healthy or just. The use of or abstention from alcohol became a powerful symbolic act in the 1930s. Prohibition and the associated propaganda and surveillance campaigns divided Indians as much as it unified them, perhaps explaining the persistence of both, the wide availability of drink in contemporary India and the heated debates surrounding it.

Notes

1 Prohibition Department, Bombay, 'Report of the Prohibition Department', in *A.I.C.C. Bombay*, 1938, Nehru Memorial Library, Delhi (henceforth NML). It is noteworthy that the burning of the drink effigy is almost identical to the Dashara festival during which the *rakshasa*, Ravana, is burned, symbolizing the triumph of good over evil.
2 K.N. Katju, 'The Hon'ble Minister of Excise on Prohibition', *Public Information, United Provinces, Lucknow*, vol. II, no. 9, 1938, 7.
3 R. Guha, 'Discipline and mobilize: hegemony and elite control in nationalist campaigns', in idem (ed.) *Dominance without Hegemony: history and power in colonial India*, Cambridge: Harvard University Press, 1997, p. 103.
4 I. Munshi, 'On drinking and "drunkenness": history of liquor in colonial India', in M. and R. Maloni Dossal (eds) *State Intervention and Popular Response: western India in the nineteenth century*, Mumbai: Popular Prakashan, 1999. See also chapter two of my forthcoming dissertation, 'A world without drink: temperance in modern India'.
5 L. Carroll, 'The Temperance Movement in India: politics and social reform', *Modern Asian Studies* 10, 3, 1976.
6 See chapter three of my forthcoming dissertation, 'A world without drink: temperance in modern India'.
7 D. Fahey and P. Manian, 'Poverty and purification: the politics of Gandhi's campaign for Prohibition, *Historian* 67, 3, 2005, 489–506.
8 I.R. Tyrrell, *Woman's World/Woman's Empire: the Woman's Christian Temperance Union in international perspective, 1800–1930*, Chapel Hill: University of North Carolina Press, 1991, p. 165.
9 See chapter two of my forthcoming dissertation, 'A world without drink: temperance in modern India', on Bombay's 1878 Abkari Act.
10 Rajaji described the drinking classes as 'Almost all the castes comprising the three groups of Backward classes and more than one-fifth of the total population.' See C. Rajagopalachari, 'Dr. Ambedkar and Drink Evil', in *C. Rajagopalachari Papers*, 2, 1931, NML.
11 F. Grubb, *Fifty Years Work in India: my temperance jubilee*, 1st edn, London: H.J. Rowling and Sons, 1942, p. 11.
12 Beginning with the Swadeshi movement in 1905, the anti-alcohol agitation was marked by interventions in public, accessible spaces. The drinking of elite Indians in the privacy of their homes and clubs thus largely receded from the public discourse surrounding drink. See chapter three of my forthcoming dissertation, 'A world without drink: temperance in modern India'.
13 More on the rules for picketing can be found below.
14 Premchand, *Greatest Stories*, Jaipur: Apollo Prakashan, 2006, p. 163. The story was originally published in 1932, at the height of the Civil Disobedience Movement. See P.C. Gupta, *Makers of Indian Literature: Premchand*, Delhi: Sahitya Akademi, 1998, p. 5.
15 *Abkari* refers to tax policies regarding the production, sale, or possession of alcohol. The name, *Abkari*, was also adopted as the title for the quarterly journal of the Anglo-Indian Temperance Association.
16 C. Rajagopalachari, 'Picketing in Madras Presidency, a Few Experiences', in *C. Rajagopalachari Papers*, 1931, NML.
17 Premchand, *Greatest Stories*, p. 164.
18 R. Guha, 'Discipline and mobilize', in idem, *Dominance without Hegemony*, p. 101.
19 C. Rajagopalachari, 'Picketing: Our Experiences', in *C. Rajagopalachari Papers*, 6, 1931, NML.
20 Ibid.
21 Ibid.
22 C. Rajagopalachari, 'Anti Drink Movement, a Report from South India', in *C. Rajagopalachari Papers*, 1931, NML.

23 Government of Madras, 'Excise – Arrack – Administration – Proposals for 1935–36 – Orders Passed', ed. Revenue Dpt. Madras, 1935, G.O. No. 148, National Archives of India, Delhi. *Arrack* is distilled country liquor.

24 C. Rajagopalachari, 'Illegal Sales – a Narrow Escape', in *C. Rajagopalachari Papers*, 1931, NML.

25 —, 'Dr. Ambedkar and Drink Evil'. Ambedkar generally urged Dalits to 'abandon customs and practices associated with the stereotype of the untouchable'. Drinking alcohol was one of these practices. See H.C. Sadangi, *Emancipation of Dalits and the Freedom Struggle*, Delhi: Isha Books, 2008, p. 274.

26 C. Rajagopalachari, 'Instructions for Picketing', in *C. Rajagopalachari Papers*, 2, 1931, NML. These rules were published in key newspapers and periodicals like *The Hindu* and Gandhi's *Young India*. They were also sent to state and local Congress Committees.

27 — 'Instructions for Picketing. Gandhiji's Instructions', in *C. Rajagopalachari Papers*, 2, 1931, NML.

28 — 'Dr. Ambedkar and Drink Evil'.

29 —, 'On Prohibition', in *C. Rajagopalachari Papers*, 1931, NML.

30 — 'Anti Drink Movement, a Report from South India'.

31 — 'Advice to Picketers', in *C. Rajagopalachari Papers*, 1931, NML.

32 —, 'Letter To "Mr. Raja", Local Congressman', in *C. Rajagopalachari Papers*, 1931, NML.

33 —, 'Letter to Vaidyanathier', in *C. Rajagopalachari Papers*, 3, 1931, NML.

34 —, 'On Prohibition'.

35 —, 'An Arrack Shop-Keeper's Penitence in Nagapatam', in *C. Rajagopalachari Papers*, 1, 1931, NML.

36 Unknown, 'Mass Arrests at Ahmedabad', *Times of India*, 7 February 1931, p. 11.

37 Unknown, 'Ban on Picketing in Mysore from *the Hindu*', in *C. Rajagopalachari Papers*, 1931, NML.

38 Charles Henderson, 'Flag Hoisting on Dt. Board Office – E. Godavari Collector's Letter to President', in *C. Rajagopalachari Papers*, 1931, NML.

39 C. Rajagopalachari, 'Anti Drink Movement, a Report from South India'.

40 —, 'On Prohibition'.

41 The violence of Chauri Chaura began with an attack on a liquor shop. More on this episode appears in chapter two of my forthcoming dissertation, 'A world without drink: temperance in modern India'.

42 H.W. Emerson, Secretary to the Government of India (Home), 'Letter to Home Secretary to the Government of Bombay', Government of Bombay, Home Department, Special, 2, 1931, Maharashtra State Archives, Mumbai.

43 D. Mirpurkhas, Secretary Congress Committee, 'Press Telegram', in *All India Congress Committee Papers*, 2, 1931, NML.

44 Ghanashyam, untitled telegram, in *All-India Congress Committee Papers*, NML, Reel 8585, file no. G-18, 1931.

45 C. Rajagopalachari, 'Encouraging Results', in *C. Rajagopalachari Papers,* 1931, NML.

46 —, 'An Arrack Shop-Keeper's Penitence in Nagapatam', in *C. Rajagopalachari Papers*, 1931, NML.

47 Ibid.

48 Ibid.

49 The Pune temperance 'riot' of 1908 is discussed in greater detail in chapter three of my forthcoming dissertation, 'A world without drink: temperance in modern India'.

50 C. Rajagopalachari, 'Instructions for Picketing', in *C. Rajagopalachari Papers*, 1931, NML.

51 —, 'Mr. Cox's Durbar Speech, C.R.'S Indictment', in *C. Rajagopalachari Papers*, 1931, NML.

52 D. Mirpurkhas, Secretary Congress Committee, 'Press Telegram', in *All India Congress Committee Papers*, 1931, NML.

53 Ibid. This occurred despite significant resistance from male nationalists, Gandhi among them. See R. Kumar, *The History of Doing: an illustrated account of movements for women's rights and feminism in India, 1800–1990*, Delhi: Kali for Women, 1993, pp. 74–95.

54 Secretary to the Government of Madras, 'Letter Exchange with C. Rajagopalachari', in *C. Rajagopalachari Papers*, 1931, NML.

55 C. Rajagopalachari, 'Peaceful Picketing of Toddy and Arrack Shop Auctions', in *C. Rajagopalachari Papers*, 1931, NML.

56 Ibid.

57 A hint of what these activities may have involved can be found in the text of a ban on picketing in Bangalore. The magistrate explicitly forbade 'the public utterance of cries, singing of songs, playing music, delivery of harangues and use of gestures or mimetic representations, and the preparation, exhibition or dissemination of pictures, symbols and placards'. See Unknown, 'Ban on Picketing in Mysore from *the Hindu*'.

58 C. Rajagopalachari, 'Encouraging Results'.

59 Ibid.

60 —, 'On Prohibition'.

61 For the role of coercion in nationalist resistance to British rule, see R. Guha, 'Colonialism in South Asia', in idem, *Dominance without Hegemony*, pp. 1–99.

62 C. Rajagopalachari, 'Letter to Un-Named Member of the Press', in *C. Rajagopalachari Papers*, 1931, NML.

63 — , 'Revenue Divisional Officer Namakkal Order', in *C. Rajagopalachari Papers*, 1931, NML.

64 — 'On Prohibition'.

65 Frederick Grubb, 'National Congress launches prohibition propaganda', *Abkari: The Quarterly Organ of the Anglo-Indian Temperance Association*, I, no. 157, 1929.

66 C. Rajagopalachari, 'Anti Drink Movement, a Report from South India'.

67 —, 'On Prohibition'.

68 B. Chandra et al., *India's Struggle for Independence, 1857–1947*, [New Delhi:] Viking, 1988, p. 276.

69 This conclusion is at odds with popular interpretations of toddy-tree cutting. Chandra et al. describe it as 'obviously connected with the popular tradition of regarding abstinence as a virtue and symbol of respectability'. See ibid.

70 Some scattered evidence for resistance against this economic pressure is discernible in nationalist celebrations of their successes. Rajaji complained that 'reports are coming from many places that Excise officials mark trees for making fermented toddy without the permission of the owners'. See C. Rajagopalachari, 'Anti Drink Movement, a Report from South India'.

71 Ibid.

72 —, 'Letter to Santhanam', in *C. Rajagopalachari Papers*, 1931, NML.

73 — 'Letter To "Mr. Raja", Local Congressman'.

74 —, 'Illegal Sales - a Narrow Escape'.

75 Ibid.

76 —, 'Instructions for Picketing'.

77 —, 'Letter to Ramanujachariar', in *C. Rajagopalachari Papers*, 1931, NML.

78 —, 'Letter', in *C. Rajagopalachari Papers*, 1931, NML.

79 —, 'Letter to Kumaraswami Reddier', in *C. Rajagopalachari Papers*, 1931, NML. Despite the nationalist aspirations of most Indian prohibition activists, Rajaji sometimes preferred to verify the temperance credentials of nationalists such as when one Niranjan Singh was recommended for a paid position with the League. Though Rajaji knew him to have been 'in the non-cooperation movement and in gaol in 1921', he wrote to a friend asking 'what sort of gentleman Mr. Niranjan Singh is from our point of view?'. See his 'Letter to Shri Prakash', in *C. Rajagopalachari Papers*, 1931, NML.

80 —, 'Advice to Picketers'.

81 —, 'Mr. Cox's Durbar Speech, C.R.'S Indictment'.

82 N.S.R. Iyengar, 'Letter', in *C. Rajagopalachari Papers*, 1931, NML.
83 C. Rajagopalachari, 'Letter'.
84 Ibid.
85 Local option was a system in which local boards were established, comprised of picked government men along with a few 'leading' men of a given locality. These boards technically had the power to institute prohibition within the boundaries of their city; however, government officials and men hand-picked by the local collector assured that these boards would never vote in favour of prohibition.
86 —, 'On Prohibition'.
87 G.F.S. Collins, Home Dept. (special), Bombay, 'Untitled, Regards Police Response to Women', in Home Department, Special, Bombay, 1930, Maharashtra State Archives, Mumbai (henceforth MSA).
88 A.S., 'Secret Memo to Home Department (Political)', in Home Department, Special, Bombay, 1929, MSA. See also A.O. Koreishi, District Magistrate, Broach, 'Letter to Commissioner, Northern Division, Ahmedabad, Broach, J.H. Garrett', in Home Department, Special, Bombay, 1930, MSA.
89 The continued picketing of liquor shops during the period of the Gandhi-Irwin Pact kept up the fight for temperance. More importantly, it also provided an avenue for continued activism for vast numbers of nationalist reformers, many of whom were unhappy with the agreement. Picketing of liquor shops was largely halted by the end of 1932.
90 C. Rajagopalachari, 'Mr. Cox's Durbar Speech, C.R.'S Indictment'.
91 Government of Madras, 'Letter to Rajagopalacharia', in *C. Rajagopalachari Papers*, 1931, NML.
92 —, 'Letter Exchange with C. Rajagopalachari,' in *C. Rajagopalachari Papers*, 1931, NML.
93 Ibid.
94 C. Rajagopalachari, 'Local Government and the Gandhi/Irwin Pact', in *C. Rajagopalachari Papers*, 1931, NML.
95 —, 'Letter to Vaidyanathier'.
96 —, 'On Prohibition'.
97 This was against Rajaji's wishes as stated in 1932 when he argued that 'the method of experimenting in one or two districts' did not appeal to him. He wanted total prohibition across the entirety of India immediately. Piecemeal implementation was a compromise position for him. See ibid.
98 Government of India, 'Bill(S) - the Orissa Prohibition Bill, 1939', edited by Excise and Opium Central Board of Revenue, Delhi, 1939.
99 Hattie Menzies, 'Prohibition in the making', *The India Temperance Record and the White Ribbon* XXXIII, 3, 1939.
100 Ibid.
101 C. Rajagopalachari, 'On Prohibition'. Rajaji's perception of America's support for prohibition was likely skewed in this regard. Americans interested in global temperance like W.E. 'Pussyfoot' Johnson sought him out during their Indian tours to discuss temperance. That being the case, it is hardly surprising that the Americans he met expressed faith in America's experiment with prohibition. See A.S. Iyengar, *Role of the Press and Indian Freedom Struggle*, New Delhi: Kulbushan Nangia, 2001, p. 69.
102 C. Rajagopalachari, 'On Prohibition'. Here we see Rajaji's faith that in a state with its 'own government', rather than colonial rule, the success of prohibition was assured; the fundamental purity of Indians assured the success of prohibition, as far as he was concerned.
103 Ibid.
104 Government of Bihar, 'Bihar Prohibition Act, 1938', edited by Legislative Department, Patna, Bihar: Superintendent, Government Printing, 1938.
105 Ibid.
106 Ruth Robinson, *The India Temperance Record and the White Ribbon* XXXIII, 7, 1939, 2.
107 B.G. Holdsworth, 'Press Communique - Prohibition Department', 1–15, edited by Revenue Department, Madras: Government of Madras, 1938. *Niro* is the unfermented juice from

toddy trees, sweet in flavour with no alcohol content. Many former toddy tappers moved to the production of *niro*.

108 Salem District Collector, Madras, 'Prohibition in Salem district: extracts from the report of the collector of Salem district', *The India Temperance Record and the White Ribbon* XXXII, 4, 1939, 9–12.

109 W.S. Caine, 'Letters from India', *Abkari: The Quarterly Organ of the Anglo-Indian Temperance Association* I, no. 28, 1897, 59.

110 Kailas Nath Katju, 'Dr. K.N. Katju inaugurates prohibition in Jaunpur, Ministry of Industries, Kadhi Seller', *Public Information, United Provinces, Lucknow* II, no. 3, 1939, 28.

111 Ruth Robinson, *The India Temperance Record and the White Ribbon* XXXIII, 7, 1939, 2.

112 Prohibition Department, Bombay, 'Report of the Prohibition Department', p. 2, in *A.I.C.C. Bombay*, 1938, NML.

113 Ibid., p. 13.

114 Ibid., p. 29.

115 Ibid.

116 Ibid., p. 15.

117 Ibid.

118 Ibid., p. 4.

119 K.N. Katju, 'Message from Hon'ble Minister of Excise', *Public Information, United Provinces, Lucknow* II, no. 2, 1939, 2.

120 Unknown, *Public Information, United Provinces, Lucknow* II, no. 5, 1939, 6.

121 Department of Public Information, United Provinces, 'Prohibition movement', *Public Information, United Provinces, Lucknow* I, no. 6, 1938, 4.

122 Women's Christian Temperance Union, 'The progress of prohibition', *The India Temperance Record and the White Ribbon* XXXII, 7, 1938, 2.

123 'Report of the Collector of Salem on the working of the Madras Prohibition Act, 1937 up to the end of June, 1938 is published', *Public Information, United Provinces, Lucknow* I, no. 7, 1939, 6.

124 Prohibition Department, Bombay, 'Report of the Prohibition Department', p. 19, in *A.I.C.C. Bombay*, 1938, NML.

125 Ibid., p. 24.

126 Unknown, 'How prohibition will work in Bombay', *Public Information, United Provinces, Lucknow* II, no. 3, 1939, 2.

127 Government of India, 'Bills – Indian Prohibition Bill – Legislative Assembly – Wajihuddin (Khan Bahadur Haji), M.L.A. – Proposal for the Introduction of – Refusal by H.E. The Governor General to Accord the Necessary Previous Sanction', edited by Excise and Opium Central Board of Revenue, Delhi: Government Printing, 1933.

128 Undersecretary West Godawari District Congress Committee, Lakshmana Acharyia, 'Prohibition in the Central Provinces and Berar', *The India Temperance Record and the White Ribbon* XXXIII, 6, 1939, 1.

129 Government of Bihar, 'Bihar Prohibition Act, 1938', edited by Legislative Department, Patna, Bihar: Superintendent, Government Printing, 1938.

130 The judge's opinion, supported through subsequent appeals, was that under the 1935 Government of India Act, the legislative assemblies of the provinces had every right to regulate alcohol use, but not to outlaw it entirely because it would infringe on the right of the central (British) government to regulate international trade and trade between Indian states. Bombay's Prohibition Act 'could not be used to prohibit possession of liquor imported across a frontier or intended for export so as to prevent or impede import or export. We are clear that in practice prohibition could not be enforced in these conditions.' See 'Excise Supplement to the Bombay Police Gazette', edited by Appellate Side Bombay High Court, Bombay: Government of Bombay, 1940.

131 P.J. Thomas, 'A statistical analysis of the shift of expenditure in a prohibition area', *Shankhya: The Indian Journal of Statistics* 4, 4, 1939.

Part IV

Postcolonial India: The legacy of prohibitionist politics

9 The culture of prohibition in Gujarat, India

Carolyn Heitmeyer and Edward Simpson

The idea of Gujarat conjures a number of contradictory and paradoxical images. In the field of political culture, for example, there is a sharp and well-known contrast between the Gandhian past and modern politicized and assertive Hinduism. A recent analysis has also drawn attention to the conflicting relation between the forces of altruism and egoism in much of the state's history.[1] It might be tempting to view prohibition as something a society does because there is a general consensus that alcohol is a bad thing, either in an absolute sense, or because people need to be protected from its seductive charm. In this chapter, however, we wish to suggest something different: that prohibition is a symptom of some of the underlying cultural and historical contradictions in the social makeup of Gujarat.

Alcohol has unique and unusual properties as both a subject of consumption and as an object of politics. It is worth pointing out from the outset that we think the politics of prohibition in Gujarat speak to some profound cultural under-currents. In much of the world, self-prohibition, or going 'dry', is the initial part of the antidote for alcoholism. Those who crave alcohol, for whatever reason, often cannot lighten their relationship with the substance without totally excluding it. The idea, especially in some treatment regimes, is that the relationship between the individual and their drink is all or it is nothing. What then does it mean for an entire region to impose an official policy of prohibition?

In this chapter, we will stop just short of suggesting that the Gujarat is culturally alcoholic. We will however suggest that alcohol plays a very important role on a number of significant social fault lines in the region. Prohibition in Gujarat, we suggest, is about denial, self-loathing and fear of others, as much as it is to be understood as an affirmative step towards the making of a better society. Prohibition speaks to a general fear of addiction in the region, which has found expression over the centuries in various reform and devotional movements. Prohibition also continues in Gujarat because of the weight of more recent history. Even though many of the conditions that put prohibition in place have shifted, to lift or even ease prohibition policy would simply appear insulting to the memory of Gandhi, for whom prohibition was such an important political and philosophical stance.

We do not see prohibition simply as the legal position of the state towards the consumption of a particular substance. Rather, prohibition is also a statement on acceptable and unacceptable forms of public sociality, and, perhaps more significantly for our purposes, prohibition policies in Gujarat have created vast ambiguous, shadowy, zones of commerce and behaviour. Indeed, prohibition policies have created a politically and symbolically rich imaginative space in the state in which demons can fatten, inequalities can grow, and lies can be incubated.

Going dry amid the floods

Alcohol is not an anodyne substance with a fully predictable set of effects. Alcohol interacts with the condition of the physical and emotional bodies as it finds them. Amongst other things, alcohol distorts, enlivens, suppresses and deludes. These qualities were well-known to Ransome, a character from the novel *The Rains Came* by Louis Bromfield set in Baroda of the 1930s, who, along with most of the other European residents of the city, is pickled by alcohol for the most part of most days (brandy is his love). For the first part of the novel, he believes that he drinks because it makes him happy. As he staggers from one social event to another, he loathes and mocks those he sees around him. Suddenly, the city is rattled by an earthquake, which is followed by a flood and a terrible plague.

In the aftermath, Ransome is separated from his brandy. The forced sobriety allows him to see that what he thought was happiness was, in the eyes of others, boorishness. Those around him, many of whom he loathed, are there because they care for him and tolerate him. Consequently, and now seeing Baroda in new light, he donates his liquor to the hospital to aid the wounded. The characters in this wonderful drama can be seen to represent the decadence of the late colonial era, while others stand for the optimism of modern India and the hold of submerged traditions in the face of catastrophe. As Ransome sobers up, a new and enlightened ruler comes to the throne in Baroda. The clarity, fairness and sense of progress the new ruler brings to the throne are parallels to the way Ransome is now able to engage soberly with the world.

Although Bromfield, the author of the novel, was an American, he had spent time in Baroda in the first half of the twentieth century, and the plot of his novel is clearly influenced by the ethos prevailing in the city during that period. The sense of moral improvement and progress that Ransome so poignantly embodies in his abstemiousness continues to be a combination of ideas commonly brought into association in Gujarat.

In the following sections, we chart the historical, social and political meanings of alcohol and prohibition in the region.

'Killer brew'

The region's all-or-nothing relationship to alcohol, at least in state-led policy, is also emblematic of a wider cultural (social) ethos governing other facets of life. A major mercantile hub of the Indian Ocean, homeland of

Gandhi, the 'laboratory of Hindutva' in the early years of this century, and, more recently, location for delinquent industrial expansion, Gujarat's cultural uniqueness stems from the assemblage or encompassment of multiple forms of religion, morality and ideas of what is good and proper. Although the idea of a Gujarati identity or ethos is strong outside Gujarat – peaceful, shrewd, conservative, money-minded, and vegetarian – those who know Gujarat well also know that this is an illusion. In political terms, we might say that Gujarat is currently headed by a coalition of caste and class interests which, although a minority, have simply been more successful than all the other minorities in ensuring that their interests are synonymous with the reputation of the state. Within Gujarat, there remain a wide-range of caste traditions, languages, religious practices and a mishmash of more general ideas about the world that contradict the prevalent image of the state. There are probably more non-vegetarians in Gujarat than vegetarians, and prohibition is a state policy rather than a cultural reality.

Prohibition policies in Gujarat have unquestionably (and despite what we claim towards the end of this article) contributed to the creation of networks of criminality and encouraged the unregulated production of alcohol. In July 2009, 136 people died as a result of drinking alcohol, which contained lethal substances. In 1989, 132 people perished in Vadodara under similar circumstances. In 1977, the Laththa Commission (*laththa*, Gujarati or Hindi for 'hooch') was appointed to investigate the death of 101 people and the hospitalization of many others after they had consumed 'killer brew'. The commission found that liquor containing lethal doses of methyl alcohol had come from four localities in Ahmedabad, with evidence that the alcohol had been distributed by well-known bootleggers who had been operating 'openly and continuously' in the city.[2]

The report is of interest because it is one of the few official acknowledgements that bootlegging is an active industry in Gujarat, despite prohibition policy. The commission's recommendations are similarly interesting because they reflect the enduring institutional uncertainty within the state on the question of alcohol. The sale and consumption of alcohol in Gujarat, the report suggests implicitly, is an open secret that the state cannot acknowledge. On one hand, the report claims that the illegal sale of foreign and country liquor does *not* constitute a problem 'on a large scale' in Ahmedabad[3] and, further to this, the distillation of country liquor 'is more or less under control'. Rather, according the report, the main problem is the illegal sale and consumption of *laththa*.[4] Several pages later, however, the observation is made that in most police stations in the city as many as five to ten bootleggers were operating on an open and continuous basis. The 'nefarious activities' which led to the deaths and hospitalizations in 1977 had, as such, been committed on such a scale that people from surrounding areas knew the exact places where illicit alcohol could be procured and consumed, suggesting an overall openness in the way in which the business operated. The Commission suggested that measures on the level of a 'war footing' should be taken to completely eliminate the 'institution' of bootlegging.[5]

The Laththa Commission report contained no suggestion that prohibition policy might have contributed to the tragedy, and saw no evidence that reform to the law was required.[6] In the final analysis, it recommended that the state take greater control over the sale of methyl alcohol.[7] Resources were to be made available to assist social workers in spreading the message on the perils of drinking, and various measures were to be made to strengthen the local police and the Special Prosecution Squads set up to combating bootlegging. Unlike later reports, which make a direct connection with the criminal underworld of bootleggers with corruption in the police forces, the 1977 Commission only drew tenuous and localized ties between the legal and illegal sides of the liquor trade.[8]

Prohibition policy then has a thorny presence in patterns of governance in Gujarat. Drink and drinking are open secrets which the state cannot acknowledge because to do so would be to also acknowledge the limits of its own power and effectiveness and thus to undermine its own legitimacy. However, in other ways, prohibition policy is useful to the state as a means through which it can conjure a normative Gujarati citizen, one opposed to the consumption of liquor for either religious and moral reasons. Through the maintenance of such an image, profound differences and expectations among those subject to its rule can be ignored, in much the same way as the ideology of secularism has been used elsewhere. Prohibition produces the impression of a citizen who, when we see a state formed of particular caste and class influences, is comprehensible by dint of the fact that they do not engage in activities such as drinking, which run counter to the public values of the ruling elites. Large numbers of people going blind at weddings or dying at festivals is a sad symptom of such a policy.

Alcohol and prohibition in context

That the academic literature on alcohol in the Indian state of Gujarat remains so slight is surprising, especially given the larger symbolic value of alcohol (both in its absence as well as in its illicit presence) in the region. Today, Gujarat, Manipur, Mizoram and Nagaland remain the only states in India in which various levels of prohibition are enforced. While other states such as Andhra Pradesh, Tamil Nadu and Haryana have experimented with prohibition policies at various points, Gujarat remains the one region amongst all Indian states which has prohibition in place continually and over the longest period of time. The policy of prohibition was first imposed in the erstwhile Bombay State (present-day Gujarat and Maharashtra), shortly after India gained independence from the British through the Bombay Prohibition Act, 1949, which outlawed the consumption, selling and buying of alcohol. There had previously been periods of prohibition in some of the region's Princely States.

Today, despite laws outlawing the sale and consumption of alcohol, it is widely argued that the policy of prohibition fails miserably in the context of Gujarat in its aim to deter its use and trade.[9] Both 'Indian Made Foreign Liquor' as well as foreign brands are easily available to members of the middle and upper classes who rely on local bootleggers to provide a home delivery service.[10] The poor, on the other hand, as we have seen, must resort to non-branded brews, which are also commonly available: hooch, moonshine, or country liquor, as they are known in Gujarat. Drinking in Gujarat, as elsewhere, has a class dimension.

The production and sale of alcohol in Gujarat have inevitably become part of the broader networks of criminal activity in the state. However, we have no access to statistics on this issue, any more than we have statistics relating to levels of alcohol consumption within Gujarat or in relation to other states without regulated prohibition.[11] We mention these factual deficits, not to deprecate our ethnographic approach to the subject, but to draw attention to the fact that no one has access to this information and, therefore, caution should be exercised when dealing with sources that make claims on these issues. It strikes us that so little is known about drinking in Gujarat that almost anything can be said. The 'bootlegger' has become synonymous in popular imagination with organized crime gangs and other anti-social elements, and this as we have already seen is a narrative enlivened by the state. This is particularly true for the principal city of Ahmedabad, where, even in academic work, the figure of the bootlegger is woven uncritically into master narratives of violence, communalism, and corruption. Needless to say, however, and we shall return to this later, given the shady nature of the bootlegger's work, such claims are usually based on scant sociological evidence, to say the least.

As we have said, it is often claimed that prohibition policies in Gujarat have 'failed'. We think however such a claim is misleading, first, because it conflates the reasons for imposing sanctions for moral and political reasons (primarily associated with Gandhi and his legacy) with the 'problem' of the rise of black market economies. Secondly, it assumes that the role of prohibition policies in Gujarat is to outlaw alcohol and to prevent Gujaratis from drinking. We want to suggest that this is not the case, at least not in any straightforward sense.

Colonial pre-cursors

In his colourful memoirs on life in the Foreign Service during the last years of the British Raj, Sir Kenneth Fitze recalls visiting the then-Residency of Baroda where the Maharaja had recently instituted a ban on liquor, in keeping with the wartime policy set by Buckingham Palace. Fitze cites this as an instance of 'praiseworthy self-denial' but which 'was hardly conducive to the maintenance of cordial relations with the officers of the regiment'.[12] He notes that the displeasure on the part of the officers was particularly apparent in the fact that the dinner parties at the Residency of the Maharaja were wont to break up at an unconventionally early hour: the thirsty officers, with unconvincing references to the exigencies of midnight inspections and early morning parades, falling over each other in their eagerness to regain the oasis of the regimental mess.[13]

The ban might have derived from the Maharaja's own rather abstemious character. However, Fitze also recalls that all four of the Maharaja's sons succumbed to the seduction of dipsomania. The eldest son, whose death had resulted from overconsumption, Fitze notes, was ironically memorialized by a plaque at the Club House bar which he had 'all too generously patronised'.[14]

Beyond the walls of elite Baroda, the wider political economy of drinking in Gujarat was also a highly contested issue in the colonial era due to the fact that a sizable portion of the government's revenue came from excise duty on the production and sale of liquor. As the historian David Hardiman has argued,[15] control over the manufacturing and distribution of both toddy and *daru* (liquor) played a fundamental role in local systems of economic and political exploitation in southern Gujarat in the late 1800s and early 1900s. Until the late 1800s, Adivasis had traditionally manufactured the country liquor they consumed at home. The rights to excises on alcohol production and sale were, under a system inherited from the Maratha period, distributed once a year by auction and the successful bidder was then responsible for selecting local-level manufacturers and distributors who paid an excise duty to him (usually in the form of a lump sum). Hardiman notes that, under this system, the overall level of duty paid had been negligible, an issue which no doubt contributed to motivating British administrators to overhaul it through the 1878 Bombay Abkari Act. This new legislation set in place a much more tightly regulated system which banned the village-level manufacturing of alcohol and confined it to central distilleries where, prior to being sold, an excise duty was to be paid.[16] While cloaked within a larger moral discourse centred on the benefits of temperance, the main objective of the 1878 Bombay Abkari Act was to increase the revenue from alcohol consumption which the colonial authorities could then claim.[17]

The Bombay Abkari Act of 1878 was disastrous for many Adivasis in southern Gujarat who, given their status as largely lower class peasants, could neither afford to purchase *daru* or toddy any longer from the central distilleries, nor could they legally produce their own. Despite disagreements within the colonial administration about the nature of the impact of the new policies, Hardiman suggests that ultimately the taxes imposed did not lead to a reduction in either the amount of alcohol produced or consumed. Rather, by rendering toddy and *daru* financially inaccessible to poor peasants in south Gujarat, these measures ultimately served to further increase the political and economic power of the Parsis who acted as middlemen in the liquor trade and controlled much of the distribution of licit alcohol. Also gaining significantly from the new excises was the colonial administration which profited handsomely from the policies: Hardiman reports how by 1938, Abkari revenue in the Bombay Presidency equalled land revenue.[18]

Given that many Adivasis were no longer able to afford liquor, they initially resorted to purchasing illicitly-brewed alcohol. Further legislation in the form of the Mahua Act of 1892 (and successive amendments) made it illegal to store or sell the *mahua* flowers from which *daru* was made. This legislation led to the further deterioration in the quality of liquor available and, eventually, the replacement of toddy with low-quality *daru* made from sugar rather than *mahua* flowers.

The complex combination of economic factors relating to the imposition of state monopolies over alcohol excises, political infighting between colonial administrators over policies and, finally, local consumption patterns and exigencies also needs to also be understood in light of local religious and self-reform movements taking place during this period. As Hardiman[19] has documented in his study of the cult which emerged in the 1920s around the goddess Devi and which gained particular popularity among Adivasis in South Gujarat, abstinence from alcohol became an important means of social reform within this community as well as, according to him, a way through which traditional hierarchies were contested. While this movement was ultimately short-lived, the rejection of alcohol by Adivasis during this period also served to destabilize the power of the local Bania moneylenders as well as the Parsi liquor dealers, both of whom had become submerged in relations of dependence and debt. In Hardiman's study, we see the emergence of a democratizing and egalitarian Adivasi, who rejects alcohol consumption, to be contrasted with the often corrupt and exploitative figures of the moneylender and 'bootlegger' who promote the culture of alcohol dependence (and the wider hierarchies to which such practices of consumption were related). The Devi movement also took on nationalistic overtones and Gandhi, also a staunch proponent of abstinence, became a secondary deity in the movement. In the next section we explore further the central connections between Gujarat, Gandhi and the nationalist movement in relation to prohibition.

'Drugs, drink and devil': Gandhi and alcohol

Today, Gandhi remains the single most important figure in the prohibition debate in Gujarat. In addition to being born in the city of Porbandar in the Saurashtra region of the state, he also based many of the earlier *satyagraha*s and campaigns for Indian independence in Gujarat. Gandhi spoke out against the consumption of liquor on moral grounds, as well as suggesting abstinence should be a key political tactic in the nationalist struggle for independence. Gandhi's hostility to both alcohol and meat-eating, while originally informed by moral prohibitions and taboos imposed by his caste association, became increasingly reliant on scientific and health rationales during his early years in England, and later on during his tenure in South Africa where he joined other activists and campaigners to popularize the struggle.[20]

Much like temperance movements elsewhere in the world during this period, middle-class (and, in the Indian context, upper-caste) moralities played a significant role in adding further fuel to demands for prohibition. These efforts took on added momentum with the Indian nationalist movement, as many nationalist leaders viewed the consumption of alcohol as an inherently 'Western' import rather than a practice indigenous to 'Indian culture'.[21] According to Fahey and Manian,[22] Gandhi's condemnation of alcohol derived from his own deeply held personal convictions on the evil moral consequences of alcohol consumption, as well as his belief that prohibition was necessary if India was to gain independence from the British Empire. It was through his influence that the Indian National Congress integrated prohibition as a core component of its political platform and strategy for independence. As he wrote in an article entitled 'Drugs, Drink and Devil' published in *Young India* on 22 April 1926:

> If I were appointed dictator for one hour for all India, the first thing I would do would be to close without compensation all the liquor shops, destroy all the toddy palms such as I know them in Gujarat, compel factory owners to produce humane conditions for their workmen and open refreshment and recreation rooms where these workmen would get innocent drinks and equally innocent amusements.[23]

Gandhi's rationale for linking the sale and consumption of alcohol to the position of subservience that the Indian people held in relation to the British was derived from two key ideas. From the perspective of advancing the nationalist agenda, the abstinence from alcohol would diminish the revenues collected by the colonial administration. From a moral standpoint, Gandhi and other nationalist leaders argued that India could best achieve independence from the British as a 'pure' nation and that, pursuant to this, prohibition was key in bringing about such purity. In particular, Gandhi's insistence on the need for prohibition was also linked to his belief that it was largely India's poor who were the most affected by the consumption of liquor. He argued that drinking stood second only to untouchability as the greatest social scourge that the nation needed to address. Once independence had finally been achieved, however, the ideal of prohibition was ultimately written into the Indian Constitution at Gandhi's prompting. This was done, however, more as a gesture rather than a legally-binding clause: Prime Minister Jawaharlal Nehru left it up to individual states to legislate the degree to which this clause was to be enforced given the substantial amount of revenue gained through excise on alcohol.[24]

As evident from the struggles over excise on alcohol in South Gujarat recounted by Hardiman, there are clear class and caste dimensions to drinking patterns in India, both historically as well as in the present. Apart from Kshatriyas, few members of the upper Hindu castes openly consume liquor, whereas local brews of *daru* and toddy remain much more common among poorer and lower caste Indians. Scholars such as Fahey and Manian[25] have argued that Gandhi's opposition to drinking, in this sense at least, broadly reflected upper caste cultural practices, as well as a rather paternalistic perspective towards the poor, who had to be protected from themselves.

Given, however, what were widely perceived as the noble aims of Gandhi's call for personal and institutional prohibition, any attempt to dilute prohibition policies in the state today would appear to devalue the things Gandhi himself stood for. While the hold of the Gandhi-inspired sections of Congress have lost much of their power in the state, they have not disappeared entirely. Prohibition was an anti-colonial stand for self-improvement, and, rather loosely (and perhaps most problematically today) held as a reflection of the core values of elite society in Gujarat. Any attempt to ease prohibition against such a background will inevitably run into difficulty, given how it would appear to be a refutation of values that elite Gujaratis themselves have placed at the heart of what it means to be Gujarati.

Liquor in Adivasi Gujarat

While the social elites of the state have connived to present a certain idea of Gujarat, there are other forms of society in which alcohol plays a key role in social intercourse and libation. As we discussed in relation to the formation of regimes of taxation on alcohol in Gujarat, in the early twentieth century toddy and *daru* still formed a central component in the religious, social and nutritional life of the Adivasi populations. Alcohol was used to propitiate the gods and to mark life-ritual events such as birth, marriage and death. Hardiman has also suggested that liquor contributed significantly to physical sustenance and nutrition.[26]

Recent anthropological research has charted the changing ways in which liquor is a sign of the symbolic violence embodied by Adivasi communities in Gujarat, as they continue lifestyles which demean them in the eyes of the wider populace. In her account of Adivasis in central Gujarat, Alice Tilche[27] describes a series of initiatives aimed at refining the consumption habits of Adivasis. Some of these initiatives come from inside the community, while others are external impositions by civil society organizations and proselytizing Hindus aiming for the 'social upliftment' and 'Hinduisation' of the Adivasi population. The focus of these campaigns invariably falls onto the role of alcohol and meat in daily life. However, Tilche points out that such substances continue to be important for Adivasis despite the constant pressure and the familiar discourses on the evils of such habits. This puts the Adivasi population in something of a bind, as, on the one hand, the consumption of meat and alcohol are seen as central markers of Adivasi identity, while on the other, such practices also mark their 'backwardness' in the eyes of broader society in Gujarat. Thus, though dominant discourses on identity in Gujarat identify vegetarianism and abstemiousness as central values, the work of Hardiman and Tilche reminds us that there is more than one Gujarat, and that for the Adivasi populations alcohol remains central to many important aspects of life while simultaneously contributing to their continued marginalization.

In the case of Muslims (constituting around 12 per cent of the population), the situation is rather different. In Gujarat, the dominant Hindu population would like to think of Adivasis as Hindus in-the-making while, in contrast, Muslims are generally thought of as being beyond any such redemptive transformation. Consequently, self-identity among Muslims is generally defined more in opposition to the dominant Hindu population. The consumption of meat is often an assertion of their identity as Muslims rather than an embodied sign of their inferiority. While this consumption of meat is often used by Hindus as an illustration of the backwardness of Muslims, there is a notable silence on the fact that with regard to the consumption of alcohol, Muslims are aligned more closely with Gandhi than many of Gujarat's Hindu populations.

While the emphasis on vegetarianism and the ban on alcohol consumption can be at least partly ascribed to the influence of Gandhi's beliefs, this in itself cannot fully explain the widespread, and, at times militant, rhetoric about meat-eating and alcohol consumption. Our discussion in this section illustrates how alcohol and meat are substances that both divide and unite sections of the Gujarat population. In the following section, we turn to look at a broader range of associations between the worlds of humans and non-human substances. Of the many ways in which this discussion could be taken, we have chosen to focus on Hindu notions of caste, rather than differences between Hindus and Muslims, because we think at this level we can say something more general about Gujarat.

Liquor in a constellation of substances

In many other parts of the world, the equation of meat-eating with something akin to drinking alcohol is absent. It almost certainly did not occur to the mayor of Chicago, for example, to shut down steak houses while upholding the senate's outlawing of liquor in the 1930s. However, as Tilche firmly notes with respect to her Adivasi informants, meat-eating and alcohol consumption are seen as generally going together in Gujarat. In a pragmatic sense, consuming one without the other lessens the enjoyment; however, there is also an element of subversion in such consumption in that both substances contravene dominant moralities and lifestyles. Both substances also inhabit both the centre and periphery of Gujarati society: each is readily available to anyone with sufficient know-how or connections to 'unpalatable' characters (be they criminals, butchers or bootleggers) – connections of all types are highly valued in Gujarat; at the same time, each substance is consumed in the shadows – or behind closed doors – away from the glare of respectable society. However, there seems to us to be slightly more to it than that, as each substance falls into a similar moral and symbolic category, with particular kinds of enflaming and distorting potentials.

In his study of the Saurashtra region of Gujarat, the anthropologist Harald Tambs-Lyche[28] captures something of what we have in mind. As we have implied, the Bania-Brahmin coalition of castes has become so powerful in Gujarat that they are able to inculcate recognition of the legitimacy of their own culture to others – a view in which all others embody their own inferiority. For Tambs-Lyche, the character that has come to represent all that is proper and good in Gujarat is part of a wider mercantile ethos, in particular that derived from the Hindu-Bania castes, which shun violence in favour of asceticism and renunciation, to which we can add here abstemiousness and vegetarianism.

However, there is more to Tambs-Lyche's analysis for he suggests that the traders' values have become so clear because they exist in opposition to the values of others, which, although inferior, give further legitimacy to the culture of the trader. In addition, the distinction between the two groups, now traders opposed to rulers, is enforced by both religious and symbolic alliances. He reasons:

> Hinduism in Saurashtra is not a unitary phenomenon. Its constituent elements may be interpreted to form a 'unity in diversity' – a view held particularly by Brahmans in the traditional set-up – but, on the regional level, Hinduism tends to dissolve into several mutually conflicting subsystems. The chief opposition, here, parallels the structure of power and economic relations; it divides the merchants from most other communities. Thus there is a structural contradiction between rulers and merchants, parties which are nevertheless dependent on each other in forming traditional Saurashtrian society. Behind the rulers stand the rural, agricultural population, in an alliance known as the *ter tansali* or 'thirteen castes'. The opposition between merchants and rulers, then, is more than just a conflict between the elite; it integrates the rulers with 'the people' and isolates the merchants from them.[29]

In this view, social division is not of equal competitive groups but a force that alienates (but elevates) traders from the political mandate of rulers and vassal. Tambs-Lyche's 'merchant–ruler opposition'[30] is a difference of 'two world views'[31] that encompasses residence, attitude, profession, social status, religious propriety and transactional preference. This division persuasively conforms to social stereotypes held in western India about the character of the traditional rulers and the accompanying 'trading' cohort. Rulers are famously known as 'Rajputs' of the *varna* category of Kshatriya. Traders are infamous as 'Vanias' or 'Banias' of the lower *varna* category of Vaishya (although their caste mythology generally makes them out to be 'cooled' Rajputs), and tend to actually rank higher than rulers because, as we have suggested, they have established the values against which hierarchy is measured and understood.

Rather crudely, in the cosmology of substances we have derived from Tambs Lyche's work, each of these opposed estates is associated with a set of substances which are either 'hot' or 'cool', not 'cold' exactly. 'Hot' substances are associated primarily with the rulers, but also with the goddess and worship which evokes power and sacrifice. Meat and liquor are 'hot' and libidinous substances, as are opium and tobacco. Tambs-Lyche suggests that 'hot' substances such as liquor (as well as meat) are viewed as inciting violence which, while important to members of the warrior castes, should be avidly avoided by merchants whose ethos revolves around non-violence and abstention. The hot then signals the lack of control, indiscipline ultimately manifesting in violence.

For a region which has been historically dominated by trade and traders and which remains one renowned for its business-minded population, it is not surprising that the lifestyle and moralities of the merchant castes extend into wider-Gujarati society. It is common to hear in public discourse that abstention from hot substances is a positive individual and social practice. Freeing people from such vices, as various devotional Hindu movements aim to do, is seen as meritorious.

As Ghassam-Fachandi[32] notes, both are also part of a larger set of vices which are seen by many Gujaratis as reflecting inner corruption or social backwardness. Moreover, in the popular imagination, alcohol and meat-eating remain clearly associated with collective violence. Common to most narratives of violence are rumours about the distribution of meat and alcohol to rioters as a form of instigation and incitement. Those at the front line of riots are usually members of the lower castes and classes, who in their 'backwardness' are easy pawns for manipulative elites, but they are also naturally more prone to such activities to begin with. Alcohol in such narratives thus acts as a natural lubricant for violence, a practice which, while not unique to Gujarat, stands out given the wider contradictions of a Gandhian legacy of non-violence and the fact that Gujarat has one of the worst records for urban mass violence in the post-independence period.

The bootlegger

In Gujarat everyone knows that bootleggers are part of organized crime networks, in cahoots with corrupt police, and involved in many of the other 'hot' activities associated with alcohol. As we have said, it is beyond doubt that the political economy of liquor smuggling and the black market is enmeshed in the local criminal underworld. But, as we have also suggested, prohibition policies have created a vast grey area of unregulated and unknown activity. As a consequence, no one knows exactly the scale, scope or nature of bootlegging and smuggling in Gujarat, nor the relation between this activity, other legal/illegal activities and the role of the state.

For the middle class Ahmedabadi having a bottle of whiskey with his friends on a Friday night, the bootlegger is not the man who lives below him and picks up the odd bottle from someone he works with. The bootlegger is far more sinister than this in the popular imagination. The (literal and metaphorical) bootlegger then allows things in rumour and politics to happen; in short, he is a terrible convenience, with magical powers and superhuman abilities. He can run enormous networks of people, manipulate the state, and connive and conspire with other anti-social elements. The bootlegger is every rumour-monger's friend.

In his analysis of the causes behind the 1985 communal riots in Ahmedabad, Howard Spodek[33] has suggested that from that time forward bootleggers built strong alliances with smugglers on the one hand, and with police and politicians on the other. It is simple to imagine how such partnerships flourished under the prohibition policies: bootleggers rely on the police and politicians for protection while providing funds and 'strong armed thugs' when necessary in exchange. Spodek links the rise in power of this criminal underbelly of Ahmedabad's economy in the older part of the city to the departure of local leaders who had helped foster cross-communal and -caste sentiment: 'Criminal activity flourished as civic order declined.'[34] Again, while this is all utterly plausible, Spodek does not provide any evidence for these claims, other than having perhaps derived a sense of this truth from his friends and informants in Ahmedabad.

While scholars, as well as people on the street, cite the role of liquor in inciting violence, could the opposite instead be possible? Could the prevalence of communal riots, at least in Ahmedabad, be a convenient cloak for the extensive networks which smuggle, peddle and distribute illegal liquor in the city and the handsome profits that are reaped by criminals and government servants alike? Shani[35] argues that this is in fact the case and presents particular instances of 'communal' violence in Ahmedabad which, she argues, at closer inspection had very little to do with competing religious ideologies. Rather, the front of communalism allowed skirmishes over patronage of bootleggers and other 'anti-social elements' along with control of particular black markets to cover up the role of local politicians and law enforcers with criminal activity.

This move becomes possible because, on one hand, bootleggers are often assumed to be Muslim in the public imagination, making it easy to imagine that instances of violence against a majority Hindu police might be cast as communal in nature (an obvious example of this is Don Latif, a Muslim bootlegger at the center of various corrupt and illegal ventures who died in police custody under suspicious circumstances). At the same time, Shani[36] also suggests that it wasn't until the mid-1980s that trade in illicit liquor took on a communal tone as the inter-religious relations became more delicate. At a more general level, the role of the mysterious and unknown bootlegger has become a resource for those wishing to attribute mischief to others: bootleggers are easy to blame for all manner of ills and disturbances because no one knows who they are. Bootlegging has become a realm onto which all manner of myth and half-truth can be grafted, because the truth is not known.

Conclusion

In this chapter we have confined ourselves to outlining the main subjects which link prohibition policy to society in Gujarat. We have pointed to the state's inability to acknowledge the widespread consumption of alcohol because to do so would be to undermine its own legitimacy. Gandhi's Gujarat, we have claimed, is not everyone's Gujarat, but the legacy of Gandhi is a principle reason for the continuation of the policy (a cynic might argue that the policy continues because the profits are so great for those who keep the policy in place, although there is no evidence whatsoever to support this). We have placed alcohol within a broader cosmology of substances, which, we have suggested, also animates the principle divisions and tensions within local society. We have explored the role of the super human figure of the bootlegger in myth making and casting blame for general ills within the state.

As we have discussed, alcohol and stories of those who trade alcohol lubricate social fault-lines and allow things to happen in Gujarat. The profundity of the anxiety over abstinence in the state is a striking feature of religious and moral life. Much of Gujarat is constantly struggling with itself; Gujarat is constantly 'giving up' something, which, aside from underlining the perceived importance of self-control, also suggests the power and attractiveness of the vices that need to be combatted. Perhaps public prohibition was a gross manifestation of the battle between allure and abstinence. Despite commissions set up in the wake of successive mass deaths due to 'killer brews' there has been little political will, or public expectation for reasons we have explored. The one exception has been the recent brief campaign launched by the so-called 'Malt Marchers' in Ahmedabad, who called for a lifting of the ban on alcohol. The Malt Marchers claimed that drinking was a fundamental human right. The name of the organization was a parody of Gandhi's almost sacred march against colonial taxation policies; he marched however against tax on salt, not malt. Many people in Gujarat claimed to find this disrespectful to the Mahatma.

Such campaigns begin to suggest that prohibition is on the wane, along perhaps with some of the political conditions that put it in place originally. There is a new shop selling liquor to international travellers arriving at the Ahmedabad airport, complimenting the much older 'permit shops' in some upmarket hotels in the state. Despite vehement opposition by local Congress politicians,[37] there is talk of loosening the rules on drink and drinking in the state's many new Special Economic Zones. Most ominously of all however, the current state is trying to instil new values and new heroes to replace those associated with Gandhi. Fierce Gujarati freedom fighters have been resurrected from history by the state sponsorship and their names advertised to excess in an attempt to hasten the weakening grip Gandhi has on the imagination of the state.

Notes

1 See E. Simpson, 'Introduction: Two historians, a research society and a freedom fighter: on the life of the sociological ideas in the mesocephalic province of Gujarat', in idem (ed.) *Society and History of Gujarat since 1800: a select bibliography of the English and European language sources*, New Delhi: Orient Blackswan, 2010, pp. xiii–xxxvi.

2 N.M. Miabhoy, *Report of the Laththa Commission of Inquiry (Second)*, Ahmedabad: Government of Gujarat, 1978, p. 34.

3 Ibid., p. 33.
4 Ibid.
5 Ibid., p. 36.
6 Ibid., p. 51.
7 Methyl alcohol is a 'tincture' commonly used by carpenters to finish wood, and is often used in manufacturing illicit liquor.
8 Compare with N.M. Miyanbhai, *Report of the Commission of Inquiry into the Prohibition Policy in Gujarat*, Ahmedabad: Government of Gujarat, 1983.
9 L. Rahman, 'Alcohol prohibition and addictive consumption in India', unpublished thesis, London School of Economics and Political Science, 2003. Online. Available HTTP: <http://viking.nottingham.ac.uk/shared/shared_levevents/conferences/2003_PG_Rahman_paper.pdf> (accessed 20 October 2011).
10 N. Mishra, 'Modi methylated', *Outlook India*, 27 July 2009. Online. Available HTTP: <http://www.outlookindia.com/article.aspx?250530> (accessed 12 September 2011).
11 A study conducted in 1994 by the National Council of Applied Economic Research surveying human development indicators across 15 Indian states (including Gujarat) included a question on whether household members consumed alcohol or tobacco 'often' (cited in A. Mahal, 'What works in alcohol policy? Evidence from rural India', *Economic and Political Weekly* 35, 45, 2000, 3959–68.). This study unfortunately tells us little of what people actually do, and nothing whatsoever of the broader structures which allow alcohol into people's homes in Gujarat.
12 K. Fitze, *Twilight of the Maharajas. An account of the author's experiences in the Indian Civil Service*, 1911–47, London: John Murray, 1956, pp. 60–1.
13 Ibid.
14 Ibid., p. 63.
15 D. Hardiman, 'From custom to crime: the politics of drinking in colonial South Gujarat', in R. Guha (ed.) *Subaltern Studies IV*, New Delhi: Oxford University Press, 1985, pp. 165–228; D. Hardiman, *The Coming of the Devi: Adivasi assertion in western India*, Delhi: Oxford University Press, 1987.
16 Hardiman, *The Coming of the Devi*, pp. 110–11.
17 *Abkari* is the Indian term for the excise tax on intoxicants, including alcohol as well as drugs such as opium (ibid., p. 497).
18 D. Hardiman, 'From custom to crime', in Guha, *Subaltern Studies IV*, p. 498.
19 Hardiman, *The Coming of the Devi*.
20 D.M. Fahey and P. Manian. 'Poverty and purification: the politics of Gandhi's campaign for prohibition', *The Historian* 67, 2005, 489–506.
21 As several scholars have pointed out, however, there is significant evidence that alcohol has deep roots in the religious traditions of South Asia. See ibid.; G. Gaunekar et al., 'Drinking patterns of hazardous drinkers: a multicenter study in India', in A. Haworth and R. Simpson (eds) *Moonshine Markets: issues in unrecorded alcohol beverage production and consumption*, New York, Hove: Brunner-Routledge, pp. 125–44; D. Mandelbaum, 'Alcohol and culture', *Current Anthropology* 6, 3, 1965, 281–93.
22 Fahey and Manian, 'Poverty and purification'.
23 Quoted in ibid., p. 500.
24 Article 47 of the Indian Constitution encouraged the government 'to bring about prohibition of the consumption except for medical purposes of intoxicating drinks and of drugs which are injurious to health'.
25 Fahey and Manian, 'Poverty and purification'. p. 490.
26 Hardiman, *The Coming of the Devi*, pp. 99–109.
27 A. Tilche, 'In search of an Adivasi worldview: identity, development and the Museum of Voice in western India', unpublished thesis, SOAS, University of London, 2011.
28 H. Tambs-Lyche, *Power, Profit, and Poetry: traditional society in Kathiawar, western India*, Delhi: Manohar, 1997, p. 232.
29 Ibid., p. 10.

30 Ibid., p. 228.
31 Ibid., p. 224.
32 P. Ghassam-Fachandi, 'The hyperbolic vegetarian: notes on a fragile subject in Gujarat', in J. Borneman and A. Hammoudi (eds) *Being there: the fieldwork encounter and the making of truth*, Berkeley: University of California Press, 2010, p. 99.
33 H. Spodek, 'From Gandhi to violence: Ahmedabad's 1985 riots in historical perspective', *Modern Asian Studies* 23, 4, 1989, 765–95.
34 Ibid., p. 785.
35 O. Shani, 'Bootlegging, politics and corruption: state violence and the routine practices of public power in Gujarat (1985–2000)', *South Asian History and Culture* 1, 4, 2010, 494–508.
36 Ibid., p. 503.
37 Congress leader Shakarsinh Vaghela went on a 52-hour hunger strike to protest against the Modi-led government's decision in 2007 to relax the prohibition policy in Gujarat's Special Economic Zones (SEZs), suggesting that this constituted a first step in relaxing the ban of alcohol in the rest of the state ('Vaghela against lifting prohibition in Gujarat SEZs', *The Economic Times*, 1 February 2007. Online. Available HTTP: <http://articles.economictimes.indiatimes.com/2007-02-01/news/28385953_1_prohibition-gujarat-sezs-industrial-houses> (accessed 4 November 2011).

Afterword

Claude Markovits

This varied collection of articles opens up different analytical perspectives on the history of alcohol and drugs in South Asia, a topic generally neglected both by historians of intoxicants and historians of South Asia. Rather than assessing the strengths and weaknesses of the papers presented here, I intend to offer a few general reflections inspired by the topic to a historian of colonial South Asia without a prior interest in the question, with the exception of a small foray into the history of the opium trade.[1]

What is striking to anyone attempting to situate the South Asian case within a broader, 'global' framework, is how specific it is. If, to use David Courtwright's catchy phrase, the last six centuries have witnessed the unfolding on a global scale of a 'psychoactive revolution'[2] characterized by the greater availability of intoxicants in different forms to an ever greater part of the world's population, then South Asia, with its fifth of the world population, somewhat bucks the trend. For it appears that intoxicants, whether in the form of beverages or drugs, were always widely available in the region. Moreover, as Maria Moritz's fascinating paper reminds us, it was precisely the availability of cheap drugs, in the form of *ganja*, one of the concoctions of cannabis, that attracted to India, as early as in the late nineteenth century, Westerners in search of a self-revelatory 'spiritual' experience which they thought would be facilitated by the use of psychotropes, such as the German theosophist Wilhelm Hübbe-Schleiden. Although this particularly tortured individual failed to find what he was looking for, the kind of drug-fuelled 'spiritual quest' in which he launched himself, with the help of an Indian guru, became a mass trend in the 1960s with the advent of the 'hippie revolution' and the well-trodden trail leading to Katmandu and Goa.

Not that India was necessarily self-sufficient in the production of intoxicants. While it was probably historically the largest producer both of opium and cannabis, its position was less prominent in the field of alcoholic beverages. Various forms of *arrack* made from toddy as well as other plants were available in India since early times, as mentioned by James McHugh in his article, but India produced little wine, and of poor quality. Hence the rise, from the sixteenth century onwards, of a trade in imported wines, which the Portuguese and other Europeans were only too happy to supply. Thus the wayward Danish pietist missionary Früchtenicht, who is the focus of Tobias Delfs' wonderful micro-study, got drunk on imported European wines, easily available in the settlements of Serampore and Tranquebar, rather than on the cheaper, but admittedly more lethal Indian 'country liquors' with which low class Europeans, like soldiers and sailors (leaving aside tinkers and tailors), found their Nirvana. His story is even sadder than that of Hübbe-Schleiden, since, once he had been sent back to Denmark, he ended up by committing suicide.

Low-class Europeans and their drinking habits, long tolerated by their upper-class employers, who saw no serious harm in them, became a major preoccupation, one century later, for the British rulers of India, wary of the potentially disastrous effect of their unruly behaviour for the prestige of the white race in the eyes of the mass of their colonial subjects. Harald Fischer-Tiné brings into sharp relief the multiple ironies of a situation in which an upper-class group with its own strong drinking habits, such as the British ruling group in India, sought to discipline a lower-class group for which drink was the only derivative to a life of drudgery. The importation of British class differences and its attendant snobbery was not without dangers to a ruling class that ultimately had to depend on the bodies of such low-class Europeans to protect it from the wrath of its Indian subjects, as happened at the time of the Great Revolt of 1857. It benefited however by the growth of temperance movements, inspired by religious and radical reformers in Britain, which targeted the soldiery and obtained certain results in the second half of the nineteenth century. The enormous consumption of spirits which characterized British soldiers in the first half of the century was somewhat curbed under the dual influence of temperance campaigns and of the greater availability in India of beer, which was deemed less intoxicating. The ghost of an alcohol-fuelled 'White Mutiny', one of the worst nightmares of the ruling class, was not however completely laid at rest, and, in 1893, when, following the *de facto* devaluation of the rupee *vis-à-vis* sterling, the India Office and the Treasury were engaged in complex negotiations regarding the fixing of a new exchange rate between the two currencies, the War Office, which had ultimate authority over the British Army in India, cynically agitated the prospect of British soldiers going 'berserk in the bazaars' in case the new exchange rate would suddenly result in a drop in the purchasing power of their pay, making it more difficult for them to procure their beer and the services of the prostitutes to whom they, as unmarried men, had regularly recourse. Such a mutiny of course never took place, and there remained the problem of vagrants or 'loafers', that did at no point really endanger the Raj, even if it generated a certain amount of panic amongst the ruling circles.

Alcoholic beverages were without doubt at the heart of the colonial order, not only in having the potential of symbolically undermining it, but also of impacting it in a more material way, much as excise represented a large share of government revenue. Here the British were hoisted with their own petard, as temperance movements, which often had their origins in Britain, became a powerful weapon in the hands of the Indian middle class in its struggle to limit the power of the colonial state. The upper caste Hindus as well as the Ashrafs amongst Muslims claimed to have always been temperate drinkers, or even teetotallers, which allowed them to occupy the high moral ground *vis-à-vis* the British rulers, even if it is a claim that a look at textual evidence for the pre-colonial period easily belies. McHugh's brief but sharp survey of the allusions to alcoholic beverages in Sanskrit literature demonstrates convincingly that ancient India had developed a sophisticated and fundamentally ambivalent approach to the question of intoxicating drinks. While they were appraised for their capacity to procure happiness, sexual potency and corpulence, as well as convenient means of intelligence-gathering for rulers who subjected drinking dens to constant surveillance, the dangers inherent to their excessive use were well perceived. The same ambivalence was noticeable in the elite culture of Mughal India, as rapidly evoked by McHugh. All in all Indian nationalists' claims that British colonialism had introduced the evil of drink to an abstemious people seem highly dubious. What remains true is that the colonial state was probably more dependent upon *abkari* (excise) revenue than earlier state formations. The state's proclaimed objective of deriving maximum revenue from minimal consumption was admirable on paper, but difficult to implement on the ground, as local officials were inevitably under pressure from their superiors to maximize revenue, be it at the cost of the health of those they were supposed to protect. This was a conundrum that even the official excise committee of 1905–6 acknowledged.[3] Therefore the state opened itself to the criticism of the middle class upper-caste intelligentsia, and drink became a central issue in the struggle between the Congress and the colonial government after 1919. This culminated at the time of the Civil Disobedience movement of 1930–1 in a widespread picketing of liquor shops, resulting in a sharp fall in excise revenue, as shown by Robert E. Colvard in an article based on a meticulous research through the archives. The author's great merit is to have been able to pierce through the often strident rhetoric deployed by Indian nationalists in their condemnation of the drinking habit to reveal the class character of the movement. For resistance to it did not come only from those who were involved in the liquor trade, an altogether not negligible constituency, but also from ordinary lower-class Indians who needed the comfort of drink to go through everyday life. Both were equally tarred with the brush of being enemies of the nation and stooges of imperialism. Here we find an interesting parallel with the episode analyzed by Fischer-Tiné. In both cases, we note that social elites used the medium of an anti-drink campaign in the service of a disciplinary project aimed at subaltern groups. It would probably be possible to develop a kind of more general Foucauldian argument about the link between governability and drink control, but the authors, perhaps rightly, stop short of it.

The article by Carrie Heitmeyer and Edward Simpson on the politics of drink in Gujarat, the only state in post-independence India to have consistently enforced prohibition, is an insightful probe into the complexities of a policy whose most visible outcome has been the emergence of a strong nexus between the state and criminal groups. Gujarat deserves particular attention inasmuch as attempts at imposing similar prohibition in other states of India, in particular in Andhra Pradesh and Haryana, failed miserably in the 1990s, in spite of being supported by large sections of the population, especially lower-class women, sick of being beaten to pulp by drunk husbands. Which by the way should alert us to the crucial gender dimension of the alcohol problem, perhaps not taken sufficiently into consideration in the volume. To come back to the case of Gujarat, the resilience of the prohibitionist agenda of the state government across six decades in the face of massive evidence that not only did it fail to check consumption but also allowed criminal networks to thrive, is explained on the one hand by pointing to the strength of the Gandhian legacy and also by a rapid probing into the tortured psyche of the Gujarati Hindu middle class. As an aside, it will be interesting to watch whether, in case the present Chief Minister of Gujarat, Narendra Modi, becomes the next Prime Minister of India after the next election, as predicted by some, he will try to extend prohibition nationwide. It seems highly doubtful.

Of the 'big three' addictions in Courtwright's classification, alcohol takes central place in the volume, which is easily explained by its crucial role in the political economy of colonial and post-Independence India. Tobacco and caffeine would undoubtedly also deserve attention if one aimed at a comprehensive survey. Both were introduced from outside, and became mass addictions in the post-colonial age, although, as far as tobacco is concerned, a British official of the early nineteenth century already deplored its 'excessive use' in India.[4] Actually, if one looks for evidence of a 'psychoactive revolution' in South Asia, tobacco and tea are the two substances that should top the list. It would be worth looking for instance at the competition between industrial cigarettes and hand-made *bidis* for the loyalty of Indian smokers, and also exploring some of the religious undertones of the tobacco question in India. To take but one example, why did the tenth Sikh guru, Gobind Singh, when he founded the *Khalsa* at the end of the seventeenth century, forbid smoking to his disciples? Closer to the present, it would also be interesting to reflect on the spectacular rise in the domestic consumption of tea in India since independence, which, apart from displacing other drinks (including *bhang*?) has also negatively impacted the traditional place of the country as the top world exporter to the advantage of Kenya and Sri Lanka.

The volume has on the other hand quite a lot to say on two of the 'little three' (Courtwright), i.e. opium and cannabis, in which India has always occupied an important place both as a producing and a consuming country. While cannabis mostly served domestic consumption in its three forms of *bhang*, *ganja* and *charas*, opium became an export product at an early stage. Portuguese sources of the early sixteenth century report a trade in 'Cambay' opium from the West Coast of India towards the Indonesian archipelago. That trade was partly captured by the Dutch East India Company (VOC) in the seventeenth century, and the opium, that the Dutch increasingly procured from Patna in Bihar, found its way to Batavia, where it became one of the biggest sources of profit to the VOC. There is therefore nothing surprising to the fact that, when the English had evicted their Dutch rivals from the Canton tea trade by the 1740s, they sought also to dominate the trade in Patna opium. But the novelty was that they started selling it not to Indonesia, but to China. Sales of opium, although declared illegal in 1729 by the Chinese imperial authorities, soon boomed as certain classes of South Chinese society quickly acquired the opium habit. This allowed the East India Company to pay for the increasing quantities of tea it bought in China with Indian opium, thus avoiding the need to transfer specie to Canton, a blessing for what was basically a mercantilist concern. This story is well known, but the growth of a parallel export market in so-called 'Malwa' opium grown in the Indian states of Central India (mostly Indore and Gwalior) and shipped through the ports of Portuguese India (Damao mostly) was not as well-known till the publication of Amar Farooqui's book.[5] In the volume, Farooqui provides a well-rounded summary of his findings, with a particular focus on the role of the Central Indian native states where the poppy was grown and refined into opium. He detects a whiff of 'subversion' in the defiance shown by the native rulers towards the East India Company and its attempt at monopolizing the China opium trade, firstly by trying to interdict the trade in Malwa opium, and, later, when that proved impossible, by controlling it. I have taken him to task about his use of the term 'subversion' and he offers a spirited response, that fails however to remove my doubts. Not wanting to try the patience of the reader by dwelling too much on this minor polemic, I shall simply state that the disagreement between us is more taxonomic than substantive, as the evidence accumulated by Farooqui is too massive to be ignored.

If the role of India as a major exporter of opium has not failed to attract the attention of a variety of scholars, less has been written about the domestic consumption of the drug and attempts by the state to regulate it. Two papers in the volume seek to close the gap. One, by Kawal Deep Kour, is focused on the case of the province of Assam, an area that figures little in the historical literature on India. The use of opium appears to have been common in the province amongst the labouring classes, especially the workers in the tea gardens, that became in the nineteenth century the backbone of the provincial economy. By the end of the century, there emerged amongst the tiny Assamese English-educated middle class intelligentsia an anti-opium movement. It grew in the twentieth century and became linked up with nationalist agitation, in the same way as the anti-drink campaign analyzed by Colvard. Thus in Assam the non-cooperation movement of 1920–2 coincided with a campaign at the grassroots level against the use of opium. In spite of the reticence of the provincial government, anxious not to lose opium revenue, a scheme was implemented resting on the registration of habitual users. After Congress formed a coalition ministry in 1937, a move started towards prohibition, and it took another twenty years for consumption to cease. An aspect on which the paper does not dwell is the way opium users reacted to the campaign and to the measures taken by the state to curb consumption.

Maria Framke's paper looks at the links between international anti-opium campaigns, in which the League of Nations was a driving force, and the rise of anti-opium legislation in India. At first the colonial government, with an eye to fiscal revenues, was reticent to embark upon a policy of regulation, but after 1925 it gave way to international pressure. So India participated in the great world-wide movement that increasingly stigmatized and even criminalized drug users, the forerunner of the 'war on drugs' declared by the US administration in the last decades. It seems however that cannabis users were on the whole left undisturbed. This lenient attitude goes back to the colonial period, when the authorities decided that the use of cannabis was on the whole not harmful, a stand that was made official in the report of the committee on hemp drugs submitted in1893–4.[6] Thus, while India has joined the global community of states fighting drug addiction in the form of opium and heroin, its toleration of cannabis has allowed it to become a magnet for a vast international community of users of that drug. However the two real scourges affecting the health of India's population, drink and tobacco, continue undisturbed their deadly work, as elsewhere.

To bring this short piece to a rapid conclusion, I find that this volume is a real breakthrough in a hitherto largely neglected field of research. It shows the diversity of forms of intoxicants that developed in South Asia, and the varied responses they drew from elites and states at different moments in history. It opens up vast perspectives for further research. Let me name a few. Firstly, we need a more comprehensive coverage of the whole range of intoxicants, by bringing in tobacco and caffeinated drinks, which remain largely unexplored domains. Secondly, and more importantly, we need a detailed social mapping of the use of intoxicants. Who exactly took what and when? It is known that in present-day India, there is a clear social hierarchy in the use of drinks: imported foreign liquors, mostly whisky, are for the upper-middle class, 'Indian-made foreign liquors' (IMFL) for the lower rungs of the middle class, 'country liquor' for the mass of the poor (with no doubt subtle internal gradations in that vast category). When and how did this hierarchy come about, and what about the status of beer and wine, which are becoming increasingly common in India? It would also be interesting to go beyond India and look at the way 'Muslim' states in South Asia like Pakistan and Bangladesh have dealt with these questions, particularly drink. Pakistan offers a fascinating case study in double language, as it is an officially prohibitionist state ruled by an elite whose alcohol-guzzling reaches remarkable proportions. The study of intoxicants in South Asia is decidedly a promising field, and it is to be hoped that this volume will be followed by others of similar quality.

Notes

1 C. Markovits, 'The political economy of opium smuggling in early 19th century India: leakage or resistance?', *Modern Asian Studies* 43, 1, 2002, 89–111.

2 D.T. Courtwright, *Forces of Habit: drugs and the making of the modern world*, Cambridge MA, London: Harvard University Press, 2001.

3 *Report of the India Excise Committee 1905–1906*, Madras: Government Press, 1906, p. 114: 'temperance leaders themselves acknowledge that the policy of responsible officers of Government is in agreement with the best temperance sentiment. Their complaint is directed against the subordinates and is that the lower one goes the more the revenue point of view comes into prominence'.

4 Papers of Sir Henry Miers Elliott, Foreign Secretary to the Government of India, British Library Additional Manuscripts, Add 30788, f.81.

5 A. Farooqui, *Smuggling as Subversion: colonialism, Indian merchants and the politics of opium*, New Delhi: New Age International, 1998.

6 *Report of the India Hemp Drugs Commission 1893–94*, Simla: Government Press, 1895. See also J.H. Mills, *Cannabis Britannica: empire, trade, and prohibition 1800–1928*, Oxford: Oxford University Press, 2003.

Index